PAGES 106–111
Street Finder maps
1, 2 & 5

PAGES 68–87
Street Finder maps
2, 4, 5 & 6

Stephansdom
Quarter

Hofburg
Quarter

PAGES 88–105
Street Finder maps
3, 4 & 5

Belvedere
Quarter

PAGES 140–155
Street Finder
map 4

KU-350-415

EYEWITNESS *TRAVEL GUIDES*

VIENNA

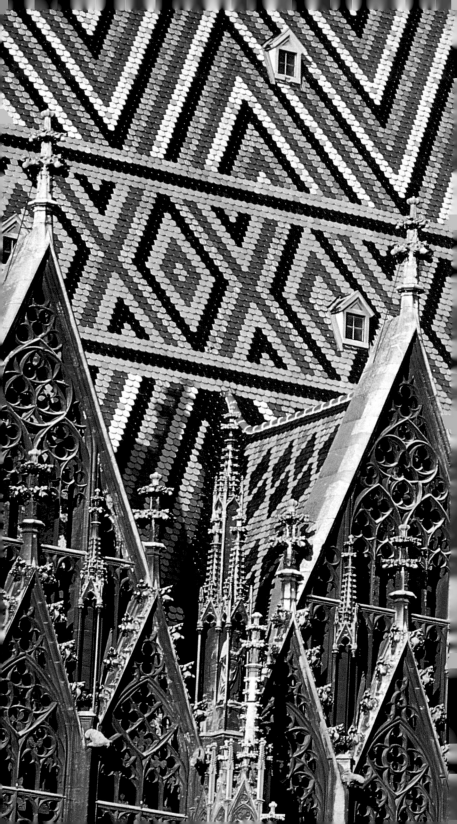

DK EYEWITNESS *TRAVEL GUIDES*

VIENNA

Main Contributor: STEPHEN BROOK

DORLING KINDERSLEY
LONDON • NEW YORK • MUNICH
MELBOURNE • DELHI
www.dk.com

A DORLING KINDERSLEY BOOK

www.dk.com

PROJECT EDITOR Carolyn Pyrah
ART EDITOR Sally Ann Hibbard
EDITORS Marcus Hardy, Kim Inglis
DESIGNERS Vanessa Hamilton, Andy Wilkinson
DESIGN ASSISTANT Elly King

PRODUCTION Hilary Stephens
PICTURE RESEARCH Ellen Root
DTP DESIGNER Adam Moore

CONTRIBUTORS
Gretel Beer, Caroline Bugler, Deirdre Coffey, Fred Mawer

PHOTOGRAPHER
Peter Wilson

ILLUSTRATORS
Richard Draper, Stephen Gyapay, Chris Orr,
Robbie Polley, Ann Winterbotham

Reproduced by Colourscan, Singapore
Printed and bound by L. Rex Printing Company Limited, China

First published in Great Britain in 1994
by Dorling Kindersley Limited
80 Strand, London WC2R 0RL

**Reprinted with revisions 1994, 1995, 1996, 1997,
1998, 1999, 2000, 2001, 2002**

Copyright 1994, 2002 © Dorling Kindersley Limited, London
A Penguin Company

A CIP CATALOGUE RECORD IS AVAILABLE FROM THE BRITISH LIBRARY.
ISBN 0-7513-4674-8

The information in every
DK Eyewitness Travel Guide is checked regularly.
Every effort has been made to ensure that this book is as
up-to-date as possible at the time of going to press. Some
details, however, such as telephone numbers, opening hours,
prices, gallery hanging arrangements and travel information
are liable to change. The publishers cannot accept responsibility
for any consequences arising from the use of this book, nor
for any material on third party websites, and cannot guarantee
that any website address in this book will be a suitable source
of travel information. We value the views and suggestions of
our readers very highly. Please write to: Senior Publishing
Manager, DK Eyewitness Travel Guides, Dorling Kindersley,
80 Strand, London WC2R 0RL.

CONTENTS

Karl V, Holy Roman Emperor
from 1519 to 1556 *(see p24)*

INTRODUCING
VIENNA

Bronze and copper Anker Clock
in Hoher Markt *(see p84)*

Façade of Schönbrunn Palace *(see pp170–73)*

Grinzing restaurant *(see pp215–17)*

Sachertorte *(see p207)*

The Vienna Boys' Choir *(see p39)*

Karlskirche in the Belvedere Quarter *(see pp146–7)*

HOW TO USE THIS GUIDE

THIS EYEWITNESS travel guide helps you get the most from your stay in Vienna with the minimum of difficulty. The opening section, *Introducing Vienna*, locates the city geographically, sets modern Vienna in its historical context and describes events through the entire year. *Vienna at a Glance* is an overview of the city's main attractions. *Vienna Area by Area* starts on page 66. This is the main sightseeing section,

Plotting the route

which covers all the important sights, with photographs, maps and illustrations. It also includes day trips from Vienna, a river trip and four walks around the city. Carefully researched tips for hotels, restaurants, cafés and bars, markets and shops, entertainment and sports are found in *Travellers' Needs*. The *Survival Guide* has advice from how to make a telephone call to using the transport system and its ticket machines.

FINDING YOUR WAY AROUND THE SIGHTSEEING SECTION

Each of the six sightseeing areas in the city is colour-coded for easy reference. Every chapter opens with an introduction to the part of Vienna it covers, describing its history and character, followed by a Street-by-Street map illustrating a typical part of the area. Finding your way around each chapter is made simple by the numbering system used throughout. The most important sights are covered in detail in two or more full pages.

Each area has colour-coded thumb tabs.

A locator map shows where you are in relation to other areas in the city centre.

Locator map

A suggested route takes in some of the most interesting and attractive streets in the area.

1 Introduction to the area
For easy reference, the sights in each area are numbered and plotted on an area map. To help the visitor, this map also shows underground stations, train stations and parking areas. The area's key sights are listed by category: Churches and Cathedrals; Museums and Galleries; Streets and Squares; Markets; Historic Buildings and Parks and Gardens.

The area shaded pink is shown in greater detail on the Street-by-Street map on the following pages.

2 Street-by-Street map
This gives a bird's eye view of interesting and important parts of each sightseeing area. The numbering of the sights ties in with the area map and the fuller descriptions on the pages that follow.

The list of star sights recommends the places that no visitor should miss.

VIENNA AREA MAP

THE COLOURED AREAS shown on this map *(see inside front cover)* are the six main sightseeing areas used in this guide. Each is covered in a full chapter in *Vienna Area by Area (pp66–177)*. They are highlighted on other maps throughout the book. In *Vienna at a Glance (pp40–61)*, for example, they help you locate the top sights. They are also used to help you find the position of the four guided walks *(pp178–87)*.

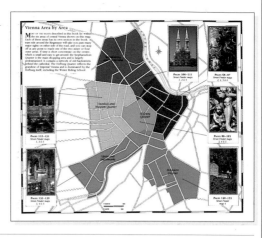

Numbers refer to each sight's position on the area map and its place in the chapter.

Practical information provides all the information you need to visit every sight. Map references pinpoint each sight's location on the *Street Finder* map *(pp262–7)*.

The visitors' checklist provides all the practical information needed to plan your visit.

3 Detailed information on each sight
All the important sights in Vienna are described individually. They are listed in order, following the numbering on the area map at the start of the section. Practical information includes a map reference, opening hours, telephone numbers, admission charges and facilities available for each sight. The key to the symbols used is on the back flap.

Stars indicate the features no visitor should miss.

4 Vienna's major sights
Historic buildings are dissected to reveal their interiors; museums and galleries have colour-coded floorplans to help you find important exhibits.

A timeline charts the key events in the history of the building.

INTRODUCING VIENNA

Putting Vienna on the Map

V IENNA HAS A POPULATION of just over 1.5 million and covers an area of 415 sq km (160 sq miles). The River Danube flows through it and the Danube Canal flows through the city centre. It is the capital of the Republic of Austria, of which it is also a federal state, and is the country's political, economic, cultural and administrative centre. At the heart of Central Europe, it makes a good base from which to explore cities such as Bratislava, Prague, Budapest, Zagreb, Salzburg and Munich, as well as many Austrian towns.

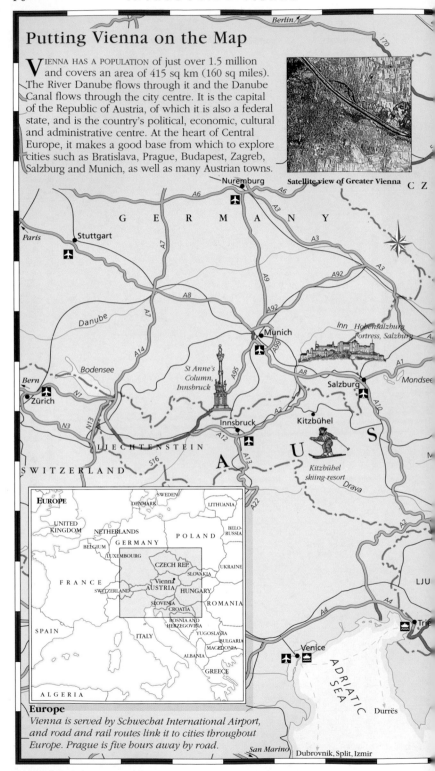

Satellite view of Greater Vienna

Europe

Vienna is served by Schwechat International Airport, and road and rail routes link it to cities throughout Europe. Prague is five hours away by road.

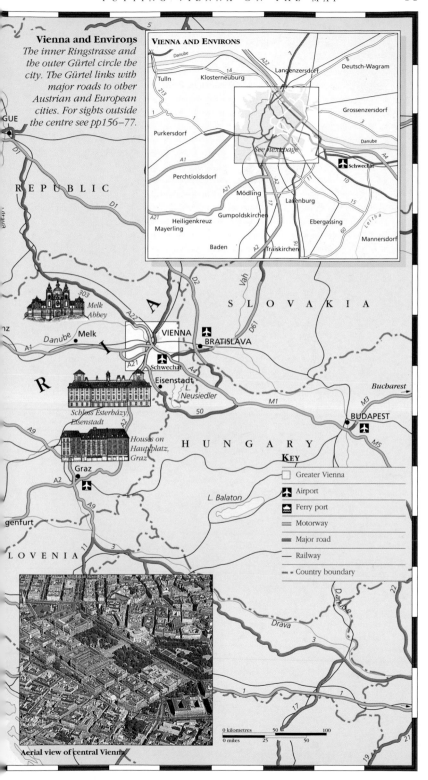

Vienna and Environs
*The inner Ringstrasse and
the outer Gürtel circle the
city. The Gürtel links with
major roads to other
Austrian and European
cities. For sights outside
the centre see pp156–77.*

VIENNA AND ENVIRONS

Danube
Tulln
Klosterneuburg
Langenzersdorf
Deutsch-Wagram
14
A22
Grossenzersdorf
Purkersdorf
Danube
See next page
Schwechat
Perchtoldsdorf
A21
Mödling
A2
Laxenburg
Gumpoldskirchen
17
Heiligenkreuz
Mayerling
Ebergassing
Baden
Traiskirchen
Mannersdorf
Leitha

Melk
Abbey
303
Danube
Melk
A22
A1
A21
Schwechat
Eisenstadt
L.
Neusiedler
Schloss Esterházy,
Eisenstadt
A2
Houses on
Hauptplatz,
Graz
A9
Graz
A2
A9
genfurt
L O V E N I A   11
3

A
VIENNA
BRATISLAVA
D2
Vah
S L O V A K I A
D61
M1
Bucharest
M3
BUDAPEST
M5
H U N G A R Y
KEY

L. Balaton

KEY

| | Greater Vienna |
| Airport |
| Ferry port |
| Motorway |
| Major road |
| Railway |
| Country boundary |

Danube
Drava
3

Aerial view of central Vienna

0 kilometres   50   100
0 miles   25   50

1
17
1
19
21
22

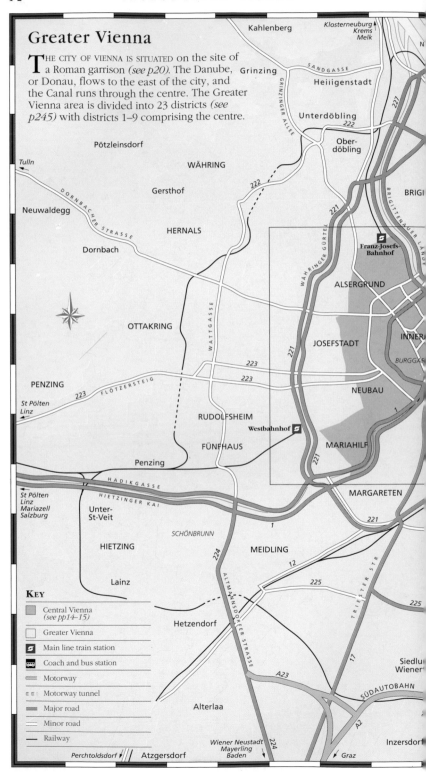

Greater Vienna

THE CITY OF VIENNA IS SITUATED on the site of a Roman garrison *(see p20)*. The Danube, or Donau, flows to the east of the city, and the Canal runs through the centre. The Greater Vienna area is divided into 23 districts *(see p245)* with districts 1–9 comprising the centre.

Kahlenberg

Klosterneuburg
Krems
Melk

Grinzing

SANDGASSE

Heiligenstadt

GRINZINGER ALLEE

Unterdöbling
222

Ober-
döbling

227

BRIGI

BRIGITTENAUER LÄNDE

Pötzleinsdorf

Tulln

WÄHRING

DORNBACHER STRASSE

Gersthof

Neuwaldegg

222

221

HERNALS

Dornbach

WÄHRINGER GÜRTEL

Franz-Josefs-
Bahnhof

ALSERGRUND

OTTAKRING

WATTGASSE

221

JOSEFSTADT

INNER

PENZING

223

FLÖTZERSTEIG

223

223

BURGGA

St Pölten
Linz

RUDOLFSHEIM

NEUBAU

Westbahnhof

221

FÜNFHAUS

MARIAHILF

Penzing

HADIKGASSE

MARGARETEN

St Pölten
Linz
Mariazell
Salzburg

HIETZINGER KAI

Unter-
St-Veit

221

SCHÖNBRUNN

1

HIETZING

224

MEIDLING

ALTMANNSDORFER STRASSE

12

Lainz

225

TRIESTER STR

225

Hetzendorf

A23

17

Siedlu
Wiener

SÜDAUTOBAHN

Alterlaa

A2

Inzersdor

Wiener Neustadt
Mayerling
Baden

224

Graz

Perchtoldsdorf Atzgersdorf

KEY

Central Vienna
(see pp14–15)

Greater Vienna

Main line train station

Coach and bus station

Motorway

Motorway tunnel

Major road

Minor road

Railway

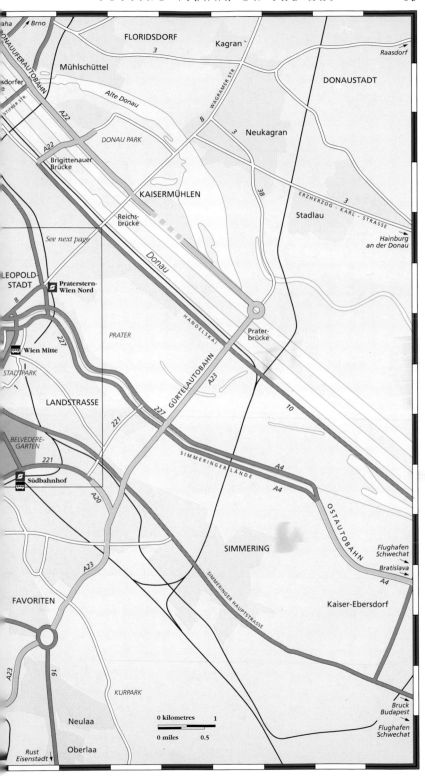

Central Vienna

THIS BOOK DIVIDES VIENNA into six areas in the centre of town, and has further sections for sights on the outskirts of the city, suggested walks and day trips, as well as practical information. Each of the six main areas has its own chapter, and contains a selection of sights that convey some of that area's history and distinctive character, such as the Stephansdom in the Stephansdom Quarter and the imperial buildings in the Hofburg Quarter. Most of the city's famous sights are in or close to the city centre and are easy to reach on foot or by public transport.

Detail on the door of the Pallavicini Palace (1784) in Josefsplatz

Bars in Sterngasse
Sterngasse, in the Jewish Quarter (see p84), *is packed with lively bars like these spilling out into the street* (see *Restaurants, Cafés and Bars on p217*).

KEY

▢	Major sight
Ⓤ	U-Bahn station
⌖	Badner Bahn stop
P	Parking
ℹ	Tourist information office
▣	Police station
✝	Church

0 metres   500

0 yards   500

**View over the Roof-
tops from Am Hof**
*Am Hof, the largest
enclosed square in
Vienna, is circled by
a number of inter-
esting houses, some
with statuary on
their roofs and
pediments (see p87).*

Rathauskeller Façade
*The city has plenty of wine
cellars – many associated with
old vineyards – where wine,
beer and simple food is served.
This one is located beneath
the city ball (see pp128
and 213).*

Pallas Athene Fountain
*The figure of Pallas Athene
by Karl Kundmann was
placed on the fountain in
front of the Parliament
building in 1902
(see p125).*

THE HISTORY OF VIENNA

VIENNA WAS ORIGINALLY a Celtic settlement on the site of the present-day city. Under the Romans it became the garrison of Vindobona, supporting the nearby town of Carnuntum. Its location on the edge of the Hungarian plains, however, made it vulnerable to attack, and Barbarian invasions reduced the town to ruins by the early 5th century. In the 10th century, the German Babenberg dynasty acquired Vienna, and during their reign of almost three centuries the city became a major trading centre. Later, in the 13th century, Vienna came under the control of the Habsburgs. In the 16th century, Turkish invasions threatened Vienna and devastated its outskirts. Only in 1683 were the Turks finally defeated, allowing Vienna to flourish. Immense palaces were built around the court within the city, and in the

Maximilian I shield

liberated outskirts, and by the 18th century Vienna was a major imperial and cultural centre. Napoleon's occupation of Vienna in 1809 shook the Habsburgs' confidence, as did the revolution of 1848 – the year Franz Joseph came to the throne. By 1914, Vienna's population had expanded to two million, as people from all over the Habsburg Empire flocked to this vibrant centre. After World War I, the Habsburg Empire collapsed and Vienna's role as the Imperial capital ended. In the following years a strong municipal government – "Red Vienna" – tried to solve the social problems of the city. Austria was annexed by Nazi Germany in the Anschluss of 1938 and then, following Hitler's defeat in 1945, came under Allied control. Vienna regained its independence in 1955, when Austria became a sovereign state.

Circular plan of Turkish siege, from 1529

◁ Detail from *The Marriage of Joseph II to Isabella of Parma* (1760) by the Martin van Meytens School

Vienna's Rulers

VIENNA EMERGED from the Dark Ages as a German outpost controlled by Babenberg dukes, who brought great prosperity to the city by the 12th century. There followed a period of social disorder, and intermittent Bohemian rule known as the Interregnum. Vienna fell into Habsburg hands in the 13th century and remained the cornerstone of their domains until the dynasty's downfall in 1918. From 1452 until 1806, Habsburg rulers were almost invariably elected as Holy Roman Emperor, enabling Vienna to develop as an Imperial capital on the grandest scale.

1278–82 Rudolf I of Germany is regent of Austria.

Duke Friedrich II with falconer

1246–50 Interregnum under Margrave Hermann of Baden after death of Duke Friedrich II

900	1000	1100	1200	1300	14●
BABENBERG RULERS				**HABSBURG RULERS**	
900	1000	1100	1200	1300	14●

976 Leopold of Babenberg

1198–1230 Duke Leopold VI

1177–1194 Duke Leopold V

1358–65 Duke Rudolf IV

1141–77 Duke Heinrich II Jasomirgott

1251–76 Interregnum under Přemysl Ottakar II

1637–57 Emperor
Ferdinand III

1452–93 Friedrich V
crowned as Holy Roman
Emperor Friedrich III)

1485–90 King Matthias
Corvinus of Hungary
occupies Vienna

1493–1519 Emperor
Maximilian I

1612–19
Emperor Matthias

1576–1612
Emperor
Rudolf II

1657–1705 Emperor Leopold I

1705–11 Emperor
Joseph I

1711–40
Emperor Karl VI

*Emperor
Franz
Joseph I*

1835–48
Emperor
Ferdinand I
of Austria

1848–1916 Emperor
Franz Joseph I

1500	1600	1700	1800	1900

1500	1600	1700	1800	1900

1619–37 Emperor
Ferdinand II

1564–76 Emperor Maximilian II

1556–64 Emperor
Ferdinand I

1792–1835 Emperor
Franz II (becomes
Franz I of Austria
in 1806)

1918
Habsburgs
exiled

1916–18 Emperor
Karl I

1790–92 Emperor
Leopold II

1780–90 Emperor
Joseph II

1519–1556
Emperor Karl V

1740–80 Empress Maria Theresa

Early Vienna

Roman urn

THE REGION AROUND VIENNA was first inhabited in the late Stone Age, and Vienna itself was founded as a Bronze Age settlement in about 800 BC. Settled by Celts from about 400 BC, the Romans incorporated it into the province of Pannonia in 15 BC, establishing the garrison of Vindobona by the 1st century AD. Later overrun by Barbarian tribes, Vindobona diminished in importance until the 8th century, when the Frankish Emperor Charlemagne made it part of his Eastern March and part of the Holy Roman Empire.

EXTENT OF THE CITY

▨ *150 AD*   ☐ *Today*

Hallstatt Idol
The Iron-Age Hallstatt culture flourished around Vienna from 750 to 400 BC.

Main defensive wall

VINDOBONA
Established around 100 AD, the garrison of Vindobona was allied to the town of Carnuntum.

Vindobona   Carnuntum

Venus of Willendorf
Now in the Natural History Museum (see p126), this late Stone Age figurine was found at Willendorf, close to Vienna, in 1906.

Roman Map
This map of Pannonia shows the position of Roman towns and forts along the Danube.

TIMELINE

2000 BC Indo-Germanic settlements on northwest wooded slopes	**800 BC** Bronze Age settlements on what is now Hoher Markt	**750 BC** Hallstatt culture **400 BC** Celtic culture		*Marcus Aurelius* **180** Roman Emperor Marcus Aurelius dies in Vindobona	**280** Ror Emperor Pro authorizes w growing in Danube a
5000	2000	800	0	100	200
5000 BC Late Stone Age culture		*Preserved shoe from the Hallstatt culture*	**15 BC** Celtic region of Noricum occupied by Romans		**250** Vindobona, developed as a garrison town, has a population of 20,000

☐ **Early Vienna**

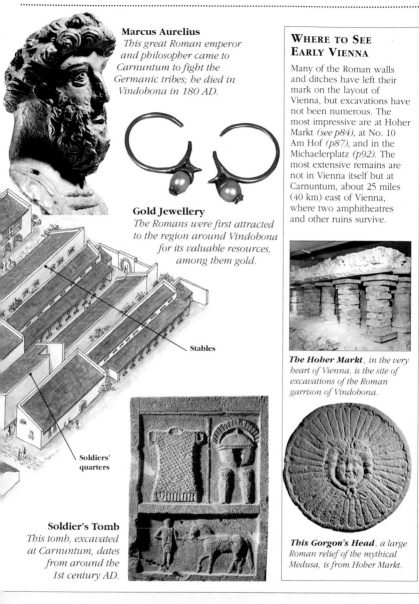

Marcus Aurelius
This great Roman emperor and philosopher came to Carnuntum to fight the Germanic tribes; he died in Vindobona in 180 AD.

Gold Jewellery
The Romans were first attracted to the region around Vindobona for its valuable resources, among them gold.

Stables

Soldiers' quarters

Soldier's Tomb
This tomb, excavated at Carnuntum, dates from around the 1st century AD.

WHERE TO SEE EARLY VIENNA

Many of the Roman walls and ditches have left their mark on the layout of Vienna, but excavations have not been numerous. The most impressive are at Hoher Markt *(see p84)*, at No. 10 Am Hof *(p87)*, and in the Michaelerplatz *(p92)*. The most extensive remains are not in Vienna itself but at Carnuntum, about 25 miles (40 km) east of Vienna, where two amphitheatres and other ruins survive.

The Hoher Markt, *in the very heart of Vienna, is the site of excavations of the Roman garrison of Vindobona.*

This Gorgon's Head, *a large Roman relief of the mythical Medusa, is from Hoher Markt.*

395 First Barbarian invasions approach Vindobona

405 Romans withdraw from Vindobona

500–650 Repeated invasions by Langobards, Goths, Avars and Slav tribes

0	400	500	600	700	800

433 Vindobona destroyed by Huns

Barbarian horseman

883 First mention of Wenia (Vienna) on the borders of the Eastern March founded by Charlemagne

Medieval Vienna

IN 955 THE HOLY ROMAN EMPEROR Otto I expelled Hungarian tribes from the Eastern March *(see p20)*. In 976 he made a gift of Vienna to the German Babenbergs, who, despite further incursions by the Hungarians, restored the city's importance as a centre of trade and culture. Following Friedrich II's death in 1246 and the ensuing Interregnum *(see p18)*, the Habsburgs began centuries of rule over Austria. Vienna became a major European city and hub of the Holy Roman Empire.

EXTENT OF THE CITY

☐ *1400*   ☐ *Today*

St Ruprecht
St Ruprecht was the patron saint of salt merchants, who brought this precious commodity along the Danube from salt mines in western Austria. Today his statue overlooks the Danube canal.

DEATH OF FRIEDRICH II

Duke Friedrich II was the last of the Babenbergs to rule Vienna. He died in battle against invading Hungarian forces in 1246.

Stephansdom

The Nobility
Often elected as Holy Roman Emperors, the Habsburgs attracted nobility from all over their huge empire.

Duke Friedrich II

Coronation Robe
This magnificent medieval robe (1133), originally from Palermo, formed part of the Habsburg's imperial regalia.

TIMELINE

955 Otto I of Germany defeats the Hungarians, restoring Christianity and re-establishing the Eastern March ("Ostmark", later renamed Ostarrichi)	**1030** The Hungarians besiege Vienna	**1147** Stephansdom consecrated
		1136 Death of Margave Leopold III
900	**1000**	**1100**
909 Eastern March invaded by Hungarian forces	**976** Otto I makes Leopold of Babenberg Margrave of the Eastern March, initiating Babenberg rule	**1137** Vienna becomes a fortified city
		1156 Heinrich II Jasomirgott moves his court to Vienna; builds Am Hof *(see p87)*

☐ **Medieval Vienna**

Richard the Lionheart
In 1192, Richard I of England, returning from the crusades in the Holy Land, was captured and held to ransom by Duke Leopold V.

Tributary of the River Danube

Medieval city wall

WHERE TO SEE MEDIEVAL VIENNA

Gothic churches include the Stephansdom (*see pp76–9*), Maria am Gestade (*p85*), the Burgkapelle, Minoritenkirche (*p103*), Ruprechtskirche (*p81*) and Augustinerkirche (*p102*). The Michaelerkirche (*p92*) includes some Gothic sculptures and the Schottenkirche medieval art (*p110*). Surviving medieval houses include the Basiliskenhaus in Schönlaterngasse (*p74*).

Verduner Altar
This masterpiece forms part of the treasury of the huge abbey at Klosterneuburg (see p159). Its 51 panels were completed in 1181 by Nikolaus of Verdun. The abbey itself was consecrated in 1136.

Stained glass *(about 1340) in the Cathedral Museum (p74).*

Hungarian encampment

University
Vienna's University was founded in 1365 by Duke Rudolf IV. This miniature (about 1400) shows the medieval university building and some of the tutors and their students.

1278–82 Rudolf I becomes ruler of Austria after defeating Ottakar II; 640 years of Habsburg rule follow

1288 Viennese uprising against Habsburgs crushed

1359 Rudolf IV lays foundation stone of the Stephansdom tower

1365 University founded

1477 Friedrich III's son Maximilian I marries Mary of Burgundy, heiress to the Low Countries

eal of emysl akar II

1200	1300	1400

1246 Death of Friedrich II followed by Interregnum, during which emysl Ottakar II rules Vienna

1273 Count Rudolf of Habsburg crowned Rudolf I of Germany

1278 Vienna granted a city charter

1330 The first Gothic section of Maria am Gestade built

1438 Albrecht V elected Holy Roman Emperor; Vienna made seat of Empire

1452 Friedrich V crowned as Holy Roman Emperor Friedrich III

1485 Vienna occupied by King Matthias Corvinus of Hungary

Renaissance Vienna

UNDER MAXIMILIAN I, Vienna was transformed into a centre for the arts. The Habsburgs were invariably elected Holy Roman Emperor, and by the 16th century their mighty empire had expanded into Spain, Holland, Burgundy, Bohemia and Hungary. But it was under constant threat: from Turkish attacks, the plague, and disputes between Protestants and Catholics that destabilized the city until 1576, when the Jesuits spearheaded the Counter-Reformation.

EXTENT OF THE CITY

☐ *1600*   ☐ *Today*

Book Illustration
This Renaissance war wagon (1512) is from Maximilian I's collection of books of engravings and illustrations.

Viennese Enamel Casket
This ornate enamel and crystal casket is typical of the skilful craftsmanship practised in Vienna in the 16th century.

Maximilian I married Mary of Burgundy in 1477 and acquired the Burgundian domains.

Imperial Crown
This beautiful crown was made by Bohemian craftsmen in 1610 for Rudolf II and can now be seen in the Hofburg Treasuries (see pp100–1).

Ferdinand I married Anna of Bohemia and Hungary, and inherited Bohemia in 1526. It wa a Habsburg domain until 1918.

TIMELINE

1516 Maximilian's grandson, Karl V, inherits Spain

1519 Karl V inherits Burgundy titles and is elected Holy Roman Emperor; his brother Ferdinand I becomes Austria's archduke

1533 Ferdinand I moves his court to the Hofburg in Vienna

1556 Karl V's son, Philip II, inherits Spain; Ferdinand I takes Bohemia, Austria, Hungary, and imperial title

1571 Protestan Maximilian II allows religious freedom; 80% c city is Protestan

1500	1520	1540	1560	15

1498 Emperor Maximilian I founds Vienna Boys' Choir

1493 Maximilian I expels Hungarians from Vienna

Suleiman the Magnificent

1541 Plague

1529 Graf Niklas Salm vanquishes Turkish army besieging Vienna

1551 Jesuits start Counter-Reformation

1572 Spanish Riding School founded

1577 Protestant services forbidden by Rudolf II

☐ **Renaissance Vienna**

Triumphal Arch of Maximilian I

The German artist Albrecht Dürer (1471–1528) paid homage to Maximilian I in a famous volume of engravings, which included this design for a triumphal arch.

Philip I married Juana of Castile and Aragon in 1496 and acquired Spain.

WHERE TO SEE RENAISSANCE VIENNA

The Schweizertor (see p97) in the Hofburg is the most colourful surviving remnant of Renaissance Vienna, though the Salvatorkapelle portal (p85) surpasses it in elegance. Also in the Hofburg is the Renaissance Stallburg (p93). Some courtyards, such as those at No. 7 Bäckerstrasse (p75) and the Mollard-Clary Palace (p94), preserve a few Renaissance features.

THE FAMILY OF MAXIMILIAN I

Painted by Bernhard Strigel (around 1520), this portrait can be read as a document of how, by marrying into prominent European families, the Habsburg family was able to gain control of almost half of Europe.

Mary of Burgundy was married to Maximilian I and was Duchess of the Burgundian domains.

Karl V inherited Spain from his mother, Juana of Castile and Aragon, in 1516.

The Schweizertor, built in the 16th century, forms the entrance to the Schweizerhof of the Hofburg (p97).

Alte Burg

The medieval core of the Hofburg was constantly being rebuilt. This engraving shows its appearance in the late 15th century, before Ferdinand I had it rebuilt in the 1550s.

edallion ommemorating aximilian II

1618 Bohemian rebellion starts Thirty Year's War

1629 Plague claims 30,000 lives

1643 Swedish forces threaten Vienna

1673–9 War with France over the Low Countries

| 1600 | 1620 | 1640 | 1660 |

1598–1618 Protestantism is banned

1620 Ferdinand II defeats Protestant Bohemian aristocracy; Counter-Reformation spreads throughout Habsburg domains

1621 Jews expelled from Inner City

17th-century French infantry

Baroque Vienna

T HE TURKISH THREAT TO VIENNA ended in 1683 when Kara Mustapha's forces were repelled. Under Karl VI the city expanded and the Karlskirche and the Belvedere palaces were constructed. Around the Hofburg, mansions for noble families sprang up, built by architects such as Johann Bernhard Fischer von Erlach *(see p147)* and Johann Lukas von Hildebrandt *(see p150)*. Vienna was transformed into a resplendent Imperial capital.

J B Fischer von Erlach

EXTENT OF THE CITY

☐ *1700*   ☐ *Today*

WINTER PALACE OF PRINCE EUGENE
J B Fischer von Erlach and Johann Lukas von Hildebrandt designed the Winter Palace *(see p80)* for Prince Eugene, hero of the Turkish campaign.

Plague
This lithograph depicts the plague of 1679, which killed around 30,000 Viennese.

Turkish Bed
Ornamented with martial emblems, this bed was designed for Prince Eugene in 1707.

Coffee Houses
The first coffee houses opened in Vienna in the mid-17th century and they have been a prized institution ever since.

Baroque Architecture
Baroque architecture was at its most prolific in Vienna in the early 18th century.   **Trautson Palace** *(see p117)*

TIMELINE

1683 Turkish siege of Vienna by 200,000 soldiers, under Kara Mustapha, from 14 July to 12 September

1700–14 The war of the Spanish Succession

1680	1690	1700

1679 Plague in Vienna

1683–1736 Prince Eugene of Savoy wins more victories over Turks and French, restoring Austria's fortunes

Kara Mustapha

The war of the Spanish Succession: Battle of Blenheim

 Baroque Vienna

Turkish Siege

The defeat of the Turks in 1683 was crucial, not only for Vienna, but for Central Europe, which was spared the prospect of Ottoman rule.

Baroque statues

Elaborate window hoods

Baroque porticos

Prince Eugene's entourage

Dome ornamentation on the Karlskirche (pp146–7)

Window hood on the Zwölf Apostelkeller (p74)

WHERE TO SEE BAROQUE VIENNA

The Baroque is everywhere in Vienna. Hardly a street in the old city or inner suburbs is without a Baroque mansion or church. Fine examples of Baroque architecture include the Belvedere Palaces (see pp150–55), the Prunksaal (p102), the Karlskirche (pp146–7), the Leopold-inischer Trakt in the Hofburg (pp96–7), the Winter Riding School (pp98–9) and the Bohemian Court Chancery (p84–5). Beautiful Baroque houses line many streets, including Naglergasse (p94) and Kurrentgasse (p86).

The Prunksaal (1721–6) was built by J B Fischer von Erlach.

Prince Eugene

Best remembered for his role in defeating the Turks, Prince Eugene showed great military prowess in the ensuing decades, and died in 1736 laden with honours.

1713 Karl VI proclaims Pragmatic Sanction, allowing succession through the female line

1719 Karlskirche begun

Statue of Maria Theresa holding Pragmatic Sanction

1716 Lower Belvedere completed

1713–14 Last plague in Vienna

1722 Vienna becomes an archbishopric

1724–6 Prunksaal and Upper Belvedere completed

Upper Belvedere

1720

1730

Vienna under Maria Theresa

THE LONG REIGN OF MARIA THERESA was a time of serenity, wealth and sensible administration, despite a background of frequent wars. The vast palace of Schönbrunn was completed by the Empress, who also presided over Vienna's development as the musical capital of Europe. She was succeeded by Joseph II, who introduced many reforms, including religious freedom and public health measures. However, these reforms made him unpopular with his subjects, including the nobility who were angered by the way he handed out titles to bankers and industrialists.

Empress Maria Theresa

EXTENT OF THE CITY
☐ 1775   ☐ Today

Rococo Table
Wilhelm Martitz designed this Rococo table in 1769 for Maria Theresa, who employed artists committed to the elaborate Rococo style.

Karlskirche   Stephansdom

Young Mozart
Mozart often performed for the Habsburgs, who were highly receptive to his genius.

Burgtheater Programme
This programme was printed for the first performance of Mozart's The Marriage of Figaro *in 1786, which took place in the original Burgtheater on Michaelerplatz.*

TIMELINE

Christoph von Gluck

1744–9 Schönbrunn Palace is extensively altered by Maria Theresa's court architect, Nikolaus Pacassi

1754 Vienna's first census records a population of 175,000

1740	1750	1760

1740 Maria Theresa comes to the throne; war of the Austrian Succession

Schönbrunn Palace

1762 First performance of Christoph von Gluck's *(see p38) Orpheus and Eurydice* in the Burgtheater

1766 Prater, formerly an imperial game reserve, opened to the public by Joseph II

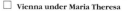

☐ **Vienna under Maria Theresa**

Damenkarussell
This painting by Martin van Meytens depicts the Damenkarussell (1743), which was held at the Winter Riding School (see pp98–9) to celebrate the defeat of the French army at Prague.

VIEW FROM THE BELVEDERE

Under Maria Theresa, the Viennese were able to enjoy a prosperous city. This townscape by Bernardo Bellotto (1759–61) shows them sauntering through the gardens of the Belvedere, with the palaces and churches of the city in the distance.

Belvedere Gardens

The Pope
In 1782 Pope Pius VI came to Vienna in an attempt to undo the religious reforms of Joseph II.

WHERE TO SEE MARIA THERESA'S VIENNA

Schönbrunn Palace (see pp172–3) and the Theresianum (p149) date from the reign of Maria Theresa. Joseph II later commissioned the Josephinum (p111) and the Narrenturm (p111), and opened the Augarten (p162) and Prater (pp160–61) to the public. A Rococo organ is in the Michaelerkirche (p92), and some of Maria Theresa's tableware is in the Hofburg Treasuries (pp100–1).

Schönbrunn Palace *is filled with Rococo interiors commissioned by Maria Theresa.*

The Rococo high altar *which is in the Michaelerkirche dates from around 1750.*

1781 Joseph II's Edict of Toleration

Allgemeine Krankenhaus

1784 Joseph II founds the Allgemeine Krankenhaus and Narrenturm *(see p111)*

1775 Augarten opened to the public by Joseph II

1782 Pope Pius VI in Vienna

0   **1780**   **1790**

1786 First performance of Mozart's *The Marriage of Figaro* in the Burgtheater

1790–2 Emperor Leopold II

1791 First performance of Mozart's *The Magic Flute*

Biedermeier Vienna

EXTENT OF THE CITY

☐ *1830*   ☐ *Today*

N
APOLEON'S DEFEAT OF AUSTRIA was a humiliation for Emperor Franz I. The French conqueror briefly occupied Schönbrunn Palace, demolished part of the city walls, and married Franz I's daughter. After the Congress of Vienna, Franz I and his minister, Prince Metternich, imposed autocratic rule in Austria. The middle classes, excluded from political life, retreated into the artistic and domestic pursuits that characterized the Biedermeier age.

Early 19th-century dress

Revolution in 1848 drove Metternich from power but led to a new period of conservative rule under Franz Joseph.

Prince Metternich
The architect of the Congress of Vienna, Metternich gained political supremacy of Austria over four decades. In 1848 revolutionary mobs drove him from Vienna.

THE CONGRESS OF VIENNA

After the defeat of Napoleon in 1814, the victorious European powers gathered in Vienna to restore the established order that had been severely disrupted by the French emperor. The crowned heads and elected rulers of Europe spent a year in the city, where the court and nobility entertained them with a succession of balls and other diversions. The outcome was the restoration of reactionary rule across Europe that, although repressive in many countries, managed to maintain the peace until a series of revolutions swept across Europe in 1848.

The singer Michael Vogl

Franz Schubert playing the piano

TIMELINE

1800 Vienna's population 232,000

1806 The Holy Roman Empire ends after Franz II abdicates and becomes Emperor Franz I of Austria

1805 First performance of Beethoven's Eroica Symphony and *Fidelio* in Theater an der Wien. Napoleon wins victory at Austerlitz

Napoleon Bonaparte

1811 Austria suffers economic collapse and state bankruptcy

1812–14 Napoleon defeated by Russia, Prussia, England and Austria

1809 Napoleon moves into Schönbrunn Palace and marries Franz I's daughter Maria-Louisa

1815–48 Period of political suppression known as the Vormärz

1814–15 Congress of Vienna held under Presidency of Metternich; Austria loses Belgium but gains parts of Northern Italy

Franz Grillparzer

1825 Johann Strauss the Eld forms first wal orchest

1800   **1810**   **1820**

☐ **Biedermeier Vienna**

The 1848 Revolution

This painting from 1848 by Anton Ziegler shows the revolution in Vienna, when the middle classes and workers fought together against Metternich.

Biedermeier Chair

This style of furniture characterized the domestic aspirations of Vienna's middle classes in the 1820s.

WHERE TO SEE BIEDERMEIER VIENNA

Napoleon's partial demolition of the city walls led to the creation of the Burggarten *(p102)* and the Volksgarten *(p104)*. Domestic architecture flourished – Biedermeier houses include the Geymüller Schlössl *(p158)* and the Dreimäderlhaus *(p129)* – as did the applied arts *(pp82–3)*.

The Geymüller Schlössl, dating from 1802, is home to Vienna's Biedermeier museum.

SCHUBERTIADE

Franz Schubert *(see p38)* wrote over 600 songs. These were often performed at musical evenings such as the one shown in this painting, *An Evening at Baron von Spaun's,* by Moritz von Schwind (1804–71).

The Grand Gallop

Waltzes, popularized by Johann Strauss I (the Elder) (see p38), were extremely popular in the 1820s.

1827 Death of Beethoven

1828 Death of Schubert

1831 The dramatist Franz Grillparzer completes *Des Meeres und der Liebe Wellen*

1830 Vienna's population reaches 318,000

1831–2 Cholera epidemic

1830

1837 First railway constructed

1846 Johann Strauss the Younger becomes music director of the court balls until 1870

1845 Gas lighting introduced

1840

1848 Revolution in Vienna; Metternich forced from office, and Emperor Ferdinand I abdicates to be replaced by Franz Joseph

1850 City population reaches 431,000

Ringstrasse Vienna

THE EMPEROR FRANZ JOSEPH ushered in a new age of grandeur, despite the dwindling power of the Habsburgs. The city's defences were demolished and a circular boulevard, the Ringstrasse, was built, linking new cultural and political institutions. Vienna attracted gifted men and women from all over the empire, as well as traders from Eastern Europe. However, the resulting ethnic brew often resulted in over-crowding and social tension.

Franz Joseph

EXTENT OF THE CITY

☐ *1885*   ☐ *Today*

Votivkirche (1856–79) *p111*
Heinrich Ferstel

Neues Rathaus (1872–83) *p128*
Friedrich von Schmidt

Parliament (1874–84) *p125*
Theophil Hansen

The Natural History Museum (1871–1890) *pp126–7, Gottfried Semper*

Kunsthistorisches Museum (1871–1890) *pp118–23 Gottfried Semper*

THE SUICIDE OF ARCHDUKE RUDOLF AT MAYERLING

In 1889 the 30-year-old heir to the throne was found dead with his mistress Mary Vetsera. The Archduke's suicide was more than a social scandal. It was a blow to the Habsburg regime, since he was a progressive and intelligent man. His despair may have been aggravated by court protocol that offered no outlet for his ideas.

Theophil Hansen
This Danish-born architect (1813–91) studied in Athens before settling in Vienna. The Greek influence is most evident in his Parliament building on the Ringstrasse.

TIMELINE

Excavation for the Ringstrasse

1867 First performance of *The Blue Danube* by Strauss in Vienna. Hungary granted autonomy, leading to Dual Monarchy with separate governments

1850	1855	1860	1865

Anton Bruckner

1868 Anton Bruckner *(see p39)* moves from Linz to Vienna

1869 Johannes Brahms settles in Vienna as conductor of the Gesellschaft der Musikfreunde. Opera House opens on Ringstrasse

1857–65 Demolition of fortifications and the building of the Ringstrasse

☐ **Ringstrasse Vienna**

The Danube
The River Danube often flooded its banks, so its course was altered and regulated in the 1890s by a system of canals and locks.

Vienna Café Society
In the 19th century, Vienna's cafés became the haunts of literary and political cliques.

Museum of Applied Arts (1867–71) *pp82–3, Heinrich Ferstel*

Horse-drawn Trams
Trams appeared on the Ringstrasse in the 1860s. Horseless trams ran along it by the end of the 19th century.

Stadtpark

Opera House (1861–69) *pp138–9*
Eduard van der Nüll and August Sicardsburg

RINGSTRASSE
This great boulevard, built on the orders of Franz Joseph, separates the Stephansdom and Hofburg Quarters from the suburbs. Completed in the 1880s, the Ringstrasse is as grand now as it was then.

The Opening of the Stadtpark
Laid out on either side of the River Wien, the Stadtpark was inaugurated in 1862.

1874 First performance of Strauss's *Die Fledermaus* at the Theater an der Wien. Opening of Central Cemetery

1889 Suicide of Archduke Rudolf at Mayerling

1875

1880

1885

1873 Stock market crash

1879 Lavish historical parade along the Ringstrasse celebrates Franz Joseph's silver wedding

1872 Death of Austrian poet and dramatist Franz Grillparzer

1890 The suburbs are incorporated into the city

Vienna in the 1900s

THE TURN OF THE CENTURY was a time of intellectual ferment in Vienna. This was the age of Freud, of the writers Karl Kraus and Arthur Schnitzler, and of the Secession and Jugendstil *(see pp54–7)*. At this time artists such as Gustav Klimt and the architects Otto Wagner and Adolf Loos *(see p92)* created revolutionary new styles. This was all set against a decaying Habsburg empire, which Karl I's abdication in 1918 brought to an end. After World War I Austria became a republic.

Engel Apotheke sign

EXTENT OF THE CITY

▨ *1912*   ☐ *Today*

Wiener Werkstätte
Josef Hoffmann (see p56), designer of this chair, was the principal artist and founder of this Viennese arts workshop (see p83).

KIRCHE AM STEINHOF
This stupendous church was designed by Otto Wagner and decorated by Kolo Moser *(see p57)*.

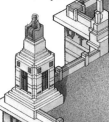

Loos Haus
The restrained elegance of this former tailoring firm is typical of Loos's style (see p92).

The Secession
This poster by Kolo Moser (see p57) was used to publicize the Secession's exhibitions.

Angels by Othmar Schimkowitz

TIMELINE

1899 First issue of Karl Kraus's periodical *Die Fackel*

1903 Wiener Werkstätte founded

1906 Arnold Schönberg's *Chamber Symphony* and works by Anton von Webern and Alban Berg performed at the Musikverein, provoking a riot

1895	1900	1905

1897 Secession established when 19 painters and architects break with the Künstlerhaus. Karl Lueger becomes mayor

1902 Gustav Klimt paints the *Beethoven Frieze*. Tramways are electrified

1905 Franz Lehár's operetta *The Merry Widow* first performed. Anti-Semitic riots at the university

1896 Death of the composer Anton Bruckner

Gustav Klimt

☐ **Vienna in the 1900s**

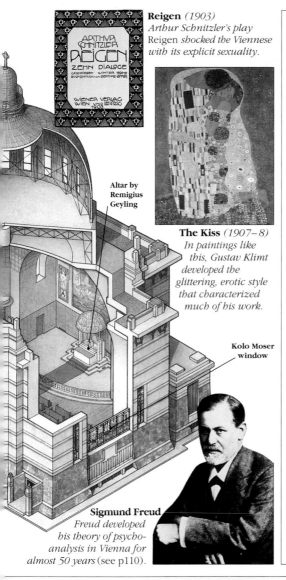

Reigen *(1903)*
Arthur Schnitzler's play
Reigen *shocked the Viennese
with its explicit sexuality.*

**Altar by
Remigius
Geyling**

The Kiss *(1907–8)*
*In paintings like
this, Gustav Klimt
developed the
glittering, erotic style
that characterized
much of his work.*

**Kolo Moser
window**

Sigmund Freud
*Freud developed
his theory of psycho-
analysis in Vienna for
almost 50 years (see p110).*

WHERE TO SEE 1900s VIENNA

Otto Wagner designed
the Karlsplatz Pavilions
(see p144), the Wagner
Apartments *(p137)*, and the
Kirche am Steinhof *(p158)*.
Adolf Loos *(p92)* designed
Loos Haus *(p92)* and the
American Bar *(p105)*. Subur-
ban architecture includes
the Wagner Villas *(p158)*.
Paintings by Klimt, Schiele,
and Kokoschka are displayed
at the Upper Belvedere
(pp152–3) and the Museum
of Modern Art *(p111)*.

The Secession Building *is
where Gustav Klimt's Beethoven Frieze is exhibited (p55).*

The Wagner Apartments *are
decorated with Jugendstil motifs
(p56) by Kolo Moser (p57).*

7 Gustav Mahler gns as director Court Opera. er studies art in nna	**1911** Death of Gustav Mahler	**1914** Archduke Ferdinand assassin-ated in Sarajevo; international crisis follows resulting in World War I
1910		**1915**
1910 Death of Karl Lueger		**1916** Death of Franz Joseph
1908 *The Kiss* by Klimt is first exhibited		**1918** Declaration of Austrian Republic after abdication of Emperor Karl I. Austria shrinks from an empire of 50 million to a state of 6.5 million

Modern Vienna

Two decades of struggle between the left and right political parties followed World War I, ending with the union of Austria with Germany – the Anschluss – in 1938. After World War II Vienna was split among the Allies until 1955, when Austria regained its independence.

1929 Ludwig Wittgenstein, a prominent member of the Vienna circle, leaves Vienna for England

1955 On 15 May the Austrian State Treaty brings to an end the Allied occupation. Austria granted independence and declares itself to be permanently neutral

1927 Workers, angered by deaths of bystanders during political violence, storm the Palace of Justice

1951 The First Festival of Vienna

1922 Karl Kraus publishes his immense drama *The Last Days of Mankind*

1944 Allied bombing of Vienna begins

1920	1930	1940	1950

1920	1930	1940	1950

1922 Death in Madeira of exiled Karl I, last Habsburg emperor

1939 Death of novelist Joseph Roth

1945 World War II ends. The second Austrian republic is declared, but Vienna remains divided between the four Allied powers

1918–20 Severe food shortages and an influenza epidemic afflict the Viennese

1933 Chancellor Dollfuss dissolves Parliament and forms a fascist regime, but refuses to accommodate Hitler

1934 Street fighting in Vienna between socialists and government troops; socialists banned. Murder of Chancellor Dollfuss by the Nazis

1919 Richard Strauss appointed joint director of the State Opera

1920–34 Socialism prevails in so-called "Red Vienna", despite conservative Catholic rule in Austria

1938 Chancellor Schuschnigg resigns. Hitler enters Vienna and pronounces Anschluss

1955 Reopening of Opera House and Burgtheater

1956 Atomic Energy Agency located in Vienna

1959 Ernst Fuchs and Arik Braue establish the school of fantastic realisr

1989 Death of Empress Zita, the last Habsburg to have ruled Austria

1988 Irmgard Seefried, star of the Vienna Opera House, dies

1986 The controversial Kurt Waldheim elected president; Franz Vranitzky elected Chancellor

1979 East-West summit held between Leonid Brezhnev and Jimmy Carter

1983 Pope John Paul visits Vienna

1970–83 Socialist Bruno Kreisky is Chancellor

1978 U-Bahn system opened

1992 Fire in the Hofburg Palace

0	1970	1980	1990	2000

0	1970	1980	1990	2000

1967 UN Industrial Development Organization (UNIDO) comes to Vienna

1995 Austria joins the European Union

1989 Velvet Revolution in Czechoslovakia heralds Austria's growing economic influence in the new democratic central Europe. Completion of Hans Hollein's Haas Haus in Stephansplatz

1985 Hundertwasser Haus by Friedensreich Hundertwasser completed

1979 UNO city opened

1961 John F Kennedy meets Nikita Khrushchev at East-West summit in Vienna

Music in Vienna

FROM THE LATE 18TH to the mid 19th centuries Vienna was the music capital of Europe. At first the Habsburg family and the aristocracy were the city's musical paymasters, but with the rise of the middle classes during the Biedermeier period *(see pp30–31)* music became an important part of bourgeois life. Popular music also flourished as migration from all parts of the Habsburg Empire brought in richly diverse styles of music and dance.

The Waltz became popular following the Congress of Vienna in 1814

a state occasion. The music of Franz Schubert (1797–1828) was little known in his short lifetime. He mostly performed chamber works, piano music and songs at Biedermeier *Schubertiaden* – evenings of music with friends. His music became more popular following his death. After this, "serious" music went through a

CLASSICISM

IN THE 18TH century, Vienna's musical life was dominated by the Imperial Court. Christoph Willibald Gluck (1714–87) was Court *Kapellmeister* (in charge of the court orchestra) to Maria Theresa until 1770, and wrote 10 operas specially for Vienna, including *Orpheus and Eurydice* (1762). His contemporary Wolfgang Amadeus Mozart (1756–91) later built on these foundations. Joseph Haydn (1732–1809) moved to Vienna in the 1790s from Prince Esterházy's palace in Eisenstadt *(see pp174–5)*, and wrote masterpieces such as *The Creation*.

Performance of *The Creation* (1808) on Haydn's birthday

ROMANTICISM

WITH THE arrival of Ludwig van Beethoven (1770–1827) in Vienna in the mid-1790s, the age of the composer as romantic hero was born. Beethoven was a controversial figure in his time, and many of his most innovative works were only successful outside Vienna. His funeral, however, attended by more than 10,000 people, was

Biedermeier *Schubertiade* evening

fallow period in Vienna, but Johann Strauss I (1804–49) and Joseph Lanner (1801–43) began creating dance music, centred on the waltz.

Performance of *The Magic Flute* (1791) by Mozart

TIMELINE

1700	1725	1750	1775	1800	1825
1714–1787 Christoph Willibald Gluck	**1732–1809** Joseph Haydn	*Joseph Haydn*	*Ludwig van Beethoven*	**1797–1828** Franz Schubert	*Johannes Brahms*
					1833–97 Johannes Brahms
	Christoph Willibald Gluck	**1756–91** Wolfgang Amadeus Mozart	**1770–1827** Ludwig van Beethoven	**1804–49** Johann Strauss I	**1825–99** Johann Strauss II
				1801–43 Joseph Lanner	**1824–96** Anton Bruckner

AGE OF FRANZ JOSEPH

A NEW ERA of high musical art began in the 1860s. Johannes Brahms (1833–97) came to Vienna in 1862, and incorporated popular musical styles into works such as his Liebeslieder waltzes and Hungarian Dances. The Romantic composer Anton Bruckner (1824–96) came to the city from Upper Austria in 1868. Johann Strauss II (1825–99) rose to the status of civic hero, composing nearly 400 waltzes, including his famous operetta *Die Fledermaus*. One popular offshoot of the period was *Schrammel* music, named after Joseph Schrammel (1850–

Jugendstil poster (1901) for the Waltz depicting Johann Strauss II

93) and characterized by an ensemble of guitars, violins and accordion. Popular music also influenced Gustav Mahler (1860–1911), director of the Vienna Opera for 10 years.

THE MODERNS

T HE EARLY YEARS of the 20th century saw the rise of the Second Viennese School: Alban Berg (1885–1935), Arnold Schönberg (1874–1951) and Anton von Webern (1883–1945). These composers were not well received in Vienna, and Schönberg found he had to start his own society to get his works, and those of his colleagues, heard. In 1933 he emigrated to the USA. Since World War II no composers of comparable stature have arisen, though Kurt Schwertsik (born 1935) and H K Gruber (born 1943) now attract international attention. However, the Vienna Philharmonic, established in 1842, is still one of the finest orchestras in the world. The State Opera continues to enjoy a strong reputation, while the Vienna-based Alban Berg Quartet is one of the world's most sought-after chamber ensembles.

The Johann Strauss II orchestra at a Court ball

Concert poster (1913) for Arnold Schönberg

1860–1911 Gustav Mahler	1874–1951 Arnold Schönberg	
	1875	
1883–1945 Anton von Webern	1885–1935 Alban Berg	
50–93 eph hrammel		

VIENNA BOYS' CHOIR

The world-famous Vienna Boys' Choir, the Wiener Sängerknaben, was founded in 1498 by that great patron of the arts, Maximilian I. Today the boys perform masses by Mozart, Schubert or Haydn on Sundays and church holidays at the Burgkapelle *(see p103).* To obtain a seat you need to book at least eight weeks in advance.

VIENNA AT A GLANCE

VIENNA IS A COMPACT city and most of its sights are contained within a small area. However, the city boasts an astonishing array of monuments, palaces, parks and museums, which themselves house an impressive array of art and artefacts from all over the world and from all periods of history. Nearly 150 sights are listed in the *Area by Area* section of this book, but to help make the most of your stay, the next 20 pages offer a guide to the very best that Vienna has to offer. As well as churches, palaces, museums and galleries, there are sections on Jugendstil art and coffee houses. Many of the sights listed have a cross-reference to their own full entry. To start with, some of Vienna's top tourist attractions are listed below.

VIENNA'S TOP TOURIST ATTRACTIONS

Opera House
See pp138–9.

Burgtheater
See pp130–31.

Prater
See pp160–61.

Karlskirche
See pp146–7.

Schönbrunn *See pp170–73.*

Winter Riding School
See pp98–9.

Kunsthistorisches Museum
See pp118–23.

Stephansdom *See pp76–9.*

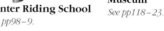

Café Central
See p61.

MuseumsQuartier
See p117.

Belvedere
See pp150–55.

◁ The façade of Otto Wagner's Majolikahaus *(see p137)* on the Linke Wienzeile

Vienna's Best: Historic Houses and Palaces

BAROQUE MANSIONS DOMINATE the streets of the Stephansdom Quarter, while outside the centre of Vienna are the grand summer palaces where the Habsburg emperors and aristocracy lived during warm Middle European summers. The interiors of several of the houses can be visited, while others can only be admired from the outside or from their inner courtyards and staircases. Further details can be found on pages 44–5.

Sigmund Freud's House
This waiting room in the house on Berggasse, where Sigmund Freud lived from 1891 to 1938, has been lovingly restored.

Schottenring and Alsergrund

Kinsky Palace
This mansion (1713–16) by Johann Lukas von Hildebrandt (see p150), was built for the Daun family, and is sometimes called the Daun Kinsky Palace. Wirch Philip Daun was commander of the city garrison, and his son Leopold Joseph Daun was Maria Theresa's field marshal.

Museum and Townhall Quarter

Hofburg
The apartments here are made up of over 20 rooms; among them are ceremonial halls and living quarters which were once occupied by Franz Joseph (see pp32–3) and the Empress Elisabeth.

0 kilometres 0.5

0 miles 0.25

Opera and Naschmarkt

Schönbrunn Palace
This palace, by J B Fischer von Erlach, was built on a scale to rival the palace of Versailles outside Paris. Parts of it were later redesigned by Maria Theresa's architect Nikolaus Pacassi (see p170).

Neidhart Fresco House
Frescoes dating from 1400, depicting the songs of the medieval minnesinger Neidhart van Reuenthal, decorate the dining room of this former house of a wealthy clockmaker.

Figarohaus
Mozart lived in this Baroque building for three years between 1784 and 1787, and composed one of his most famous works, The Marriage of Figaro, *here.*

Winter Palace of Prince Eugene
J B Fischer von Erlach and Johann Lukas von Hildebrandt designed this Baroque palace, with its spectacular staircase, for the war hero Prince Eugene (see pp26–7).

Zum Blauen Karpfen
A stucco relief of a blue carp and a frieze of putti *adorn the façade of this 17th-century house on Annagasse.*

Belvedere Quarter

Belvedere
Designed by Johann Lukas von Hildebrandt, Prince Eugene's summer palaces, built on what were originally the southern outskirts of Vienna, now house important museums of Austrian art.

Exploring Vienna's Historic Houses and Palaces

A STROLL AROUND VIENNA'S streets offers the visitor an unparalleled choice of beautifully-preserved historic buildings, from former imperial residences to humbler burgher's dwellings. The majority date from the 17th and 18th centuries, and illustrate the various phases of Baroque architecture. In most cases their original function as residences of the rich and famous has been superseded; a number have now been turned into museums, and their interiors are open to the public.

Façade of the Schönborn-Batthyány Palace

TOWN PALACES

T HE MOST EXTENSIVE town palace is the **Hofburg**, with its museums and imperial apartments. The staircase of the magnificent **Winter Palace of Prince Eugene** is on view to the public, and the 19th-century Neo-Gothic **Ferstel Palace** (1860) houses the Café Central *(see p58)*. The **Obizzi Palace** is home to the Clock Museum *(see p86)*. Town palaces which can be admired from the outside only are the **Kinsky Palace** (1713–16), **Trautson Palace**, **Schönborn-Batthyány Palace**, **Lobkowitz Palace**, and **Liechtenstein Palace** (1694–1706), the winter home of the Liechtenstein family.

GARDEN PALACES

A LTHOUGH IT SEEMS strange that palaces within the city limits should be termed garden palaces, when they were built they were outside the city boundaries, and offered a cool refuge during the hot summer months. The most famous example is **Schönbrunn Palace**, where the state apartments can be seen as part of a guided tour. The **Belvedere**, to the south of the city, houses museums of Austrian art, and many of the rooms retain their original splendid decoration. The nearby **Schwarzenberg Palace** is now a luxury hotel and is open to hotel guests only. The **Hermes Villa** (1884), a cross between a hunting lodge and a villa, was commissioned by Franz Joseph for his wife Elisabeth. The interior of the Neo-Classical **Rasumofsky Palace** (1806–7), now occupied by the Institute of Geology, can sometimes be seen on special occasions. The **Liechtenstein Garden Palace** houses the Museum of Modern Art *(see p111)*.

Frescoed ceiling of the Liechtenstein Garden Palace

SUBURBAN VILLAS

T HE DÖBLING regional museum is housed in the Biedermeier **Villa Wertheimstein** (1834–5), where the interior is furnished in its original flamboyant and overcrowded manner. By contrast, the **Geymüller Schlössl**, containing the Sobek Collection of clocks and watches, is a model of taste and restraint. In Hietzing, the **Villa Primavesi** (1913–15) is a small Jugendstil masterpiece designed by Josef Hoffmann *(see p56)* for the banker Robert Primavesi.

BURGHERS' HOUSES

O N TUCHLAUBEN, the **Neidhart Fresco House** is decorated with secular frescoes from around 1400. Charming Baroque houses of modest dimensions can be seen on **Naglergasse** and **Kurrentgasse** and in inner districts such as **Spittelberg** and **Josefstadt**. A particularly fine example of external decoration can be seen on the Baroque inn **Zum Blauen Karpfen** in Annagasse *(see p80)*. The **Dreimäderlhaus** in Schreyvogelgasse, built in an intermediate style between Rococo and Neo-Classicism, is also worth visiting.

Façade and gardens of the Hermes Villa

MEMORIAL HOUSES

VIENNA ABOUNDS in the former residences of famous composers. They are not all of great architectural merit, and their interest tends to reside mainly in the exhibits they contain. The **Pasqualati Haus** was one of Beethoven's many Viennese residences – it was here that he composed the opera *Fidelio* – and the museum here houses portraits and other mementoes of the great composer. The rooms of the **Heiligenstadt Testament House**, where Beethoven stayed in an attempt to cure his deafness, are now a memorial. The first-floor apartment of the **Haydn Museum** in Haydngasse is

Courtyard of the Heiligenstadt Testament House

pleasantly furnished and filled with letters, manuscripts, personal possessions and the composer's two pianos. Mozart and his family lived from 1784–7 in the **Figarohaus**. This is where Mozart wrote *The Marriage of Figaro*.

The **Freud Museum** houses furnishings, documents and photographs, and the waiting room is as it looked when Freud used to see his patients. It is also a study centre.

DECORATIVE DETAILS

Many of the historic houses and palaces of Vienna were built during a period corresponding to the Baroque and late Baroque styles of architecture. Details such as window hoods and pediments over doorways were often extremely ornate.

Caryatid on the doorway of the Liechtenstein Palace

Decorative window hood on the façade of the Trautson Palace

Decorative urns on the Lobkowitz Palace

Decorative pediment with shield on the Schönborn-Batthyány Palace.

Stucco *putti* on the façade of Zum Blauen Karpfen

WHERE TO FIND THE PALACES AND HOUSES

Vienna's Best: Museums and Galleries

VIENNA BOASTS an astonishing number of museums, and many of the collections are housed in elegant former palaces or handsome buildings specially commissioned for the purpose. Some of the museums are of international importance, while others are of more local or specialist interest. Further details can be found on pages 48–9.

Natural History Museum
This museum has displays of fossils, ethnography, mineralogy and a much-visited dinosaur hall.

Sacred and Secular Treasuries
The Ainkurn sword (around 1450) can be seen in the Imperial Treasuries in the former imperial palace of the Hofburg.

Schottenring and Alsergrund

Kunsthistorisches Museum
Hans Holbein's portrait of Jane Seymour (1536) is one of hundreds of Old Master paintings displayed in this fine art museum.

Museum and Townhall Quarter

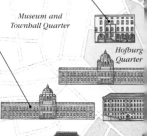

Hofburg Quarter

Opera and Naschmarkt

MuseumsQuartier
This vast cultural centre contains the largest Egon Schiele collection in the world, including this Self-portrait with Lowered Head *(1912).*

Albertina
This museum has a constantly changing display of drawings and graphic works, such as Albrecht Dürer's The Hare *(1502).*

Historical Museum of the City of Vienna

Stained-glass windows from the Stephansdom (around 1390) are among the many items here documenting Vienna's history.

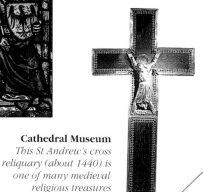

Cathedral Museum

This St Andrew's cross reliquary (about 1440) is one of many medieval religious treasures on display here.

Austrian Museum of Applied Arts

The applied arts of Vienna, such as this early 19th-century beaker and Wiener Werkstätte furniture (see pp54–7), are among the varied artefacts on display in this museum.

Museums of Baroque and Medieval Art

The Lower Belvedere houses two museums devoted to Austrian art up to the 18th century. Among the collections is the medieval Schotten-altar, which dates from around 1470.

Stephansdom Quarter

Museum of 19th- and 20th-Century Art

Ferdinand Waldmüller's Roses in the Window (1832) is one of several Biedermeier canvases on show here. There are also works by Klimt, Schiele and Kokoschka.

Belvedere Quarter

Heeresgeschichtliches Museum

Paintings of battles and military commanders, such as Sigmund L'Allemand's portrait of Field Marshal Gideon-Ernst Freiherr von Laudon (1878), are part of this museum's collection.

ilometres   0.5

iiles   0.25

Exploring Vienna's Museums and Galleries

VIENNA'S MUSEUMS EXHIBIT an amazing variety of fine, decorative and ethnic art from all periods of history and from different regions of the world. The visitor can see artefacts from all over the ancient world as well as more recent collections, from medieval religious art to 19th- and 20th-century paintings. Silverware is displayed in the city's imperial collections, and Vienna is also unrivalled for its turn-of-the-century exhibits.

Interior of Friedensreich Hundert-wasser's Kunsthaus Wien

ANCIENT AND MEDIEVAL ART

VIENNA HAS marvellous collections of medieval art. The **Neidhart Fresco House** contains medieval secular frescoes, while a number of superb Gothic altarpieces can be seen in the **Museum of Medieval Art**. Displayed in the **Cathedral Museum** are outstanding Gothic sculptures as well as masterpieces of applied art; the highlight is a 9th-century Carolingian Gospel. The **Sacred and Secular Treasuries** in the Hofburg are awash with precious medieval objects, including the insignia and crown of the Holy Roman Empire, and a unique collection of medieval objects and Gothic paintings is on display in the treasury of the **Deutschordenskirche**. The splendours of the Verduner Altar at **Klosterneuberg**

await those prepared to make a short journey out of the centre of Vienna. The **Ephesos Museum** of the Hofburg houses ancient Roman and Greek antiquities unearthed at the turn of the century.

OLD MASTERS

THE PICTURE GALLERY in the **Kunsthistorisches Museum** has one of the best collections of Old Masters in the world, reflecting the tastes of the many generations of Habsburg collectors who formed it. There are works by Flemish and Venetian artists, and the best collection of Bruegels on display in any art gallery, as well as Giuseppe Arcimboldo's (1527–93) curious portraits composed of fruit and vegetables. The **Academy of Fine Arts** houses some fine examples of Dutch and Flemish works, its prize exhibit being Hieronymos Bosch's triptych of the *Last Judgement*,

which contains some of the most horrifying images in Christan art. There are also paintings by Johannes Vermeer (1632–75) and Peter Paul Rubens (1577–1640). The **Museum of Baroque Art** focuses on Austrian paintings and sculptures from the 17th and 18th centuries. The building that the museum is housed in is a masterpiece of Baroque architecture.

19TH- AND 20TH-CENTURY ART

A PERMANENT display of 19th- and 20th-century Austrian art is housed in the **Museum of 19th- and 20th-Century Art**. The most famous exhibits are by Gustav Klimt, and his newly-restored *Beethoven Frieze* can be seen in the **Secession Building**. The **Museum of Modern Art** has recently moved from the Liechtenstein Garden Palace to the new MuseumsQuartier (*see p117*). It contains exhibits by 20th-century European artists, including recent works by the Viennese avant garde, and a huge Egon Schiele collection. The work of Friedensreich Hundertwasser, perhaps Vienna's best-known modern artist, is on show at his gallery, the **Kunsthaus Wien**. The **Albertina's** prints and collotypes are currently housed in the Akademiehof near the Academy of Fine Arts.

Parthian monument (around AD 170) in the Ephesos Museum

THE APPLIED ARTS AND INTERIORS

O N DISPLAY IN THE **Austrian Museum of Applied Arts** is a rich collection of the decorative arts, including Oriental carpets, medieval ecclesiastical garments, Biedermeier and Jugendstil furniture, and the archives of the Wiener Werkstätte. The **Historical Museum of the City of Vienna** houses a reconstructed version of the poet Franz Grillparzer's apartment as well as Adolf Loos's (*see p92*) drawing room. In the **Silberkammer** of the Hofburg is a dazzling array of dinner services collected by the Habsburgs. The **Lobmeyr Museum** exhibits glassware designed by Josef Hoffmann.

Glass by Josef Hoffmann in the Lobmeyr Museum

Picture clock in the Clock Museum

SPECIALIST MUSEUMS

C LOCK ENTHUSIASTS can visit the **Clock Museum** and the Sobek Clock and Watch Collection at the **Geymüller Schlössl**. Music is celebrated at the **Sammlung Alter Musikinstrumente**, while the darker side of life can be seen at the **Kriminalmuseum**, and at the **Bestattungsmuseum** which houses exhibits to do with Viennese funeral rites. The **Heeresgeschichtliches Museum** houses reminders of Austria's military past. The **Hofjagd und Rüstkammer** exhibits historical weaponry. Other specialist museums include the **Österreichisches Filmmuseum** and the **Doll and Toy Museum**.

NATURAL HISTORY AND SCIENCE

S TILL OCCUPYING the building constructed for it in the 19th century is the **Natural History Museum**, which has displays of mineralogy, dinosaur skeletons and zoology. The **Josephinum** houses a range of wax anatomical models, while the **Technical Museum** documents the contribution Austria has made to developments in technology, ranging from home-made items such as an amateur wooden typewriter, to the invention of the car.

ETHNOLOGY AND FOLKLORE

V IENNA'S Museum of Ethnology in the Hofburg, the **Völkerkundemuseum**, contains objects from all over the world. There are artefacts from Mexico and a collection of musical instruments, masks and textiles from the Far East. The Benin collection from Africa is now back on display in the museum (*see p95*). There is also a section on Eskimo culture. The **Museum für Volkskunde** in Josefstadt houses fascinating exhibits on Austrian folklore and rural life over the centuries.

Benin carving in the Völkerkundemuseum

Vienna's Best: Churches

Vienna's most potent symbol is its cathedral – the Stephansdom – a masterpiece of Gothic architecture which stands out in a city where the overwhelming emphasis is on the Baroque. After the defeat of the Turks in 1683 *(see pp26–7)*, many churches were built or remodelled in the Baroque style, although it is often possible to detect the vestiges of older buildings beneath later additions. Many church interiors are lavishly furnished, and several have fine frescoes. Churches are generally open during the day except when mass is being held. Stage concerts or organ recitals are given in the evenings in some churches. A more detailed overview of Vienna's churches is on pages 52–3.

Peterskirche
The tall dome of this late Baroque church dominates the view as you approach from the Graben.

Michaelerkirche
This church has one of the most impressive medieval interiors in Vienna. The Neo-Classical façade and this cascade of Baroque stucco angels over the high altar were later additions.

Schottenring and Alsergrund

Museum and Townhall Quarter

Hofb
Qua

Maria Treu Kirche
A statue of Mary Immaculate graces the square in front of this Baroque church (1716). Its façade dates from 1860.

Opera and Naschmarkt

0 kilometres   0.5

0 miles   0.25

Augustinerkirche
Antonio Canova's (1753–1822) tomb for Archduchess Maria Christina is in the Gothic Augustinerkirche, which once served as the Habsburgs' parish church.

Maria am Gestade
Dating from the 14th century, this church was restored in the 19th century. This 15th-century Gothic panel, shows The Annunciation.

Ruprechtskirche
Vienna's oldest church has a Romanesque nave and bell tower, a Gothic aisle and choir, and stained-glass windows which date back to the turn of the 14th century.

Stephansdom
The richly-carved Wiener Neustädter Altar from 1447 was a gift from Friedrich III (see p19).

Jesuitenkirche
A series of twisted columns rise up to support the vault of the Jesuitenkirche (1623–31), which also features a trompe l'oeil dome.

Stephansdom Quarter

Belvedere Quarter

Karlskirche
J B Fischer von Erlach's eclectic Baroque masterpiece (1714–39) boasts a dome, minarets and two Chinese-inspired lateral pavilions.

Franziskanerkirche
The dramatic high altar (1707) by Andrea Pozzo features a Bohemian statue of the Virgin Mary as its centrepiece.

Exploring Vienna's Churches

MANY OF VIENNA'S CHURCHES have undergone modifications over the centuries, and they often present a fascinating mixture of styles, ranging from Romanesque to Baroque. The great era for church building in the city was in the 17th and 18th centuries, when the triumphant Catholic church, in a spate of Counter-Reformation fervour, remodelled several early churches and built new ones. A number of churches were also constructed after the Turks were defeated in 1683 (see pp26–7), and the city as a whole was able to spread out beyond its earlier confines.

MEDIEVAL CHURCHES

AT THE HEART OF THE CITY is the **Stephansdom**. Parts date from Romanesque times but most of the cathedral is Gothic; it contains a collection of Gothic sculpture, including a pulpit by Anton Pilgram (see p78). Vienna's oldest church is the **Ruprechtskirche**, which stands in its own square in the Bermuda Triangle (see p84); its plain façade contrasts with the delicate Gothic tracery of **Maria am Gestade**, which has a filigree spire and a lofty, vaulted interior. The early interior of the **Deutschordenskirche** contains a number of heraldic blazons. A late Romanesque basilica with Gothic modifications lurks behind the façade of the **Michaelerkirche**. The 14th-century

Madonna and Child in the Minoritenkirche

Augustinerkirche contains the hearts of the Habsburg families (see pp24–5) down the centuries as well as Antonio Canova's tomb for Maria Christina (see p102). Behind the façade of the **Minoritenkirche** is a newly-restored Gothic interior; the same is true of the **Burgkapelle**.

17TH-CENTURY CHURCHES

THERE IS LITTLE Renaissance architecture in Vienna, but a number of churches built before the Turkish siege survive. The **Franziskanerkirche**, with its gabled façade and theatrical high altar, and the **Jesuitenkirche** are fine examples of the architecture inspired by the Counter-Reformation (see p24). The **Ursulinenkirche**, built between 1665 and 1675, has a high-galleried interior and **Annakirche** is notable for its beautiful Baroque tower. The **Dominikanerkirche** has a majestic early Baroque façade built in the 1630s by Antonio Caneval. Although it dates back to Romanesque times,

the bulk of the rather squat **Schottenkirche** was built between 1638 and 1648. In the middle of the Baroque square of Am Hof is the impressive façade of the **Kirche am Hof**. It was founded by the Carmelites and is also known as "Church of the Nine Choir Angels".

Carving of St Anne (about 1505) in Annakirche, attributed to Veit Stoss

LATE BAROQUE AND NEO-CLASSICAL CHURCHES

AFTER THE Turkish defeat (see pp26–7), a number of Viennese High Baroque churches were built. The most exotic is the **Karlskirche**, and just off the Graben is the great **Peterskirche**. The tiny, ornate **Stanislaus-Kostka Chapel** was once the home of a Polish saint. Two graceful 18th-century churches are to be found on the edge of the inner city: the majestic **Maria Treu Kirche** and the **Ulrichskirche**. Joseph Kornhäusel's **Stadttempel** has a Neo-Classical interior.

TOWERS, DOMES AND SPIRES

Vienna's skyline is punctuated by the domes, spires and towers of its fine churches. Topping **Maria am Gestade** is a delicate openwork lantern, while the **Ruprechtskirche** tower is characteristically squat. The towers of the **Jesuitenkirche** are Baroque and bulbous, and **Karlskirche** has freestanding columns. **Peterskirche** has an oval dome and small towers.

Ruprechtskirche

Maria am Gestade

Jesuitenkirche

**The frescoed interior of the late
Baroque Stanislaus-Kostka Chapel**

19TH-CENTURY
CHURCHES

DURING THE 19TH century
the prevailing mood of
Viennese architecture was
one of Romantic historicism.
Elements of past styles were
adopted and re-created, for
churches and for many other
municipal buildings, specifically on the Ringstrasse *(see
pp32–3)*. The **Griechische
Kirche** on Fleischmarkt, took
its inspiration from Byzantine
architecture, and the inside is
replete with iconostases and

frescoes. The **Votivkirche**,
built just off the Ringstrasse
as an expression of gratitude
for Franz Joseph's escape
from assassination, is based
on French Gothic architecture;
its richly-coloured interior
contains the marble tomb of
Count Niklas Salm, who
defended Vienna from the
Turks during the siege of
1529 *(see p24)*. On Lerchenfelder Strasse the red-brick
Altlerchenfelder Kirche is
a 19th-century architectural
hodge-podge of Gothic and
Italian Renaissance styles.

20TH-CENTURY
CHURCHES

A MASTERPIECE of early 20th-
century church archi-
tecture is Otto Wagner's *(see
p57)* massive **Kirche am
Steinhof**, built to serve a
psychiatric hospital. The
interior has a slightly clinical
air, since it is tiled in white,
but the austerity is relieved
by Kolo Moser's *(see p57)*
stained-glass windows and

**The haphazard, sculpted blocks of
the modern Wotruba Kirche.**

mosaics. The **Dr-Karl-Lueger-
Kirche**, located in the Central
Cemetery, was built by a
protégé of Otto Wagner,
Max Hegele, and has the
same monumental feel about
it. For true devotees of the
modern, there is the **Wotruba
Kirche** on Georgsgasse in the
suburb of Mauer, designed by
the sculptor Fritz Wotruba.
Not universally liked, this
looks as if it is a haphazard
assembly of concrete blocks.

19th-century interior of the Altlerchenfelder Kirche

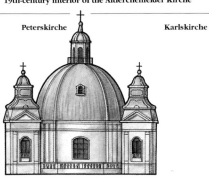

Peterskirche   Karlskirche

WHERE TO FIND THE
CHURCHES

Vienna's Best: Jugendstil

A STROLL AROUND Vienna's streets will reveal the richness of the city's turn-of-the-century architecture. Some of the buildings are well known and instantly recognizable, and a few of the public ones, such as the Secession building, can be seen inside. However, it can be just as rewarding to discover the lesser-known buildings and monuments of the period and to savour the variety of finely-crafted architectural details. Further details can be found on pages 56–7.

Strudelhof Steps
The setting for a famous novel of the same name by Heimato von Doderer (1896–1966), these magnificent steps were built by Theodore Jäger in 1910.

Schotten and Alsergru

Kirche am Steinhof
Commissioned for the grounds of a lunatic asylum on the outskirts of the city, this church with its grand copper dome was designed by Otto Wagner in 1905. The stained-glass windows are by Kolo Moser.

Museum ar Townball Quarter

Opera and Naschmarkt

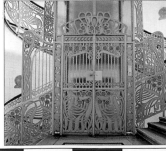

Wagner Apartments
Otto Wagner's two apartment blocks (1899) overlook the River Wien. No. 40, the Majolikahaus, is covered with ceramic decoration. No. 38 has gold Jugendstil motifs.

Kaiser Pavilion
Otto Wagner's imperial station pavilion (1899) was built as a showcase for his work.

Anker Clock
This clock, created by the artist Franz Matsch in 1911, sits on a bridge spanning two buildings on the Hoher Markt. Every hour, on the hour, moving figures parade across the clock face.

Postsparkasse
One of Otto Wagner's masterpieces, this post office savings bank exhibits the finest workmanship outside, and inside. Even the interior ventilator shafts are by Wagner.

Stadtpark Portals
The city's municipal park is adorned with magnificent portals (1903–7), designed by Friedrich Ohmann as part of a project to regulate the flow of the River Wien.

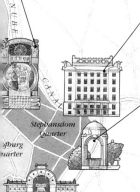

Stephansdom
Quarter

Hofburg
Quarter

Belvedere
Quarter

Karlsplatz Pavilions
Two recently-restored pavilions standing in Karlsplatz were built as part of Otto Wagner's scheme for Vienna's turn-of-the-century underground system.

0 kilometres 1

0 miles 0.5

Secession Building
Nicknamed the Golden Cabbage because of its golden filigree dome, the Secession Building was designed at the turn of the century by Joseph Maria Olbrich for exhibitions of avant-garde art. In the basement is Gustav Klimt's Beethoven Frieze.

Exploring Viennese Jugendstil

THE TURN OF THE CENTURY saw a flowering of the visual arts in Vienna. A new generation of avant-garde artists formed the Secession in 1896 and, together with architects and designers, forged close ties between the fine and decorative arts, and created new architectural styles.

PAINTING AND DRAWING

VIENNESE ART at the turn of the century did not conform to one particular style, but there were common elements: an obsession with line and rich surface pattern, as well as themes such as the *femme fatale*, love, sex and death. The finest collection of paintings from this period is in the **Museum of 19th- and 20th-Century Art** where pictures by Gustav Klimt (1862–1918) and Egon Schiele (1890–1918) feature prominently. Paintings by both artists and their contemporaries also form part of the permanent display at the **Historical Museum of the City of Vienna**. Further examples are at the **Museum of Modern Art** in the new MuseumsQuartier. The **Albertina** sometimes shows Schiele drawings. Klimt's *Beethoven Frieze* is in the **Secession Building**, and the decorative schemes he produced for the **Burgtheater** and **Kunsthistorisches Museum** are still in situ.

Hoffman tea service (1903) in the Austrian Museum of Applied Arts

Decoration (1891) by Gustav Klimt in the Kunsthistorisches Museum

APPLIED ARTS

THE WIENER WERKSTÄTTE – an arts and crafts studio – was founded by Josef Hoffmann (1870–1956) in 1903, and produced jewellery, fabrics, ceramics, metalwork, cutlery, bookbinding and fashion accessories with the same artistic consideration normally given to painting or sculpture. An outstanding collection is in the **Austrian Museum of Applied Arts**, which also houses a document archive open to researchers. Glass designed by Hoffmann for the Viennese firm of Lobmeyr is displayed in the **Lobmeyr Museum**.

FAVOURITE JUGENDSTIL MOTIFS

Jugendstil motifs were similar to those employed by the French Art Nouveau movement, but were generally made up of a more rigorous, geometric framework. Decorations based on organic plant forms such as sunflowers were very popular, as were female figures, heads and masks. Abstract designs made up of squares and triangles were also used to great effect.

Sunflower motif from the Karlsplatz Pavilions by Otto Wagner

Postcard designed by Joseph Maria Olbrich from *Ver Sacrum*

FURNITURE

THE LEADING Secession designers, such as Hoffmann and Kolo Moser (1868–1918), wanted interior design to return to the simple lines of Biedermeier style *(see pp30–1)* after the excesses of the Ringstrasse era. The **Austrian Museum of Applied Arts** has several interesting displays of their work, as well as that of the Thonet firm, which made the bentwood furniture admired by the Wiener Werkstätte. Furniture was often conceived as just one element of interior design. Unfortunately, many interiors have disappeared or are not open to the public, but the **Historical Museum of the City of Vienna**, which also has some pieces of Jugendstil furniture, has a re-creation of Adolf Loos's *(see p92)* living room. This is a rare example of a progressive Viennese interior from the turn of the century, created before the architect finally broke with the Secession.

Writing desk and chair by Kolo Moser (1903) in the Austrian Museum of Applied Arts

Altar in the Kirche am Steinhof (1905–7)

ARCHITECTURE

ANYONE WALKING around Vienna will notice several buildings with charming Jugendstil details. By the 1890s young architects were beginning to react against buildings of the Ringstrasse era, many of which were pastiches of earlier historical styles. The leading architects at this time were Otto Wagner (1841–1918) and Joseph Maria Olbrich (1867–1908), who collaborated on a number of projects, notably the design and installation of a new city railway and its stations, the most famous examples of which are the **Kaiser Pavilion** at Hietzing and the **Karlsplatz Pavilions**, as well as the **Wagner Apartments** on the Linke Wienzeile. Working independently, Wagner produced the extraordinary **Kirche am Steinhof** as well as the **Postsparkasse**, while Olbrich designed the

Secession Building as an exhibition space for radical artists and designers. Hoffmann created a number of houses for Secession artists in **Steinfeld-gasse**. There are also some Jugendstil houses in **Hietzing**, while the **Anker Clock** by Franz Matsch (1861–1942) is an example of the late flowering of the style. Other examples of street architecture are the **Strudelhof Steps** (1910) by Theodore Jäger and the **Stadt-park Portals** by Friedrich Ohmann (1858–1927) and Joseph Hackhofer (1868–1917).

WHERE TO FIND JUGENDSTIL VIENNA

Postcard design by Joseph Maria Olbrich from *Ver Sacrum*

Gold leaf detail from the Wagner Apartments

Lettering by Alfred Roller from *Ver Sacrum*

Abstract fabric design by Josef Hoffmann

Vienna's Best: Coffee Houses

COFFEE HOUSES HAVE BEEN an essential part of Viennese life for centuries. The coffee house is more than just a place to go to drink coffee. It is a meeting place, somewhere to linger over a snack or a light lunch, and a refuge from city life. Each coffee house attracts its own particular clientele and has its own unique atmosphere. Most of them also serve alcohol. Further details of what coffee houses have to offer can be found on pages 60–61.

Landtmann
This comfortable and formal coffee house used to be frequented by Sigmund Freud. Today it is visited by theatregoers and actors from the nearby Burgtheater, and by journalists and politicians.

Schottenring and Alsergrund

Central
Once the meeting place of writers and free thinkers, the most splendid of all the coffee houses in Vienna has now been restored to its former grandeur.

Museum and Townhall Quarter

Hofburg Quarter

Sperl
Just outside the city centre, the Sperl has a faithful clientele, including many young people who come here for the billiard tables and hot strudels.

Opera and Naschmarkt

Eiles
Its location near various government offices has made the Eiles a favourite haunt of officials and lawyers.

Museum
The Museum is not as stylish as when it boasted an interior by Adolf Loos (see p92), but it is still packed with students and artists, making it smoky and noisy but atmospheric.

Hawelka
This famous coffee house has long cultivated its bohemian image. The atmosphere is warm and theatrical, and no visit to Vienna is complete without a late-night cup of coffee or a drink here.

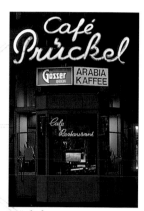

0 kilometres 0.5

0 miles 0.25

bansdom Quarter

DANUBE CANAL

Prückel
The Prückel has been shabby and run down for as long as anyone can remember, but it has become a mecca for bridge players and locals who crowd into its back room.

Kleines
One of the smallest, quaintest coffee houses in Vienna, the Kleines still attracts a loyal clientele of actors.

Belvedere Quarter

Frauenhuber
The oldest coffee house in Vienna, this is where Mozart once performed. Its location off Kärntner Strasse makes it handy for shoppers and for tourists visiting the nearby Stephansdom.

Exploring Vienna's Coffee Houses

THE VIENNESE COFFEE HOUSE serves many functions and to make the best of the institution it helps to understand the many roles it plays in the lives of local people. In a coffee house you can read the newspapers, share a simple lunch with a friend, or in some play a game of bridge or billiards. Most places serve wines, beers and spirits as well as coffee. The coffee house is a priceless urban resource and, though no longer unique to Vienna, it is here that it has flourished in its most satisfying form. Vienna also has many Café-Konditoreien *(see p215).*

Waiter at the Dommayer café

THE HISTORY OF THE COFFEE HOUSE

LEGEND MAINTAINS that the first coffee house opened its doors after the defeat of the Turks in 1683 *(see p26).* However, historians insist that coffee was known in the city long before this date. Coffee houses took the form we know today in the late 18th century. They reached their heyday in the late 19th century, when they were patronized by cliques of like-minded politicians, artists, writers, composers, doctors or civil servants. In 1890, for instance, the controversial literary

18th-century Viennese girl holding a coffee grinder

group Jung Wien met regularly at the **Griensteidl**, while the essayist Peter Altenberg was reputed to have never been seen outside his favourite café, the **Central**. Today, as in the past, the **Ministerium**, **Museum**, **Frauenhuber**, **Raimund**, **Eiles**, **Schwarzenberg** and **Zartl** continue to attract their own specific clientele.

COFFEE HOUSE ETIQUETTE

THERE IS A SIMPLE but formal etiquette attached to a coffee house. A waiter, almost certainly dressed in a tuxedo, however shabby the coffee house, will take your order, which will often be served with a plain glass of water. Once

you have ordered you are free to occupy your table for as long as you like. A cup of coffee is not cheap, but entitles you to linger for an hour or two and to read the newspapers which are freely available. The grander coffee houses, such as the **Landtmann** and **Central**, will also have a selection of foreign newspapers and periodicals.

WHAT COFFEE HOUSES HAVE TO OFFER

COFFEE HOUSES often function as local clubhouses. At the **Sperl** you can play billiards, at the **Prückel** there are bridge tables, and at the

TYPES OF COFFEE

Just as the coffee house is a Viennese institution, so too are the extraordinary varieties of coffee that are available. Just asking for a cup of coffee in Vienna will not always guarantee a result, as the Viennese are exceedingly particular about how they take their coffee; over the centuries they have devised their own specific vocabulary to convey to the waiter precisely how they like their beverage served. The list that follows will cover most variations of the Viennese cup of coffee, although you may well find local ones.

Türkischer: plain, strong black Turkish coffee served in the traditional manner.

Brauner:
coffee with milk (small or large).
Melange:
a blend of coffee and hot milk.
Kurz:
extra strong.
Obers:
with cream.
Mokka:
strong black coffee.

Kapuziner:
black coffee with a dash of milk, usually frothed.
Schwarzer:
black coffee (small or large).
Konsul:
black coffee with a dash of cream.
Kaffeinfreier Kaffee:
decaffeinated coffee.

Espresso: strong black coffee made by machine. Ask for it *gestreckt* for a weak one.

Dommayer you can attend literary readings. The **Central** and **Bräunerhof** both offer live piano music with your coffee. The **Kleines** is, as its name suggests, too tiny to offer entertainment, but still draws a regular crowd. The **Imperial** is part of the hotel of the same name. Coffee houses outside the city centre include the excellent **Westend**.

Coffee house sign

WHAT TO EAT

MOST COFFEE HOUSES offer snack foods throughout the day, simple lunches and occasional specialities, such as pastries, which are served at particular times. The **Hawelka** serves hot jam-filled buns *(Buchteln)* late at night, and the **Sperl** often has fresh strudel late morning. Larger coffee houses, such as **Diglas** and **Landtmann**, offer extensive lunchtime menus as well as a range of excellent pastries made on the premises.

COFFEE PLAIN AND SIMPLE

THERE ARE times when you quite simply want a good cup of coffee – when newspapers or a table of your own are luxuries you can dispense with. On such occasions you should keep an eye out for an Espresso bar, where you can lean informally against a counter and order coffee at a half or a third of the price you would normally expect to pay at a coffee house. The Café-Konditoreien belonging to the Aida chain *(see p217)*, apart from serving delicious cakes and pastries, also function as Espresso bars.

Old Viennese coffee machine in Diglas

Pharisäer: strong black, with whipped cream on top, served with a small liqueur glass of rum.

Schlagobers: strong black coffee served with either plain or whipped cream.

Einspänner: large glass of coffee with whipped cream on top.

Kaisermelange: black coffee with an egg yolk and brandy.

WHERE TO FIND THE COFFEE HOUSES

Bräunerhof
Stallburggasse 2. **Map** 5 C3.
🎵 *Sat & Sun afternoons.*

Central
Palais Ferstel, Herrengasse 14.
Map 2 D5 & 5 B2. 🎵

Diglas
Wollzeile 10. **Map** 6 D3. ⊞

Dommayer
Dommayergasse 1, Hietzing.
⊞ 🎵 *first Sat of month.*

Eiles
Josefstädter Strasse 2. **Map** 1 B5.

Frauenhuber
Himmelpfortgasse 6.
Map 4 E1 & 6 D4.

Griensteidl
Michaelerplatz 2.
Map 2 D5 & 5 B3.

Hawelka
Dorotheergasse 6.
Map 2 D5 & 5 C3.

Imperial
Hotel Imperial,
Kärntner Ring 16.
Map 4 E2 & 6 D5. ⊞ 🎵

Kleines
Franziskanerplatz 3. **Map** 6 D4.

Landtmann
See p129. ⊞

Ministerium
Georg-Coch-Platz 4.
Map 2 F5 & 6 F3. ⊞

Museum
Friedrichstrasse 6.
Map 4 D2. ⊞

Prückel
Stubenring 24. **Map** 6 F3.
⊞ 🎵 *evenings.*

Raimund
Museumstrasse 6.
Map 3 B1. ⊞

Schwarzenberg
Kärntner Ring 17.
Map 6 D5. ⊞

Sperl
Gumpendorfer Strasse 11.
Map 3 A4. ⊞

Westend
Mariahilfer Strasse 128.
Map 3 A3.

Zartl
Rasumofskygasse 7,
Landstrasse. 🎵

VIENNA THROUGH THE YEAR

SPRING OFTEN ARRIVES unexpectedly, with a few days of sunshine and warmth. The climax of spring is the Wiener Festwochen in May. Summers are long and hot, and ideal for swimming and for river trips on the Danube (see pp176–7) during July and August, when some venues officially close. Vienna comes alive again in September when the most important theatres reopen. More often than not, there is an Indian summer at this time, and it is still warm enough to sit in the Stadtpark. As autumn turns to winter, the streets fill with stalls selling chestnuts and by the feast of St Nicholas on 6 December, snow has often fallen. Christmas is a family occasion, but the New Year is celebrated in style as it heralds the start of the carnival season. The Wiener Fremdenverkehrsamt (see p237) has details of important events.

SPRING

VIENNA IS beautiful in spring and is the time for the **Wiener Festwochen** (see May). It is also a season that brings a few days of balmy weather, and when beautiful colours appear in the parks and the Prater woods (see pp160–61). This is the best time of the year to visit the Stadtpark (see p98) with its open-air bandstand and much-photographed resident peacock. The Volksgarten, Burggarten and the great parks of the Belvedere and Schönbrunn also come into their own and there are some splendid views of the city from the Stephansdom tower.

A collection of life-sized dolls on display during the Wiener Festwochen

MARCH

Easter Market (two weeks before Easter), held at the Freyung. Items on sale include arts, crafts and traditional food.

APRIL

Volksprater Funfair (1 Apr–31 Sep), held in the Prater woods (pp160–61).

Runners taking part in the annual Spring Marathon

Spring Marathon (1st Sun Apr) starts from the main entrance of Schönbrunn Palace (pp170–71), passing the Hofburg, Ringstrasse and Opera House, and ends at the Neues Rathaus (Town Hall).
Frühlingsfestival (2nd week Apr to mid-May). Classical music performances which each year alternate between the Musikverein (p144) and the Konzerthaus (p227).
Spanish Riding School (until Jun). Performances of the Lipizzaner horses start again in the Winter Riding School (pp98–9).
Hofburg Orchestra (until Oct). Concerts at Musikverein (p144) and Hofburg (pp96–7).
Kursalon (until end Oct). Open-air concerts (p227).
Flat racing at the Freudenau (until mid-Nov) in the Prater (pp160–61).

MAY

Tag der Arbeit (1 May). Public holiday. Labour day celebrated with parades on Rathausplatz and Ringstrasse.
Maifest (1 May), in the Prater (pp160–61) with music and children's programmes.
Vienna Music Festival (6 May–12 Jun), part of Wiener Festwochen programme which begins a few days earlier at the Theater an der Wien (p136) and the Messepalast (p117).
Dancing on the Vindobona (15 May to end Sep). Board the boat at Schwedenplatz for a cruise on the Danube.
Schönbrunn Zoo (until Sep). The oldest zoo in the world opens its doors (p171).
Wiener Festwochen (mid-May to mid-Jun), Vienna's greatest festival with operas, plays and performing arts.

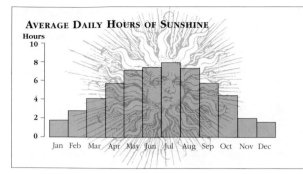

AVERAGE DAILY HOURS OF SUNSHINE

Hours
10
8
6
4
2
0

Jan Feb Mar Apr May Jun Jul Aug Sep Oct Nov Dec

Sunshine Chart
*June, July and August
are the hottest months
in Vienna, with
between six and eight
hours of sunshine
each day, but summer
can also be quite
damp and humid.
Although the city cools
down in September,
Indian summers are
quite common.*

SUMMER

SUMMER CAN BE both the
busiest and most relaxing
time in Vienna. The great
theatres may be closed
officially, but the Jazz Festival
is on at the Opera House and
the Volkstheater in July, and
Mozart operas are performed
in Schönbrunn Park until mid-
August. The Danube beaches
are ideal for sunbathing,
swimming and other
watersports on sunny days.

Summer outside the Votivkirche

JUNE

Corpus Christi *(2 Jun)*. Public
holiday. Catholic festival in
honour of the Eucharist.
Vinova *(2nd week Jun)*, wine
fair in the Prater *(pp160–61)*.

Klangbogen Wien *(until
early Sep)*. Music festival with
concerts in some of Vienna's
most attractive venues.
The Concordia Ball *(2nd Fri
in Jun)* takes place at the
Neues Rathaus *(p128)*.
Ball der Universität *(18 Jun)*
held at the University *(p128)*.

JULY

**Outdoor films, operas and
concerts** *(until Sep)* on a
giant screen in Rathausplatz.
Seating is provided free.
Jazzfest *(1st two weeks Jul)*,
part of Klangbogen Wien.
Venues include the Opera
House *(pp138–9)*, the
Volkstheater *(p228)* and the
arcaded courtyard of the
Neues Rathaus *(p128)*.
Festival Wiener Klassik
(Jul–Sep). Orchestral, chamber
and solo concerts held at
various historical venues.
Spectaculum *(throughout Jul)*.
Part of Klangbogen Wien with
seldom-performed religious
operas and unusual ballets at
the Jesuitenkirche *(p73)*.
International Dance Weeks
(mid-Jul to 3rd week Aug) at
the Universitäts Sportzentrum,
Schmelz; Volkstheater *(p228)*.
**Summer Dance Festival
(Im Puls)** *(end-Jul to 3rd

Bathing beside the Danube

week Aug)* is held at the Volks-
theater *(p228)* and Universitäts
Sportzentrum at Schmelz.
**Mozart im Schönbrunner
Schlosspark** *(until mid-Aug)*.
Mozart operas are performed
by the Kammeroper *(p227)*
against the reproduction
Roman Ruins *(p170)*.
Soirée bei Prinz Orlofsky
(until mid-Aug) at the Schön-
brunner Schlosstheater.
Operetta by the Kammeroper.
Seefestspiele Mörbisch
*(weekends mid-Jul to end
Aug)*. Operetta festival in Mör-
bisch, 40 km (25 miles) away.

AUGUST

Maria Himmelfahrt *(15
Aug)*, public holiday. Catholic
festival which celebrates the
assumption of the Madonna.

Seefestspiele Mörbisch, an annual operetta festival performed against the backdrop of Lake Neusiedl

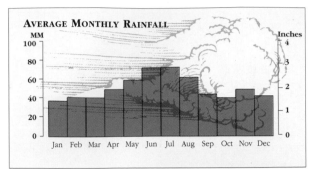

Rainfall Chart

The summer months are not only the hottest but also the wettest, helping to keep the city cool. During spring and autumn, days can be mild, with some drizzle, until November, which can be very wet. Around 600 mm (23 inches) of rain falls annually.

AUTUMN

IN VIENNA, AUTUMN means a new start. The theatres, and particularly Vienna's great opera houses, reopen once again. Shops get ready to tempt buyers with their range of autumn fashions. Then, almost overnight, all the shop windows seem to be filled with figures of St Nicholas and his wicked companion Krampus. This cute little furry devil appears everywhere. It is only after 6 December that the shop windows are finally cleared for Christmas displays.

SEPTEMBER

Spanish Riding School performances *(until end Oct)* and training sessions of the Lipizzaner horses *(pp98–9)*.
Vienna Boys' Choir *(mid-Sep to Dec)* perform at Mass at the Burgkapelle *(p103)* on Sundays.
Trotting in the Krieau *(until Jun)*. Trotting races at the Prater *(pp160–61)*.

OCTOBER

Küche und Keller *(1st week Oct)*. Hotel and food fair, at the Messegelände *(pp160–61)*.

The Vienna Boys' Choir performing at the Konzerthaus

Krampus, the wicked furry devil who accompanies St Nicholas

National Holiday *(26 Oct)*. Celebrations to mark passing of the Neutrality Act in 1955.
Viennale *(end Oct)*, film festival at Gartenbau, Parkring 12; Metro, Johannesgasse 4; Künstlerhaus, Akademiestrasse 13; and Stadtkino, Schwarzenbergplatz 7–8.
Wien Modern *(until end Nov)*. Modern music festival at the Konzerthaus *(p227)* or Musikverein *(p144)*.

NOVEMBER

Allerheiligen *(1 Nov)*. Public holiday. Catholic festival celebrating All Saints Day.
Antik-Aktuell *(2nd week Nov)*, art and antiques fair held at the Hofburg.
Schubertiade *(3rd week Nov)* at the Musikverein *(p144)*.
Mozart Festival *(last week Nov to 3rd week Dec)* at the Konzerthaus *(p227)*.
Krippenschau *(until mid-Dec)*, display of historic mangers at Peterskirche *(p87)*.
Christkindlmarkt *(2nd Sat Nov to end Dec)*, Christmas market and children's workshop by the Rathaus *(p128)*.
Christmas markets *(from last Sat Nov)* held at the Freyung, Heiligenkreuzerhof and Spittelberg.
International choirs *(last Sat Nov)* at the Rathaus *(p128)*.

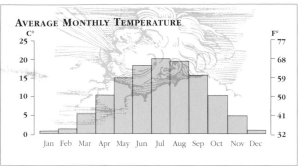

AVERAGE MONTHLY TEMPERATURE

Temperature Chart
The chart shows the average temperatures each month. Top temperatures in July and August can reach 25˚ C (77˚ F) although May and September are also quite warm. Winters are icy, and temperatures can be as low as −1.4˚ C (29.5˚ F) in January.

WINTER

ROASTING CHESTNUTS over hot coals is a regular winter sight on Vienna's streets. As Christmas draws near, stalls offer mulled wine and hot snacks and shops enter into the festive spirit putting up lights and decorations.

The Viennese celebrate Christmas Eve with a traditional meal consisting of *Fisch-beuschelsuppe*, a creamy fish soup, followed by fresh fried carp. The usual dish which is eaten on Christmas Day is goose, although turkey is becoming more popular.

New Year also marks the start of Fasching, Vienna's famous Carnival season.

DECEMBER

Christmas markets
(continue from November).

PUBLIC HOLIDAYS

New Year's Day (1 Jan)
Epiphany (6 Jan)
Easter Sunday
Easter Monday
Tag der Arbeit (1 May)
Ascension Day (6th Thu after Easter)
Whit Monday (6th Mon after Easter)
Corpus Christi (2 Jun)
Maria Himmelfahrt (15 Aug)
National Holiday (26 Oct)
Allerheiligen (1 Nov)
Maria Empfängnis (8 Dec)
Christmas Day (25 Dec)
Stefanitag (26 Dec)

Chestnut-roasting in winter

Maria Empfängnis *(8 Dec)*. Public holiday. Catholic festival celebrating the Immaculate Conception.
Midnight Mass *(Christmas Eve)* held in the Stephansdom *(pp76–7)*. No tickets needed but arrive early for seats.
Stefanitag *(26 Dec)*. Public holiday for Boxing Day.
New Year's Eve performance of *Die Fledermaus* *(31 Dec)* at the Opera House *(pp138–9)* and Volksoper *(p227)*. The performance is shown on a large screen in Stephansplatz *(p70)*.
New Year's Eve concerts at the Konzerthaus *(p227)* and Musikvereinsaal *(p144)*.
Kaiserball *(31 Dec)* at the Hofburg *(pp96–7)*.
New Year's Eve in the city centre: a street party with snacks and drink. Marquees provide music and cabaret.

JANUARY

New Year's Concert *(31 Dec & 1 Jan)* by the great Vienna Philharmonic at the Musik-verein *(p144)*. Tickets are very difficult to obtain, and requests should be received on precisely 2 January for next year's concert *(p226)*. Or you may watch it live on television.
Beethoven's Ninth Symphony *(31 Dec & 1 Jan)* is performed at the Konzert-haus *(p227)*.
Fasching *(6 Jan to Ash Wed)*, the Vienna Carnival includes the **Heringschmaus** *(Ash Wed)*, a hot and cold buffet.
Holiday on Ice *(mid- to end Jan)*. This is held at the Stadthalle, Vogelweidplatz.
Resonanzen *(2nd to 3rd week Jan)*. Festival of ancient music at the Konzerthaus *(p227)*.

FEBRUARY

Opera Ball *(last Thu before Shrove Tue)*, one of the grand-est balls of Fasching *(p139)*.
Wintertanzwoche *(5–13 Feb)*. Part of the dance festival *(see below)*. Events are held at Messepalast 7.
Dance Festival *(17 Feb to 27 Mar)*, includes classic and jazz dance at the Universitäts Sportzentrum at Schmelz.
Haydn Tage *(3rd week Feb to 1st week Mar)*. Haydn's music at the Konzerthaus *(see p227)*.

The Christkindlmarkt, in front of the Neues Rathaus

VIENNA AREA
BY AREA

STEPHANSDOM QUARTER

Plaque on No. 19 Sonnenfelsgasse, once part of the university

THE WINDING STREETS and spacious squares of this area form the ancient core of Vienna. Following World War II, subterranean excavations uncovered the remains of a Roman garrison from 2,000 years ago, and every succeeding age is represented here, from the Romanesque arches of the Ruprechtskirche to the steel and glass of the spectacular Haas Haus in Stephansplatz. Many of the buildings in the area house government offices, businesses, taverns and stylish shops. Dominating the skyline is the Stephansdom, the focus of the city at its geographical centre.

SIGHTS AT A GLANCE

Streets and Squares
- Blutgasse 3
- Domgasse 4
- Grünangergasse 6
- Schönlaterngasse 10
- Sonnenfelsgasse 12
- Bäckerstrasse 14
- Annagasse 18
- Fleischmarkt 22
- Griechengasse 23
- Jewish District 25
- Hoher Markt 26
- Judenplatz 30
- Kurrentgasse 32
- Am Hof 35

Historic Buildings
- Academy of Sciences 9
- Heiligenkreuzerhof 13
- Haas Haus 15
- Winter Palace of Prince Eugene 17
- Postsparkasse 21
- Bohemian Court Chancery 27
- Altes Rathaus 28

Churches and Cathedrals
- *Stephansdom pp76–9* 1
- Deutschordenskirche 2
- Dominikanerkirche 7
- Jesuitenkirche 8
- Franziskanerkirche 16
- Annakirche 19
- Ruprechtskirche 24
- Maria am Gestade 29
- Kirche am Hof 34
- Peterskirche 36

Museums and Galleries
- Figarohaus 5
- Cathedral Museum 11
- *Austrian Museum of Applied Arts pp82–3* 20
- Museum Judenplatz 30
- Clock Museum 31
- Doll and Toy Museum 33

GETTING THERE

This area is served by the Stephansplatz (lines U1, U3), Stubentor (line U3) and Schwedenplatz (lines U1, U4) U-Bahn stations. Trams 1 and 2 go along Franz-Josefs-Kai and the Ringstrasse. Buses 1A, 2A and 3A stop at the junction of Hoher Markt and Marc-Aurel-Strasse.

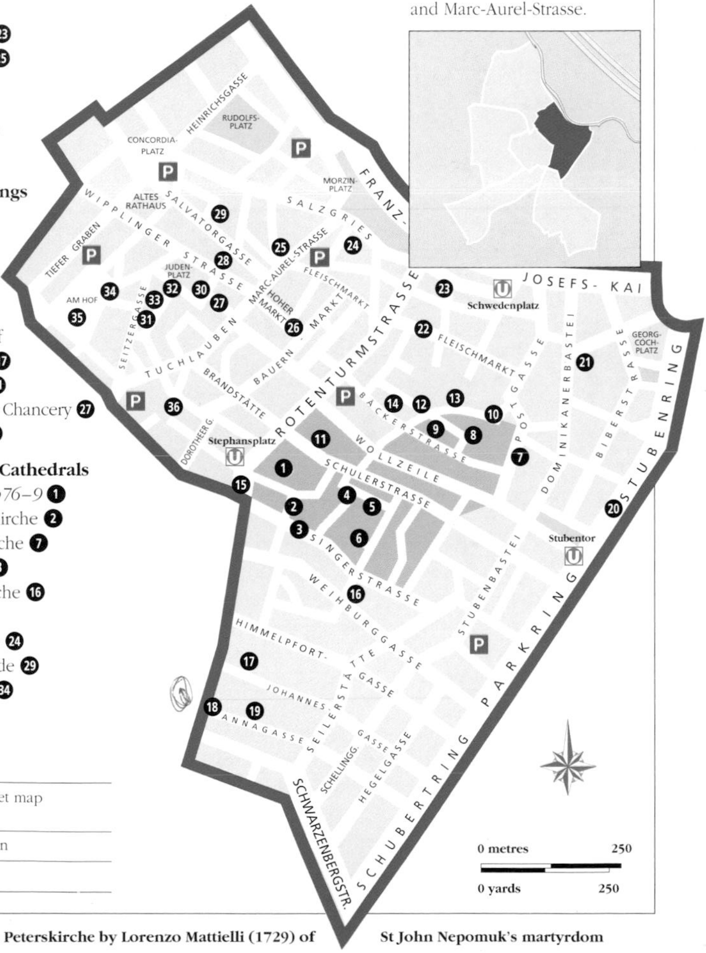

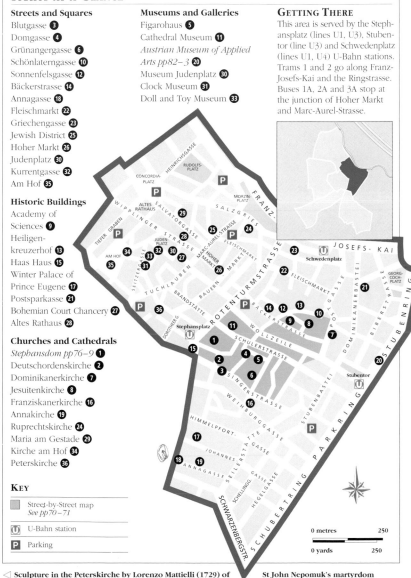

KEY

- Street-by-Street map *See pp70–71*
- U-Bahn station
- Parking

◁ Sculpture in the Peterskirche by Lorenzo Mattielli (1729) of St John Nepomuk's martyrdom

Street-by-Street: Old Vienna

THIS PART OF THE INNER CITY retains its medieval layout, offering a complex of lanes, alleys and spacious courtyards. The influence of the church is particularly evident. You can find remains of monastic orders such as the Dominicans and feudal orders such as the Teutonic Knights, as well as ideological orders, for example the Jesuits. Yet there is nothing ossified about the area: at night the bars and restaurants on Bäckerstrasse and Schönlaterngasse are thronged with people until the early hours of the morning. Dominating everything is the 137-m high (450-ft) spire of the Stephansdom cathedral in the very heart of Vienna.

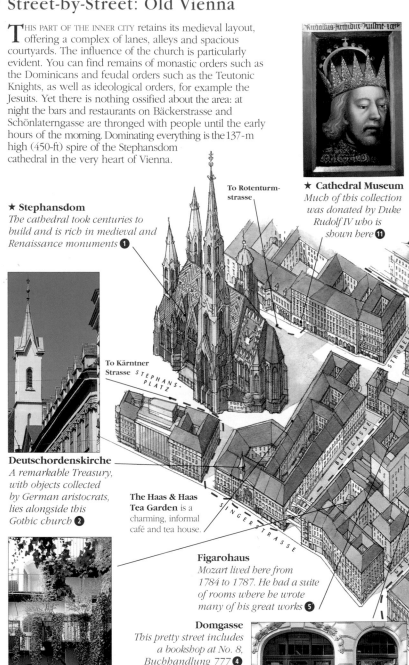

★ Cathedral Museum
Much of this collection was donated by Duke Rudolf IV who is shown here **⓫**

To Rotenturm-strasse

★ Stephansdom
The cathedral took centuries to build and is rich in medieval and Renaissance monuments **❶**

To Kärntner Strasse STEPHANS-PLATZ

Deutschordenskirche
A remarkable Treasury, with objects collected by German aristocrats, lies alongside this Gothic church **❷**

The Haas & Haas Tea Garden is a charming, informal café and tea house.

Figarohaus
Mozart lived here from 1784 to 1787. He had a suite of rooms where he wrote many of his great works **❺**

Domgasse
This pretty street includes a bookshop at No. 8, Buchhandlung 777 **❹**

Blutgasse
Courtyards like this are typical of the tenement houses on Blutgasse **❸**

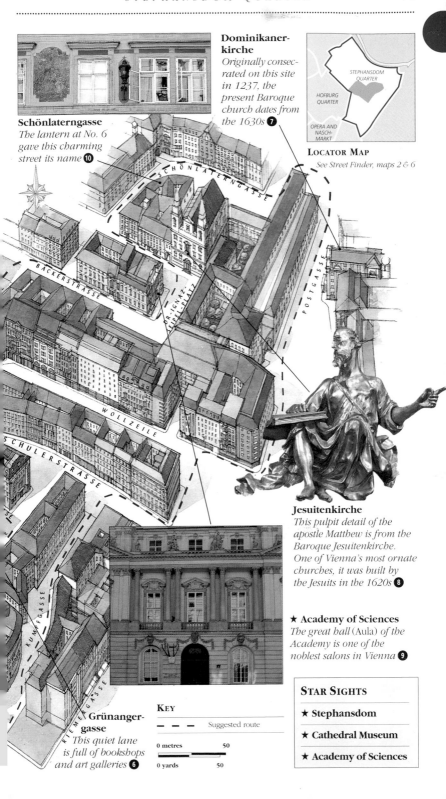

Schönlaterngasse
The lantern at No. 6 gave this charming street its name ⑩

Dominikaner-kirche
Originally consecrated on this site in 1237, the present Baroque church dates from the 1630s ❼

LOCATOR MAP
See Street Finder, maps 2 & 6

Jesuitenkirche
This pulpit detail of the apostle Matthew is from the Baroque Jesuitenkirche. One of Vienna's most ornate churches, it was built by the Jesuits in the 1620s ❽

★ Academy of Sciences
The great hall (Aula) of the Academy is one of the noblest salons in Vienna ❾

Grünanger-gasse
This quiet lane is full of bookshops and art galleries ❻

KEY

- – – Suggested route

0 metres   50

0 yards   50

STAR SIGHTS

★ Stephansdom

★ Cathedral Museum

★ Academy of Sciences

Stephansdom ❶

See pp76–9.

Deutschordens-kirche ❷

Singerstrasse 7. **Map** 2 E5 & 6 D3.
[5121065. **Ⓤ** *Stephansplatz.*
Church ◯ *7:00am–6:00pm daily.*
◙ Treasury ◯ *10am–noon Mon &
Thu, 3–5pm Wed & Fri, 10am–noon
3–5pm Sat.* ● *Tue & Sun.* ◙

Tʜɪs ᴄʜᴜʀᴄʜ belongs to the
Order of Teutonic Knights,
a chivalric order which was
established in the 12th century.
It is 14th-century Gothic, but
was restored in the 1720s by
Anton Erhard Martinelli.
Numerous coats of arms of
teutonic knights and memorial
slabs are displayed on the
walls. The altarpiece from
1520 is Flemish and
incorporates panel paintings
and carvings of scenes from
the Passion beneath some very
delicate traceried canopies.
  The Order's Treasury is
situated off the church's
courtyard and now serves as
a museum, displaying various
collections acquired by its
Grand Masters over the
centuries. The starting point is
a room which houses a large
collection of coins, medals and
a 13th-century enthronement
ring. This leads into the second
room which contains chalices
and Mass vessels worked
with silver filigree. Following
this is a display of
maces, daggers
and ceremonial

Inner courtyard of No. 9 Blutgasse, the Fähnrichshof

garb. The final exhibits show
some Gothic paintings and a
Carinthian carving of *St George
and the Dragon* (1457).

Blutgasse ❸

Map 2 E5 & 6 D3. **Ⓤ** *Stephansplatz.*

A ʟᴏᴄᴀʟ ʟᴇɢᴇɴᴅ relates that
this street acquired its
gruesome name – Blood Lane
– after a massacre in 1312
of the Knights Templar (a
military and religious order)
in a skirmish so violent that
the streets flowed with blood.
But there is no evidence to
support this story and the
street's name belies its charm.
  Its tall apartment buildings
date mostly from the 18th
century. Walk into No. 3 and
see how the city's restorers
have linked up the buildings
and their courtyards. No. 9,
the Fähnrichshof,
is particularly
impressive.

Domgasse ❹

Map 2 E5 & 6 D3. **Ⓤ** *Stephansplatz.*

Iɴ ᴀᴅᴅɪᴛɪᴏɴ to the Figarohaus,
Domgasse boasts some
interesting buildings, including
the Trienter Hof, with its airy
courtyard. No. 6 is a house of
medieval origin called the
Kleiner Bischofshof or small
bishop's house: it has a 1761
Matthias Gerl façade. Next
door is the site of the house
where Franz Georg Kolschitzky
lived and, in 1694, died. It is
said that he claimed some
Turkish coffee beans as a
reward for his bravery in the
1683 Turkish siege, and later
opened Vienna's first coffee
house. The truth of this story,
however, is doubtful.

Figarohaus ❺

Domgasse 5. **Map** 2 E5 & 6 D3.
[5136294. **Ⓤ** *Stephansplatz.*
◯ *9am–6pm Tue–Sun.* ◙ ◙

Mᴏᴢᴀʀᴛ and his family
occupied a flat on the
first floor of the Figarohaus
from 1784 to 1787. Of Mozart's
11 Viennese residences, this is
the one where he is said to
have been happiest, and
where he composed some of
his masterworks: the exquisite
Haydn quartets, a handful of
piano concerti, and *The
Marriage of Figaro* – after
which the building was named.
Since Mozart died impover-
ished and left few effects, the
museum is spartan, displaying
a small number of prints on the
walls, and a few documents
and photocopies of scores.

**Winged altar-
piece in the
Deutschordens-
kirche (1520)**

Elaborate nave of the Dominikanerkirche

Grünangergasse ❻

Map 4 E1 & 6 D3. Ⓤ *Stephansplatz.*

THIS QUIET LANE takes its name from the creperie Zum Grünen Anker at No. 10, a tavern frequented by Franz Schubert in the 19th century.

No. 8's portal has crude carvings of rolls, croissants and pretzels. It is known as the Kipferlhaus after a Viennese crescent-shaped roll. The former Fürstenberg Palace, from 1720, has a Baroque portal with carved hounds racing to the top of the keystone.

Dominikaner-kirche ❼

Postgasse 4. **Map** 2 E5 & 6 E3. 📞 5129174. Ⓤ *Stephansplatz, Schwedenplatz.* ⏱ 7am–7pm Mon–Sat, 7am–9pm Sun. 📷

THE DOMINICAN order of monks came to Vienna in 1226, and by 1237 they had consecrated a church here. In the 1630s Antonio Canevale designed their present church, which boasts a majestic and really rather handsome Baroque façade. The interior is equally imposing. The central chapel on the right has swirling Rococo grilles and candelabra, and there is a very beautiful gilt organ above the west door. Its casing dates from the mid-18th century. The frescoes by Tencala and Rauchmiller are especially noteworthy, as is the high altar.

Jesuitenkirche ❽

Dr-Ignaz-Seipel-Platz 1. **Map** 2 E5 & 6 E3. 📞 5125232. Ⓤ *Stubentor, Stephansplatz, Schwedenplatz.* ⏱ 7am–6:30pm daily. 📷

ANDREA POZZO, an Italian architect, redesigned the Jesuitenkirche between 1703 and 1705 and its broad, high façade dominates the Dr-Ignaz-Seipel-Platz. In the 1620s the Jesuits decided to move their headquarters here in order to be near the Old University, which they controlled. The Jesuit order was the dominant force behind the Counter-Reformation. The Jesuits were not afraid of making a statement, and the church's grand design and high façade reflects this dominance.

The interior is gaudy, with plump marble columns screening the side chapels. Pozzo's ceiling frescoes are cleverly executed using a *trompe l'oeil* effect and the pews are richly carved.

Academy of Sciences ❾

Dr-Ignaz-Seipel-Platz 2. **Map** 2 E5 & 6 E3. Ⓤ *Schwedenplatz, Stubentor.* 📞 515810. ⏱ 8am–5pm Mon–Fri.

ONCE THE CENTREPIECE of the Old University, the Akademie der Wissenschaften has an impressive Baroque façade. Designed in 1753 by Jean Nicolas Jadot de Ville-Issey as the *Aula,* or great hall, it has recently been restored. A double staircase leads up to a huge salon that, despite its reconstruction after a fire in 1961, is still one of the great rooms of Vienna.

Elaborate frescoes adorn the ceilings of the Ceremonial Hall and the walls are composed of marble embellished with Rococo plasterwork. Haydn's *Creation* was performed here in 1808 in the presence of the composer: it was the eve of his 76th birthday and his last public appearance.

Fountain by Salomon Kleiner on the Academy of Sciences (about 1755)

The Baroque Bernhardskapelle *(left)*, seen from Schönlaterngasse

Schönlaterngasse ⓾

Map 2 E5 & 6 E3. Ⓤ *Stephansplatz, Schwedenplatz.* **Alte Schmiede**
Ⓒ *5124446.* ◯ *10am–3pm Mon–Fri.*

THE ATTRACTIVE CURVING lane derives its name (Pretty Lantern Lane) from the handsome wrought-iron lantern which is clamped to No. 6. This is a copy of the 1610 original which is now in the Historical Museum of the City of Vienna *(see p144)*. At No. 4, a solid early 17th-century house guards the curve of the street. No. 7, the Basiliskenhaus, which is of medieval origin, displays on its façade an artist's impression of a mythical serpent, dating from 1740. A serpent is reputed to have been discovered in 1212 in a well by the house.

The composer Robert Schumann lived at No. 7a from 1838 to 1839. No. 9 is the Alte Schmiede – the large smithy from which it takes its name has been reassembled in the basement. This complex also contains an art gallery and a hall used for poetry readings and musical workshops.

Cathedral Museum ⓫

Stephansplatz 6. **Map** 2 E5 & 6 D3.
Ⓒ *515523560.* Ⓤ *Stephansplatz.*
◯ *10am–5pm Tue–Sat.* ● *24 & 31 Dec, Maundy Thu & Easter Mon.* 🎟 📷 ♿

KNOWN IN GERMAN as the Dom und Diözesanmuseum, its exhibits include 18th-century religious paintings by important Austrian artists such as Franz Anton Maulbertsch, and some 16th- and 17th-century rustic carvings. There are also works by the Dutch painter Jan van Hemessen. Not to be missed is the display of medieval carvings, many of which are of the Madonna and Child.

The Treasury is spectacular as many of the items were the personal gift of Duke Rudolf IV to the Cathedral. His shroud is housed here as well as a famous portrait of him by a Bohemian master dating from the 1360s *(see p70)*. Other items include the St Leopold reliquary from 1592, which is encrusted with figures of saints and coats of arms, and some outstanding enamels from the 12th-century.

Sonnenfelsgasse ⓬

Map 2 E5 & 6 E3. Ⓤ *Stephansplatz, Schwedenplatz.*

FINE HOUSES line this pleasant street. Though by no means uniform in style, most of the dwellings on the north side of the street are solid merchant and patrician houses dating from the late 16th century. No. 19, which was built in 1628 and renovated in 1721, was once part of the Old University *(see p73)*. No. 11 has an impressive courtyard. Many of the balconies overlooking the courtyard have been glassed in to their full height so as to provide extra living space. No. 3 has the most elaborate façade, and contains a *Stadtheuriger* called the Zwölf Apostelkeller *(see p217)*. This is an urban equivalent of the *Heurige*, the wine growers' inns found in the villages outside Vienna *(see p216)*.

The street was named after a soldier called Joseph von Sonnenfels. He became Maria Theresa's legal adviser and under his guidance, she totally reformed the penal code and abolished torture.

Gothic Madonna (1325) in the Cathedral Museum

Heiligenkreuzerhof ⓭

Schönlaterngasse 5. **Map** 2 E5 & 6 E3. *5125896.* *Schwedenplatz.* *6am–9pm Mon–Sat, 7am–9pm Sun.* ***Bernhardskapelle*** *on request*

In the Middle Ages, the rural monasteries expanded by establishing a presence in the cities. Secularization in the 1780s diminished such holdings, but this one, belonging to the abbey of Heiligenkreuz *(see p174)*, survived.

The buildings around the courtyard housing the city's Applied Arts College present a serene 18th-century face. On the south side of the courtyard is the Bernhardskapelle. Dating from 1662, but altered in the 1730s, the chapel is a Baroque gem. Across from the chapel a patch of wall from Babenberg times *(see pp22–3)* has been exposed to remind you that, as so often in Vienna, the building is much older in origin than it at first appears.

Fresco at No. 12 Bäckerstrasse

Bäckerstrasse ⓮

Map 2 E5 & 6 D3. *Stephansplatz.*

Nowadays people visit this street, which used to house the city's bakers in medieval times, to sample its nightlife rather than its bread. The architecture is also of considerable interest: No. 2 sits beneath a 17th-century tower, and has a pretty courtyard. Opposite, at No. 1, is the site of the Alte Regensburgerhof, the outpost of Bavarian merchants who were given incentives to work in Vienna in the 15th century. No. 8 is the former palace of Count Seilern dating from 1722, and No. 7 is famous for its arcaded Renaissance courtyard and stables, which is the only surviving example in Vienna. Two other houses of Renaissance origin are located at Nos. 12 and 14.

Haas Haus ⓯

Stephansplatz 12. **Map** 2 E5 & 6 D3. *5356083.* *Stephansplatz.* *6am–2am daily.*

Commissioning a modern building directly opposite the Stephansdom was a sensitive task, and the city entrusted its design to one of Austria's leading architects, Hans Hollein. The result is the 1990 Haas Haus, a shining structure of glass and blue-green marble that curves elegantly round right into the Graben. The building has a very pleasing asymmetrical appearance, with decorative elements such as lopsided cubes of marble attached to the façade, a protruding structure high up resembling a diving board and a Japanese bridge inside. The atrium within is surrounded by cafés, shops, a restaurant, Do & Co *(see p212)* and offices.

Franziskanerkirche ⓰

Franziskanerplatz 4. **Map** 4 E1 & 6 D4. *5124578.* *Stephansplatz.* *6:30am–noon & 2–5:30pm Mon–Sat, 7am–5:30pm Sun.*

The Franciscans were fairly late arrivals in Vienna and one of their first tasks was to build a church on the site of a former medieval convent. Dating from 1603, the church totally dominates the Franziskanerplatz.

The façade is in South German Renaissance style, and is topped by an elaborate scrolled gable with obelisks.

Detail from Andrea Pozzo's altar (1707) in the Franziskanerkirche

The Moses Fountain in front of the church was designed by the Neo-Classicist Johann Martin Fischer in 1798.

The interior is in full-blown Baroque style and includes a finely-modelled pulpit dating from 1726, and richly-carved pews. A dramatic high altar by Andrea Pozzo rises to the full height of the church. Only the front part of the structure is three-dimensional – the rest is *trompe l'oeil*. Look out for a 1725 *Crucifixion* by Carlo Carlone among the paintings in the side altars.

You usually have to ask a passing monk for permission to see the church organ. It is worth being persistent, as this is the oldest organ in Vienna (1642), designed by Johann Wöckerl. It has statues of angel musicians and beautifully painted doors on religious themes.

Gleaming façade of Haas Haus (1990)

Stephansdom ❶

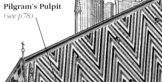

Carving of Rudolf IV

Ｓ ITUATED IN THE CENTRE of Vienna, the Stephansdom is the soul of the city itself; it is no mere coincidence that the urns containing the entrails of some of the Habsburgs lie in a vault beneath its main altar. A church has stood on the site for over 800 years, but all that remains of the original 13th-century Romanesque church are the Giants' Doorway and Heathen Towers. The Gothic nave, choir and side chapels are the result of a rebuilding programme in the 14th and 15th centuries, while some of the outbuildings, such as the Lower Vestry, are Baroque additions.

★ Giants' Doorway and Heathen Towers
The entrance and twin towers apparently stand on the site of an earlier heathen shrine.

The North Tower, according to legend, was never completed because its master builder, Hans Puchsbaum, broke a pact he had made with the devil, by pronouncing a holy name. The devil then caused him to fall to his death.

Pilgram's Pulpit *(see p78)*

Entrance to the catacombs

STAR FEATURES

★ Giants' Doorway and Heathen Towers

★ *Steffl* or Spire

★ Tiled Roof

★ Singer Gate

The symbolic number "O5" of the Austrian Resistance Movement was carved here in 1945.

Main entrance

★ Singer Gate
This was once the entrance for male visitors. A sculpted relief above the door depicts scenes from the life of St Paul.

Lower Vestry

★ Steffl or Spire
The 137-m high (450-ft) Gothic spire is a famous landmark. From the Sexton's Lodge (see p79), visitors can climb the stairs as far as a viewing platform.

★ Tiled Roof
Almost a quarter of a million glazed tiles cover the roof; they were meticulously restored after the damage caused in the last days of World War II.

JOHANNES CAPISTRANO

On the exterior north-eastern wall of the choir is a pulpit built after the victory over the Turks at Belgrade in 1456. It was from here that the Italian Franciscan, Johannes Capistrano, (1386–1456) is said to have preached against the Turkish invasion in 1451. The 18th-century Baroque statue above it depicts the triumphant saint trampling on a defeated Turkish invader.

South-eastern entrance

TIMELINE

1147 The first Romanesque building on the site consecrated by the Bishop of Passau		**1304** Duke Rudolf IV initiates work on High Gothic Albertine Choir		**1515** Anton Pilgram carves his pulpit		**1711** Pummerin bell cast from remains of guns left by Turks on their retreat from Vienna		**1948** Reconstruction and restoration carried out	
1100	**1200**	**1300**	**1400**	**1500**	**1600**	**1700**	**1800**	**1900**	**2000**
1230 Second Romanesque building erected on the same ground	**1359–1440** Main aisle, southern arches and southern tower built	**1515** Double wedding of grandchildren of Maximilian with children of the King of Hungary takes place		**1556** North Tower is roofed over **1783** Stephansdom churchyard closed after plague			**1916** Emperor Franz Joseph's funeral	**1945** Cathedral catches fire during bombing	

Inside the Stephansdom

THE LOFTY VAULTED INTERIOR of the Stephansdom contains an impressive collection of works of art spanning several centuries. Masterpieces of Gothic sculpture include the fabulously intricate pulpit, several of the figures of saints adorning the piers, and the canopies or baldachins over many of the side altars. To the left of the High Altar is the early 15th-century winged Wiener Neustädter Altar bearing the painted images of 72 saints. The altar panels open out to reveal delicate sculpture groups. The most spectacular Renaissance work is the tomb of Friedrich III, while the High Altar adds a flamboyant Baroque note.

The Catacombs
A flight of steps leads down to the catacombs, which extend under the cathedral square.

Christ with Toothache (1420) is the irreverent name of this figure; an old legend has it that Christ afflicts mockers with toothache.

Lift to the Pummerin Bell

Portrait of Pilgram
Master craftsman Anton Pilgram left a portrait of himself, holding a square and compass, below the corbel of the original organ.

Bishop's Gate

The Tirna Chapel houses the grave of the military hero Prince Eugene.

The Statue of Crucified Christ above the altar has, according to legend, a beard of human hair that is still growing.

Main entrance

★ Pilgram's Pulpit
Pilgram's intricate Gothic pulpit is decorated with portraits of the Four Fathers of the Church (theologians representing four physiognomic temperaments), while Pilgram himself looks out from a "window" below.

Organ Gallery and Case
In 1960 this modern organ was installed in the loft above the entrance. A more recent organ is in the south choir area.

The Canopy with Pötschen Madonna is a 16th-century canopy that shelters a 1697 icon of the Madonna, to which Prince Eugene's victory over the Turks at Zenta was attributed. It comes from Pecs, a village in Hungary.

★ **Wiener Neustädter Altar**
Friedrich III commissioned the elaborate altarpiece in 1447. Painted panels open out to reveal an earlier carved interior showing scenes from the life of the Virgin Mary and Christ. This panel portrays the Adoration of the Magi *(1420).*

Albertine Choir

Exit from crypt

Emperor Friedrich III's tomb is made from ornate red marble and has a lid bearing a life-like carved portrait of the Emperor. It dates from the 15th century.

The Sexton's Lodge houses the stairs that lead up the steeple.

Chapel of St Catherine

The Madonna of the Servants

The Füchsel Baldachin is a fine Gothic canopy.

The Trinity Altar probably dates from around 1740.

★ **High Altar**
Tobias Pock's altarpiece shows the martyrdom of St Stephen. The sculptures were fashioned by Johann Jakob Pock in 1647.

STAR SIGHTS

★ **Pilgram's Pulpit**

★ **Wiener Neustädter Altar**

★ **High Altar**

THE PUMMERIN BELL

The bell that hangs in the North Tower, known as the *Pummerin* or "Boomer", is a potent symbol for the city reflecting Vienna's turbulent past. The original bell was made from melted-down cannons abandoned when the Turks fled Vienna in 1683. The bell crashed down through the roof in 1945 when fire swept through the Stephansdom, so a new and even larger bell was cast using the remains of the old.

Statuary in the hall of the Winter Palace of Prince Eugene

Winter Palace of Prince Eugene ⑰

Himmelpfortgasse 3. **Map** 4 E1 &
6 D4. [51433. [U] Stephansplatz.
Vestibule [8am–4pm Mon–
Fri. [o]

Now the Ministry of Finance
(Bundesministerium für
Finanzen), the Winter Palace
was commissioned in 1694 by
Prince Eugene of Savoy *(see
p27)*, hero of the 1683 Turkish
siege. It was begun by Johann
Bernhard Fischer von Erlach
(see p147) and taken over by
Johann Lukas von Hildebrandt
(see p150) in 1702. The result
is an imposing town mansion,
considered one of the most
magnificent Baroque edifices in
Vienna. Maria Theresa bought
it for the state in 1752. Access
is limited, but you can view
the Baroque staircase *(see p43)*
and glance into the courtyard
with its lovely Rococo fountain.

Annagasse ⑱

Map 4 E1 & 6 D4. [U] Stephansplatz.
Zum Blauen Karpfen [●] to the public.

Now splendidly Baroque,
Annagasse dates from
medieval times. It is pedestrianized and a pleasant place to
browse in the bookshops.

　Of note are the luxurious
Mailberger Hof and the stucco-
decorated Römischer Kaiser
hotels *(see p197)*. No. 14's
lintel has a Baroque carving of
babes making merry, while
above this is a relief of the
blue carp that gives the house,
once a pub, its name: Zum
Blauen Karpfen. No. 2 is the
17th-century Esterházy Palace,
which is now a casino. Until a
few years ago you could see
the Countess Esterházy
sweeping her front doorstep!

Annakirche ⑲

Annagasse 3b. **Map** 4 E1 & 6 D4.
[5124797. [U] Stephansplatz.
[6am–7pm daily. [o]

There has been a chapel in
Annagasse since 1320, but
the present Annakirche dates
from 1629 to 1634, and it
was renovated by the Jesuits
during the early 18th century.
Devotion to St Anne has deep
roots in Vienna and this very
intimate church is often full of
quiet worshippers.

　The finest exterior feature
of the church is the moulded
copper cupola over the tower.
Daniel Gran's ceiling frescoes
are now fading and his richly-
coloured painting glorifying St
Anne on the High Altar is more
striking. Gran, together with
Franz Anton Maulbertsch,
was a leading painter of the
Austrian Baroque period. The
first chapel on the left houses
a copy of a carving of St Anne
from about 1505 – the original
is in the cathedral museum
(see p74). St Anne is portrayed
as a powerfully maternal figure
and shown with her daughter,
the Virgin Mary, who in turn
has the baby Jesus on her
knee. The carving is attributed
to the sculptor Veit Stoss.

Austrian Museum of Applied Arts ⑳

See pp82–3.

Postsparkasse ㉑

Georg-Coch-Platz 2. **Map** 2 F5 & 6 F3.
[514000. [U] Schwedenplatz.
[8am–3pm Mon–Wed & Fri,
8am–5:30pm Thu. [o]

This building is the Austrian
Post Office Savings Bank
and is a wonderful example
of Secession architecture *(see
pp54–57)*. Designed between

Moulded copper cupola over the tower of the Annakirche

Detail on the façade of the Griechische Kirche on Griechengasse

1904 and 1906 by Otto Wagner, it still looks unashamedly modern. The building features the architect's characteristic overhanging eaves, spindly aluminium columns supporting a canopy, heroic sculptures of angels and ornament-like nailheads protruding from the surface of the building.

Wagner was a pioneer in incorporating many functional elements into the decorative scheme of a building. Inside the large glass-roofed banking hall the metal columns are clad in aluminium, and tubular warm-air heating ducts encircle the hall. Wagner also designed some of the bank's furnishings including the office stools which are still in use.

Fleischmarkt ㉒

Map 2 E5 & 6 D2–E3. **⊓** Schweden-platz. **Griechische Kirche**
☎ 5332965. **◯** 9am–4pm Mon–Fri.

FLEISCHMARKT, THE FORMER meat market, dates from 1220. The small cosy inn called the Griechenbeisl (see p211) is its best-known landmark. On its façade is a woodcarving of a bagpiper known as Der liebe Augustin (Dear old Augustin). Rumour has it that during the 1679 plague, this bagpiper slumped drunk into the gutter one night and, taken for dead, was put in the plague pit. He woke, attracted attention by playing his pipes and was

rescued. Miraculously he did not catch the plague. Many major 19th-century musicians have patronized the Beisl, including Brahms and Wagner.

Next to the Griechenbeisl is the Neo-Byzantine Griechische Kirche (Greek church of the Holy Trinity). The versatile architect Theophil Hansen (see p32) created its rich, gilt appearance in the 1850s.

A passage links the Griechen-beisl to Griechengasse.

Griechengasse ㉓

Map 2 E5 & 6 E2. **⊓** Schwedenplatz.
Griechische Kirche. **☎** 5332965.
◯ by appt, 9am–4pm Mon–Fri,
10am–1pm for mass only Sat & Sun.

THIS STREET NAME refers to the Greek merchants who settled here in the 18th century and it leads up from Rotenturmstrasse. The house on the right dates from 1611 but has since been altered. Opposite is the Griechische Kirche (St George's), not to be confused with the Griechische Kirche in Fleischmarkt, though mass does alternate between the two churches. This one was built in 1803 but the gable was added later, in 1898. No. 7 is a 17th-century house. The façade was rebuilt in the late 18th century, with a Baroque Madonna in a niche and an iron lantern beneath. Within the courtyard passage are two wooden panels with inscriptions in Ottoman, possibly dating from the 17th century when the Turks besieged Vienna. In the courtyard is a 13th-century watchtower.

Ruprechtskirche ㉔

Ruprechtsplatz. **Map** 2 E5 & 6 D2.
☎ 5356003. **⊓** Schwedenplatz.
◯ 9:30–11:30am Mon–Fri & for mass 5pm Sat & 10:30am Sun; Jul–Aug: for mass 6pm Sat only. **◉** **&**
Donation expected.

Ivy-clad façade of Ruprechtskirche

ST RUPRECHT (see p22) was the patron saint of Vienna's salt merchants and the church that takes his name overlooks the merchants' landing stage on the Danube canal. There is a statue of the saint holding a tub of salt at the foot of the Romanesque tower. Salt was a valuable commodity in the Middle Ages, and evidence suggests that the church dates back to the 11th century, making it the oldest church in Vienna. The interior is less interesting, having been restored at various times, but the chancel has two panes of Romanesque stained glass. The choir is 13th century, the vault-ed south aisle 15th century.

Carving of the bagpiper on the façade of the Griechenbeisl, Fleischmarkt

Austrian Museum of Applied Arts ⓴

THE RENOVATED MAK (Museum für angewandte
Kunst) acts both as a showcase for Austrian
decorative arts and as a repository for fine objects
from around the world. Originally founded in 1864
as a museum for art and industry, it expanded and
diversified over the years to include objects
representing new artistic movements. The museum
has a fine collection of furniture, including some
classical works of the
German cabinet-maker
David Roentgen, textiles,
glass, Islamic and East
Asian art and fine
Renaissance jewellery.
In 1993 the museum was
completely renovated
and each room was re-
designed by a different
leading artist. The result
is a series of displays
that lend the exhibits a
unique, unusual flavour.

**★ Wiener Werk-
stätte Collection**
*Kolo Moser created
this brass vase, inlaid
with citrines (false
topaz), for the
Wiener Werkstätte
in 1903.*

★ Dubsky Porcelain Room
*A reassembly of a room (around 1724) in
the Dubsky Palace at Brno, Czech Republic.*

Stairs to
second
floor

First
floor

First floor
mezzanine

**Romanesque,
Gothic and
Renaissance Room**
*Blue walls set off the
furniture and ceramics
in display cases designed
by Matthias
Esterházy in
1993.*

Entrance to MAK
Café *(see p211)*

Entrance
hall

Stubenring
entrance

MUSEUM GUIDE
*The basement houses the
individual collections, and the
extension is used for special
exhibitions. Most of the permanent
collection is displayed in the
ground-floor galleries, although
the Wiener Werkstätte collection is
on the first floor. A flight of stairs
in the west wing leads to the
contemporary architecture and
design rooms on the second floor.*

KEY

☐	Romanesque, Gothic, Renaissance
☐	Baroque, Rococo
☐	Wiener Werkstätte
☐	Art Nouveau, Art Deco
☐	Islamic Art
☐	Biedermeier
☐	20th-century design
☐	Individual collections
☐	Temporary exhibition space
☐	Non-exhibition space

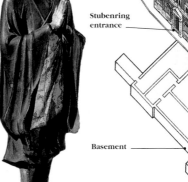

Basement

Monk of the Nichiren Sect
*This Japanese wooden
sculpture of a praying
monk dates from the
Muromachi Period
(around 1500).*

THE WIENER WERKSTÄTTE

In 1903 Josef Hoffman (pictured) and Kolo Moser founded a co-operative arts and crafts workshop, the Wiener Werkstätte. This promoted all aspects of design from postage stamps and book illustrations to fabric, furniture, jewellery and interiors. The museum houses its archives, which include sketches, fabric patterns and fine pieces.

VISITORS' CHECKLIST

Stubenring 5. **Map** 2 F5 & 6 F3.
711360. Stubentor. 1A, 74A. 1, 2. Landstrasse.
10am–midnight Tue, 10am–6pm Wed–Sun. 1 Jan, 1 May, 1 Nov, 25 Dec (24 & 31 Dec: 10am–3pm). W www.MAK.at

Lecture Hall

Library

Ground floor

Mundus Chair

Bentwood furniture was made popular by the 19th-century designer, Michael Thonet (1796–1871), who pioneered bentwood furniture techniques in the 1830s. This example was manufactured by Mundus in 1910.

Knotted Mameluke Carpet

This 16th-century Egyptian silk rug is the only known surviving example of its kind.

STAR FEATURES

★ **Dubsky Porcelain Room**

★ **Wiener Werkstätte Collection**

★ **Biedermeier Room**

★ **Biedermeier Room**
This cherrywood sofa (1825–30), designed and manufactured by Danhauser'sche Möbelfabrik, is an outstanding example of Viennese Empire-style Biedermeier design (see pp30–31). The original upholstery has been reproduced.

Jewish District ㉕

Map 2 F5 & 6 D2. 🚇 *Schwedenplatz.*
Stadttempel 📞 *531040.* 🕐
*Mon–Thu (am) by appointment or
for tours at 11:30am and 3pm.*

The Anker Clock in Hoher Markt

V IENNA'S JEWISH DISTRICT is
more famous today for its
area of bars and discos called
the Bermuda Triangle than
for its Jewish community.
Judengasse is now a bustling
lane lined with clothes shops
and bars. There are some
solid Biedermeier apartment
blocks and on Ruprechts-
platz, in the former town
hall, a kosher restaurant, the
Arche Noah. Behind it is a
jutting tower, the Korn-
häuselturm. Named after Josef
Kornhäusel, an architect from
the Biedermeier period *(see
pp30–31)*, it was apparently
built as a refuge from his wife.

Close to Arche Noah is
Sterngasse. This street has an
English-language bookshop
called Shakespeare & Co *(see
p223)* and the Neustädter-Hof,
a Baroque palace built by
Anton Ospel in 1734. A
Turkish cannonball, fired in
1683, is embedded in its façade.

Vienna's oldest surviving
synagogue, the Stadttempel,
designed by Kornhäusel in
the 1820s, is on Seitenstettengasse. On the same street is
the headquarters of Vienna's

Jewish community. It used to
house the Jewish museum,
which is now located in
Dorotheergasse *(see p93)*.

Hoher Markt ㉖

Map 2 E5 & 6 D2. 🚇 *Stephansplatz,
Schwedenplatz.* **Roman ruins**
📞 *5355606.* 🕐 *9am–12:15pm,
1–4:30pm Tue–Sun.*

H OHER MARKT IS the oldest
square in Vienna. In
medieval times fish and cloth
markets were held here, and
so were executions. Today it
is possible to view the subterranean ruins of a former
Roman garrison beneath it *(see
p21)*. Discovered after World
War II, the ancient foundations
show groups of houses bisec-
ted by straight roads leading
to the town gates. It seems
probable that they were 2nd-
and 3rd-century officers'
houses. The excavations are
well laid out and exhibits of
pottery, reliefs and tiles
supplement the ruins.

In the centre of the square is
the Vermählungsbrunnen
(Nuptial Fountain), or Josefs-
brunnen. Emperor Leopold I
vowed to commemorate the
safe return of his son Joseph
from the Siege of Landau
and commissioned Johann
Bernhard Fischer von Erlach
to design this monument,
which was built by von
Erlach's son Joseph Emanuel
between 1729 and 1732. The
fountain celebrates the
betrothal of Joseph and Mary
and bears figures of the high
priest and the couple, with gilt
urns, statues of angels, and
fluted columns supporting an
elaborate canopy.

Linking two office buildings
on the square is the bronze
and copper sculptural clock,
known as the Anker Clock.
Commissioned by the Anker
Insurance Company, and
designed by Franz Matsch, it
was completed in 1914. Every
hour a procession of cut-out
historical figures, ranging from
the Emperor Marcus Aurelius
and Duke Rudolf IV to Joseph
Haydn, glide from one side of
the clock to the other to the
sound of organ music. Noon
is the best time to see it, as all
the figures are on display then.

Bohemian Court Chancery ㉗

Judenplatz 11. **Map** 2 D5 & 5 C2.
📞 *53122.* 🚇 *Stephansplatz.*
🕐 *8am–3:30pm Mon–Fri.*

H ABSBURG RULERS were also
kings of Bohemia, which
was governed from this magnificent palace (1709–14). Its
architect was the finest of the
day: Johann Bernhard Fischer
von Erlach *(see p146)*.

VIENNA'S JEWS – PAST AND PRESENT

A Jewish community has thrived in Vienna since at least the
12th century, with Judenplatz and, later, the Stadttempel at
its core. Unfortunately, the Jews' commercial success caused
envy and in 1421, after a charge of ritual murder, almost the
entire Jewish population was burnt to death, forcibly baptised
or expelled. Thereafter Jewish fortunes fluctuated, with periods
of prosperity alternating with expulsions. The 1781 Edict of
Tolerance lifted legal constraints that had applied to Jews and
by the late 19th century the city's cultural and intellectual life
was dominated by Jews. Anti-Semitism spread in the early
20th century and burgeoning Nazism forced many Jews to
leave. Of those who remained, 65,000 were murdered. In
1938 170,000
Jews lived in the
city; 50 years
later there were
7,000. Now East-
ern European
Jews are adding
to the number.

**The interior of
the Stadttempel**

Matthias Gerl enlarged the Chancery between 1751 and 1754 to accommodate the Ministry of the Interior. Its glory is the huge Baroque portals, yet the building is as subtle as it is powerful. The elegantly-curved window frames on the first floor are particularly noteworthy.

The building's interior, now a courthouse, and its two courtyards, are less impressive, partly due to reconstruction undertaken after serious bomb damage in World War II.

Altes Rathaus 28

Wipplinger Strasse 8. **Map** 2 D5 & 6 D2. **U** Schwedenplatz. **Salvatorkapelle** **C** 5337133. **Q** 9–11am Mon, Wed, Sat, or by appointment. **Austrian Resistance Archive C** 53436779. **Q** 9am–5pm Mon, Wed & Thu.

A FTER THE GERMAN brothers Otto and Haymo of Neuburg conspired to overthrow the Habsburgs *(see p22)* in 1309, their property

Ironwork at the Rathaus entrance

was confiscated and donated to the city. Over the centuries the site was expanded to form the complex of buildings that until 1883 served as the city hall or *Rathaus*.

The entrance of the Altes Rathaus is festooned with ornamental ironwork. The building is now occupied by offices and shops. The District Museum, which deals with the first municipal district of Vienna (roughly covering the area within the Ring), is also here. Of much greater interest is the Austrian Resistance Archive on the first floor, where

Portal figure by Lorenzo Mattielli in the Bohemian Court Chancery

Austrian resistance to Nazism is documented. Although many Austrians welcomed Hitler's takeover in 1938, a distinguished minority fiercely resisted it, and this exhibition pays tribute to them.

In one corner of the Altes Rathaus is the Andromeda Fountain. Located in the main courtyard, it was the last work by sculptor Georg Raphael Donner who designed it in 1741. The relief shows Perseus rescuing Andromeda.

At No. 5 Salvatorplatz is a late 13th-century chapel, the Salvatorkapelle, the only surviving building of the original medieval town house. It has since been enlarged and renovated, but retains its fine Gothic vaults. The walls are lined with old marble tomb slabs, some from the 15th century. Its pretty organ dates from around 1740 and is sometimes used for recitals in the chapel. On the outside wall on Salvatorgasse is an exquisite Renaissance portal dating from 1520 to 1530 – a rare example of Italianate Renaissance style in Vienna.

Maria am Gestade 29

Salvatorgasse 12. **Map** 2 D5 & 5 C2. **C** 5339594. **U** Schwedenplatz, Stephansplatz. **Q** 7am–6pm daily & inside at rear by appointment only.

O NE OF THE CITY'S oldest sights is this lofty, Gothic church with its 56-m high (180-ft) steeple and immense choir windows. Mentioned as early as 1158, the present building dates from the late 14th century. It was restored in the 19th century. The church has had a chequered history and during the occupation of Vienna by Napoleon in 1809 his troops used it as an arsenal.

Inside, the nave piers are enlivened with Gothic canopies sheltering statues from various periods: medieval, Baroque, and modern. The choir contains two High Gothic panels (1460): they depict the Annunciation, the Crucifixion and the Coronation of the Virgin. Behind the high altar the windows contain medieval stained glass, much of which is patched with surviving fragments. Tucked away on the north side of the choir is a chapel with a beautiful painted stone altar dated 1520. The main parts of the interior are visible from the front entrance, but to walk around inside you need to make an appointment.

Gothic canopies in the Maria am Gestade church

Holocaust memorial in Judenplatz

Judenplatz **30**

Map 2 D5 & 5 C2. Ⓤ *Stephansplatz, Herrengasse.* **Museum Judenplatz**
☏ *5332265.* ◯ *10am–6pm Sun–Thu, 10am–2pm Fri.* ● *on main Jewish holidays.* 🖼 ♿ *except to synagogue.* 📷 🎟 *free 5pm Tue & Thu, 11:30am & 2:30pm Sun.* 🅦 *www.jmw.at*

JUDENPLATZ WAS THE SITE of the Jewish ghetto in medieval times. In the centre of the square stands a statue of the German playwright and critic Ephraim Lessing by Siegfried Charoux. The Nazis took great offence to this tribute to a writer whose works plead for toleration towards Jews, and they destroyed it in 1939. It was later redesigned by the same sculptor and reinstated in the square in 1982.

In 1996 British artist Rachel Whiteread was the controversial winner of a competition to design a monument for the Jewish victims of the Nazi regime, to be unveiled in the square on 9 November 1999, the anniversary of Kristal Nacht. A heated public debate ensued and following many changes, including the repositioning of

the proposed monument by one metre, Judenplatz was reopened on 25 October 2000 as a place of remembrance. It now contains Whiteread's memorial, the new Museum Judenplatz at No. 8, and the excavated remains of the medieval synagogue that lie beneath the square. The museum celebrates the vibrant Jewish quarter that was centred on the square until the expulsion of the Jews in 1421, an event gleefully recorded in an inscription, *Zum Grossen Jordan,* on the façade of No. 2. The museum also houses a public database of the 65,000 Austrian Jews killed by the Nazis and, in the basement, the excavated synagogue.

Clock Museum **31**

Schulhof 2. **Map** 2 D5 & 5 C2.
☏ *5332265.* Ⓤ *Stephansplatz.* ◯ *9am–4:30pm Tue–Sun.* ● *25 Dec, 1 Jan.* 📷 🅦 *www.museum.vienna.at*

YOU DON'T HAVE to be a clock fanatic to enjoy a visit to this wonderful and fascinating museum. Located in the beautiful former Obizzi Palace (1690), the museum contains

a fine collection of clocks which were accumulated by an earlier curator, Rudolf Kaftan, as well as those of the novelist Marie von Ebner-Eschenbach. The first floor displays the mechanisms of tower clocks from the 16th century onwards, painted clocks, grandfather clocks and pocket watches. On the floors above are huge astronomical clocks and various novelty ones. There are more than 3,000 exhibits.

Kurrentgasse **32**

Map 2 D5 & 5 C2. Ⓤ *Stephansplatz.* **Grimm bakery** ◯ *7am–6:30pm Mon–Fri, 7am–noon Sat.*

THIS NARROW street is shaded by elegant tall Baroque houses, their lower floors filled with cosy bars and pricey Italian restaurants. It's a pleasant place to while away an afternoon. The Grimm bakery at No. 10 is one of the best in Vienna and offers an astonishing variety of breads. No. 12, a house dating from 1730, has an attractive pink cobbled courtyard filled with numerous plants and trees.

Doll and Toy Museum **33**

Schulhof 4. **Map** 2 D5 & 5 C2.
☏ *5356860.* Ⓤ *Stephansplatz, Herrengasse.* ◯ *10am–6pm Tue–Sun.* 📷

ONE OF VIENNA'S more unexpected museums is housed in this fine Baroque building. Originally a private collection, it was opened to the public in 1989 and comprises dolls and toys from the past two centuries. The dolls are mainly of French and German origin. Particularly intriguing are the early 20th-century "exotic" dolls or Südsee-Babies (South Sea babies); they are black, Polynesian and Oriental models.

Among the exhibits are some astonishingly opulent dolls' houses from the turn of the century, and some teddy bears. There is also a shop which sells historic dolls.

Musical doll from the Doll and Toy Museum

Statue on top of No. 10 Am Hof

Kirche am Hof ❸

Schulhof 1. **Map** 2 D5 & 5 C2.
📞 5338394. 🚇 Herrengasse.
🕐 7am–noon, 4–6pm daily. 📷 ♿

THIS CATHOLIC CHURCH, which is picturesquely dedicated to the Nine Choirs of Angels, was founded by Carmelite friars in the late 14th century. The façade, at present being renovated, was redesigned by the Italian architect Carlo Carlone in 1662 to provide space for a large balustraded balcony. The church is now used for services by Vienna's large Croatian community.

It is also worth taking a walk behind the church into Schulhofplatz to look at the tiny restored shops which snuggle happily between the buttresses of the Gothic choir.

Am Hof ❸

Map 2 D5 & 5 C2.
🚇 Stephansplatz, Schottentor.

THIS IS THE LARGEST enclosed square in Vienna. The Romans established a garrison here and, later, the Babenberg ruler Duke Heinrich II Jasomirgott built his castle close to where No. 2 Am Hof stands. In the centre of the square you can see the Mariensäule (Column of Our Lady), a monument that commemorates the end of

the threat of Swedish invasion during the Thirty Years War (see p25). Dating from 1667, it was designed by Carlo Carlone and Carlo Canevale.

There are a number of interesting houses around the square. Opposite the church is the palatial Märkleinisches Haus which was designed by Johann Lukas von Hildebrandt (see p150) in 1727. Its elegant façade was wrecked by the insertion of a fire station on the ground floor in 1935. The 16th-century red house next door is the headquarters of Johann Kattus, a producer of sparkling wine. No. 10, designed by Anton Ospel, is the Bürgerliche Zeughaus, the citizens' armoury, where the city's fire services are now permanently based. The façade is dominated by the Habsburg coat of arms and military emblems. The allegorical statues above are by Lorenzo Mattielli.

At No. 12 the bay-windowed Urbanihaus dates from the 1730s, and its iron inn sign dates from the same period. Next door is the Collalto Palace – it was here, in 1762, that Mozart made his first public appearance aged just six (see p38).

Peterskirche ❸

Petersplatz 6. **Map** 2 D5 & 5 C3.
📞 5336433. 🚇 Stephansplatz.
🕐 7am–6pm daily. 📷

A CHURCH HAS STOOD here since the 12th century, but the oval structure you see today dates from the early 18th century. It was modelled on St Peter's in Rome and a number of architects collaborated on the design, notably Gabriele Montani. The interior is amazingly lavish, and there's an exuberant, eye-catching pulpit (1716) by the sculptor Matthias Steindl. The richly-clothed skeletons on the right and beneath the altar are the remains of early Christian martyrs originally deposited in the catacombs in Rome. The frescoes inside the huge dome, depicting the Assumption of the Virgin, are by J M Rottmayr.

In 1729 Lorenzo Mattielli designed the sculpture of St John Nepomuk to the right of the choir. This priest earned his sainthood by being thrown into the River Vltava in Prague in 1393 after he refused to reveal the secrets of the confessional to King Wenceslas IV; his martyrdom by drowning later became a favourite subject of artists.

18th-century engraving of Peterskirche

HOFBURG QUARTER

W HAT BEGAN AS a modest city fortress has grown over the centuries into a vast palace, the Hofburg. The palace was still expanding up until a few years before the Habsburgs fell from power in 1918. The presence of the court had a profound effect on the surrounding area. The former gardens of the palace are now

Portal detail in Josefsplatz

the Volksgarten and Burggarten, and some of the buildings are now splendid museums. Streets such as Herrengasse and Bankgasse are lined with the palaces that the nobility built in their eagerness to be as close as possible to the centre of imperial power. This area is bustling with tourists by day, but at night it is almost deserted.

SIGHTS AT A GLANCE

Streets and Squares

GETTING THERE
This area is served by the Herrengasse (line U3) U-Bahn station. Trams 1 and 2 run along the Burgring and Dr-Karl-Renner-Ring. Buses 2A and 3A run along Herrengasse and bus 1A goes from Stubentor to the Graben.

0 metres 250

0 yards 250

KEY

- Street-by-Street map *See pp90–91*
- Ⓤ U-Bahn station
- Ⓟ Parking

◁ **Detail of Danubius fountain by Johann Meixner (1869)** outside the Albertina

Street-by-Street: Imperial Vienna

THE STREETS AROUND the Hofburg are no longer filled with the carriages of the nobility. Most of the palaces have become offices, embassies or apartments. Yet this district remains the most fashionable in Vienna, crammed with elegant shops, art galleries and coffee houses, which offer enjoyable interludes between visits to the many museums and churches in the area.

Herrengasse
This was a prime site for the palaces of the nobility **⑬**

Herrengasse U-Bahn

Demel Konditorei
This Café-Konditorei offers delightful décor and exquisite pastries **⑪**

Grosses und Kleines Michaelerhaus
Joseph Haydn (see p38) once lived in rooms overlooking the handsome courtyard of the Grosses Michaelerhaus **❸**

Mollard-Clary Palace
This mansion, built at the end of the 17th-century, has a façade designed by J L Hildebrandt **⑭**

Michaelerplatz
Roman remains were recently excavated here **❶**

★ Loos Haus
Built in 1912, this unadorned design outraged the conservative sensibilities of the ornament-loving Archduke Franz Ferdinand (see p164) **❷**

★ Michaelerkirche
The crypt of this church contains well-preserved corpses from the late 18th century **❹**

STAR SIGHTS

★ Loos Haus

★ Michaelerkirche

★ Pestsäule

KEY

– – – Suggested route

0 metres	50
0 yards	50

Josefsplatz
An equestrian statue of Joseph II stands at the centre of this elegant square **❻**

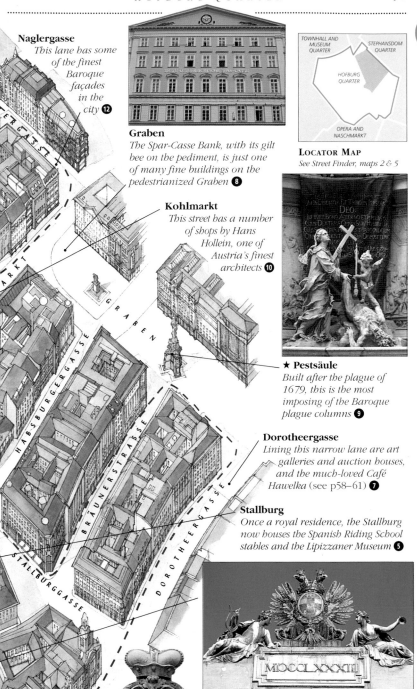

Naglergasse
This lane has some of the finest Baroque façades in the city ⑫

Graben
The Spar-Casse Bank, with its gilt bee on the pediment, is just one of many fine buildings on the pedestrianized Graben ⑧

Kohlmarkt
This street has a number of shops by Hans Hollein, one of Austria's finest architects ⑩

LOCATOR MAP
See Street Finder, maps 2 & 5

★ **Pestsäule**
Built after the plague of 1679, this is the most imposing of the Baroque plague columns ⑨

Dorotheergasse
Lining this narrow lane are art galleries and auction houses, and the much-loved Café Hawelka (see p58–61) ⑦

Stallburg
Once a royal residence, the Stallburg now houses the Spanish Riding School stables and the Lipizzaner Museum ⑤

The Palffy Palace, built in the 16th century, was later the venue for a private performance of Mozart's *The Marriage of Figaro.*

The Pallavicini Palace is a late 18th-century aristocrats' palace, strategically located opposite the Hofburg.

Michaelerplatz ❶

Map 2 D5 & 5 C3. 🚇 *Herrengasse.*

Michaelerplatz faces the grandiose entrance into the Hofburg, the Michaelertor. Opposite are the Michaelerkirche and Loos Haus. On one side of Michaelerplatz is the Michaelertrakt, commissioned by Franz Joseph in 1888 when the new Burgtheater *(see pp130–31)* on the Ringstrasse opened, and the original theatre dating from 1751, which occupied this site, was demolished. An old design by Joseph Emanuel Fischer von Erlach *(see p147)* was used as the basis for a new design by Ferdinand Kirschner (1821–96). It was finished in 1893, complete with gilt-tasselled cupolas and statuary representing Austria's land and sea power.

Recent excavations have uncovered remains of a Roman encampment, as well as some medieval foundations.

Loos Haus ❷

Michaelerplatz 3. **Map** 2 D5 & 5 C3. 📞 53173455. 🚇 *Herrengasse.* 🕐 *8am–3pm Mon–Wed & Fri, 8am–5:30pm Thu.* ♿

Erected opposite the Michaelertor in 1910–12, and designed by Adolf Loos, this building so outraged Franz Ferdinand *(see p164)* that he declared he

Adolf Loos

Unlike his contemporary Otto Wagner *(see p57)*, Adolf Loos (1870–1933) loathed ornament for its own sake. Instead, he used smooth lines and exquisite interior decoration; his buildings' lack of "eye-brows" (the window hoods on many of Vienna's buildings) scandalized Viennese society. Surviving interiors include Knize *(see p93)* and the American Bar *(see p105)*.

would never use the Michaelertor again. Today it's hard to understand why: the outside is unexceptional but the inside is a lesson in stylish elegance.

Grosses und Kleines Michaelerhaus ❸

Kohlmarkt 11 & Michaelerplatz 6. **Map** 2 D5 & 5 C3. 🚇 *Herrengasse.* ● *to the public.*

At no. 6 Michaelerplatz a footpath leads to the Baroque Kleines Michaelerhaus (1735). Look out for a vivid painted relief of Christ on the Mount of Olives with a crucifixion in the background (1494) on the side of the Michaelerkirche. The Baroque façade of the Grosses Michaelerhaus is at No. 11 Kohlmarkt. It has a

Michaelerplatz fountain

handsome courtyard and coach house. From here there is a fine view of the older parts of the Michaelerkirche. The buildings around the courtyard were erected in about 1720, and the composer Joseph Haydn *(see p38)* is said to have lived in an unheated attic here in 1749.

Michaelerkirche ❹

Michaelerplatz 1. **Map** 2 D5 & 5 C3. 📞 5338000. 🚇 *Herrengasse.* 🕐 *6:30am–6pm daily.* 📷 ♿ 🕐 *May–Oct: 11am, 1pm, 2pm, 3pm, 4pm; Nov–Apr: 11am, 3pm.*

The Michaelerkirche was once the parish church of the court. Its earliest parts were built in the 13th century, and the choir dates from 1327–40. The Neo-Classical façade is from 1792. Its porch is topped by Baroque statues (1724–25) by Lorenzo Mattielli depicting the Fall of the Angels. Inside are Renaissance and 14th-century frescoes, and a glorious, vividly-carved organ from 1714 by Johann David Sieber. The main choir (1782), replete with tumbling cherubs and sunbursts, is by Karl Georg Merville. The altarpiece of the north choir (1755) is by Franz Anton Maulbertsch.

Off the north choir is the crypt entrance. In the 17th and 18th centuries parishioners were frequently buried beneath their church. Corpses clothed in their burial finery, well-preserved due to the constant temperature, can still be seen in open coffins.

Baroque organ (1714) in the Michaelerkirche

Stallburg ❺

Reitschulgasse 2. **Map** 4 D1 & 5 C3.
Ⓤ *Stephansplatz, Herrengasse.*
Lipizzaner Museum 🎫 *5337811.*
Ⓞ *9am–6pm daily.* 📷 🎦 *after gala performances only.*

THE STALLBURG WAS BUILT in the mid-16th century for Archduke Maximilian. Later converted to stables for the Hofburg, these are ranged around a large courtyard with arcades on three storeys. You can view the horses in their stables, which are open to the public as part of the Lipizzaner Museum. The museum also contains objects from the Imperial Collection, as well as exhibits on the history of the Lipizzaner horses and art which portrays the Spanish Riding School *(see pp98–9).*

Josefsplatz ❻

Augustinerstrasse. **Map** 4 D1 & 5 C4.
Ⓤ *Stephansplatz, Herrengasse.*

IN THE CENTRE OF the Josefs-platz is an equestrian statue (1807) of Joseph II by Franz Anton Zauner. Despite his reforms, Joseph II was a true monarchist, and during the 1848 revolution *(see p31)* loyalists used the square as a gathering place.
   Facing the Hofburg are two palaces. No. 5 is the Pallavicini Palace (1783–4), a blend of Baroque and Neo-Classical styles by Ferdinand von Hohenberg.
No. 6 is
the 16th-

century Palffy Palace. On the right of the Prunksaal *(see p102)* is the Redoutensaal. It was built from 1750–60 and was the venue for masked balls in imperial times. To the left is an extension to the library which was built a few years later. Both are by Nikolaus Pacassi, a favourite architect of Maria Theresa.

Dorotheergasse ❼

Map 4 D1 & 5 C4. Ⓤ *Stephansplatz.*
Jewish Museum 🎫 *5350431.*
Ⓞ *10am–6pm Mon–Wed, Fri & Sun, 10am–8pm Thu.* Ⓦ *www.jmw.at*

AT NO. 11 OF THIS street is the Eskeles Palace, now home to the Jewish Museum (Jüdisches Museum) which, along with its new extension in Judenplatz *(see p86)*, chronicles the city's rich Jewish heritage. At No. 27 is the Dorotheum *(see pp222–3)*, from the 17th century. A pawnbrokers and, more importantly, an auction house, it has branches all over Vienna. Halfway along the street is the Evangelical church (1783–4), originally by Gottlieb Nigelli. Towards the top end, close to Graben, are two immensely popular Viennese gathering places, Café Hawelka at No. 6 *(see pp58–61)*, and the Buffet Trzesniewski at No. 1 *(see p217)*.

Baroque plague column (Pestsäule)

Graben ❽

Map 2 D5 & 5 C3. Ⓤ *Stephansplatz.*
Neidhart Fresco House Ⓞ *9am–12:15pm, 1–4:30pm Tue–Sun.*

FACING No. 16 of this pedestrianized street is the Joseph Fountain by Johann Martin Fischer. Further along is his identical Leopold Fountain (both 1804). No. 13, the clothing shop Knize *(see p221)*, is by Adolf Loos. No. 10, the Ankerhaus by Otto Wagner, is topped by a studio used by Wagner himself and, in the 1980s, by Friedensreich Hundertwasser *(see p162)*. No. 21 is Alois Pichl's Spar-Casse Bank from the 1830s. Just off the Graben at No. 19 Tuchlauben is the Neidhart Fresco House, containing medieval frescoes. *(See pp54–7).*

Pestsäule ❾

Graben. **Map** 2 D5 & 5 C3.
Ⓤ *Stephansplatz.*

DURING THE PLAGUE of 1679, Emperor Leopold I vowed to commemorate Vienna's eventual deliverance. The plague over, he commissioned Matthias Rauchmiller, Lodovico Burnacini and the young Johann Bernhard Fischer von Erlach *(see p147)* to build this Baroque plague column. Devised by the Jesuits, its most striking image shows a saintly figure and an angel supervising the destruction of a hag representing the plague, while above the bewigged Emperor prays.

Statue in Josefsplatz of Joseph II by Franz Anton Zauner (1746–1822)

Exterior of Schullin shop (see p223)

Kohlmarkt ❿

Map 2 D5 & 5 C3. Ⓤ *Herrengasse.*

SOME OF VIENNA's most exclusive shops line the pedestrianized Kohlmarkt. On the corner of Wallnerstrasse is the show room of Thonet, creator of shapely black chairs that were a hallmark of Viennese design at the turn of the century. Further along are the jewellers Rothe & Neffe (1980), and Schullin (1982) and Retti (1965), which both have striking abstract shopfronts designed by the architect Hans Hollein *(see p91)*. No. 9, the Jugendstil Artaria Haus (1901), is by Max Fabiani (1865–1962), a protégé of Otto Wagner *(see p57)*.

Demel Konditorei ⓫

Kohlmarkt 14. **Map** 2 D5 & 5 C3. 📞 53517170. Ⓤ *Stephansplatz.* ◯ *10am–7pm daily.* 📷 ♿

THIS FAMOUS pastry shop at No. 14 Kohlmarkt still bears its imperial patent – K.u.k. Hof-Zuckerbäcker – proudly lettered above the shopfront.

The pastry shop was founded in Michaelerplatz in 1785 and acquired by the pâtissier Christoph Demel in 1857, before moving to its present site on Kohlmarkt in 1888. Its many small rooms are in an ornate late 19th-century style.

Naglergasse ⓬

Map 2 D5 & 5 C2. Ⓤ *Herrengasse.*

DURING THE Middle Ages needle-makers had their shops here, which is how the street acquired its name. This narrow lane also follows the line of a wall that used to stand here in Roman times. Today Naglergasse is lined with a succession of gorgeous Baroque houses. The delightful Renaissance bay window of No. 19 is ornamented with carved cherubs. No. 13 dates from the 16th century but has been considerably altered since. No. 21 (1720) is now an inn with a particularly snug and cosy interior.

Herrengasse ⓭

Map 2 D5 & 5 B2. Ⓤ *Herrengasse.*

FLANKING THE HOFBURG, this street was the prime location for the palaces of the Habsburg nobility. In 1843 a visiting writer, J G Kohl, wrote of the street's "silent palaces", and today little has changed.

The base of the provincial government of Lower Austria, the Landhaus, is at No. 13; the façade of the present building dates from the 1830s.

In the courtyard a tablet from 1571 warns visitors not to carry weapons or to fight here. The injunction was famously ignored when the 1848 Revolution *(see p31)* was ignited on this very spot.

The long, low Neo-Classical façade of No. 7 received its present appearance from Ludwig Pichl and Giacomo Quarenghi in 1811. At No. 5 Anton Ospel (1677–1756) gave the Wilczek Palace (built before 1737) an original façade, with angled pilasters lending the central bays an illusion of perspective.

Coat of arms in the courtyard of the Mollard-Clary Palace

Mollard-Clary Palace ⓮

Herrengasse 9. **Map** 2 D5 & 5 B3. Ⓤ *Herrengasse.* ⬤ *to the public.*

AT NO. 9 HERRENGASSE is the former Mollard-Clary Palace, a mansion constructed by Domenico Martinelli in 1698. The façade, which also dates from 1698, was the first commission for Johann Lukas von Hildebrandt *(see p150)*.

From 1923 until 1997 the palace housed the Lower Austrian Provincial Museum, or Landesmuseum. Today the building houses offices.

Visible throught the courtyard gates are an elaborate, 16th-century wrought-iron well cover and a carved stone coat of arms (1454).

Hofburg Complex ⓯

See pp96–101.

Inside the ornately-decorated Demel Konditorei

Neue Burg 16

Burgring. **Map** 4 D1 & 5 B4.
52524484. Volkstheater,
Herrengasse. 10am–6pm Mon,
Wed–Sun. www.khm.at

THE NEUE BURG, a massive
curved building situated
on Heldenplatz, was added
to the Hofburg Complex in
1881–1913. It embodies the
last gasp of the Habsburg
Empire as it strained under
aspirations of independence
from its domains, when the
personal prestige of Emperor
Franz Joseph was all that
seemed able to keep it intact.
It was not the perfect moment
to embark on an extension to
the Hofburg, but the work was
undertaken nevertheless, and
the Neue Burg was built to
designs by the Ringstrasse
architects Karl von Hasenauer
(1833–94) and Gottfried
Semper (1803–79). Five years
after its completion, the
Habsburg empire ended.

In 1938, Adolf Hitler stood
on the terraced central bay to
proclaim the Anschluss – the
union of Austria and Germany
– to tens of thousands of
Viennese (see p36).

Today the Neue Burg is
home to the reading room of
the National Library, as well
as a number of museums
(see following entries).

Ephesos Museum 17

As Neue Burg. 52524484.
10am–6pm Mon, Wed–Sun.

FOR DECADES Austrian archaeologists have been
excavating the
Greek and
Roman site of
Ephesus in
Turkey. Since
1978 their discoveries
have been on display in
the main block of the Neue
Burg. Also on show are finds
from the Greek island
of Samothrace, excavated in
the 1870s. The main exhibits
include a colossal frieze
commemorating Lucius
Verus's victory over
the Parthians in AD 165, as
well as a substantial number
of architectural fragments.

Armour at Hofjagd und Rüstkammer

Sammlung Alter Musikinstrumente 18

As Neue Burg.

PIANOS THAT belonged to
Beethoven, Schubert and
Haydn, among countless
other items, are housed in the
musical instrument museum.
More important, however, is
the collection of Renaissance
instruments, widely believed
to be the finest in the world.
The claviorgan (1596), the
oldest surviving example of
this instrument, is particularly
fascinating, and features stops
used to create special effects
such as birdsong.

**Renaissance cittern
from the Sammlung
Alter Musikinstrumente**

Hofjagd und Rüstkammer 19

As Neue Burg.

THE HOFBURG'S weapons
collection is impressive
both for its size and for the
workmanship of its finest
items: ivory and filigree inlay
on weapons, medieval ceremonial saddles and jewelled
Turkish and Syrian maces.
Particularly resplendent are
the 16th-century ceremonial
suits worn by the Habsburgs
for tournaments and military
parades, and the decorative
fighting and hunting weapons.

The museum was based on
the personal armouries of the
Habsburg emperors and, not
surprisingly, houses one of the
finest collections in Europe.

Völkerkunde- museum 20

As Neue Burg. 534300.
10am–6pm Mon, Wed–Sun.

RANGED AROUND an arcaded
Italian Renaissance-style
courtyard is Vienna's ethno-
logical museum. It is situated
at the west end of the Neue
Burg. To one side are the
Oriental collections: lacquer
screens, clothes, furniture,
weapons, ceramics, farm tools,
masks and musical instruments.
In a neighbouring room are
African figurines and masks.
The artefacts from Benin are
the highlight of the African
collection. Australasia and
Polynesia dominate the
displays upstairs, with fabrics
from Bali, weapons from
Borneo and many musical
instruments from the Far East.

The large pre-Columbian
collection from Mexico
includes an Aztec feather
headdress. A recent addition
to the permanent collection is
a section on Eskimo culture.

The Hofburg Complex ⑮

THE VAST HOFBURG COMPLEX contains the former imperial apartments, several museums, a chapel, a church, the Austrian National Library, the Winter Riding School and the President of Austria's offices. It was the seat of Austrian power for over six centuries, and successive rulers were all anxious to leave their mark. Seven centuries of architectural development can be seen in the 10 or so buildings, ranging from Gothic to late 19th-century historicism.

Burggarten
(see p102)

Albertina
(see p102)

Augustiner-
kirche *(see p102)*

★ **Prunksaal**
The showpiece of the Austrian National Library (1722–35) is the flamboyant, wood-panelled Prunksaal, or Hall of Honour.

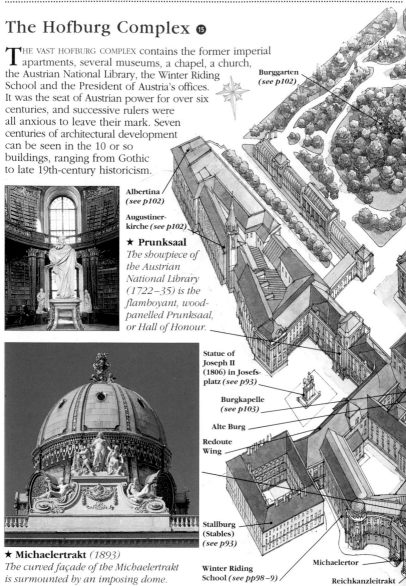

Statue of Joseph II (1806) in Josefs-platz *(see p93)*

Burgkapelle *(see p103)*

Alte Burg

Redoute Wing

Stallburg (Stables) *(see p93)*

★ **Michaelertrakt** *(1893)*
The curved façade of the Michaelertrakt is surmounted by an imposing dome.

Winter Riding School *(see pp98–9)*

Michaelertor

Reichkanzleitrakt

TIMELINE

1275 First fort built on site of the Schweizerhof		**1558–65** Stallburg built – a Renaissance palace, later a mews	**1729–35** J E Fischer von Erlach's Winter Riding School built	**1938** Hitler proclaims annexation of Austria from the Neue Burg
	Statue of the angel Gabriel in the Burgkapelle	**1575–1611** Amalienburg built	**1881–1913** Neue Burg built	
1300	**1500**		**1700**	**1900**
	1547–52 Ferdinand I reconstructs the Alte Burg	**1552–3** Schweizertor built	**1728** Work begun on J E Fischer von Erlach's Reichskanzleitrakt	**1992** The banqueting hall and ball-room in the Redoute Wing destroyed by fire
1447–9 Alterations carried out on the Burgkapelle under Friedrich III		**1660–80** Leopoldinischertrakt built under Leopold I	**1889–93** Construction of Michaelertrakt and Michaelertor	

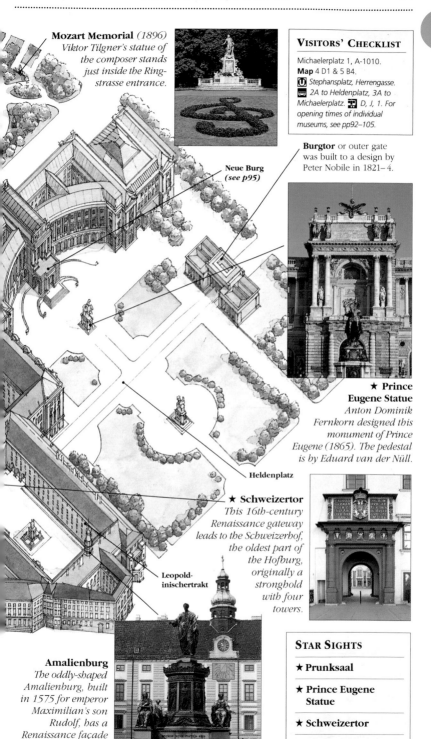

Mozart Memorial *(1896)*
Viktor Tilgner's statue of the composer stands just inside the Ringstrasse entrance.

Neue Burg
(see p95)

VISITORS' CHECKLIST

Michaelerplatz 1, A-1010.
Map 4 D1 & 5 B4.
Ⓤ *Stephansplatz, Herrengasse.*
🚌 *2A to Heldenplatz, 3A to Michaelerplatz.* 🚋 *D, J, 1. For opening times of individual museums, see pp92–105.*

Burgtor or outer gate was built to a design by Peter Nobile in 1821–4.

★ Prince Eugene Statue
Anton Dominik Fernkorn designed this monument of Prince Eugene (1865). The pedestal is by Eduard van der Nüll.

Heldenplatz

★ Schweizertor
This 16th-century Renaissance gateway leads to the Schweizerhof, the oldest part of the Hofburg, originally a stronghold with four towers.

Leopold-inischertrakt

Amalienburg
The oddly-shaped Amalienburg, built in 1575 for emperor Maximilian's son Rudolf, has a Renaissance façade and an attractive Baroque clock tower.

STAR SIGHTS

★ **Prunksaal**

★ **Prince Eugene Statue**

★ **Schweizertor**

★ **Michaelertrakt**

Winter Riding School 26

THE ORIGINS OF THE Spanish Riding School are obscure, but it is believed to have been founded in 1572 to cultivate the classic skills of *haute école* horsemanship. By breeding and training horses from Spain, the Habsburgs formed the Spanische Reitschule. Today, 80-minute shows take place in the building known as the Winter Riding School. Commissioned by Karl VI, it was built from 1729 to 1735 to a design by Josef Emanuel Fischer von Erlach. There are two entrances to the building – one from door 2, Josefsplatz, the other from the Michaelerkuppel.

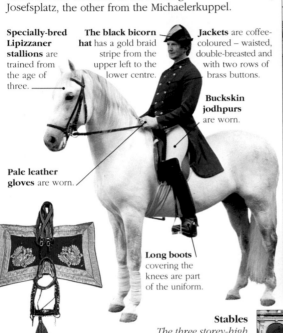

Specially-bred Lipizzaner stallions are trained from the age of three.

The black bicorn hat has a gold braid stripe from the upper left to the lower centre.

Jackets are coffee-coloured – waisted, double-breasted and with two rows of brass buttons.

Buckskin jodhpurs are worn.

Pale leather gloves are worn.

Long boots covering the knees are part of the uniform.

Tack
The elegant saddle with embroidered cloth differs from modern versions and complements the historical dress of the riders; the curb rein is generally used.

Stables
The three storey-high Renaissance former palace of the Stallburg is across the road from the Winter Riding School. It is now home to the Lipizzaner Museum (see p93) as well as providing stabling for the horses.

THE HORSES' STEPS

The steps made by the horses and riders are part of a carefully orchestrated ballet. Many derive from exercises that were developed during the Renaissance period by cavalrymen, who needed agile horses capable of special manoeuvres.

The Croupade: the horse leaps into the air with hind legs and forelegs bent under its belly.

Levade: the horse stands on its hind legs with hocks almost touching the ground.

VISITORS' CHECKLIST

Josefsplatz 1, A-1010.
Map 4 D1 & 5 C4. 🄲 5339032.
🚌 3A to Habsburgergasse, 2A to
Michaelerplatz. 🄾 for performances (see annual programme).
⬤ 1 Jan, 6 Jan, 1 May, Ascension
Day, Corpus Christi, 15 Aug,
26 Oct, 1 Nov, 8 Dec, 25–26 Dec.
🄰 🚫 ♿ some areas.

Portrait of Karl VI

*An equestrian portrait of
Emperor Karl VI who
commissioned the building,
hangs in the royal box.
Whenever a rider enters the
hall, he must express his
respect to the founder of the
school by raising his bicorn
hat to the portrait.*

THE LIPIZZANER HORSES

The stallions that perform their athletic feats on the sawdust
of the Winter Riding School take their name from the stud
at Lipizza near Trieste in Slovenia *(see below)*, which was
founded by Archduke Karl in 1580. Today the horses are
bred on the Austrian National Stud Farm at Piber near Graz.
The breed was originally produced by crossing Arab, Berber
and Spanish horses. The horses are renowned for their grace
and stamina. You may be able to obtain a ticket without a
reservation to see them at their morning training session.

Interior of the Winter Riding School

*The gracious interior is lined
with 46 columns and adorned
with elaborate plasterwork,
chandeliers and a coffered
ceiling. At the head of the
arena is the court box.
Spectators sit here or watch
from upper galleries.*

Capriole: this is a
leap into the air with
a simultaneous kick
of the hind legs.

The Piaffe: the horse
trots on the spot, often
between two pillars.

State Apartments and Treasuries ㉗

THE STATE APARTMENTS in the Reichkanzleitrakt (1723–30) and the Amalienburg (1575) include the rooms occupied by Franz Joseph from 1857 to 1916, Empress Elisabeth's apartments from 1854 to 1898 and the rooms where Tsar Alexander I lived during the Congress of Vienna in 1815. The sacred and secular treasures amassed during centuries of Habsburg rule are displayed in 21 rooms. They include relics of the Holy Roman Empire, the crown jewels and liturgical objects of the imperial court.

Entrance Treasuries

★ 10th-Century Crown
The insignia of the Holy Roman Empire includes this crown set with enamel plaques and cabochons.

Emperor Maximilian I
(around 1500)
This portrait by Bernhard Strigel hangs in the room containing Burgundian treasure. Emperor Maximilian married Mary, Duchess of Burgundy in 1477.

Cradle of the King of Rome
Designed by the French painter Prud'hon, Maria Louisa gave this cradle to her son, the King of Rome (see p173).

Ticket office

Entrance through the Michaelerkuppel to State Apartments and Silberkammer

STAR FEATURES	KEY	
★ **10th-Century Crown**	☐ Franz Joseph's State Apartments	
★ **Imperial Dining Hall**	☐ Elisabeth's State Apartments	
★ **Empress Elisabeth by Franz Xaver Winterhalter**	☐ Alexander's State Apartments	
	☐ Sacred Treasury	
	☐ Secular Treasury	
	☐ Non-exhibition space	

Crucifix after Giambologna
(around 1590)
This type of crucifix, a Cristo Morto, can be traced back to a similar model by Giambologna which is in Florence.

THE SILBERKAMMER

On display in the ground-floor rooms of the court tableware and silver depot is a dazzling array of items – gold, silver and the finest porcelain – that were once used at the Habsburg state banquets. One of the highlights is a 33-m long (100-ft) gilded bronze centrepiece with accompanying candelabra from around 1800. Visitors can also admire the mid-18th-century Sèvres dinner service that was a diplomatic gift from Louis XV to Maria Theresa.

Goblet from the Laxemburg Service (around 1821)

VISITORS' CHECKLIST

Map 4 D1 & 5 B3.
State Apartments (Kaiser-appartements) & Silberkammer
Michaelerkuppel. 5337570.
9am–5pm daily. Sat & Sun. www.schoenbrunn.at ***Secular & Sacred Treasuries (Schatzkammer)***
Schweizerhof. 5337931.
10am–6pm Mon, Wed–Sun; 31 Dec: 10am– 1pm. 1 Jan, 1 May, 1 Nov, 24–25 Dec. www.khm.at

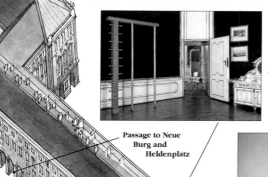

Elisabeth's Gymnastic Equipment
The Empress was a fitness enthusiast, and the bars at which she exercised are still in place in her dressing room.

Passage to Neue Burg and Heldenplatz

Entrance through the Kaisertor to State Apartments and Silberkammer

★ Imperial Dining Hall
The table is laid as it used to be in Emperor Franz Joseph's day (see p32–3), in the room where the Imperial family used to dine.

Exit from apartments

GUIDE TO TREASURIES
Entering the Secular Treasury, Rooms 1–8 contain items from the Austrian Empire (with Room 5 commemorating Napoleon). Rooms 9–12 exhibit treasures from the Holy Roman Empire, while the Burgundian Inheritance is displayed in Rooms 13–16. Rooms I–V, furthest from the entrance, house the Sacred Treasury. (There is one route through the State Apartments, starting with Franz Joseph's rooms.)

★ Empress Elisabeth
Winterhalter's portrait of the Empress (1865) with stars in her hair hangs in the large drawing room.

Greenhouses in the Burggarten by Friedrich Ohmann (1858–1927)

Burggarten ㉑

Burgring/Opernring. **Map** 4 D1 & 5 B4.
Ⓤ *Babenbergerstrasse.* ☐ *Apr–Sep: 6am–10pm; Oct–Mar: 6am–8pm daily.*

BEFORE LEAVING Vienna, Napoleon showed his contempt for the Viennese by razing part of the city walls which had proved so ineffective at preventing his entry. Some of the space left around the Hofburg was later transformed by the Habsburgs into a landscaped garden, planted with a variety of trees. It was opened to the public in 1918.

Overlooking the garden are greenhouses (1901–7) by the Jugendstil architect Friedrich Ohmann, and near the Hofburg entrance is a small equestrian statue (1780) of Emperor Franz I by the sculptor Balthasar Moll. Closer to the Ringstrasse is the Mozart Memorial (1896) by Viktor Tilgner.

Albertina ㉒

Augustinerstrasse 1. **Map** 4 D1 & 5 C4. 【 534 83 0 Ⓤ *Karlsplatz, Stephansplatz.* ● *for renovation until spring 2003.* Ⓦ www.albertina.at

HIDDEN AWAY in a corner of the Hofburg is the Albertina, housing one of the world's finest collections of prints, watercolours and drawings. The palace once belonged to Maria Theresa's daughter, Maria Christina, and her husband Duke Albert of Sachsen-Teschen, after whom the gallery is named.

Of the Albertina's one million prints and over 45,000 watercolours and drawings, the most famous are collotypes, skilful copies, made decades ago. The gems of the collections are by Dürer, but there are works by Rubens and Michelangelo. Nineteenth and early 20th-century art is well represented too.

The renovation programme is intended to restore the building's historic façades, including the magnificent Burggarten façade, that were damaged during World War II. In addition, the central courtyard will be returned to how it was in the 19th century, with reconstructed façades to designs by Joseph Korhäusel and Solnhofen slate paving.

The grand rooms of this, the largest of the Hapsburg's residencies, will also be restored to their former magnificence, with silk wall coverings, extensive guilding and inlayed floors, and opened to the public for the first time in over a century.

A new modern extension, situated between the Burggarten front and the greenhouses, will include a study centre, library and large hall for temporary exhibitions.

Augustinerkirche ㉓

Augustinerstrasse 3. **Map** 4 D1 & 5 C4. 【 5337099. Ⓤ *Stephansplatz.* ☐ *8am–5pm daily.* ⊙

THE AUGUSTINERKIRCHE has one of the best-preserved 14th-century Gothic interiors in Vienna; only the modern chandeliers strike a jarring note. The church also houses the Loreto Chapel, which is currently closed for restoration. The chapel contains the silver urns that preserve the hearts of the Habsburg family *(see pp24–5).* Here too is one of the most powerful works by the Italian Neo-Classical sculptor Antonio Canova, the tomb of Maria Christina, favourite daughter of Maria Theresa. Like the tomb of Leopold II, which is also here, Maria Christina's tomb is empty; the royal remains lie in the Kaisergruft *(see p104).*

The church is also celebrated for its music, including masses by Schubert or Haydn held here on Sundays.

Prunksaal ㉔

Josefsplatz 1. **Map** 4 D1 & 5 C4. 【 53410397. Ⓤ *Herrengasse.* ☐ *10am–2pm daily.* ⊙
Ⓦ www.oub.ac.at

COMMISSIONED AS the court library by Karl VI, the main hall, or Prunksaal, of the National Library was designed by Johann Bernhard Fischer von Erlach *(see p147)* in 1719. After his death in 1723, the building was completed by his son. The collection consists of approximately 2.6 million books, and includes the personal library of Prince Eugene *(see pp26–7),* as well as books that were taken from monastic libraries closed during the religious reforms of Joseph II *(see p29).*

The Prunksaal is 77 m (252 ft) long and is the largest Baroque library in Europe. Paired marble columns frame the domed main room, and bookcases line the walls. Spanning the vaults are frescoes by the Baroque painter Daniel Gran (1730), which were restored by Franz

Domed interior of the Prunksaal in the National Library building

Anton Maulbertsch (1769). The many fine statues, including the likeness of Karl VI in the centre of the hall, are the work of Paul Strudel (1648–1708) and his brother Peter (1660–1714).

Burgkapelle 25

Wiener Hofburg, Schweizerhof. **Map** 4 D1 & 5 B4. 5339927. Herrengasse. 11am–3pm Mon–Thu, 11am–1pm Fri. 1 Nov, 8 Dec, 1 Jan. **Vienna Boys' Choir** Jan–Jun & Sep–Dec: 9:15am Sun (book by phone).

F ROM THE SCHWEIZERHOF, steps lead up to the Burgkapelle, or Hofburg Chapel, originally constructed in 1296 but modified 150 years later on the orders of Friedrich III. On Sundays, visitors can hear the Wiener Sängerknaben, the Vienna Boys' Choir (see p39). The chapel interior has Gothic statuary in canopied niches and Gothic carvings, and boasts a bronze crucifix (1720) by Johann Känischbauer.

Winter Riding School 26

See pp98–9.

State Apartments and Treasuries 27

See pp100–1.

Bundeskanzleramt 28

Ballhausplatz 2. **Map** 1 C5 & 5 B3. 531150. Herrengasse. to the public.

T HE BUNDESKANZLERAMT (1717–19), the Austrian Chancery and Foreign Ministry, was designed by Johann Lukas von Hildebrandt (see p150). It was expanded to its present size in 1766 by Nikolaus Pacassi. Major events that shaped Austria's history have taken place here, including meetings of the Congress of Vienna (see p30) in 1814–15, the final deliberations in 1914 that led to

No. 4 Minoritenplatz

the outbreak of World War I, and the murder of Chancellor Dollfuss by Nazi terrorists in 1934 (see p36).

Minoritenplatz 29

Map 2 D5 & 5 B3. Herrengasse.

A T NO. 1 MINORITENPLATZ is the Baroque-style State Archives building (the archives are no longer housed here), built on to the back of the Bunderskanzleramt in 1902. There are a number of palaces around the square. No. 3 is the former Dietrichstein Palace of 1755, an early building by Franz Hillebrand. It now contains the offices of the Federal Chancellor and the Foreign Office. No. 4 is the side of the Liechtenstein Palace (see p104). The mid-17th-century Starhemberg Palace is at No. 5. Now housing ministry offices, it was the residence of Count Ernst Rüdiger von Starhemberg, a hero of the 1683 Turkish siege (see p27) when he led the Austrian forces within the city.

Minoritenkirche 30

Minoritenplatz 2. **Map** 1 C5 & 5 B3. 5334162. Herrengasse. 9am–6pm daily.

T HIS ANCIENT CHURCH was established here by the Minor Friars in around 1224, although the present structure dates from 1339. The tower was given its odd pyramidal

shape during the Turkish siege of 1529, when shells sliced the top off the steeple. In the 1780s the Minoritenkirche was restored to its original Gothic style, when Maria Theresa's son, Joseph II (see p28), made a gift of the church to Vienna's Italian community. The church retains a fine west portal (1340) with statues beneath traceried canopies; the carvings above the doorway are modern.

The interior of the church is unexpectedly bright and large and contains a mosaic copy of Leonardo da Vinci's *Last Supper*. Napoleon Bonaparte commissioned Giacomo Raffaelli to execute this work as he proposed to substitute it for the original in Milan and remove the real painting to Paris. Following Napoleon's downfall at Waterloo in 1815, Raffaelli's version was bought by the Habsburgs. In the south aisle is a painted statue of the Madonna and Child (dating from around 1350), while at the same spot in the north aisle is a faded fragment of a 16th-century fresco of St Francis of Assisi.

Gothic statue (about 1400) of Leopold III in the Burgkapelle

Bankgasse ❸

Map 1 C5 & 5 B3. Ⓤ *Herrengasse.*
Liechtenstein Palace ☐ *10am–*
6pm Wed–Mon.

FEW STREETS IN VIENNA are
more crammed with the
palaces of the nobility.

At Nos. 4–6 is the former
Strattmann-Windischgrätz
Palace (1692–1734), originally
designed by Johann Bernhard
Fischer von Erlach *(see p147).*
The present façade (1783–4)
is by Franz Hillebrand, who
expanded the building by
incorporating the palace next
door. Today, it houses the
Hungarian Embassy.

Nos. 5–7 are the back of the
Starhemberg Palace. No. 9 is
the Liechtenstein Palace, built
as a town residence for the
Liechtenstein family by Dome-
nico Martinelli (1694–1706).
No. 2 is the Schönborn-
Batthyány Palace (1695).

Volksgarten ❸

Dr-Karl-Renner-Ring. **Map** 1 C5 &
5 A3. Ⓒ *5339083.* Ⓤ *Herrengasse.*
☐ *Apr–Nov: 6am–10pm daily;*
Dec–Mar: 6:30am–10pm daily. ▣ ▤

LIKE THE BURGGARTEN land-
scaped garden *(see p102),*
the Volksgarten was created
after the destruction of the

Statuary above the portal to the Lobkowitz Palace

city walls by Napoleon, and
opened up a space previously
occupied by fortifications.
Unlike the Burggarten, the
Volksgarten was opened to
the public soon after its completion in 1820. The formal
plantations, especially the
splendid rose gardens, are
matched in grandeur by the
garden's ornaments, notably
the Temple of Theseus (1823)
by Peter von Nobile. It was
built to house Canova's statue
of the Greek god, which now
graces the staircase of the
Kunsthistorisches Museum.
Other compositions include
Karl von Hasenauer's
monument to the poet Franz
Grillparzer *(see p33)* and the
fountain memorial to the
assassinated Empress Elisabeth
(1907) by Friedrich Ohmann
(see p57) and the sculptor
Hans Bitterlich.

Lobkowitz Palace ❸

Lobkowitzplatz 2. **Map** 4 D1 & 5 C4.
Ⓤ *Karlsplatz.* ☐ *10am–5pm Tue–Sun.*
▣ ▢ ▤ Ⓦ www.theatermuseum.at

THIS LARGE PALACE WAS built
for Count Dietrichstein in
1685–7 by Giovanni Pietro
Tencala and altered by Johann
Bernhard Fischer von Erlach
(see p147) in 1710. In 1753 it
was acquired by the Lobkowitz
family, who were among
Beethoven's patrons. Balls
were held here during the
Congress of Vienna *(see p30).*

Since 1991 the palace has
been the Austrian Theatre
Museum, which houses a
model of the first Hofburg
theatre and the Eroica-Saal
(1724–29) – where many first
performances of Beethoven's
work took place, such as the
Eroica symphony in 1804.
The main exhibits chronicle
Austrian theatre in the 1940s.

Kapuzinerkirche
und Kaisergruft ❸

Tegetthoffstrasse 2. **Map** 4 D1 & 5 C4.
Ⓒ *5126853.* Ⓤ *Stephansplatz.*
Kaisergruft ☐ *9:30am–4pm daily.*
Kapuzinerkirche ☐ *6am–6pm*
daily. ▣

BENEATH THE Kapuziner-
kirche are the vaults of
the Kaisergruft, the imperial
crypt founded in 1619 by the
Catholic Emperor Matthias.
Here lie the remains of 138
Habsburgs, including Maria
Theresa and her husband
Franz Stephan in a large tomb
by Balthasar Moll (1753). The
most poignant tomb is that of
Franz Joseph, flanked by his
assassinated wife Elisabeth
and their son Rudolf, who

Formal rose garden in the Volksgarten

Tomb of Karl VI by Balthasar Moll

committed suicide *(see p32)*. The last reigning Habsburg, Empress Zita, died in 1989 and her remains are also buried in the crypt.

Neuer Markt ⑳

Map 4 D1 & 5 C4. Ⓤ *Stephansplatz.*

K NOWN AS THE Mehlmarkt or flour market until around 1210, the Neuer Markt was also used as a jousting area. Of these origins nothing is left, though a few 18th-century houses remain. In the middle of the Neuer Markt is a replica of the Donner Fountain (1737–9) by Georg Raphael Donner, a symbolic celebration of the role played by rivers in the economic life of the Habsburg Empire. The four figures denote tributaries of the Danube, while the central figure represents Providence. The original figures are in the Lower Belvedere *(see p155)*.

Kärntner Strasse ㊱

Map 4 D1 & 5 C5. Ⓒ 5120508. Ⓤ *Stephansplatz.* **Malteserkirche** Ⓞ *8am–6pm daily.* **Lobmeyr Museum** Ⓞ *9am–6pm Mon–Fri, 10am–5pm Sat.*

T HIS PEDESTRIANIZED STREET was the main highway to Carinthia in medieval times. Now it is the old city's principal shopping street. Day and night, it is packed with

people shopping, buying fresh fruit juice from stands, pausing in cafés, or listening to the street musicians.

No. 37 is the Malteserkirche. This church was founded by the Knights of Malta who were invited to Vienna early in the 13th century by Leopold VI. The interior retains lofty Gothic windows and vaults.

At No. 1 is the Lobmeyr Museum, which houses glass designed by Josef Hoffmann *(see p56)*, among others, for the Viennese firm of Lobmeyr.

Around the corner at No. 5 Johannesgasse is the superb Questenberg-Kaunitz Palace which dates from the early 18th century. Its design has been attributed to the architect Johann Lukas von Hildebrandt *(see p150)*.

American Bar ㊲

Kärntner Strasse 10. **Map** 4 D1 & 6 D3. Ⓤ *Stephansplatz.* *See Light Meals and Snacks p217.*

B ENEATH A GARISH depiction of the Stars and Stripes is this bar designed by Adolf Loos *(see p92)* in 1908. The interior,

The Donner Fountain in Neuer Markt

restored in 1990, is a gem. The bar is tiny, with every detail worked out by Loos, such as the tables lit from below and the exquisite glass cabinets for storing glasses. One of his hallmarks is the use of mahogany panelling, and this bar is no exception. Mirrors give the impression that the interior is larger than it actually is, and onyx and marble panels reflect a soft light.

Façade of the American Bar

Stock-im-Eisen-Platz ㊳

Map 2 D5 & 5 C3. Ⓤ *Stephansplatz.*

T HIS SQUARE is at the inter-section of Stephansplatz, Kärntner Strasse and Graben. Opposite Haas Haus *(see p75)* is the Equitable Palace (1891), once headquarters to the Equitable Life Insurance Company. There is also an old tree trunk with nails in it in the square. Passing locksmiths' apprentices would bang in a nail to ensure a safe passage home.

SCHOTTENRING AND ALSERGRUND

Relief on the façade of the Schottenkirche

THIS PART OF THE CITY is dotted with sites of interest, such as the ornate Ferstel Palace and the glass-roofed Ferstel Passage that runs through it. The Schotten-ring and the Schottentor are named after the Benedictine monks who came here in Babenberg times to found the Schottenkirche Monastery. Later rulers of Austria were responsible for the area's other monuments: Joseph II built a huge public hospital, now the Josephinum, and Franz Joseph founded the Votivkirche as a way of giving thanks after escaping assassination in 1853. To the east, nearer the Danube Canal, quiet residential streets are broken only by the imposing Liechtenstein Palace, one of many summer palaces built beyond the city gates by Vienna's nobility.

SIGHTS AT A GLANCE

Streets and Squares
Freyung Passage ❶
Freyung ❷

Churches and Cathedrals
Schottenkirche ❸
Servitenkirche ❺
Votivkirche ❾

Museums and Galleries
Freud Museum ❹
Liechtenstein Palace ❻
Josephinum ❼
Narrenturm ❽

GETTING THERE
This area is served by the Schottentor (line U2) and Rossauer Lände (line U4) U-Bahn stations. Trams 37, 38, 40, 41 and 42 go along Währinger Strasse. Bus 40A runs the length of Liechten-steinstrasse.

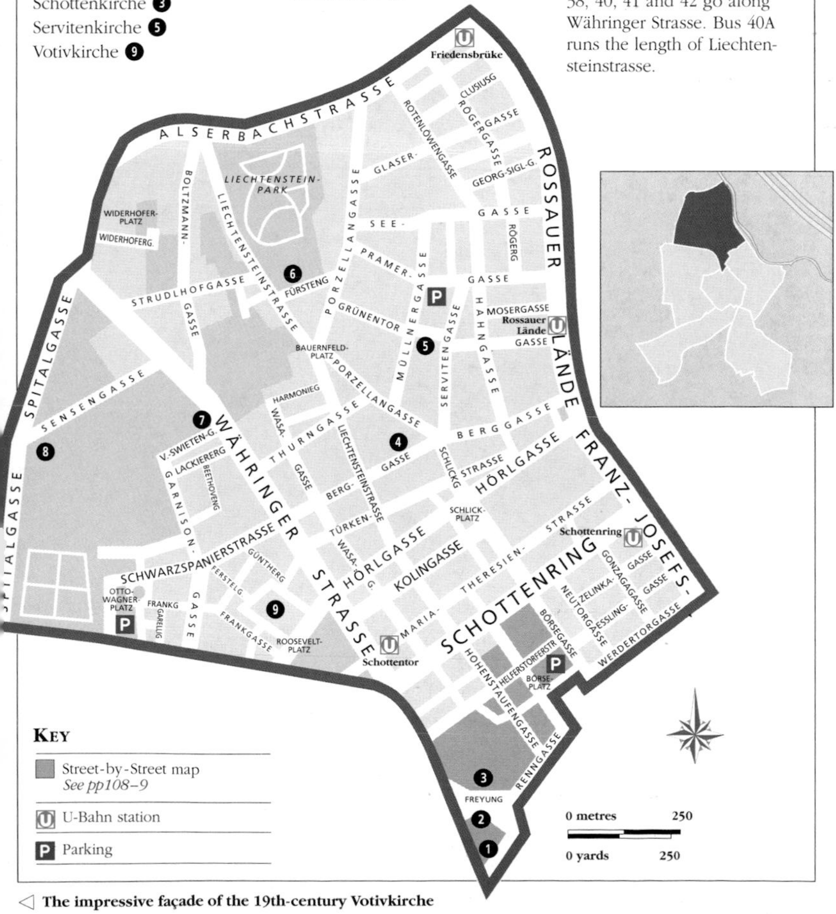

KEY

▦	Street-by-Street map See pp108–9
🚇	U-Bahn station
🅿	Parking

◁ **The impressive façade of the 19th-century Votivkirche**

Street-by-Street: Around the Freyung

Statue of Turkish soldier, south of the Freyung

AT THE CORE of this elegant part of the city is the former medieval complex of the Schottenkirche and its courtyards and school. On the other side of the Freyung square are some beautiful Baroque palaces, including Hildebrandt's Kinsky Palace (1713–16), and the Palais Ferstel. The Freyung Passage links the Freyung square with Herrengasse, which is lined with Baroque mansions as well as the city's first skyscraper. Backing onto the Schottenring is the Italianate Börse.

★ **Schottenkirche**
Founded in 1177 and redecorated in the Baroque period, this fine church has a museum and there is a famous boys' school alongside it ❸

Passageway leading from No. 2 Helferstorferstrasse to the Freyung

HELFERSTORFERSTRASSE

SCHOTTENGASSE

★ **Freyung**
This square is overlooked by fine buildings, including the former Schottenkirche priory, originally founded in 1155, then rebuilt in 1744 and, due to its appearance, known by the Viennese as the "chest of drawers house" ❷

★ **Freyung Passage**
The Freyung and Herrengasse are connected by a luxury shopping arcade ❶

FREYUNG

HERRENGASSE

The Café Central has a papier-mâché statue of the poet Peter Altenberg next to the main entrance. Altenberg spent a great deal of time in various coffee houses around the city *(see pp58–61).*

To Herrengasse U-Bahn

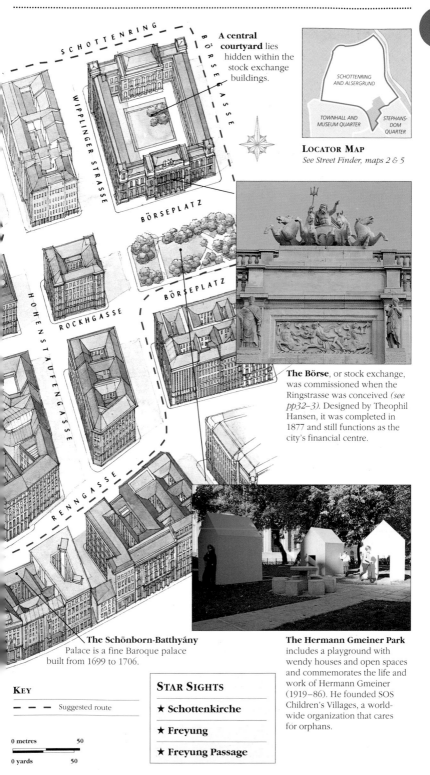

A central courtyard lies hidden within the stock exchange buildings.

SCHOTTENRING

BÖRSEGASSE

WIPPLINGER STRASSE

BÖRSEPLATZ

BÖRSEPLATZ

HOHENSTAUFENGASSE

ROCKHGASSE

RENNGASSE

LOCATOR MAP
See Street Finder, maps 2 & 5

SCHOTTENRING
AND ALSERGRUND

TOWNHALL AND
MUSEUM QUARTER

STEPHANS-
DOM
QUARTER

The Börse, or stock exchange, was commissioned when the Ringstrasse was conceived *(see pp32–3)*. Designed by Theophil Hansen, it was completed in 1877 and still functions as the city's financial centre.

The Schönborn-Batthyány Palace is a fine Baroque palace built from 1699 to 1706.

The Hermann Gmeiner Park includes a playground with wendy houses and open spaces and commemorates the life and work of Hermann Gmeiner (1919–86). He founded SOS Children's Villages, a world-wide organization that cares for orphans.

KEY

– – – Suggested route

0 metres   50

0 yards   50

STAR SIGHTS

★ **Schottenkirche**

★ **Freyung**

★ **Freyung Passage**

Freyung Passage ❶

Map 2 D5 & 5 B2. 🚇 *Herrengasse.*

FACING THE FREYUNG is the Italian-style *palazzo* known as the Palais Ferstel, dating from 1860 and taking its name from the architect, Heinrich von Ferstel. Wander in and you will find yourself in the glass-roofed Freyung Passage: lined with elegant shops, it converges on a small courtyard of which the centrepiece is a many-tiered statue portraying the lissom water-sprite of the Danube holding a fish. It then emerges on Herrengasse. As an example of civilized urban amenities, the passage is a great success. It also has an entrance into one of Vienna's grandest coffee houses, the Café Central *(see pp59–61).*

Danube Mermaid's Fountain (1861) in Freyung Passage

Freyung ❷

Map 2 D5 & 5 B2. 🚇 *Herrengasse.* **Kinsky Palace** 🏛 *to public.*

THE FREYUNG is a curiously shaped "square". Its name derives from the right of sanctuary granted to the monks of the Schottenkirche that lasted until it was abolished by Maria Theresa. Fugitives from persecution who entered the area were safe from arrest. No. 4 is the Kinsky Palace (1713–16), by Johann Lukas von Hildebrandt *(see p150).* Next door is the Porcia Palace of 1546, one of the oldest in Vienna, though much altered. At No. 3 is the Harrach Palace;

Façade of the Schottenkirche

the interior has some fine Rococo doors. Opposite stands the Austria Fountain: its four figures symbolize the major rivers of the Habsburgs' lands. Behind is the former Schottenkirche priory, unkindly known as the chest of drawers house.

Schottenkirche ❸

Schottenstift, Freyung 6. **Map** 2 D5 & 5 B2. 📞 *53498.* 🚇 *Schottentor.* **Museum** ⏰ *10am–5pm Thu–Fri, 11am–5pm Sat & Sun.* 📷 🚫

DESPITE ITS NAME (Scottish church) this 1177 monastic foundation was established by Irish Benedictines. The adjoining buildings have a fine medieval art collection that includes the famous Schotten altarpiece (1475).

The church has been altered repeatedly and has recently undergone extensive renovation. Today it presents a rather drab Neo-Classical façade, with a rich Baroque interior.

Freud Museum ❹

Berggasse 19. **Map** 1 C3. 📞 *319-1596.* 🚇 *Schottentor.* ⏰ *9am–4pm (Jul–Sep: 6pm) daily.* 📷 📷

NO. 19 BERGGASSE differs little from any other 19th-century apartment in Vienna, yet it is now one of the city's most famous addresses. The father of psychoanalysis, Sigmund Freud, lived, worked and received patients here from 1891 until his departure from Vienna in 1938.

The flat housed Freud's family as well as his practice. The catalogue lists 420 items of memorabilia on display, including letters and books, furnishings, photographs documenting Freud's long life, and various antiquities.

Although it was quickly abandoned when the Nazis forced Freud to leave the city where he had lived almost all his life, the flat still preserves an intimate domestic atmosphere. Even his hat and cane are on show.

Servitenkirche ❺

Servitengasse 9. **Map** 1 C3. 📞 *317 6195.* 🚇 *Rossauer Lände.* ⏰ *7–9am, 6–7pm Mon–Fri, 7–9am, 5–8pm Sat, 7am–noon, 5–8pm Sun.* 📷 ♿

ALTHOUGH OFF the beaten track, this Baroque church (1651–77) is well worth a visit. Inside, a riot of Baroque decoration includes elaborate stucco ornamentation, a fine wrought-iron screen near the entrance, and an exuberant pulpit (1739), partly by Balthasar Moll.

FREUD'S THEORIES

Sigmund Freud (1856–1939) was not only the founder of the techniques of psychoanalysis, but a theorist who wrote many essays and books expounding his contentious ideas. Modern concepts such as subconscious, ego, sublimation and Oedipus complex, evolved from Freudian theories. Freud posited different structural systems within the human psyche that, if seriously out of balance, result in emotional or mental disturbance.

Liechtenstin Garden Palace ❻

Fürstengasse 1. **Map** 1 C2.
📞 3176900. 🚇 *Friedensbrücke.*
⬤ *for renovation.*

DESIGNED BY Domenico Martinelli mostly in Rococo style, the Liechtenstein Garden Palace was the summer home of the Liechtenstein family. This, together with their town residence at No. 9 Bankgasse (*see p104*), also designed by Martinelli, gives a good impression of the Baroque lifestyle led by this wealthy aristocratic family. The winter was spent in town, with formal concerts, balls and receptions, while for the summer months the Garden Palace offered a more informal outdoor lifestyle, including hunting trips.

From 1979 this palace housed part of the Museum of Modern Art. The artworks were relocated to the new museum in the MuseumsQuartier (*see p117*) in 2001.

Josephinum ❼

Währinger Strasse 25/1. **Map** 1 C4.
📞 427763401. 🚇 *Schottentor.*
⬤ *9am–3pm Mon–Fri.* ⬤ *public hols.* 🈲 ♿

THE ARDENT REFORMER Joseph II (*see p28*) established this military surgical institute. Designed by Isidor Canevale in 1785, it is now a medical museum. Some rooms contain memorabilia from the 19th century, when Vienna was a leading centre for medical research, but the museum's main attraction is its unusual collection of wax anatomical models commissioned by the emperor from Tuscan artists.

Narrenturm ❽

Spitalgasse 2. **Map** 1 B3. 📞 4068672.
🚇 *Schottentor.* ⬤ *3–6pm Wed, 8–11am Thu, 10am–1pm 1st Sat of month.* 🚫 ⬤ *public hols.*

BEHIND A GREY façade along Alser Strasse are the courtyards of the Allgemeines

Detail on the Votivkirche façade

Krankenhaus, founded by Joseph II (*see p28*) in 1784. At the far end of the complex is the Narrenturm Tower, a former lunatic asylum designed by Isidor Canevale. The tower now houses the Museum for Pathological Anatomy. Exhibits include a reconstruction of an apothecary's shop, physically abnormal skeletons, specimens preserved in formaldehyde, and wax models. The few ground-floor rooms open to the public only show a small part of the collection, but serious students can enrol on a guided tour of the corridors upstairs.

Votivkirche ❾

Rooseveltplatz 8. **Map** 1 C4 & 5 A1.
📞 4061192. 🚇 *Schottentor.*
⬤ *9am–1pm, 4–6:30pm Tue–Sat, 9am–1pm Sun.* 📷 ♿ *side entrance.*

AFTER A DERANGED tailor tried but failed to assassinate Emperor Franz Joseph on 18 February 1853, a collection was made to pay for a new church to be built opposite the Mölker-Bastei, where the attempt had been made. The architect was Heinrich von Ferstel, who began the church in 1856 though it was not dedicated until 1879. The lacy steeples and spire are very attractive. Many of the church's chapels are dedicated to Austrian regiments and military heroes. The finest monument is the Renaissance sarcophagus tomb of Niklas Salm in the chapel just west of the north transept. Salm commanded Austria's forces during the 1529 Turkish siege.

Wooden pietà in Gothic style (1470) in the Servitenkirche

MUSEUM AND TOWNHALL QUARTER

Der liebe Augustin, Sankt-Ulrichs-Platz

THE EMPEROR Franz Joseph commissioned the major institutional buildings of the Habsburg empire, and the city, along the Ringstrasse in the mid-19th century *(see pp32–3).* Today these buildings remain a successful and imposing example of good urban planning. The districts to the west of the Ringstrasse are untouched, including Josefstadt, which still retains an 18th-century atmosphere with its picturesque streets, modest palaces and Baroque churches. The area's cultural institutions are vibrant: the brilliant productions of the Burgtheater and the wide-ranging exhibits of the Natural History Museum and the Kunsthistorisches Museum are all popular today.

SIGHTS AT A GLANCE

Streets and Squares
Sankt-Ulrichs-Platz **6**
Spittelberg Pedestrian Area **8**
Mölker-Bastei **18**

Historic Buildings
Alte Backstube **2**
Josefstadt Theater **4**
Trautson Palace **5**
Parliament **11**
Neues Rathaus **12**
University **14**
Café Landtmann **15**
Burgtheater pp130–31 **16**
Dreimäderlhaus **17**
Pasqualati Haus **19**

Churches and Cathedrals
Maria Treu Kirche **3**
Dreifaltigkeitskirche **13**

Museums and Galleries
Museum für Volkskunde **1**
MuseumsQuartier **7**
Kunsthistorisches Museum pp118–23 **9**
Natural History Museum pp126–7 **10**

GETTING THERE
This area is served by the Rathaus, Lerchenfelder Strasse (line U2) and Volkstheater (lines U2, U3) U-Bahn stations. Trams 5 and 31/5 run from Josefstädter Strasse to Lange Gasse, and 46 goes down Lerchenfelder Strasse. Bus 2A runs from Schwedenplatz to Volkstheater. 13A runs along Piaristengasse, and 48A along Burggasse.

KEY
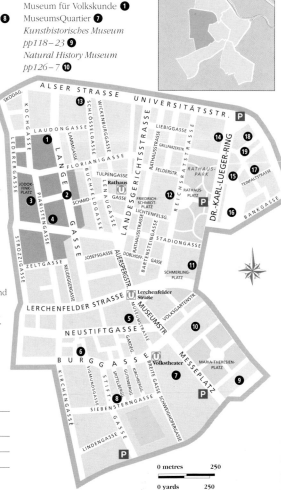

▮ Street-by-Street map
See pp114–15

Ⓤ U-Bahn station

Ⓟ Parking

0 metres 250
0 yards 250

◁ **Neues Rathaus façade by night**

Street-by-Street: Josefstadt

Tucked behind the grand museums of the Ringstrasse is the 18th-century district known as Josefstadt, named after Emperor Joseph II. Although outside the Inner City, Josefstadt has a vibrant cultural life of its own, with a popular theatre, many good restaurants, and handsome churches and museums. Students from the university and lawyers from the courthouses provide a constantly changing clientele for the district's varied establishments.

★ Maria Treu Kirche
Founded by the fathers of the Piarist order, this church was built from 1716 ❸

Josefstadt Theater
Founded in 1788, Vienna's oldest theatre has kept its doors open continuously since it was rebuilt by Josef Kornhäusel (see p84) in 1822 ❹

No. 29 Lange Gasse
Originally built for servants and workers in the 18th century, the cottages lining this courtyard have changed little over the years.

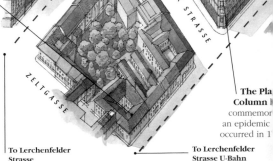

KEY

- - - Suggested route

STAR SIGHTS
★ **Maria Treu Kirche**
★ **Museum für Volkskunde**

PIARISTENGASSE

MARIA TRE

JOSEFSTÄDTER STRASSE

ZELTGASSE

The Pla Column
commemor
an epidemic
occurred in 1

To Lerchenfelder
Strasse

To Lerchenfelder
Strasse U-Bahn

LOCATOR MAP
See Street Finder, map 1

★ **Museum für Volkskunde**
The Schönborn Palace houses exhibits reflecting folklore and rural life in Austria ❶

Schönborn Park
is a secluded, leafy retreat. Among the sculptures is this bust (1974) of the composer Edmund Eysler by Leo Gruber.

No. 53 Lange Gasse has handsome statuary on its gates. It was built in the early 18th century when Vienna was expanding beyond the old city walls.

The Schnattl Restaurant,
occupying the spacious ground floor and courtyard of an old house on Lange Gasse, is one of Vienna's finest *(see p213)*.

Alte Backstube
A working bakery from 1701 to 1963, since 1965 it has been a museum and restaurant ❷

| 0 metres | 50 |
| 0 yards | 50 |

Museum für Volkskunde ❶

Laudongasse 15–19. **Map** 1 B4.
📞 4068905. 🚇 *Rathaus.*
🕙 10am–5pm Tue–Sun. ● *public hols.* 🎫 📷 ♿
🌐 *www.volkskundemuseum.at*

The charming Museum of Austrian Folklore is a reminder that Vienna is not only full of imperial grandeur. Here you will find artefacts reflecting the culture of people in Austria and neighbouring countries. Exhibits include objects dating from the 17th to 19th centuries. The museum is housed in the 18th-century Schönborn Palace, designed by Johann Lukas von Hildebrandt as a homely two-storey mansion and altered in 1760 by Isidor Canevale. Today it has a rather imposing façade with statuary running along its top.

Alte Backstube ❷

Lange Gasse 34. **Map** 1 B5.
🚇 *Rathaus.* 📞 4061101. 🕙 11am–midnight Mon–Sat, 5pm–midnight Sun. ● *mid-Jul–mid-Aug and public hols.* 📷 ♿

One of the finest middle-class houses in Vienna was built at No. 34 Lange Gasse in 1697 by the jeweller Hans Bernhard Leopold. Inside is an old bakery, the Alte Backstube, that was in continuous use from 1701 to 1963. The baking ovens were never removed, and today the rooms have been sympathetically restored and incorporated into a traditional restaurant and café. They also contain a museum dedicated to the art of baking where 300-year-old equipment is on display.

A few doors away, at No. 29, it's worth glancing into the courtyard to see the rows of single-storey houses facing each other – a rare example of working-class Vienna that is probably about 200 years old.

Maria Treu Kirche ❸

Jodok-Fink-Platz. **Map** 1 B5.
[☎] *4061453.* [Ⓤ] *Rathaus.* [◻] *for services and by appointment.* [◻]

Overlooking Jodok-Fink-Platz and flanked by monastic buildings stands the Church of Maria Treu. It was founded in 1698 by the fathers of the Piarist order.

This outstanding church was originally designed by Johann Lukas von Hildebrandt in 1716 and altered by Matthias Gerl in the 1750s. The elegant twin towers were not completed until 1854. Inside, there is a splendid Baroque frescoed ceiling in vibrant colours from 1752–3 by the great Austrian painter Franz Anton Maulbertsch. A chapel immediately to the left of the choir contains an altarpiece of the Crucifixion dating from about 1774, also painted by Maulbertsch.

Directly in front of the church and rising up from the square is a fine Baroque pillar topped with a statue of the Madonna, attended beneath by statues of saints and angels. Like many such columns in Vienna, it was erected to commemorate an outbreak of plague, in this case the epidemic of 1713.

Ceiling frescoes above the altar in the Maria Treu Kirche

Josefstadt Theater ❹

Josefstädter Strasse 26. **Map** 1 B5.
[☎] *427000.* [Ⓤ] *Rathaus.* [◻] *by appointment only.* [ⓦ] *www. josefstadt.org*

This intimate theatre *(see p228)*, one of the oldest still standing in Vienna, has

The façade of the glorious Josefstadt Theater

enjoyed a glorious history. Founded in 1788, it was rebuilt by Joseph Kornhäusel *(see p84)* in 1822, and has been in operation ever since, accommodating ballet, opera and theatre performances. Beethoven composed and conducted his overture *The Consecration of the House* for the reopening of the theatre in 1822 after its renovation. The director Max Reinhardt supervised the restoration of this attractive theatre in 1924. Today, it puts on mostly light plays and comedies.

Trautson Palace ❺

Museumstrasse 7. **Map** 3 B1.
[Ⓤ] *Volkstheater.* [◕] *to the public.*

Set back from the street next to the Volkstheater is this elegant Baroque palace, designed in 1710 by Johann Bernhard Fischer von Erlach *(see p147)*. Most Viennese palaces have flat fronts but on this one the central bays of the façade jut out with real panache. Nor is there anything restrained about the ornamentation: above the cornice and pediment is one of the largest collections of statuary atop any palace in the whole of Vienna. This includes a large statue of Apollo playing the lyre. Passing beneath the tall portal you will see on the left an immense staircase, with carvings of bearded giants bearing its weight, by the Italian sculptor Giovanni Giuliani. This leads to the ceremonial hall.

Originally built for Count Johann Leopold Donat Trautson who was in the service of Joseph I, the palace was acquired in 1760 by Maria Theresa *(see pp28–9)*. She donated it to the Royal Hungarian Bodyguard that she had founded. It has housed the Ministry of Justice since 1961, so there is no public access to the interior.

Sankt-Ulrichs-Platz ❻

Between Neustiftgasse and Burggasse.
Map 3 B1. [Ⓤ] *Volkstheater.* **Café Nepomuk** [☎] *5263919.* [◻] *8am– 11pm Mon–Fri, 8am–10pm Sat & Sun.* **Ulrichskirche** [☎] *5231246.* [◻] *on request or for services only.*

This tiny sloping square is an exquisite survival of early Vienna. The dainty Baroque house at No. 27 is now the Café Nepomuk, and adjoining it is a Renaissance house that escaped destruction by the Turks during the sieges of the city, most probably because the Turkish commander Kara Mustafa pitched his own tent nearby.

The house partly obscures the façade of the Baroque Ulrichskirche, built by Josef Reymund from 1721–4. Handsome patrician houses encircle it, of which the prettiest is No. 2, the Schulhaus. Elaborately decorated, it dates from the mid-18th century. In the church the composer Gluck was married and Johann Strauss the Younger was christened.

MuseumsQuartier ❼

Messeplatz 1. **Map** 3 C1. 🎫 5235881.
Ⓤ Volkstheater. 🅦 www.mqw.at
Visitors Centre ⏱ 10am–7pm daily.
Architektur Zentrum Wien 🎫 522
3115. ⏱ 10am–7pm daily. 🚹 🅦
www.azw.at **Art Cult Center** 🎫 526
1716. **Kunsthalle Wien** 🎫 521 89-33.
⏱ 10am–7pm Fri–Wed, 10am–10pm
Thu. 🅦 www.KUNSTHALLEwien.at
Leopold Museum 🎫 524 48 01-32.
⏱ 10:30am–7pm Wed & Fri–Sun,
10:30am–9pm Tue & Thu. 🚹
🅦 www.leopoldmuseum.org
**Museum of Modern Art Ludwig
Foundation Vienna** 🎫 317 6900-
25. ⏱ 10am–6pm Tue–Wed & Fri–Sun,
10am–9pm Thu. 🚹 **Tanzquartier
Wien** 🎫 581 35 91. ⏱ 8pm for
performances. **ZOOM Kinder-
museum** 🎫 522 67 48 4. ⏱
8:30am–5pm Mon–Fri, 10am–5:30pm
Sat, Sun & school hols. 🚹 🅦 www.
kindermuseum.at **Vienna Festival
Office** Lehargasse 11. 🎫 589 22-0.
🅦 www.festwochen.at

Once home to the imperial
stables and carriage
houses, the Vienna
MuseumsQuartier is one of
the biggest cultural centres in
the world. It houses a diverse
range of facilities from classical
art museums to venues for
film, theatre, architecture,
dance, new media and a
children's creativity centre, as
well as shops and cafés.

As you enter the
complex through the
main gate in the
Fischer von Erlach
Wing, you will
see in front of
you the renovated
Winter Riding
School, now renamed
the Hall of Events of the
City of Vienna. This is the
central and permanent
venue for the **Vienna
Festival** that has been
taking place since 1951.
Performances include
concerts, theatre and dance
as well as events organised
by the city of Vienna.

Behind this is the red
brick building of the
Kunsthalle Wien,
home to exhibitions of
international and
contemporary art. It
focuses on experimental
architecture, video,
photography and film.

On either side there
are two diagonally
positioned buildings –
to the left is the white
limestone façade of
the **Leopold Museum**,
whilst to the right the
**Museum of Modern
Art Ludwig
Foundation Vienna**
enclosed in dark grey
basalt. The Leopold
Museum houses the
art collection of
Rudolph Leopold
encompassing over
5,000 works of art,
including major pieces
by Gustav Klimt,
together with the
world's largest Egon
Schiele collection. The
Museum of Modern
Art Ludwig
Foundation Vienna
contains one of the largest
European collections of
modern and contemporary
art, from American Pop Art to
Cubism, Expressionism and
Viennese Actionism,
as well as other
contemporary art
from Central and
Eastern Europe.

Elsewhere on
the site the **Art
Cult Center**
contains an

Kneeling Female Nude **(1910) by Egon Schiele
is in the Museum of Modern Art collection**

exhibition on tobacco, tracing
the development of the plant
from its discovery in 1492 to
its economic significance
today. The **Architektur
Zentrum Wien** is a venue
for temporary exhibitions
of modern architecture
and architectural history.
It also has a permanent
exhibition of 20th-century
Austrian architecture. The
Tanzquartier Wien is
dedicated to dance and
performance of all types
providing facilities and
training to performers
and choreographers
and presenting a
variety of dance
and other
performances to the public.

The MuseumsQuartier also
contains archives, exhibitions
and facilities for lectures,
discussions, workshops and
seminars on art and culture,
as well as Austria's first
educational centre for
international museum and
exhibition studies.

In addition, for children,
there is the **ZOOM Kinder-
museum** where children can
play, explore and learn about
various exhibition subjects.
This lively centre offers an
unconventional approach to
the world of the museum.

**Rossbändiger (1892), by Theodor
Friedl and Gustav Jahn, near
the MuseumsQuartier**

Kunsthistorisches Museum 9

MORE THAN ONE AND A HALF MILLION people visit the
Museum of the History of Art every year. Its collections
are based largely on those built up over the centuries by
generations of Habsburg monarchs. Originally the works
of art were housed in the Hofburg and the Belvedere,
but when the Ringstrasse was built *(see pp32–3)*
two magnificent buildings were erected to house
the collections of imperial art and natural
history. The former are on display in this
museum where lavish internal decoration
complements the exhibits.

Second floor

★ **Hunters in the Snow** *(1565)*
*The last painting in Pieter Bruegel the
Elder's series of the seasons shows hunters
returning to the village on a winter's day.*

First floor

★ **The Artist's Studio**
*In this 1665 allegory of art,
Johannes Vermeer shows an
artist in decorative dress
painting a model posing as
Clio, the Muse of History.*

★ **Salt Cellar** *(1540–3)*
*Benvenuto Cellini's sumptuous
gold Saliera shows the sea and
earth united, represented by a
female earth
goddess and the
sea god Neptune.*

KEY

- ☐ Egyptian and Near Eastern collection
- ☐ Collection of Greek and Roman Antiquities
- ☐ Collection of Sculpture and Decorative Arts
- ☐ Picture gallery
- ☐ Coin cabinets
- ☐ Non-exhibition space

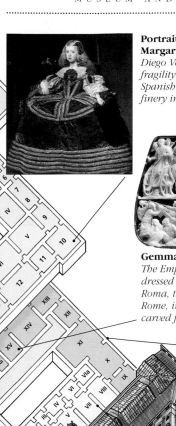

Portrait of the Infanta Margarita Teresa *(1659)*
Diego Velázquez captures the fragility of the eight-year-old Spanish princess in all her finery in this official portrait.

Gemma Augustea
The Emperor Augustus dressed as Jupiter sits next to Roma, the personification of Rome, in this Roman cameo carved from onyx.

VISITORS' CHECKLIST

Maria-Theresia-Platz, A-1010.
Map 3 C1 & 5 B5. **C** 52524.
W www.khm.at **U** Babenberger Strasse, Volkstheater. **bus** 2A, 57A to Burgring. **O** 10am–6pm Tue–Sun; picture gallery also 6–9pm Thu. **●** 1 Jan, 1 May, 1 Nov, 25 Dec. **⌖ ◎ ⚇ ⬚ ⬚ ⬚ ♫**

MUSEUM GUIDE

The ground floor houses sculpture and the applied arts. To the right of the entrance hall are the Greek and Roman, Egyptian and Near Eastern collections; to the left are later European sculpture and the decorative arts. The picture gallery occupies the whole of the first floor. Three rooms on the second floor house the impressive coin collection.

Ground floor

King Thutmosis III
Sculpted around 1460 BC, this royal portrait of King Thutmosis III is a remnant of a standing or kneeling figure.

Main entrance from Maria-Theresia-Platz

Rotunda

STAR EXHIBITS

★ **Hunters in the Snow by Bruegel**

★ **The Artist's Studio by Vermeer**

★ **Salt Cellar by Cellini**

THE APOTHEOSIS OF THE RENAISSANCE

Many prominent artists were employed to decorate the museum's interior. As part of an extravagant decorative scheme, the Hungarian painter Michael Munkácsy contributed a fabulous *trompe l'oeil* ceiling painting for the main staircase depicting *The Apotheosis of the Renaissance* (1890). It features Leonardo, Raphael, Veronese, Michelangelo and Titian and their models, presided over by Pope Julius II.

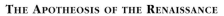

Exploring the Kunsthistorisches' Picture Collection

THE COLLECTION FOCUSES on Old Masters from the 15th to the 18th centuries, and largely reflects the personal tastes of its Habsburg founders. Venetian and 17th-century Flemish paintings are particularly well represented, and there is an excellent display of works by earlier Netherlandish and German artists. Broadly speaking, the pictures are hung following regional schools or styles of painting, although there is considerable overlap between the various categories.

The Fur (around 1635–40) by Peter Paul Rubens

FLEMISH PAINTING

BECAUSE OF THE historic links between the Habsburg monarchy and the Netherlands, there are several works from this part of Europe (present-day Belgium). The works of the early Flemish masters, who pioneered the development of oil painting, are characterized by their luminous colours and close attention to detail. This can be seen in the triptychs by Rogier van der Weyden and Hans Memling, and Jan van Eyck's *Cardinal Niccolo Albergati* (1435). The highlight for many is Room X, in which about half of all Pieter Bruegel the Elder's surviving works are displayed, including his *Tower of Babel* and most of the cycle of *The Seasons*, all from the mid-16th century.

The two rooms devoted to Rubens (Rooms XIII and XIV) include large-scale religious works such as the *Ildefonso Altarpiece* (1630–32) and *The Fur*, an intimate portrait of his wife. Rubens' collaborator and pupil, Anthony Van Dyck, is also represented here by some outstanding works in which his sensitivity to human emotion is fully portrayed.

DUTCH PAINTING

PROTESTANT HOLLAND'S newly-rich merchants of the 17th century delighted in pictures that reflected their own world rather than the hereafter. The Dutch genre scenes include works of great domestic charm such as Pieter de Hooch's lovely *Woman with Child at her Breast* (1663–5) and Gerard ter Borch's *Woman Peeling Apples* (1661) while Jacob van Ruisdael's *Great Forest* (1655–60) shows the advances made by Dutch painters in their observations of the natural world. All the

Large Self-Portrait (1652) by Rembrandt van Rijn

Rembrandts on show in Room XV are portraits; there is the picture of his mother as the prophetess Hannah (1639) and, in contrast to earlier works, the *Large Self-Portrait* shows the artist wearing a plain smock, with the emphasis on his face. The only painting by Johannes Vermeer is the enigmatic *The Artist's Studio* (Room 24). It is a complicated work with layers of symbolism; whether it is a self portrait or not has never been resolved.

ITALIAN PAINTING

THE ITALIAN GALLERIES have a strong collection of 16th-century paintings from Venice and the Veneto. In Room I the broad chronological and stylistic sweep of Titian's work, from his early *Gypsy Madonna*

Susanna and the Elders (1555) by Tintoretto

(1510) to the late *Nymph and Shepherd* (1570–5), can be seen. Other Venetian highlights include Giovanni Bellini's graceful *Young Woman at her Toilette* (1515) and Tintoretto's *Susanna and the Elders*. This is considered to be one of the major works of Venetian Mannerism. Giuseppe Arcimboldo's series of allegorical portrait heads representing the elements and the seasons are usually on show in Room 19, together with other works commissioned by Emperor Rudolf II. Italian Baroque painting includes works by Annibale Carracci and Michelangelo Merisi da Caravaggio, including the huge *Madonna of the Rosary*. Painted between 1606 and 1607, it depicts an intensely realistic Madonna advising St Dominic to distribute rosaries.

FRENCH PAINTING

ALTHOUGH THE number of French paintings on show is relatively small, there are some minor masterpieces. The minutely detailed and highly original portrait of *The Court Jester Gonella* (1440–45), is thought to be the work of Jean Fouquet. It depicts a wily old man, seemingly squeezed into the picture, believed to be a famous court jester of the time. A more formal court portrait from 1569 is that of the youthful Charles IX of France by François Clouet. *The Destruction of the Temple in Jerusalem*, a monumental work painted by Nicolas Poussin in 1638, depicts the Emperor Titus watching the Old Testament prophecy of the destruction of the Temple of Solomon come true. It combines agitated movement with thorough archaeological research. Joseph Duplessis' *Christopher Willibald Ritter von Gluck at the Spinet* shows the famous composer gazing into the heavens for inspiration.

Summer (1563) by Giuseppe Arcimboldo

BRITISH AND GERMAN PAINTING

THERE ARE FEW British works. Perhaps the most appealing is the *Landscape of Suffolk* (around 1750) by Thomas Gainsborough. There are also portraits by Gainsborough, Reynolds and Lawrence.

The German collection is rich in 16th-century paintings. There are several Albrecht Dürer works, including his *Madonna with the Pear* (1512). Other works include the *Stag Hunt of Elector Friedrich the Wise* (1529) by Lucas Cranach the Elder and seven portraits by Hans Holbein the Younger.

SPANISH PAINTING

ROOM 10 HOUSES several fine portraits of the Spanish royal family by the artist Diego Velázquez. He lived from 1599 to 1660 and was the court painter to Philip IV. His works include three portraits of Philip IV's daughter, the Infanta Margarita Teresa (in one aged three, another aged five and in a third aged eight), as well as a portrait of her sickly infant brother, Philip Prosper. Other Spanish works include paintings by Alonso Sánchez Coello and Antonio de Pereda.

Stag Hunt of Elector Friedrich the Wise (1529), by Lucas Cranach the Elder, in the German Collection

Exploring the Kunsthistorisches' Other Collections

A PART FROM THE PICTURE GALLERY, the Kunsthistorisches Museum houses several distinct collections of three-dimensional art and objects. Most of the European sculpture and decorative art is from approximately the same period as the paintings (from the 15th to the 18th centuries), but there is also a fine display of medieval objects, while exhibits on show in the Egyptian, Greek and Roman rooms provide an intriguing record of the world's earliest civilizations.

made to contain deceased souls. Other rooms house mummified animals, Egyptian scripts and everyday artefacts such as pots, bits of clothing and jewellery.

Also shown are a glazed brick relief of a lion from Babylon, and items from Arabia.

ORIENTAL AND EGYPTIAN ANTIQUITIES

S IX SPECIALLY-decorated rooms adorned with Egyptian friezes and motifs provide the perfect setting for the bulk of the museum's collection of Egyptian and Near Eastern antiquities. The nucleus of the collection was formed under the earlier Habsburg monarchs. Most of the items were either bought in the 19th century, after Napoleon's Egyptian expedition had increased interest in the area, or added early this century, when Austrian archaeologists excavated at Giza; an outstanding example is the so-called *Reserve Head* (around 26th century BC). The entire 5th-dynasty Tomb Chapel of Ka-Ni-Nisut, from the Pyramid district of Giza, and its well-preserved hieroglyphics (from around 2400 BC) are on display in Room VIA.

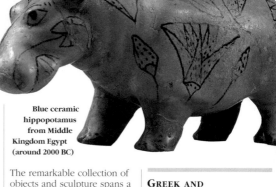

Blue ceramic hippopotamus from Middle Kingdom Egypt (around 2000 BC)

The remarkable collection of objects and sculpture spans a wide chronological period from the Pre-Dynastic era until Roman times. There is a bust of King Thutmosis III *(see p119)* as well as portraits of Egyptian gods and goddesses. In Room I, where the decorative scheme incorporates Egyptian columns from Aswan, there are items associated with the mortuary cult in Ancient Egypt, including sarcophagi, canopic jars (which used to contain the entrails of mummified corpses), scarabs, mummy cases, papyrus books of the dead, and a small blue ceramic statue of a hippopotamus. These were often found in Middle Kingdom tombs, as hippopotamus hunting was a royal privilege given to certain citizens who had won the king's favour. Many of the small-scale sculptures on display were

GREEK AND ROMAN ANTIQUITIES

O NLY PART OF the museum's Greek and Roman collection is housed in the main building; the finds from Ephesus and Samothrace are displayed in the Neue Burg *(see p95)* in the Hofburg.

If you approach the collection from the Egyptian galleries, the first room you come to (Room IX) is devoted to very early Greek sculpture and Cypriot art. Room X is dominated by the large bronze statue of the *Youth from Magdalensberg,* a 16th-century cast of a lost Roman statue, found buried in an Austrian field, that has an astonishing presence. The main gallery (Room XI) is decorated in the style of an imperial Roman villa and includes a mosaic of Theseus and the Minotaur, a Roman marble statue of Isis, numerous portrait heads and a sarcophagus with some fine relief decoration. Room XII is full of figurines and bronzes from Greece and Rome.

Etruscan art and vases, and vases from Tanagra (a town in Ancient Greece) precede Room XV, which contains a

Room I from the Egyptian galleries, with papyrus stalk columns from Aswan (around 1410 BC)

large collection of Roman cameos, jewellery, busts of Roman Emperors and Roman glass. Coptic, Byzantine and Germanic items are shown in the rest of the rooms, where pride of place goes to the Treasure of Nagyszentmiklós, a late 9th-century collection of golden vessels found in Romania in 1799.

Medal of Ulrich II Molitor (1581)

SCULPTURE AND DECORATIVE ARTS

THE COLLECTION CONSISTS OF many of the special objects and treasures bought or commissioned by Habsburg connoisseurs, particularly Rudolf II and Archduke Leopold William, for their *Kunstkammern*, or chambers of art and marvels housed in various of their Habsburg residences. In addition to sculpture, these princely treasuries contained precious items of high craftsmanship, exotic, highly unusual novelties, and scientific instruments. Among the most intriguing are some intricate automata made solely for amusement. These include a musical box in the form of a ship, and a moving clock. Some of the royal patrons worked in the studio themselves; on display is some glass blown by the Archduke Ferdinand II and embroidery sewn by Maria Theresa.

Virgin with Child (about 1495) by Tilman Riemenschneider

As in the Picture Gallery, the main emphasis is on the Renaissance and Baroque, although there is an excellent display of medieval items in Rooms XXXIV and XXXVI. These include fine, late Gothic religious carved statues by

artists such as Tilman Riemenschneider, some medieval ivories, drinking horns and communion vessels. The highlights of the Italian Renaissance rooms (Rooms XXX and XXXII) are a marble bust of a laughing boy by Desiderio da Settignano, a marble relief of Bacchus and Ariadne and a fine bronze and gilt figurine called Venus Felix after an antique marble statue. Included in the large German Renaissance collection are early playing cards and a table centrepiece, incorporating "vipers' tongues" (in fact, fossilized sharks' teeth), said to ward off poison. Other gems on display include Benvenuto Cellini's Salt Cellar *(see p118)* which was made for the French king François I, and some statuettes by Giambologna.

Youth from Magdalensberg, 16th century, cast after a Roman original

COINS AND MEDALS

TUCKED AWAY on the second floor is one of the most extensive coin and medal collections in the world. For those with a special interest in the area it is exceptional. Once again, the nucleus of the collection came from the former possessions of the Habsburgs, but it has been added to by modern curators and now includes many 20th-century items. Only a fraction of the museum's 500,000 pieces can be seen in the three exhibition rooms.

Room I gives an overview of the development of money. It includes coins from Ancient Greece and Rome, examples of Egyptian, Celtic and Byzantine money, and medieval, Renaissance and European coins, as well as the whole range of Austrian currency.

Also on display is a collection of primitive forms of money such as stone currency from Yap Island in Micronesia.

Rooms II and III house an extensive collection of 19th- and 20th-century medals. The portrait medallions are often miniature works of art in themselves. Particularly noteworthy are the unusual silver and gilt medals belonging to Ulrich Molitor, the Abbot of Heiligenkreuz, and the silver medallion which was engraved by Bertrand Andrieu and minted to commemorate the baptism of Napoleon's son. This shows the emperor as a proud father, lifting aloft his baby, the King of Rome *(see p173)*.

Spittelberg Pedestrian Area ❽

Map 3 B1. **Ⓤ** *Volkstheater.* **Amerling-
haus** ◯ *2–10pm Mon–Fri.* **Market**
◯ *Apr–Jun & Sep–Nov: 10am–6pm
Sat; Jul & Aug: 2–9pm Sat.* ◙ ♿

A GROUP OF STREETS – the pedestrianized Spittelberg-gasse, Gutenberggasse and Schrankgasse – has been well restored to present a pretty group of 18th- and 19th-century houses. Traditionally the area was lower class and very lively, home to the actors, artists and strolling players of the day. The houses were mostly tenements, without gardens or courtyards.

The charm of the district was rediscovered in the 1970s and the city authorities set about restoring the buildings. Today, it is a district of restaurants, cafés

**Façade detail at No. 20
Spittelberggasse**

and boutiques. It hosts a Christmas and an Easter market, as well as a regular arts and crafts market from April to November. The Amerlinghaus theatre at No. 8 Stiftgasse is the area's cultural centre and provides a venue for exhibitions and events. The Spittelberg is a great success, and café life keeps the cobbled streets buzzing into the early hours of the morning.

The Amerlinghaus at No. 8 Stiftgasse was the birthplace of the painter Friedrich Amerling. Today it is a community centre, theatre and *Beisl (see p201).*

No. 10 Stiftgasse has a handsome façade, decorated with statues.

Nos. 18 and 20 Spittelberg-gasse are fine examples of Baroque houses.

No. 29 Gutenberggasse is a delightfully pretty Biedermeier building.

Spittelberggasse acts as the venue for an arts and crafts market that is held on every Saturday from April to November, and daily during Easter and Christmas.

The Witwe Bolte restaurant used to be an inn in the 18th century; legend has it that Emperor Joseph II was thrown out of here in 1778.

No. 9 Spittelberggasse is a beautifully-decorated house, with skilfully-painted *trompe l'oeil* windows, dating from the 18th century.

Kunsthistorisches Museum ❾

See pp118–23.

Natural History Museum ❿

See pp126–7.

Parliament ⓫

Dr-Karl-Renner-Ring 3. **Map** 1 C5 & 5 A3. **【** 401100. **⓪** Volkstheater. **◯** for **✦** 11am, 3pm Mon–Thu, 11am, 1pm, 2pm, 3pm Fri (except when parliament is in session). **♿**

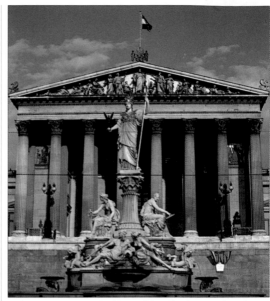

Façade of the Parliament building and the Athenebrunnen fountain

THE ARCHITECT Theophil Hansen *(see p32)* chose a strict Neo-Classical style when he designed the immense Parliament building. It was originally constructed as part of the Ringstrasse development to act as the *Reichsrat* building (the Parliament of the Austrian part of the Habsburg empire). Construction began in 1874 and finished in 1884.

The Parliament's entrance is raised above street level and approached up a broad ramp. At the foot of the ramp are the least pompous sculptures: they are the bronze Horse Tamers (1901) by sculptor Josef Lax;

the ramp itself is decorated with marble figures of Greek and Roman historians. On the roof there are chariots and impressive statues of ancient scholars and statesmen.

In front of the central portico is the Athenebrunnen, a fountain dominated by the figure of Pallas Athene, the goddess of Wisdom. It was

designed by Karl Kundmann and was placed here in 1902. In this splendid, if chilly, setting on 11 November 1918 after the collapse of the Habsburg empire, the parliamentary deputies proclaimed the formation of the republic of Deutsch-Österreich. It was renamed the Republic of Austria in 1919.

THE AUSTRIAN PARLIAMENT

The Austrian parliament is composed of two houses – the Lower House, or *Nationalrat*, and the Upper House, or *Bundesrat*. The Lower House has 183 seats and its members are elected for a four-year term by proportional representation. It comprises the governing party and the opposition. The Upper House is composed of elected representatives from Austria's nine provinces, and its function is to approve legislation passed by the Lower House. Bills may also be presented to parliament by the general public or by the Chambers of Labour (representing consumers and employees) and the Chambers of the Economy (representing employers and industry). The federal President is elected for a six-year term and is largely a figurehead. Theoretically, he or she has the power to veto bills and dissolve parliament, though this has never occurred.

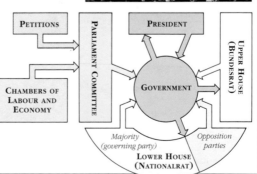

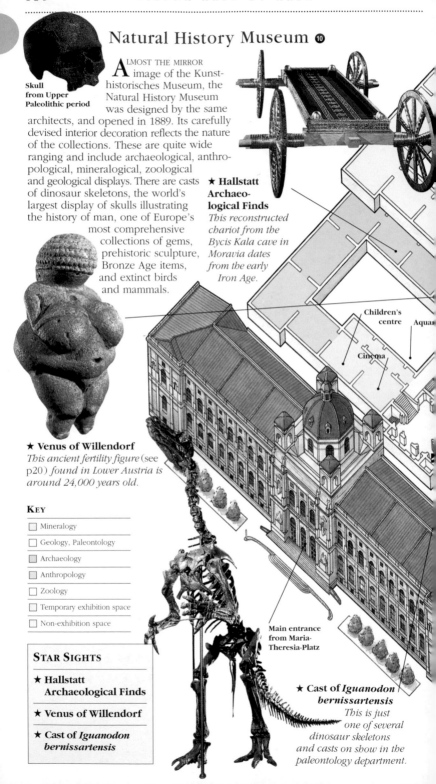

Skull from Upper Paleolithic period

Natural History Museum ⑩

ALMOST THE MIRROR image of the Kunsthistorisches Museum, the Natural History Museum was designed by the same architects, and opened in 1889. Its carefully devised interior decoration reflects the nature of the collections. These are quite wide ranging and include archaeological, anthropological, mineralogical, zoological and geological displays. There are casts of dinosaur skeletons, the world's largest display of skulls illustrating the history of man, one of Europe's most comprehensive collections of gems, prehistoric sculpture, Bronze Age items, and extinct birds and mammals.

★ Hallstatt Archaeological Finds
This reconstructed chariot from the Bycis Kala cave in Moravia dates from the early Iron Age.

Children's centre

Aqua

Cinema

★ Venus of Willendorf
This ancient fertility figure (see p20) found in Lower Austria is around 24,000 years old.

KEY

- ☐ Mineralogy
- ☐ Geology, Paleontology
- ☐ Archaeology
- ☐ Anthropology
- ☐ Zoology
- ☐ Temporary exhibition space
- ☐ Non-exhibition space

Main entrance from Maria-Theresia-Platz

STAR SIGHTS

★ **Hallstatt Archaeological Finds**

★ **Venus of Willendorf**

★ **Cast of *Iguanodon bernissartensis***

★ Cast of *Iguanodon bernissartensis*
This is just one of several dinosaur skeletons and casts on show in the paleontology department.

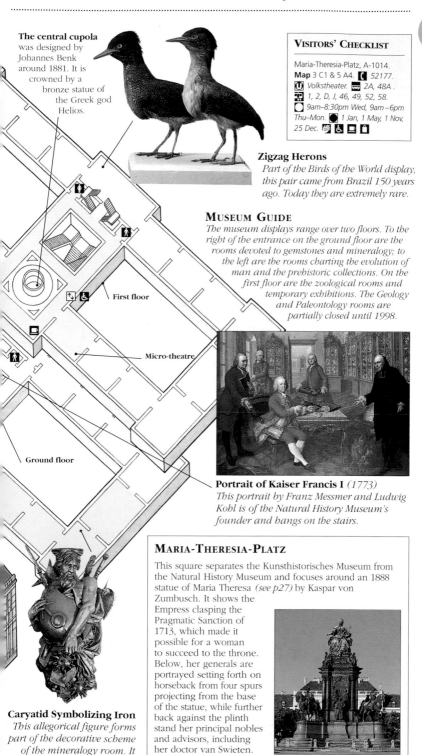

The central cupola was designed by Johannes Benk around 1881. It is crowned by a bronze statue of the Greek god Helios.

VISITORS' CHECKLIST

Maria-Theresia-Platz, A-1014.
Map 3 C1 & 5 A4. 52177.
Volkstheater. 2A, 48A.
1, 2, D, J, 46, 49, 52, 58.
9am–8:30pm Wed, 9am–6pm
Thu–Mon. 1 Jan, 1 May, 1 Nov,
25 Dec.

Zigzag Herons
Part of the Birds of the World display, this pair came from Brazil 150 years ago. Today they are extremely rare.

MUSEUM GUIDE
The museum displays range over two floors. To the right of the entrance on the ground floor are the rooms devoted to gemstones and mineralogy; to the left are the rooms charting the evolution of man and the prehistoric collections. On the first floor are the zoological rooms and temporary exhibitions. The Geology and Paleontology rooms are partially closed until 1998.

First floor

Micro-theatre

Ground floor

Portrait of Kaiser Francis I *(1773)*
This portrait by Franz Messmer and Ludwig Kohl is of the Natural History Museum's founder and hangs on the stairs.

MARIA-THERESIA-PLATZ

This square separates the Kunsthistorisches Museum from the Natural History Museum and focuses around an 1888 statue of Maria Theresa *(see p27)* by Kaspar von Zumbusch. It shows the Empress clasping the Pragmatic Sanction of 1713, which made it possible for a woman to succeed to the throne. Below, her generals are portrayed setting forth on horseback from four spurs projecting from the base of the statue, while further back against the plinth stand her principal nobles and advisors, including her doctor van Swieten.

Caryatid Symbolizing Iron
This allegorical figure forms part of the decorative scheme of the mineralogy room. It represents the metal iron.

Neues Rathaus ⑫

Friedrich-Schmidt-Platz 1. **Map** 1 B5
& 5 A2. ⓒ 52550. ① Rathaus. ◯ for
☑ 1pm Mon, Wed & Fri & through
phone bookings for groups. ⓧ

T HE NEW TOWN HALL is the
seat of the Vienna City and
Provincial Assembly. Built from
1872 to 1883 to replace the
Altes Rathaus (see p85), it is
unashamedly Neo-Gothic in
style. The architect, Friedrich
von Schmidt, was chosen by
the authorities in a competition
for the best design.

A huge central tower, topped
by the 3-m (11-ft) statue of a
knight in armour with a lance,
dominates the front façade.
Known affectionately as the
Rathausmann, it was designed
by Franz Gastell and made by
the wrought-iron craftsman
Alexander Nehr. The most
attractive feature of the façade is
the lofty loggia with its delicate
tracery and curved balconies.

The building has seven courtyards and summer concerts are
held in the Arkadenhof courtyard. At the top of the first of
the two grand staircases is the
Festsaal, a ceremonial hall that
stretches the length of the
building. Round all four sides
are Neo-Gothic arcades and
statues of Austrian worthies,
including prominent Habsburgs.

Beneath the town hall is the
Wiener Rathauskeller, a popular
restaurant (see p213).

Dreifaltigkeits-kirche ⑬

Alser Strasse 17. **Map** 1 B4.
ⓒ 4057225. ① Rathaus.
◯ 8–11:30am Mon–Sat, 8am–noon
Sun. ⓧ ♿ entrance on
Schlösselgasse for services.

B UILT BETWEEN 1685 and 1727,
the church of the Holy
Trinity contains an altarpiece
(1708) in the north aisle by the

**16th-century crucifix by Veit
Stoss, in the Dreifaltigkeitskirche**

painter Martino Altomonte,
and a graphic crucifix in the
south aisle from the workshop
of Veit Stoss. Beethoven's body
was brought here after he died
in 1827. Following the funeral
service attended by his
contemporaries, including
Schubert and the poet Franz
Grillparzer, the cortege bore
his coffin to the cemetery at
Währing on the city outskirts.

University ⑭

Dr-Karl-Lueger-Ring 1. **Map** 1 C4 &
5 A2. ⓒ 42770. ① Schottentor.
◯ 6:30am–8:30pm Mon–Fri, 8am–
1pm Sat. ⓧ ♿

F OUNDED IN 1365 by Duke
Rudolf IV, the University of
Vienna now has approximately
50,000 students. The versatile
architect Heinrich Ferstel
designed its present home
in 1883, adopting an Italian
Renaissance style.

From the entrance hall, huge
staircases lead up to the
university's ceremonial halls. In
1895 Gustav Klimt was
commissioned to decorate the
hall with frescoes, but the
nudity portrayed in some
panels proved unacceptable to
the authorities. Eventually,
Klimt returned his fee to the
government and took back the
paintings; they were destroyed
during World War II.

A spacious arcaded court-
yard, lined with busts of the
university's most distinguished
professors, is located in the

**Front elevation of the Neues Rathaus showing the Rathausmann on his
tower some 98 m (320 ft) above the ground**

centre of the building. Figures include the founder of psychoanalysis, Sigmund Freud *(see p110)*, and the philosopher Franz Brentano. Nearby are the smoke-filled and poster-daubed corridors of today's university students.

Café Landtmann ⓯

Dr-Karl-Lueger-Ring 4. **Map** 1 C5 & 5 B2. 5320621. Schottentor, Volkstheater. 8am–midnight daily.

IF THE CAFE CENTRAL *(see p58)* was, and perhaps still is, the coffee house of Vienna's intelligentsia, this café *(see p58)* is the coffee house of the affluent middle classes. With mirrors and elegant panelling, it is an exceedingly comfortable place. Established in 1873 by coffee-maker Franz Landtmann, it is still a popular café. It was Sigmund Freud's *(see p110)* favourite coffee house.

Burgtheater ⓰

See pp130–31.

The attractive Dreimäderlhaus (left) on Schreyvogelgasse

Dreimäderlhaus ⓱

Schreyvogelgasse 10. **Map** 1 C5 & 5 B2. Schottentor.

A DELIGHTFUL REMNANT of Biedermeier Vienna is found in the houses on one side of the cobbled Schreyvogelgasse. The prettiest is the Dreimäderlhaus (1803). There is a legend that Schubert had three sweethearts *(drei Mäderl)* ensconced here, but it is more likely that the house was named after the 1920s' operetta, *Dreimäderlhaus*, which uses his melodies.

One of the arcades surrounding the University courtyard

Mölker-Bastei ⓲

Map 1 C5 & 5 B2. Schottentor.

A FEW PACES AWAY from the bustling Schottentor, a quiet street has been built on to a former bastion of the city walls. It boasts some beautiful late 18th-century houses. Beethoven lived here, and the Emperor Franz Joseph nearly met his death on the bastion in 1853 when a tailor attempted to assassinate him. No. 10 is the

Plaque on the front of the Pasqualati Haus

house where the Belgian Prince Charles de Ligne lived during the Congress of Vienna in 1815 *(see p30)*. De Ligne, an elderly aristocrat, wrote a number of cynical commentaries on the various activities of the crowned heads of Europe who came to Vienna at that time. A ladies' man, he caught a fatal chill while waiting for an assignation on the bastion.

Pasqualati Haus ⓳

Mölker-Bastei 8. **Map** 1 C5 & 5 B2. 5358905. Schottentor. **Museum** 9am–12:15pm & 1–4:30pm Tue–Sun.

THE PASQUALATI HAUS is no different in appearance from any of the other houses along this lane, but it is the most famous of more than 30 places where Ludwig van

Beethoven resided in Vienna. Named after its original owner, Baron Johann von Pasqualati, it was Beethoven's home between 1804 and 1808, and 1810 and 1815. He composed many of his best-loved works here, including the Symphonies 4, 5, 7 and 8, the opera *Fidelio*, the Piano Concerto No. 4, and string quartets. Today, the rooms on the fourth floor which the composer occupied house a small museum. Various memorabilia, such as a lock of Beethoven's hair, a photograph of his grave at Währing cemetery, a deathbed engraving and early editions of his scores are on display. The museum also contains busts and paintings of Beethoven and his patron Prince Rasumofsky, the Russian ambassador to Vienna.

Liebenberg monument (1890) below the Mölker-Bastei

The Burgtheater ⑯

THE BURGTHEATER IS THE most prestigious stage in the German-speaking world *(see also p228)*. The original theatre built in Maria Theresa's reign was replaced in 1888 by today's Italian Renaissance-style building by Karl von Hasenauer and Gottfried Semper. It closed for refurbishment in 1897 after the discovery that the auditorium had several seats with no view of the stage. Forty-eight years later a bomb devastated the building, leaving only the side wings containing the Grand Staircases intact. Subsequent restoration was so successful that today its extent is hard to assess.

Two statues of the muses of music and dramatic art adorn the roof.

JOHANN
NESTROY
1801—1862

Busts of playwrights
Lining the walls of the Grand Staircases are busts of play-wrights whose works are still performed here, including this one of Johann Nestroy by Hans Knesl.

Ceiling frescoes by the Klimt brothers and Franz Matsch cover the north and south wings.

Entrance for tours

Candelabra lining the staircase

★ Grand Staircases in North and South Wings
Two imposing gala stair-cases lead up from the side entrances to the foyer. Each is a mirror image of the other.

Main entrance on Dr Karl-Lueger-Ring

STAR FEATURES

★ **Grand Staircases in North and South Wings**

★ **Der Thespiskarren by Gustav Klimt**

Foyer
The 60-m long (200-ft) curving foyer serves as a waiting area during intervals. Portraits of famous actors and actresses line its walls.

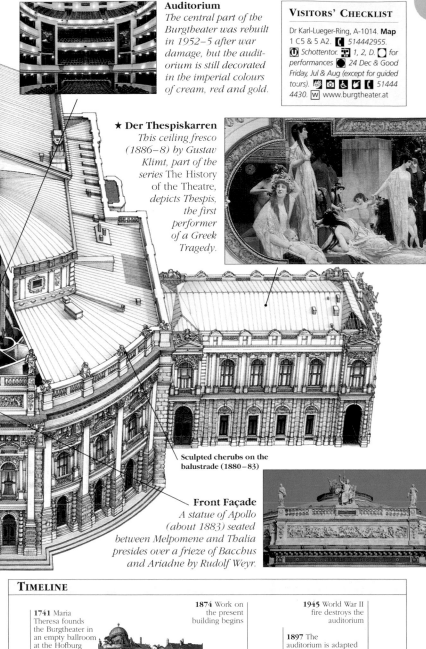

Auditorium
The central part of the Burgtheater was rebuilt in 1952–5 after war damage, but the auditorium is still decorated in the imperial colours of cream, red and gold.

★ **Der Thespiskarren**
This ceiling fresco (1886–8) by Gustav Klimt, part of the series The History of the Theatre, *depicts Thespis, the first performer of a Greek Tragedy.*

Sculpted cherubs on the balustrade (1880–83)

Front Façade
A statue of Apollo (about 1883) seated between Melpomene and Thalia presides over a frieze of Bacchus and Ariadne by Rudolf Weyr.

TIMELINE

1741 Maria Theresa founds the Burgtheater in an empty ballroom at the Hofburg

1776 Joseph II reorganizes the theatre and promotes it to the status of a national theatre

1874 Work on the present building begins

The Old Burgtheater in the mid-18th century

1888 The Burgtheater opens on 14 October in the presence of the Emperor Franz Joseph and his family

1945 World War II fire destroys the auditorium

1897 The auditorium is adapted

1955 Theatre reopens with Grillparzer's *King Ottokar*

1750	1850	1900	1950

OPERA AND NASCHMARKT

THIS IS AN AREA of huge contrasts, ranging from the stateliness of the Opera House and the opulence of the Opernring shops to the raucous modernity of Mariahilfer Strasse. This long street is lined with cinemas and department stores, drawing shoppers not just from Vienna but from much of eastern Europe. The other major thoroughfare in our area is the Linke Wienzeile, which runs parallel to the Rechte Wienzeile. Both roads stretch from

Relief on the façade of the Secession Building

just beyond the Ringstrasse to the city outskirts, following the curving and sometimes subterranean River Wien. Between these roads is the bustling Naschmarkt, which is overlooked by Otto Wagner's Jugendstil apartments on the Linke Wienzeile. Visitors wanting to escape the crowds should visit the celebrated Café Museum, located near the three great cultural institutions of the area – the Academy of Fine Arts, the Opera House and the Secession Building.

SIGHTS AT A GLANCE

Streets and Squares
Mariahilfer Strasse **8**

Historic Buildings
Opera House pp138–9 **1**
Hotel Sacher **2**
Theater an der Wien **5**
Wagner Apartments **7**

Museums and Galleries
Academy of Fine Arts **3**
Secession Building **4**
Tobacco Museum **9**
Kaiserliches Hofmobiliendepot **10**
Haydn Museum **11**

Markets
Naschmarkt **6**

GETTING THERE
This area is served by Zieglergasse (line U3), Neubaugasse (line U3) and Babenbergerstrasse (line U2) U-Bahn stations. Bus 13A runs from Josefstädter Strasse to Mariahilfer Strasse and to the southern end of the Linke Wienzeile. Bus 57A travels the length of Gumpendorfer Strasse.

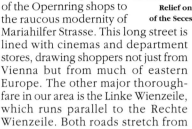

0 metres 250
0 yards 250

KEY

	Street-by-Street map *See pp134–5*
U	U-Bahn station
P	Parking

◁ **Main staircase and hallway at the Opera House**

Street-by-Street: Opernring

BETWEEN THE OPERA HOUSE and the Karlskirche, two of the great landmarks of Vienna, lies an area that typifies the varied cultural vitality of the city as a whole. Here are an 18th-century theatre, a 19th-century art academy, and the Secession Building. Mixed in with these cultural monuments are emblems of the Viennese devotion to good living: the Hotel Sacher, as sumptuous today as it was a century ago; the Café Museum (see p58), still as popular as it was in the 1900s; and the hurly-burly of the colourful Naschmarkt, where you can buy everything from oysters and exotic fruits to second-hand clothes.

★ **Academy of Fine Arts**
This Italianate building is home to one of the best collections of old masters in Vienna ❸

The Goethe Statue was designed by Edmund Hellmer in 1890.

The Schiller Statue dominates the park in front of the Academy of Fine Arts.

★ **Secession Building**
This delightful structure, built in 1898 as a showroom for the Secession artists, houses Gustav Klimt's (see p56) Beethoven Frieze ❹

Theater an der Wien
Today this 18th-century theatre is used for major musicals. It was the venue for many premieres including Beethoven's Fidelio ❺

Naschmarkt
This market sells everything from fresh farm produce to bric-a-brac. It is liveliest on Saturday mornings ❻

SCHILLERPLATZ

MAKARTGASSE

GETREIDEMARKT

MILLÖCKERGASSE

LINKE WIENZEILE

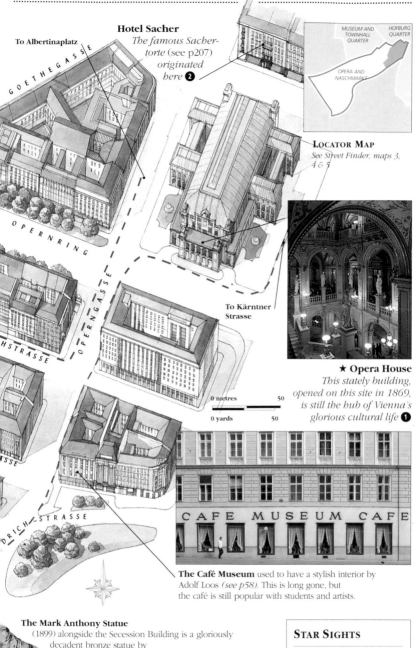

To Albertinaplatz

GOETHEGASSE

Hotel Sacher
*The famous Sacher-
torte (see p207)
originated
here* ❷

MUSEUM AND
TOWNHALL
QUARTER

HOFBURG
QUARTER

OPERA AND
NASCHMARKT

LOCATOR MAP
*See Street Finder, maps 3,
4 & 5*

OPERNRING

OPERNGASSE

**To Kärntner
Strasse**

HSTRASSE

0 metres   50

0 yards   50

★ **Opera House**
*This stately building,
opened on this site in 1869,
is still the hub of Vienna's
glorious cultural life* ❶

DRICH-STRASSE

CAFE MUSEUM CAFE

The Café Museum used to have a stylish interior by
Adolf Loos *(see p58)*. This is long gone, but
the café is still popular with students and artists.

The Mark Anthony Statue
(1899) alongside the Secession Building is a gloriously
decadent bronze statue by
Arthur Strasser.

STAR SIGHTS

★ **Secession Building**

★ **Academy of
Fine Arts**

★ **Opera House**

KEY

― ― ― Suggested route

Opera House ❶

See pp138–9.

Hotel Sacher ❷

Philharmonikerstrasse 4. **Map** 4 D1 &
5 C5. ☎ 514560. Ⓤ *Karlsplatz.*
◯ *6:30am–midnight daily.* 🅿 ♿
🔲 www.sacher.com

FOUNDED BY the son of Franz
Sacher, who, according to
some, was the creator of the
Sachertorte in 1840 *(see p207)*,
this hotel *(see p198)* came into
its own under Anna Sacher.
The cigar-smoking daughter-in-
law of the founder ran the hotel
from 1892 until her death in
1930. During her time the Sacher
became a venue for the extra-
marital affairs of the rich and
noble. It is still a discreetly
sumptuous hotel.

Academy of Fine Arts ❸

Schillerplatz 3. **Map** 4 D2 & 5 B5.
☎ 588160. Ⓤ *Karlsplatz.*
◯ *10am–4pm Tue–Sun & public hols.*
● *1 Jan, 1 May, Corpus Christi and
following Fri, 1 & 2 Nov, 24, 25 & 31
Dec.* 🎫 🅿 ♿ 🔲 www.akbild.ac.at

THEOPHIL HANSEN built the
Academy of Fine Arts in
Italian Renaissance style from
1872 to 1876. In 1907 Adolf
Hitler was barred from entrance

Façade of the Secession Building

on the grounds that he lacked
talent. Today the Academy acts
as an arts college and has a
gallery showing changing
exhibitions. These include late
Gothic and early Renaissance
works, some Rubens' pieces,
17th-century Dutch and Flemish
landscapes, as well as a 19th-
century Austrian collection.

Secession Building ❹

Friedrichstrasse 12. **Map** 4 D2.
☎ 5875307. Ⓤ *Karlsplatz.*
◯ *10am–6pm Tue–Wed, 10am–8pm
Thu.* 🎫 🅿 ♿ 🔲 www.secession.at

JOSEPH MARIA Olbrich designed
the unusual Secession Building
in Jugendstil style *(see pp54–7)*
as a showcase for the Secession
movement's artists
(see p34). The
almost windowless
building, with its
filigree globe of
entwined laurel
leaves on the roof,
is a squat cube
with four towers.
The motto of the
founders, em-
blazoned in gold
on the façade,
states, *"Der Zeit
ihre Kunst, der
Kunst ihre Frei-
heit"*, which
translates as: "To
every Age its Art, to
Art its Freedom".
Alongside the
building stands the
marvellous statue
of Mark Anthony
in his chariot being

drawn by lions (1899), by
Arthur Strasser. Gustav Klimt's
Beethoven Frieze is the
Secession's best-known exhibit.
Designed in 1902 as a decora-
tive painting, it covers three
walls and is 34 m (110 ft) long.
It shows interrelated groups of
figures and is thought to be a
commentary on Beethoven's
Ninth Symphony. *(See also p35.)*

Theater an der Wien ❺

Linke Wienzeile 6. **Map** 3 C2.
☎ 588300. Ⓤ *Kettenbrückengasse.*
◯ *for performances.*
🔲 www.musicalvienna.at

EMANUEL SCHIKANEDER founded
this theatre *(see p224)* in
1801; a statue above the entrance
show him playing Papageno in
the premiere of Mozart's *The
Magic Flute* in the forerunner
of the present theatre. The
premiere of Beethoven's *Fidelio*
was staged here in 1805.

Naschmarkt ❻

Map 3 C2–C3. Ⓤ *Kettenbrückengasse.* **Market** ◯ 6am–6:30pm Mon–
Fri, 6am–2pm Sat. **Schubert Museum**
◯ 9am–12:15pm, 1–4:30pm Tue–Sun.

Typical stall at the Naschmarkt

THE NASCHMARKT is Vienna's
liveliest market. It has
many well-established shops
and some of the best snack
bars in Vienna *(see pp215–17)*.
As you walk west it gradually
becomes less formal, with flower
vendors', wine producers' and
farmers' stalls spilling out onto
the street and offering meats,
breads and so on. This area in
turn leads into the flea market –
a chaos of makeshift stalls.
It's also worth going to No. 6
Kettenbrückengasse, by the
U-Bahn, to see the simple flat
where Franz Schubert died in
1828. It displays facsimiles,
prints and a family piano.

Columned entrance to the Theater an der Wien

The Majolikahaus, one of the Wagner Apartments

Wagner Apartments **❼**

Linke Wienzeile 38 & 40. **Map** 3 C2.
Ⓤ *Kettenbrückengasse.*

LOOKING ONTO THE Nasch-
markt are two remarkable
apartment buildings. Designed
by Otto Wagner in 1899, they
represent the apex of Jugendstil style *(see pp54–7)*. No. 38
has sparkling gilt ornament,
mostly by Kolo Moser. The
façade of No. 40 has subtle
flower patterns in pink, blue
and green. Even the sills are
moulded and decorated. No.
40, called the Majolikahaus
after the glazed pottery used
for the weather-resistant
surface decoration, is the more
striking. No. 42 next door, in
historicist style *(see pp32–3)*,
shows what Secession architects were reacting against.

Mariahilfer Strasse **❽**

Map 3 A3 & 5 A5. Ⓤ *Zieglergasse,
Kirchengasse, Babenberger Strasse.*
Stiftkirche ◯ *7:30am–6pm
Mon–Fri, 7am–11pm Sat, 8:30am–
9:30pm Sun.* **Mariahilfer Kirche** ◯
8am–7pm Mon–Sat, 8:30am–7pm Sun.

THIS IS ONE OF Vienna's
busiest shopping streets.
On the corner of Stiftgasse is
the Stiftkirche. The architect is
unknown, but the church dates
from 1739. The façade is an
austere pyramidal structure,
rising to a bulbous steeple.
There are some lively Rococo
reliefs set into the walls.
Across the street at No. 45 is
the house where the playwright
Ferdinand Raimund was born
in 1790. Its cobbled courtyard
is lined with shops.
Mariahilfer Kirche is named
after a 16th-century cult of the
Virgin Mary which was
founded at the pilgrimage of
Mariahilfer Kirche at Passau.
The Viennese church is
Baroque, dominated by two
towers with bulbous steeples.

Tobacco Museum **❾**

Mariahilfer Strasse 2. **Map** 3 C2 &
5 A5. Ⓒ *5261716.* Ⓤ *Babenberger
Strasse.* ◯ *10am–5pm Tue, Wed &
Fri, 10am–7pm Thu, 10am–2pm Sat,
Sun & public hols.* 🖼 📷
Ⓦ *www.austriatabak.com*

PART OF THE MuseumsQuartier
(see p117), the contents of
this museum are not
unexpected – smoking
kits, snuffboxes,
pipes, cigarette
boxes, and so on,
mostly from the 19th
century. In 1784,
Joseph II reorganized
the Austrian tobacco
industry into a state
monopoly. This still
survives as Austria Tabak.

Kaiserliches Hof-mobiliendepot **❿**

Andreasgasse 7. **Map** 3 A2.
Ⓒ *52433570.* Ⓤ *Zieglergasse.*
◯ *9am–5pm Tue–Sun.* 🖼

THE IMPERIAL furniture collection, founded by Maria
Theresa in 1747, gives an intimate portrait of the Habsburg
way of life as well as a detailed
historical record of Viennese
interior decoration and cabinet-
making in the 18th and 19th
centuries. Room after room is
filled with outstanding furnishings and royal domestic objects, ranging from a faithful re-
creation of Empress Elisabeth's
Schönbrunn Palace apartments
to a simple folding throne that
was used while travelling.

Haydn Museum **⓫**

Haydngasse 19. **Map** 3 A3.
Ⓒ *5961307.* Ⓤ *Zieglergasse.*
◯ *9am–12:15pm & 1–4:30pm
Tue–Sun.* ● *25 Dec, 1 Jan.* 🖼 📷

AS WITH MANY of the museums
dedicated to composers,
the Haydn Museum is not very
comprehensive: it has only a
few copies of documents and
scores, a piano and clavichord.
Haydn built this house in
what was then a new suburb
with money he had earned on
his successful visits to London
between 1791 and 1795. He
lived in the house from 1797
until his death in 1809 and
composed many major works
here, including *The Creation*
and *The Seasons*. There is
also a room with some
furniture and
mementoes
belonging to
Johannes Brahms.

**Ornate 1845
pipe from the
Tobacco Museum**

The Opera House ❶

Gustav Mahler by Rodin

V IENNA'S STATE OPERA HOUSE, or Staatsoper, was the first of the grand Ringstrasse buildings to be completed (see pp32–3); it opened on 25 May 1869 to the strains of Mozart's *Don Giovanni*. Built in Neo-Renaissance style, it initially failed to impress the Viennese. Yet when it was hit by a bomb in 1945 and largely destroyed, the event was seen as a symbolic blow to the city. With a brand new auditorium and stage incorporating the latest technology, the Opera House reopened on 5 November 1955 with a performance of Beethoven's *Fidelio*.

Reliefs of Opera and Ballet (1861–9) *Painted allegorical lunettes by Johann Preleuthner represent ballet, tragic opera and comic opera. The one here depicts comic opera.*

The Auditorium

★ **Grand Staircase**
A superb marble staircase sweeps up from the main entrance to the first floor. It is embellished with statues by Josef Gasser of the seven liberal arts (such as Music and Dancing) and reliefs of opera and ballet.

★ **Schwind Foyer**
The foyer is decorated with scenes from operas painted by Moritz von Schwind. Among the busts of famous composers and conductors is Rodin's bronze bust of Mahler (1909).

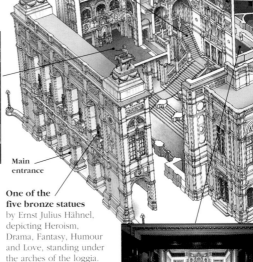

Main entrance

One of the five bronze statues by Ernst Julius Hähnel, depicting Heroism, Drama, Fantasy, Humour and Love, standing under the arches of the loggia.

★ **Tea Room**
Franz Joseph and his entourage used to spend the intervals in this graceful room, which is decorated with silk hangings bearing the Emperor's initials.

STAR FEATURES

★ Grand Staircase

★ Schwind Foyer

★ Tea Room

THE VIENNA OPERA BALL

On the last Thursday of the Vienna Carnival *(see p65)* the stage is extended to cover the seats in the auditorium to create space for the Opera Ball *(see p229)*. This is an expensive society event which opens when the cream of the *jeunesse dorée* – well-to-do girls clad in white and their escorts – take to the floor.

VISITORS' CHECKLIST

Opernring 2, A-1010. **Map** 4 D1 & 5 C5. **(** *514442955.* **Ⓤ** *Karls-platz.* **🚋** *1, 2, D, J.* **◯** *for performances.* **📷** *ring 514442613 for details.* 🎭 📷 ♿ 🖥 🎵
W www.wiener-staatsoper.at

The Architects
The architects of the Opera House were August Siccardsburg (right) and Eduard van der Nüll (left).

Fountain
On either side of the Opera House stand two graceful fountains. Designed by Hans Gasser, this one depicts the legendary siren Lorelei supported by figures representing Grief, Love and Vengeance.

***The Magic Flute* Tapestries**
One of the two side salons, the Gustav Mahler Saal, is hung with modern tapestries by Rudolf Eisenmenger illustrating scenes from The Magic Flute.

BELVEDERE QUARTER

THIS IS A GRANDIOSE and extravagant district. From the Karlsplatz, with its gardens and statues, there is a lovely view of Johann Bernhard Fischer von Erlach's Baroque Karlskirche. East of this great church, visitors can see more delights, including the two palaces of the Belvedere, now public galleries, and the Schwarzenberg Palace, now a hotel. These huge palaces and beautiful gardens were designed by Johann Lukas von Hildebrandt,

Statue of Leonardo da Vinci in the Künstlerhaus

following the crucial defeat of the Turks in 1683. Only after the Turkish threat had been removed was it possible for Vienna to expand. The turbulent history of the city is excellently documented in the Historical Museum of the City of Vienna in Karlsplatz. Just a few paces away is the Musikverein, home to the Vienna Philharmonic. There is also the Bestattungsmuseum (undertakers' museum), that chronicles the importance the Viennese attach to pomp and death.

SIGHTS AT A GLANCE

Streets and Squares
Schwarzenbergplatz ❼
Rennweg ❾

Historic Buildings
Musikverein ❸
Karlsplatz Pavilions ❹
Imperial Hotel ❻
Schwarzenberg Palace ❽
Theresianum ⓭

Museums and Galleries
Historical Museum of the City of Vienna ❷
Künstlerhaus ❺
Palaces and Gardens of the Belvedere pp150–55 ❿
Bestattungsmuseum ⓬

Parks and Gardens
Botanical Gardens ⓫

Churches
Karlskirche pp146–7 ❶

GETTING THERE
This area is served by the Karlsplatz (lines U1, U2, U4) and Taubstummengasse (line U1) U-Bahn stations. Tram 71 runs along Rennweg and Bus 4A goes from Wittelsbachstrasse to Karlsplatz.

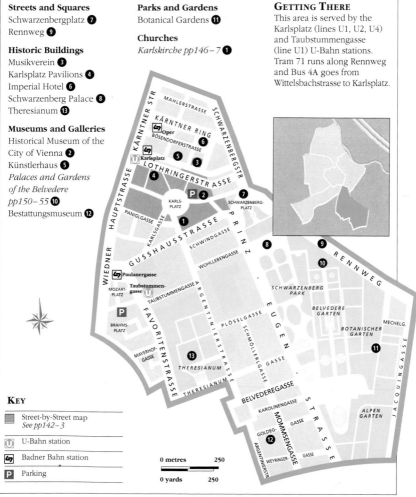

KEY

	Street-by-Street map *See pp142–3*
Ⓤ	U-Bahn station
🚃	Badner Bahn station
🅿	Parking

0 metres 250
0 yards 250

◁ **Botanical Gardens**

Street-by-Street: Karlsplatz

THIS PART OF THE CITY became ripe for development once the threat of Turkish invasion had receded for good in 1683 *(see pp26–7)*. The Ressel Park, at the front of the Karlskirche, gives an unobstructed view of this grandiose church, built on the orders of Karl VI. The park itself is lined with a variety of cultural institutions, notably the Historical Museum of the City of Vienna and, across the road, the Musikverein.

★ **Karlsplatz Pavilions**
These pavilions were built as part of the underground system of 1899 ❹

Underpass

To Karlsplatz U-Bahn

Ressel Park café

The Technical University with its Neo-Classical façade (1816) fronts on to Ressel Park, which contains busts and statues of famous 19th-century Austrian scientists and engineers.

Ressel Statue

STAR SIGHTS
★ **Karlsplatz Pavilions**
★ **Historical Museum of the City of Vienna**
★ **Karlskirche**

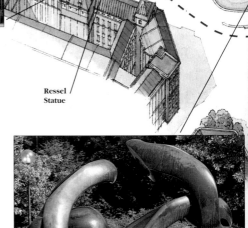

Henry Moore's Hill Arches were presented to the City of Vienna by the artist himself in 1978.

Musikverein
This Ringstrasse-style (see p144) concert hall, home of the Vienna Philharmonic Orchestra, is renowned for its superb acoustics ❸

LOCATOR MAP
See Street Finder, map 4

★ **Historical Museum of the City of Vienna**
This museum houses relics of Roman Vienna, stained glass from the Stephansdom and the reconstructed rooms of celebrated Viennese such as Adolf Loos (see p92) ❷

★ **Karlskirche**
Promised to the people during the 1713 plague, this is Vienna's finest Baroque church ❶

French Embassy

THE ART NOUVEAU FRENCH EMBASSY

Built in 1904–12 by the French architect Georges Chédanne, the Embassy is typical of French Art Nouveau, resembling houses along Rue Victor Hugo in Paris. Unaccustomed to this foreign style, some thought the building was oriental, giving rise to a rumour that its plans had been mixed up with those of the French Embassy in Istanbul.

Art Nouveau façade of the French Embassy

0 metres   50
0 yards   50

– – Suggested route

Karlskirche ❶

See pp146–7.

Historical Museum of the City of Vienna ❷

Karlsplatz. **Map** 4 E2. 📞 *5058747.* Ⓤ *Karlsplatz.* ⏲ *9am–6pm Tue–Sun.* 📷 ♿ 🎦 Ⓦ *www. museum.vienna.at*

The monumental, historicist-style façade of the Musikverein

T HE HISTORICAL MUSEUM of the City of Vienna moved to its current location in 1959. The ground floor usually has Roman and pre-Roman items, as well as exhibits from the Gothic period. These include 14th- and 15th-century gargoyles and figures, and stained glass from the Steph-ansdom, and carved portraits of early rulers of Vienna. These displays are sometimes moved for visiting exhibitions.

The first-floor 16th- and 17th-century exhibits include prints depicting Turkish sieges from 1529 onwards, as well as a portrait of the Turkish commander Kara Mustafa, captured banners and weapons, and prints of the celebrations after Austria's victory. Here too are Johann Bernhard Fischer von Erlach's original plans for the Schönbrunn Palace *(see pp170– 3)*, and the original lantern from No. 6

Schönlaterngasse *(see p74)*. On the second floor are a reconstructed 1798 room from the Caprara-Geymüller Palace in Wallnerstrasse, panelled with painted silks, and the apartment of Austria's most famous poet, Franz Grillparzer. There are displays chronicling the popularity of ballet, theatre and operetta.

Exhibits from this century include Richard Gerstl's portrait of Arnold Schönberg *(see p39)* and portraits by Egon Schiele and Gustav Klimt. There is a room (1903) from Adolf Loos's house *(see p92)* in Bösendorferstrasse, silver- and glassware by Josef Hoffmann, designs from the Wiener Werkstätte *(see p56)* and pictures of Vienna over the past hundred years.

Musikverein ❸

Bösendorferstrasse 12. **Map** 4 E2. 📞 *5058190.* Ⓤ *Karlsplatz.* ⏲ *for concerts only.* 🚫 ♿ Ⓦ *www. musikverein.at*

T HE MUSIKVEREIN building – the headquarters of the Society of the Friends of Music – was designed from 1867 to 1869 by Theophil Hansen, in a mixture of styles employing terracotta statues, capitals and balustrades. It is the home of the great Vienna Philharmonic Orchestra *(see p227)*, which gives regular performances here, and forms the orchestra of the Opera House. The concert hall seats almost 2,000. Tickets are sold on a subscription basis to Viennese music lovers, but some are also available on the day of the performance. The most famous annual event here is the New Year's Day concert *(see p65)*.

Karlsplatz Pavilions ❹

Karlsplatz. **Map** 4 D2. 📞 *5058747.* Ⓤ *Karlsplatz.* ⏲ *Apr–Oct: 1:30–4:30pm Tue–Sun.* 📷

O TTO WAGNER *(see pp54–57)* was responsible for designing and engineering many aspects of the early underground system in the late 19th century. Some of these bridges and tunnels are remarkable in themselves, but cannot match his stylish pair of underground railway exit pavilions (1898–9) alongside

Sunflower motifs on the façade of the Karlsplatz Pavilions

The enormous Hochstrahlbrunnen in Schwarzenbergplatz

Imperial Hotel ❻

Kärntner Ring 16. **Map** 4 E2 & 6 D5.
📞 *50110.* Ⓤ *Karlsplatz.* 📷 ♿
🆆 *www.luxurycollection.com*

Along with the Hotel Sacher *(see p136)*, this is the best known of the 19th-century hotels. You can sip tea to the sound of a pianist playing in the background or stay in the same room Richard Wagner occupied. Adolf Hitler made the hotel his headquarters after the Anschluss *(see p36)*.

Schwarzenberg-platz ❼

Map 4 E2. Ⓤ *Karlsplatz.*

At the centre of this square is the equestrian statue (1867) of Prince Schwarzenberg, who commanded the Austrian and allied armies against Napoleon at the Battle of Leipzig in 1813. This is one of Vienna's grandest squares, combining huge apartment and office blocks, the Ringstrasse and, at the far end of the square, the Baroque splendours of the Schwarzenberg and Belvedere palaces. At the intersection of Prinz-Eugen-Strasse and Gusshausstrasse is the Hochstrahlbrunnen (1873), a fountain which is floodlit at night in summer. Behind it stands the monument to the Red Army, commemorating its liberation of Vienna. It is in full-blown Soviet heroic style and is none too popular with older Viennese, who still recall the brutalities endured in the Russian zone until 1955.

the Karlsplatz, which are among his best-known buildings. The green copper colour of the roofs and the ornamentation complement the Karlskirche beyond. Gilt patterns are stamped onto the white marble cladding and eaves, with repetitions of Wagner's beloved sunflower motif. But the greatest impact is made by the buildings' elegantly curving rooflines. The two pavilions face each other: one is now a café, the other is used for exhibitions.

Künstlerhaus ❺

Karlsplatz 5. **Map** 4 D2 & 6 D5.
📞 *5879663.* Ⓤ *Karlsplatz.*
⏰ *10am–6pm Fri–Wed; 10am–9pm Thu.* 📷 ♿ 🆆 *www.k-haus.at*

Commissioned by the Vienna Artists' Society as an exhibition hall for its members, the Künstlerhaus was built in 1868. The society favoured grand,

academic styles of painting in tune with the historicist Ringstrasse architecture. The Künstlerhaus itself is typical of this style, which is named after the Vienna boulevard where the look is most prevalent *(see pp32–3)*. Designed by August Weber (1836–1903) in a Renaissance palazzo style, the Künstlerhaus is now used for temporary art exhibitions.

Palazzo-style façade of the Künstlerhaus (1868)

Karlskirche ❶

DURING VIENNA'S PLAGUE epidemic in 1713, Emperor Karl VI vowed that as soon as the city was delivered from its plight he would build a church dedicated to St Charles Borromeo (1538–84), a former Archbishop of Milan and a patron saint of the plague. The following year he announced a competition to design the church, which was won by the architect Johann Bernhard Fischer von Erlach. The result was a richly eclectic Baroque masterpiece: the gigantic dome and portico are borrowed from the architecture of ancient Greece and Rome, while there are Oriental echoes in the gatehouses and minaret-like columns. Building took almost 25 years, and the interior was richly embellished with carvings and altarpieces by the foremost artists of the day, including Daniel Gran and Martino Altomonte.

Angel representing the New Testament

The Pulpit
Two putti surmount the canopy of the richly-gilded pulpit, decorated with rocailles and flower garlands.

★ **High Altar**
The high altar features a stucco relief by Albert Camesina showing St Charles Borromeo being assumed into heaven on a cloud laden with angels and putti.

The two gatehouses leading into the side entrances of the church are reminiscent of Chinese pavilions.

Stairway (closed to public)

Pediment reliefs
by Giovanni Stanetti show the suffering of the Viennese during the 1713 plague.

Angel representing the Old Testament

Main entrance

STAR FEATURES

★ **High Altar**

★ **Frescoes in the Cupola**

★ **The Two Columns**

Cupola Cross

★ **Frescoes in the Cupola**
Johann Michael Rottmayr's fresco, painted between 1725 and 1730, depicts the Apotheosis of St Charles Borromeo. It was the painter's last commission.

JOHANN BERNHARD FISCHER VON ERLACH

Many of Vienna's finest buildings, including the Trautson and Schönbrunn Palaces, were designed by Fischer von Erlach (1656–1723). He died before he finished the Karlskirche and his son completed it in 1737.

★ **The Two Columns**
Inspired by Trajan's Column in Rome, they are decorated with spiralling scenes of St Charles Borromeo's life. Qualities of Steadfastness are illustrated on the left, and Courage on the right.

Visitors entrance and tickets

St Charles Borromeo
Lorenzo Mattielli's statue of the patron saint crowns the pediment.

Angel representing the New Testament

Schwarzenberg Palace and Joseph Fischer von Ehrlach's fountain

Schwarzenberg Palace **8**

Schwarzenbergplatz 9. **Map** 4 E2.
See **Where to Stay** p199.

THE PALAIS SCHWARZENBERG was built by Johann Lukas von Hildebrandt *(see p150)* in 1697 and then altered by the Fischer von Erlachs *(see p147)* in the 1720s. The main salon has a domed hall with a magnificent chandelier. Behind the palace are the lawns and shady paths of the park, focused around a pool and fountain designed by Joseph Emanuel Fischer von Erlach. Part of the building has now been converted into a luxurious hotel and restaurant, while one wing is now occupied by the Swiss Embassy. It is only open to guests of the hotel, restaurant and embassy.

The present head of the Schwarzenberg family served as an advisor to President Havel after the Velvet Revolution in Czechoslovakia in 1989.

Rennweg **9**

Map 4 E2. Karlsplatz.
Gardekirche 8am–8pm daily.

RENNWEG RUNS from the Schwarzenbergplatz along the edges of the Belvedere palaces. At No. 3, a house built by Otto Wagner *(see p57)* in 1890 is now the (former) Yugoslav Embassy. Though the façade is in shabby condition, the house remains an interesting example of Wagner's work

just as he was making the transition from Ringstrasse pomp to his later Jugendstil style of architecture.

Next door at No. 5 is where Gustav Mahler *(see p39)* lived from 1898 to 1909. No. 5a is the Gardekirche (1755–63) by Nikolaus Pacassi (1716–99), Maria Theresa's court architect. It was originally built as the church of the Imperial Hospital and since 1897 has been Vienna's Polish church. A huge dome covers the entire interior, which adds to its spaciousness. One feature of interest is the gilt Rococo embellishment over the side chapels and between the ribs of the dome. Just beyond the Belvedere palace gates at No. 6a stands a Baroque mansion, while the forecourt at No. 8 has formed part of the Hoch-

schule für Musik since 1988. At No. 10, behind splendid wrought-iron gates, stands the Salesianerinnenkirche of 1717–30. The Baroque façade is flanked by monastic buildings in the same style. The upper storey has scrolled projections that serve as the base for statues. Like the Gardekirche, this church is domed, its design partly attributed to Joseph Emanuel Fischer von Erlach *(see p147)*. Apart from the pulpit, the interior is of little interest.

At No. 27, the present-day Italian Embassy is the palace where Prince Metternich *(see p30)* lived until he was forced to flee the city in 1848.

Palaces and Gardens of the Belvedere **10**

See pp150–55.

Botanical Gardens **11**

Rennweg 14. **Map** 4 F3. 4277 54192. 71. Easter–mid-Oct: 9am–dusk daily.

THE MAIN ENTRANCE to the Botanical Gardens is on the corner of Prätoriusgasse and Mechelgasse. Other entrances are on Jacquingasse,

Detail of the façade of the Salesianerinnenkirche in Rennweg

and via a small gate at the rear of the Upper Belvedere which leads to the Alpine Garden and the Botanical Gardens. The latter contains more than 9,000 plant species. The Botanical Gardens were created in 1754 by Maria Theresa and her physician van Swieten for cultivating medicinal herbs. Expanded to their present shape in the 19th century, they remain a centre for the study of plant sciences as part of the University of Vienna's Institute of Botany. Of equal interest to amateurs, the gardens offer a quiet spot to sit and relax after sightseeing.

The Botanical Gardens created by Maria Theresa in 1754

Bestattungs-museum ⑫

Goldeggasse 19. **Map** 4 E4. 📞
501954227. ⓤ *Südtiroler Platz.* ⓞ
noon–3pm Mon–Fri (by appt only). 📷

IN VIENNA, DEATH and pomp have always been allied with one another, and even today the Viennese like to be buried in style. For the clearest insight into this fascinating feature of Viennese life, it's worth making a visit to this undertakers' museum.

One of the more eerie items, shown immediately after you enter, is the wrought-iron grille (1784) that formed the entrance to the Catholic cemetery at Matzleindorf. Its motif is of a crowned skeleton. You can see the various lanterns and staffs and liveries that were part of the pall-bearers' equipment from the 17th century onwards, as well as the special livery decked around the horses that pulled the hearse. In the 19th century, Viennese specialist couturiers provided widow's mourning attire complete with black handbag and black jewellery. As in the 19th century a bell was often attached to a rope within the coffin, allowing the recently deceased, should he or she unexpectedly reawaken, to signal the alarm. This device became unnecessary if you requested in your will to be stabbed

in the heart before the coffin lid was nailed down, and the stiletto used for this practice is on display. Other displays show how corpses were dressed up and seated on a chair for one last photograph.

The custodian of the museum will also show you one of Joseph II's *(see p28)* more eccentric innovations from the late 18th century: the economy-model coffin with a trapdoor in the bottom which allowed the shrouded corpse to be dumped into the grave and the coffin to be reused. This story partly illustrates why the tireless reformer was not universally loved by his subjects. His attempts at reform were often perceived as doing more harm than good, or as unnecessary. The emperor was soon forced to abandon this unpopular idea.

Theresianum ⑬

Favoritenstrasse 15. **Map** 4 E3.
ⓤ *Taubstummengasse.* ⓞ *to public.*

THE ORIGINAL BUILDINGS of this former imperial summer palace date from the early 17th century, but were

essentially rebuilt after the Turkish siege of 1683 in a Baroque style by the architect and theatre designer Lodovico Burnacini (1636–1707) and others. Known at that time as the Favorita, it became a favourite residence of emperors Leopold I,

Façade of the Theresianum

Joseph I and Karl VI. In 1746 Maria Theresa, who had moved into Schönbrunn *(see pp170–73),* her summer palace, handed it over to the Jesuits. They established a college here for the education of children from less well-off aristocratic families – the sons of these families were trained to be officials.

Today, the Theresianum is still a school and, since 1964, has also been a college for diplomats and civil servants. In the Theresianum park on Argentinierstrasse stands Radio House. It has a beautiful entrance hall, which was designed by Clemens Holz-meister in 1935.

Matzleindorf cemetery grille (1784) in the Bestattungsmuseum

Palaces and Gardens of the Belvedere ⑩

Statuary on a gate of Lower Belvedere

THE BELVEDERE WAS BUILT BY Johann Lukas von Hildebrandt as the summer residence of Prince Eugene of Savoy, the brilliant military commander whose strategies helped vanquish the Turks in 1683. Situated on a gently sloping hill, the Belvedere consists of two palaces linked by a formal garden laid out in the French style by Dominique Girard. The garden is sited on three levels, each conveying a complicated programme of Classical allusions: the lower part of the garden represents the domain of the Four Elements, the centre is Parnassus and the upper section is Olympus.

★ **Upper Cascade**
Water flows from the upper basin over five shallow steps into the pool below.

***Putti* on the Steps** *(1852)*
Children and cherubs representing the 12 months adorn the steps to the left and right in the middle area of the gardens.

Lower cascade

Bosquet or hedge garden

Statues of the Eight Muses

Lower Belvedere *(see pp154–5)*

Entrance to Lower Belvedere from Rennweg

JOHANN LUKAS VON HILDEBRANDT

Hildebrandt became the court architect in Vienna in 1700 and was one of J B Fischer von Erlach's greatest rivals. In addition to the Belvedere, he designed the Schönborn Palace *(see p110)*, the Kinsky Palace *(see p110)* and the Maria Treu Kirche *(see p116)*.

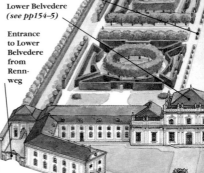

Coloured etching of the Upper Belvedere and Gardens by Karl Schütz (1784)

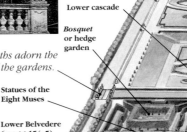

Triumphal gate to Lower Belvedere

TIMELINE

Detail on Upper Cascade

1717–19 Dominique Girard landscapes the gardens	**1765** Lower Belvedere becomes the barracks for the military guard	**1897** Archduke Franz Ferdinand, heir to the throne, moves to the Upper Belvedere		**1953** Museum of Medieval Austrian Art opens to the public
1720 Orangery built		**1781–1891** Belvedere houses the Imperial Picture Gallery, which opens to the public		
1750	**1800**	**1850**	**1900**	**1950**
1721–3 Upper Belvedere built	**1752** Habsburgs acquire the Belvedere		**1923–9** The Baroque Museum, the 19th-century Gallery and the 20th-century Gallery open to the public	**1955** The Austrian State Treaty signed in the Marble Hall
1714–16 Lower Belvedere built	**1779** Belvedere gardens open to the public			

★ **Main Gate of the Upper Belvedere**
*The Baroque iron gate (1728) by Arnold and Konrad
Küffner, with an "S" for Savoy and the cross of Savoy,
leads to the south façade of the Upper Belvedere.*

VISITORS' CHECKLIST

Map 4 F3. *Upper Belvedere
see pp152–3.* **Lower Belvedere
and Orangery** *see pp154–5.*
Gardens ◯ *6:30am–dusk all
year round.* ◉ &

★ **Upper Belvedere Façade**
*The lively façade dominates
the sweeping entrance to the
palace (see pp152–3). The
domed copper roofs of the
end pavilions resemble the
shape of Turkish tents – an
allusion to Prince Eugene's
victories over the Turks.*

**Entrance
to Upper
Belvedere
(see pp152–3)
and gardens
from Prinz-
Eugen-Strasse**

Statues of Sphinxes
*With their lion bodies
and human heads,
the imposing sphinx
statues represent
strength and
intelligence.*

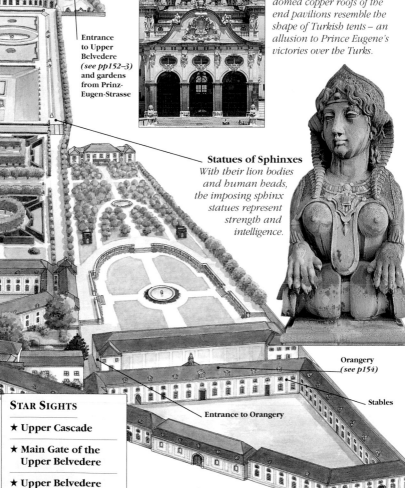

Orangery
(see p154)

Stables

Entrance to Orangery

STAR SIGHTS

★ **Upper Cascade**

★ **Main Gate of the
Upper Belvedere**

★ **Upper Belvedere
Façade**

Upper Belvedere

STANDING AT THE HIGHEST POINT of the garden, the Upper Belvedere has a more elaborate façade than the Lower Belvedere: it was intended to be a symbolic reflection of Prince Eugene's glory, and was appropriate for the festive occasions for which it was originally used. In addition to the impressive interiors of the Sala Terrena with its sweeping staircase, the chapel and the Marble Hall, the building now houses the collections of 19th- and 20th-century paintings belonging to the Austrian Gallery.

Viewing balcony for chapel

★ Chapel
The centrepiece of this brown, white and gold interior is an altarpiece, The Resurrection, *by Francesco Solimena (1723), set among statues of angels. Prince Eugene could enter the chapel from his apartments.*

Laughing Self-Portrait *(1908)*
This picture is by Richard Gerstl, the Viennese artist who was developing his own Expressionist style when he killed himself in his twenties.

GALLERY GUIDE
The ground floor houses temporary exhibitions, art from the turn of the last century is on the first floor along with 19th-century art, which extends onto the second floor where there is also a Biedermeier collection.

KEY

☐ Neo-Classicism-Romanticism

☐ Biedermeier

☐ Art at the turn of the last Century

☐ Historicism-Realism-Impressionism

☐ Temporary Exhibitions

☐ Non-exhibition space

Main entrance from gardens

★ Sala Terrena
Four Herculean figures by Lorenzo Mattielli support the ceiling vault of the Sala Terrena, while white stuccowork by Santino Bussi covers the walls and ceiling.

★ Gustav Klimt Collection
This marvellous Jugend-stil collection by Gustav Klimt is considered by some to be the Belvedere's highlight. In the work here, Judith I *(1901), Klimt depicts the Old Testament heroine as a Viennese femme fatale.*

The Tiger Lion *(1926)*
This savage beast from the 20th-century collection was painted by Oskar Kokoschka, a leading figure in Austrian Expressionism.

Second floor

Marble Hall

The Plain of Auvers *(1890)*
Van Gogh's airy landscape from the 20th-century collection captures the colours of summer fields in the south of France.

First floor

STAR SIGHTS

★ Chapel

★ Gustav Klimt Collection

★ Sala Terrena

Stairs to

Ground floor

Corpus Christi Morning *(1857)*
This bright genre scene is typical of the Austrian Biedermeier painter Ferdinand Georg Waldmüller.

Lower Belvedere and Orangery

THE MUSEUM OF AUSTRIAN BAROQUE ART is housed in the elegant rooms of the Lower Belvedere, which were used by Prince Eugene for day-to-day living. Works of art by the artists and sculptors who shaped the city during Vienna's Golden Age (approximately 1683–1780) are gathered together under its roof. There are paintings by J M Rottmayr, Martino Altomonte, Daniel Gran and Paul Troger amongst others, and sculptures by Franz Xaver Messerschmidt and Georg Raphael Donner.

Exit to Orangery, Museum of Medieval Art and stables

Prince Eugene's former bedroom

★ **Hall of Mirrors**
A statue of Prince Eugene (1721) by Balthasar Permoser stands in this room, whose walls are covered with huge gilt-framed mirrors.

The Marble Hall

Hall of Grotesques
The hall is decorated with paintings of grotesques inspired by ancient Roman frescoes of fantastical creatures. They were created by the German painter Jonas Drentwett.

KEY

☐ Museum of Baroque Art

☐ Non-exhibition space

THE ORANGERY

Next door to the Lower Belvedere is the handsome Orangery building, originally used to shelter tender garden plants in winter. The Museum of Austrian Medieval Art is housed here, and the gallery contains masterpieces of Gothic and early Renaissance painting and sculpture. Notable among the sculptures is the Romanesque Stammerberg Crucifix from the end of the 12th century, which may be the oldest surviving example of Tyrolean woodcarving. Seven painted panels by Rueland Frueauf the Elder (1490–94) show the Passion taking place in an Austrian setting.

★ **Ecce Homo** *(1508)*
Urban Görtschacher's composition shows Pontius Pilate below the judgement hall, condemning Christ.

The Orangery and gardens in winter

St Jacob's Victory over the Saracens *(1764)*
Franz Anton Maulbertsch's painting portrays St Jacob's victory at the Battle of Clavigo.

Intentional Jester *(after 1770)*
Franz Xaver Messerschmidt's Character Heads (studies in physiognomy and temperament) are one of the museum's highlights. Their exaggerated expressions represent a departure from idealized portraiture.

GALLERY GUIDE
The Museum of Austrian Baroque Art displays large works of sculpture in the Marble Hall and the Hall of Grotesques, while smaller exhibits are on show in other rooms.

Christ on the Mount of Olives *(around 1750)*
Paul Troger's painting shows Christ deep in prayer on the Mount of Olives after the Last Supper. This detail depicts him being comforted by an angel.

Library

Main entrance

To gardens

STAR SIGHTS

★ **Hall of Mirrors**

★ **Figures from the Providentia Fountain by G R Donner**

★ **Ecce Homo by Urban Görtschacher**

★ **Figures from the Providentia Fountain** *(1739)*
The original lead figures that Georg Raphael Donner made for the Providentia Fountain in the Neuer Markt (see p105) are displayed in the Marble Hall. This central statue represents Providence.

FURTHER AFIELD

FOR A CITY of almost two million inhabitants, Vienna is supatisingly compact. Nonetheless, some of the most interesting sights are a fair distance from the city centre. At Schönbrunn sprawls the immense palace and gardens so loved by Maria Theresa,

Detail on riding school (1882–6) next to Hermes Villa

and the monastery at Kloster-neuburg houses some of Austria's great ecclesiastical art treasures. Many parks and gardens, including the Prater, the Augarten and the Lainzer Tiergarten, all former private Habsburg domaines, are now open to the public.

SIGHTS AT A GLANCE

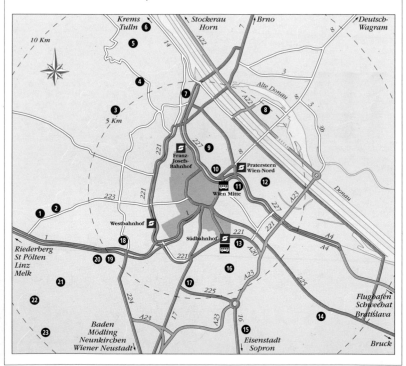

◁ **Part of the façade of the Hundertwasser Haus, built in 1985**

Detail on façade of the Villa Otto Wagner

Wagner Villas ●

Hüttelbergstrasse 26, Penzing.
[9148575. **[U]** Hütteldorf. **[]** 148,
152. **[]** 10am–5pm Mon–Fri. **[]**
[○] **[W]** www.ernstfuchs-zentrum.com

THE VILLA Otto Wagner,
designed by Wagner from
1886 to 1888 as his own residence, is stylistically midway
between his earlier Ringstrasse
architecture and the decorative
elements of Jugendstil (see
pp54–7). The house is built
on a grand scale and incorporates classical elements such
as Ionic columns, and seems
more suitable for a north Italian
hillside than for the more
austere climate of Austria. The
present owner, the painter
Ernst Fuchs (see p36), has
imposed his own personality
on the villa, adding a fertility
statue and garish colours.
   The simpler villa next door
was built more than 20 years
later. Completed in 1913, the
house is of steel and concrete
rather than brick. It is very

lightly decorated in a severe
geometrical style with deep
blue panels and nailhead
ornament. The glass ornament
is by Kolo Moser (see p57).

Kirche am Steinhof ●

Baumgartner Höhe 1, Penzing.
[9106020031. **[T]** 48A.
[] 3pm Sat or by appt. **[]** **[○]**

COMPLETED IN 1907,
this astonishing
church was Otto
Wagner's (see
pp54–7) last
commission. It
is set within the
grounds of the
Psychiatrisches
Krankenhaus, a
large mental
hospital. The
exterior is
marble clad
with nailhead
ornament and
has spindly

screw-shaped pillars, topped
by wreaths, supporting the
porch. Four stone columns
along the façade are adorned
with angels by Othmar
Schimkowitz (1864–1947).
The statues at each corner of
the façade are of St Leopold
and St Severin to the left and
right respectively. They were
designed by Richard Luksch
and are seated in chairs by
Josef Hoffmann (see pp56–7).
   The interior is a single space
with shallow side chapels.
The main decoration consists
of gold and white friezes and
square roof panels orna-
mented with gilt nailhead.
Illumination is provided by
daylight shining through
lovely blue glass windows by
Kolo Moser (see p57).

Geymüller Schlössl ●

Khevenhüllerstrasse 2, Währing.
[711360. **[]** 41A. **[T]** 41.
[] by phone appointment. **[]** **[○]**

THE GEYMÜLLER SCHLÖSSL in
Pötzleinsdorf, northwest of
the city, is a temple to Biedermeier style (see pp30–31).
Dating from 1808, the house
was built for Johann Heinrich
von Geymüller, a rich banker.
Now a branch of the Austrian
Museum of Applied Arts (see
pp82–3), it has a collection of
intricate Biedermeier and
Empire furniture, such as an
apparently simple desk that
combines a writing desk with
a water-colour cabinet.
Gadgets abound: spittoons,
still-lifes painted on porcelain,
bowls, and 200 clocks dating
from 1780 to about 1850, the
heyday of Viennese clock
manufacture.

**Jugendstil angels by Othmar Schimkowitz adorning
the façade of the Kirche am Steinhof**

Grinzing ❹

📞 5138892. Ⓤ Heiligenstadt.
🚌 38A. 🚃 38.

GRINZING IS THE most famous *Heuriger* village *(see pp186–7 & 216)*, but it is also the least authentic, as many of the inns here cater to very large groups of tourists. It is nonetheless very pretty.

It is divided into the Oberer Ort and Unterer Ort (upper and lower towns), the lower town being where you will find more authentic *Heurige* along such lanes as Sandgasse.

Grinzing was repeatedly destroyed by Turkish troops during the many sieges of Vienna *(see p26–7)*, and was again damaged by Napoleon's forces in 1809 *(see p30)*.

Kahlenberg ❺

🚌 38A.

KAHLENBERG, at 484 m (1,585 ft) *(see pp182–3)*, is the highest point of the Vienna Woods. It has a television mast at the top, as well as a church, an observation terrace and a restaurant. The views over the vineyards below and the city beyond are fabulous, with the Danube bridges to the left and the Vienna Woods to the right. The Kahlenberg played a crucial part in the city's history, in 1683 when the Polish king, Jan Sobieski, led his troops down from this spot to the rescue of Viennese forces who were fighting for the city.

Klosterneuburg ❻

Stift Klosterneuburg. 📞 022434110.
🚌 239, 340. Ⓢ Franz-Josefs-Bahnhof to Klosterneuburg-Kierling.
🕐 May–Oct: 9am–noon 1:30–4:30pm Mon–Sat; Nov–Apr: 10am–noon 1:30–4:30pm Mon–Sat; all year: 10am–noon 1:30–4:30pm Sun & public hols. 🎫 daily. 📷 📷

ABOVE THE DANUBE, 13 km (8 miles) north of Vienna, stands the vast monastery and fortress of Klosterneuburg.

The peach- and salmon-coloured façade of the Karl Marx Hof

Dating originally from the 12th century, it houses the astonishing Verduner Altar, completed in 1181 *(see p23)*. In the 18th century it was expanded by Karl VI, who intended to build a complex on the same grand scale as the Escorial palace near Madrid. The work was halted after his death in 1740.

Statue in Grinzing

Karl Marx Hof ❼

Heiligenstädterstrasse 82–92, Döbling. Ⓤ Heiligenstadt. 🚃 D.
⛔ to the public.

THE KARL MARX HOF, dating from 1927 to 1930, is an immense council block which contains 1,382 flats. It is the most celebrated of the municipal housing developments built during the period of Red Vienna *(see p36)*, when 63,000 new dwellings went up across the city between 1919 and 1934. The architect of the Karl Marx Hof was Karl Ehn, a pupil of Otto Wagner *(see p54–7)*.

Danube Park ❽

Ⓤ Alte Donau. 🚌 20B. 🕐 24 hrs daily. **Danube Tower** 📞 26335730.
🕐 9:30am–midnight daily. 📷 ♿

ADJOINING UNO-CITY *(see p37)*, the complex of United Nations agencies, is the Danube Park. Laid out in 1964, the park has cycle paths, cafés and other amenities. Rising 252 m (827 ft) above the park is the Danube Tower, with two revolving restaurants and an observation platform. The park and surrounding area are currently being redeveloped as the Danube City housing project, encompassing the Millennium Tower.

View of the Klosterneuburg monastery with its Baroque dome

Prater ⑫

ORIGINALLY AN IMPERIAL HUNTING GROUND, these woods and meadows between the Danube and its canal were opened to the public by Joseph II in 1766. The central avenue, or Hauptallee, was for a long time the preserve of the nobility and their footmen. During the 19th century the western end of the Prater became a massive funfair with booths, sideshows, beer gardens and *Wurst* stands catering for the Viennese workers.

The Miniature Railway
The Liliputbahn travels a 4-km (2½-mile) circuit.

To Praterstern station

Planetarium

Messegelände exhibition centre

Tennisplätze (Tennis Courts)

★ **Ferris Wheel**
The huge wheel circulates very slowly at a speed of about 75 cm (2½ ft) per second, allowing riders spectacular views over the park and funfair.

★ **Volksprater Funfair**
An amusement park has existed here since the last century. Today the enormous funfair is full of high-tech rides ranging from dodgem cars to ghost trains.

The Trotting Stadium
Built in 1913, the Krieau Stadium is the scene of exciting regional and international trotting races from September to June (see p229).

STAR SIGHTS

★ **Hauptallee**

★ **Volksprater Funfair**

★ **Ferris Wheel**

THE HISTORY OF THE FERRIS WHEEL

One of Vienna's most famous landmarks, the giant Ferris Wheel was immortalized in the film of Graham Greene's *The Third Man*. It was built in 1896 by the English engineer Walter Basset, but it has only half the original number of cabins as fire destroyed many of them in 1945.

VISITORS' CHECKLIST

🄾 🅂 🅕 Praterstern. 🚌 74A.
Funfair 🄾 15 Mar–end Sep:
10am–11pm daily. **Ferris Wheel**
🄾 May–Sep: 9am–midnight daily;
Oct–early Nov & Mar–Apr: 10am–
10pm daily; early Nov–early Jan &
Feb: 10am–6pm daily. ● 24 Dec.
Planetarium 🄾 for performances
3 & 5pm Sun. ● 9 Jan–18 Feb,
12 Nov–25 Dec, Aug. **Miniature
railway** 🄾 15 Mar–mid Oct:
10am–11pm daily. **Golf course**
🄾 8am– 4pm Mon–Thu. **Stadionbad** 🄾 29 Apr–16 Sept: 9am–7pm
Mon–Fri, 8am–7pm Sat & Sun.
Maria Grun Kirche 🄾 10am–
3pm Sun. **Lusthaus** 🄾 1 Apr–
end Oct: noon–11pm Mon–Tue &
Thu–Fri; all year: noon–6pm Sat,
Sun & public hols. 🄾

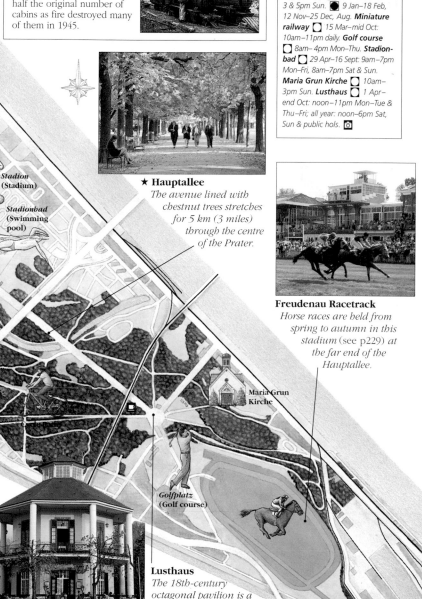

Stadion
(Stadium)

Stadionbad
(Swimming pool)

★ **Hauptallee**
The avenue lined with chestnut trees stretches for 5 km (3 miles) through the centre of the Prater.

Freudenau Racetrack
Horse races are held from spring to autumn in this stadium (see p229) at the far end of the Hauptallee.

Maria Grun Kirche

Golfplatz
(Golf course)

Lusthaus
The 18th-century octagonal pavilion is a former hunting lodge which now houses a restaurant.

Baroque façade of the Augarten Palace set amid 18th-century parkland

Augarten Palace and Park **9**

Obere Augartenstrasse 1. **Map** 2 E2.
🚋 5A. Ⓤ *Praterstern.* 🚎 *31, 32.*
◯ *6am–dusk daily.* **Porcelain Museum** ◯ *9:30am–6pm Mon–Fri, 9:30am–noon Sat.* **Ambrosi Museum** ◯ *10am–5pm Tue–Sun.* 📷 ♿

THERE HAS BEEN a palace on this site since the days of Leopold I, when it was known as the Alte Favorita, but it was destroyed by the Turks in 1683 and then rebuilt around 1700 to a design attributed to Johann Bernhard Fischer von Erlach *(see p147)*. Since 1948 it has been the home of the Vienna Boys' Choir *(see p39)* and consequently it is inaccessible to the public.

The park was planted in the second half of the 17th century, renewed in 1712, and opened to the public in 1775 by Joseph II. The handsome gates by which the public now enters the gardens were designed by Isidor Canevale in 1775. Mozart, Beethoven, and Johann Strauss I all gave concerts in the park pavilion. The Augarten was also used for royal receptions and gatherings while the Congress of Vienna *(see p30)* was taking place in 1815. The pavilion used to be the imperial porcelain factory, founded in the 18th century, but has been run since the 1920s by the municipal authorities. Its showroom has displays showing the history of Augarten porcelain. Behind the pavilion is the studio of the early 20th-century sculptor Gustinus Ambrosi, open to the public as the Ambrosi Museum.

The Augarten has the oldest Baroque garden in Vienna, with topiary lining long paths shaded by walls of foliage. In the distance, you can see two of the huge and terrifying flakturms that the Viennese are unable to rid themselves of. Built by German forces in 1942 as defense towers and anti-aircraft batteries, these enormous concrete monoliths could house thousands of troops. So thick are their walls that any explosives powerful enough to destroy them would have a similar effect on the surrounding residential areas. There are four other such flakturms still standing in other parts of the city.

Kriminalmuseum **10**

Grosse Sperlgasse 24. **Map** 6 E1.
📞 *2144678.* Ⓤ *Nestroyplatz.*
🚋 *5A.* 🚎 *N, 21.* ◯ *10am–5pm Thu–Sun.* 📷

SINCE 1991, this house of medieval origin has been the home of Vienna's museum of crime. Once known as the *Seifensiederhaus* (the soap

Hundertwasser Haus **11**

Löwengasse/ Kegelgasse.
Ⓤ *Landstrasse.* 🚎 *Hetzgasse.*
⬤ *to the public.*

THE HUNDERTWASSER HAUS is a municipal apartment block created in 1985 by the artist Friedensreich Hundertwasser *(see p37)*, who wished to strike a blow against what he saw as soulless modern architecture. The resulting building, with its irregular bands of colour and onion dome cupolas, has been controversial since its construction. While it is loved by some, others think it is more like a stage set than a block of flats.

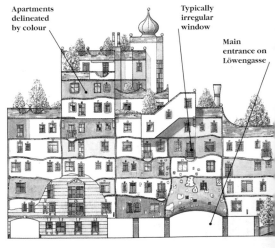

Apartments delineated by colour

Typically irregular window

Main entrance on Löwengasse

boiler's house), this museum's 20 rooms mostly chronicle violent crime, charting the murderous impulses of Vienna's citizenry from the Middle Ages to the 20th century, and the history of the judicial system.

Many of the exhibits come from the archives of the Viennese police force and are distinctly gruesome; there is a wide selection of murder weapons, mummified heads of executed criminals, death masks and case histories

Painting depicting a 1782 robbery

illustrated with photographs and prints. Many of the more unsettling exhibits give a notion of how the Viennese poor of earlier centuries were involved in crime. Political crimes, such as the lynching of a government minister during the revolution of 1848 *(see p30)*, are also covered.

This interesting museum provides a blend of documentary social history and a chamber of horrors which portrays the darker side of Viennese life with gusto.

Prater ⓬

See pp160–61.

Heeresgeschicht-liches Museum ⓭

See pp164–5.

Central Cemetery ⓮

See pp166–7.

Favoriten Water Tower ⓯

Windtenstrasse 3, Favoriten.
☎ 5995931006. Ⓤ *Reumannplatz.*
🚌 15A. 🚋 65, 65A, 7A, 15A. ⬜ *for guided tours (phone to arrange).*

A COMPLEX KNOWN as the Favoriten pumping station was constructed in 1889 by Franz Borkowitz as part of a municipal scheme for the transportation of drinking water from the Alpine foothills to the rapidly-growing city. By 1910 the construction of other installations around Vienna meant that the operations of the complex had to be scaled down, and of the seven original buildings only the highly decorative yellow-and-red-brick

water tower remains. The fascinating feature of this incongruous-looking tower that soars 67 m (220 ft) into the sky is the original pumping equipment which is still in place. Its utilitarian appearance provides a stark contrast to the ornate turrets, pinnacles and tiles of the building's superstructure. In recent years the interior has been restored and guided tours are available to the public. Nearby is the small children's funfair, the Böhmische Prater *(see p232).*

Favoriten Water Tower

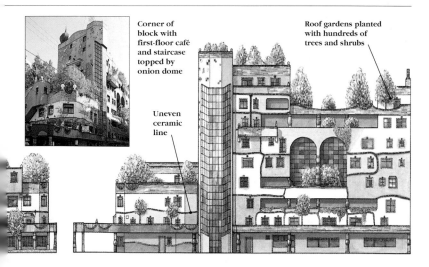

Corner of block with first-floor café and staircase topped by onion dome

Roof gardens planted with hundreds of trees and shrubs

Uneven ceramic line

Heeresgeschichtliches Museum ⓭

THIS IMPRESSIVE MUSEUM of army history is housed in a single block of the military complex known as the Arsenal. It was completed in fortress style in 1856. Theophil Hansen designed the museum itself *(see façade, right)*, which chronicles Austria's military prowess from the 16th century onwards. Exhibits relate to the Turkish siege of 1683, the French Revolution and the Napoleonic wars. Visitors should not miss seeing the car in which Archduke Franz Ferdinand was assassinated, or the modern armaments used in the war that the murder precipitated.

KEY

☐ Tank park
☐ 16th–19th centuries
☐ 19th and 20th centuries
☐ Non-exhibition space

Ground floor

Sea Power Austria

Republic and Dictatorship 1918–1945

Tank Park
Situated behind the museum are the armoured vehicles used in the Austrian army from 1955 as well as those that belonged to the German army that occupied Austria.

Main entrance from Ghegastrasse

THE ASSASSINATION OF FRANZ FERDINAND

On 28 June 1914 the heir to the throne, Archduke Franz Ferdinand, and his wife Sophie von Hohenberg paid a visit to Sarajevo. Gavrilo Princip, a Serbian nationalist, assassinated the couple, provoking an international crisis that later resulted in World War I. The museum houses the car in which the couple were killed.

MUSEUM GUIDE
The museum is housed on two floors. To view it in chronological order, begin on the first floor on the left, where exhibits relating to the Turkish siege are displayed. Other rooms chronicle the various 18th-century wars and Napoleon's victory over Austria. The 19th and 20th centuries, including heavy artillery used in World War I, are covered on the ground floor. There is also a tank park.

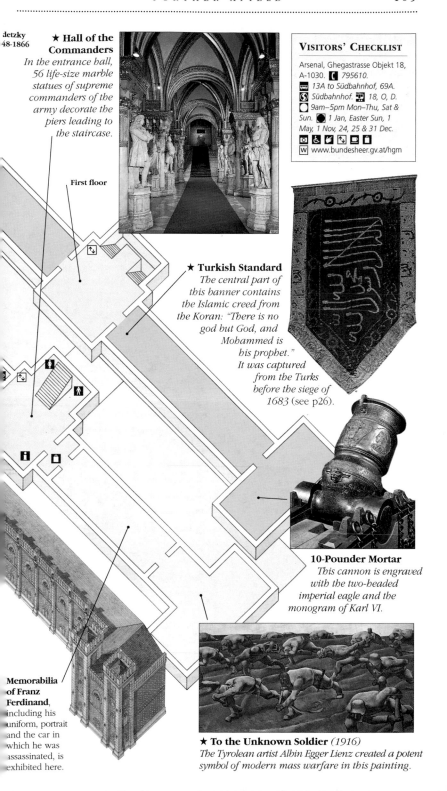

detzky
48-1866

★ Hall of the Commanders
In the entrance hall, 56 life-size marble statues of supreme commanders of the army decorate the piers leading to the staircase.

First floor

VISITORS' CHECKLIST

Arsenal, Ghegastrasse Objekt 18, A-1030. 795610.
13A to Südbahnhof, 69A.
Südbahnhof. 18, O, D.
9am–5pm Mon–Thu, Sat & Sun. 1 Jan, Easter Sun, 1 May, 1 Nov, 24, 25 & 31 Dec.
W www.bundesheer.gv.at/hgm

★ Turkish Standard
The central part of this banner contains the Islamic creed from the Koran: "There is no god but God, and Mohammed is his prophet." It was captured from the Turks before the siege of 1683 (see p26).

10-Pounder Mortar
This cannon is engraved with the two-headed imperial eagle and the monogram of Karl VI.

Memorabilia of Franz Ferdinand, including his uniform, portrait and the car in which he was assassinated, is exhibited here.

★ To the Unknown Soldier (1916)
The Tyrolean artist Albin Egger Lienz created a potent symbol of modern mass warfare in this painting.

Central Cemetery ⑭

AUSTRIA'S LARGEST burial ground, containing two and a half million graves, was opened in 1874 on the city's southern outskirts. The central section includes graves of artists, composers, architects, writers and local politicians.

Headstone of Brahms' grave

Funerals are usually quite lavish affairs, as the Viennese like to be buried in style, with the pomp appropriate to their station in life. The cemetery contains a vast array of funerary monuments varying from the humble to the bombastic, paying tribute to the city's enduring obsession with death.

★ Dr-Karl-Lueger-Kirche
Max Hegele, a pupil of Otto Wagner, designed this church dedicated to Vienna's mayor in 1907–10.

Arcades around the Dr-Karl-Lueger-Kirche

Presidential Vault
This contains the remains of Dr Karl Renner, the first President of the Austrian Republic after World War II.

Fritz Wotruba's grave (see p169)

CEMETERY LAYOUT

The cemetery is divided into specific numbered sections: apart from the central garden of honour where VIPs are buried, there are old and new Jewish cemeteries; a Protestant cemetery; a Russian Orthodox section and various war graves and memorials. It is easier to take the circulating bus that covers the whole area than to walk.

The Monument to the Dead of World War I is a powerful depiction of a mother lamenting by Anton Hanak.

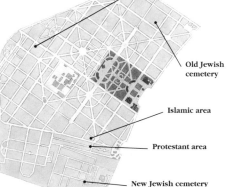

Old Jewish cemetery

Islamic area

Protestant area

New Jewish cemetery

Arnold Schönberg's Cube
The grave of the modernist Viennese composer Arnold Schönberg is marked with this bold cube by Fritz Wotruba.

STAR SIGHTS

★ Musicians' Graves

★ Dr-Karl-Lueger-Kirche

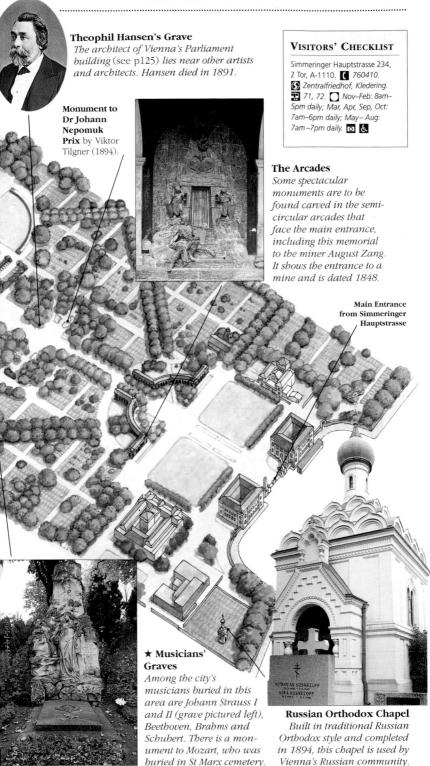

Theophil Hansen's Grave
The architect of Vienna's Parliament building (see p125) lies near other artists and architects. Hansen died in 1891.

VISITORS' CHECKLIST

Simmeringer Hauptstrasse 234,
2 Tor, A-1110. 760410.
Zentralfriedhof, Kledering.
71, 72. Nov–Feb: 8am–
5pm daily; Mar, Apr, Sep, Oct:
7am–6pm daily; May–Aug:
7am–7pm daily.

Monument to Dr Johann Nepomuk Prix by Viktor Tilgner (1894).

The Arcades
Some spectacular monuments are to be found carved in the semi-circular arcades that face the main entrance, including this memorial to the miner August Zang. It shows the entrance to a mine and is dated 1848.

Main Entrance from Simmeringer Hauptstrasse

★ Musicians' Graves
Among the city's musicians buried in this area are Johann Strauss I and II (grave pictured left), Beethoven, Brahms and Schubert. There is a monument to Mozart, who was buried in St Marx cemetery.

Russian Orthodox Chapel
Built in traditional Russian Orthodox style and completed in 1894, this chapel is used by Vienna's Russian community.

Amalienbad ⑯

Reumannplatz 23, Favoriten.
📞 6074747. ⓤ Reumannplatz. 🚌
7A, 14A, 66A, 67A, 68A. 🚊 6, 67.
Swimming pool ◯ 9am–6pm Tue,
9am–9:30pm Wed & Fri, 7am–9:30pm
Thu, 7am–8pm Sat, 7am–6pm Sun.
Sauna ◯ 1–9:30pm Tue, 9am–
9:30pm Wed–Fri, 7am–8pm Sat,
7am–6pm Sun. ♿

PUBLIC BATHS may not seem
like an obvious tourist
destination, but the Jugendstil
Amalienbad (1923–6) shows
how the municipal administration in the 1920s not only
provided essential public
facilities, but did so with
stylistic vigour and conviction.
The two designers, Otto
Nadel and Karl Schmalhofer,
were employees of the city's
architectural department.

The magnificent main pool
is covered by a glass roof that
can be opened in minutes and
is surrounded by galleries overlooking the pool. Elsewhere
in the building are saunas
and smaller baths and pools
used for therapeutic purposes.
When first opened, the baths
were one of the largest of
their kind in Europe, designed
to accommodate 1,300 people.
The interior is enlivened by
imaginative mosaic and tile
decoration, which is practical
as well as colourful. The
baths were damaged in World
War II but were impeccably
restored in 1986.

Spinnerin am Kreuz

Spinnerin am Kreuz ⑰

Triesterstrasse 10, Meidling.
ⓤ Meidling. 🚌 15A, 65A, 7A. 🚊 65.

A MEDIEVAL COLUMN marks the
southernmost boundary
of Vienna's inner suburbs.
Built in 1452 and carved on
all sides, it stands on the spot
where, according to legend, a
woman sat spinning for years
awaiting her husband's return
from the Crusades. Known as
the Spinner at the Cross, it was
designed by Hans Puchsbaum.
Pinnacled canopies shelter
groups of statuary, including a
crucifixion and a grotesque
figure placing the crown of
thorns on the head of Christ.

Technical Museum ⑱

Mariahilfer Strasse 212, Penzing.
📞 899980. ◯ 9am–6pm Mon–Wed
& Fri–Sat, 9am–8pm Thu, 10am–6pm
Sun. 📷 ♿ 🆆 www.tmw.ac.at

FRANZ JOSEPH founded the
Technisches Museum Wien
in 1908, using the Habsburgs'
personal collections as core
material; it opened its doors
10 years later. It documents all
aspects of technical progress,
from domestic appliances to
large turbines, and includes
exhibitions on heavy industry,
energy, physics and musical
instruments.

A major new section of the
museum opened in June
1999, featuring displays on
computer technology and oil
and gas drilling and refining,
as well as a reconstruction of
a coal mine.

The Railway Museum, which
is due to reopen in 2001,
forms an integral part of the
Technical Museum. It houses
an extensive collection of imperial railway carriages and
engines. One of the prize exhibits is the imperial carriage
used by Franz Joseph's wife,
the Empress Elisabeth.

Schönbrunn Palace and Gardens ⑲

See pp170–73.

Decorative, geometrically-patterned tiling from the 1920s in the Amalienbad

Kaiser Pavilion ⑳

Schönbrunner Schlosstrasse 13, Hietzing.
📞 8771571. 🚇 Hietzing. 🚌 51A,
56B, 58B, 156B. 🚉 Westbahnhof to
Penzing. 🚋 10, 60, 62.
🕐 1:30–4:30pm Tue –Sun. 📷

OTTO WAGNER *(see p57)* designed and built this railway station between Schönbrunn and Hietzing for the imperial family and royal guests in 1899. A lovely building in the shape of a white cube with green iron-work and a copper dome, it has a waiting room panelled with wood and glass, with a peach and russet asymmetrical carpet, and a stylish marble and brass fireplace. The cupola is decorated with glass and gilt flower and leaf motifs.

Wagner built the pavilion without a commission from the emperor in an attempt to showcase his work. Unfortunately, Franz Joseph used the station only twice.

The Jugendstil Kaiser Pavilion

Werkbund-siedlung ㉑

Jagdschlossgasse, Veitingergasse and Woinovichgasse, Hietzing. 🚌 54B, 55B. 🚋 60.

IN THE 13TH DISTRICT you can find the 30 or so fascinating "model" houses of the *Werkbundsiedlung* (housing estate) built in the early 1930s for the municipality by some of Europe's leading architects. They are neither beautiful nor lavish, since the idea was to produce a formula for cheap housing, with two bedrooms,

Hermes Villa in the grounds of the Lainzer Tiergarten

that was plain and functional. No. 19 Woinovichgasse is by Adolf Loos *(see p92)*, and Nos. 83–5 Veitingergasse are by Josef Hoffmann *(see p56)*. Each architect had to design a single building, placed side by side with the rest in order to evaluate the different qualities of each. Although intended to be temporary, they have luckily survived.

Lainzer Tiergarten ㉒

Lainzer Tiergarten, Hietzing. **Tiergarten**
📞 8041315. 🚌 60A. 🕐 mid-Feb–
mid-Nov: 8am–dusk daily. 📷 **Hermes
Villa and Garden** 📞 8041324.
🕐 for exhibitions 10am–6pm
Tue–Sun & public hols. 📷

THE LAINZER TIERGARTEN is a former Habsburg hunting ground which has been converted into an immense nature reserve in the Vienna Woods *(see p174)*. The Tiergarten was opened to the public in 1923 and is still encircled by its 24-km (15-mile) stone wall, protecting its herds of deer and wild boar. From the entrance, a 15-minute walk along paths through woods and meadows brings you to the Hermes Villa, built by Karl von Hasenauer in 1884. It became a retreat for the imperial family, notably the Empress Elisabeth and her husband Franz

Joseph, who had a suite of rooms on the first floor. Inside are murals of scenes from *A Midsummer Night's Dream*, as well as art and historical exhibitions.

Wotruba Kirche ㉓

Georgsgasse/Rysergasse, Mauer.
📞 8886147. 🚌 60A. 🕐 2–7:30pm
Sat, 9am–4pm Sun or 📞 888 5003 for
appointment to see the church. 📷

BUILT BETWEEN 1965 and 1976 in uncompromisingly modern style, this church stands on a hillside very close to the Vienna Woods. It forms a pile of uneven rectangular concrete slabs and glass panels, some of the latter rising to the height of the church. They provide its principal lighting and views for the congregation out on to the woods and hills. The building is raw in style, but powerful and compact. Designed by the sculptor Fritz Wotruba (1907–75), the church looks different from every angle and has a strong sculptural quality. It can accommodate a congregation of up to 250, and has a sacristy in the basement.

The exterior of the Wotruba Kirche by Fritz Wotruba, not unlike a modern sculpture

Schönbrunn Palace and Gardens ⓳

THE FORMER SUMMER RESIDENCE of the imperial family
takes its name from a beautiful spring that was found
on this site. An earlier hunting lodge was destroyed by
the Turks, so Leopold I asked Johann Bernhard Fischer
von Erlach to design a grand Baroque residence here in
1695. However, it was not until Maria Theresa employed
Nikolaus Pacassi that the project was completed in the
mid-18th century. The strict symmetry of the architecture
is complemented by the gardens with fountains
and statues framed by trees and alleyways.

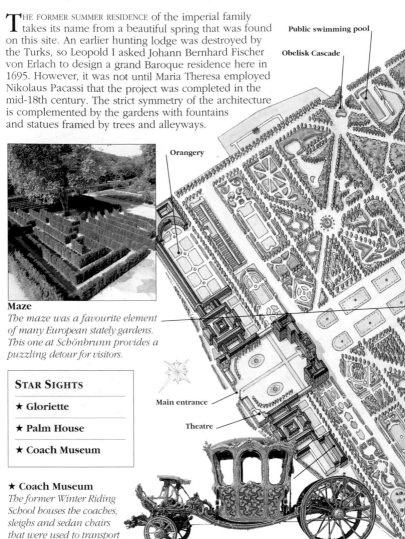

Public swimming pool

Obelisk Cascade

Orangery

Maze
*The maze was a favourite element
of many European stately gardens.
This one at Schönbrunn provides a
puzzling detour for visitors.*

Main entrance

Theatre

STAR SIGHTS

★ **Gloriette**

★ **Palm House**

★ **Coach Museum**

★ **Coach Museum**
*The former Winter Riding
School houses the coaches,
sleighs and sedan chairs
that were used to transport
the imperial family.*

TIMELINE

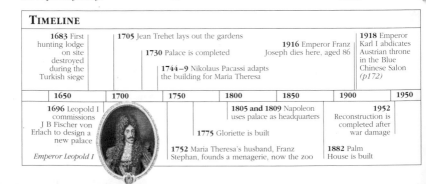

1683 First hunting lodge on site destroyed during the Turkish siege	**1705** Jean Trehet lays out the gardens					**1918** Emperor Karl I abdicates Austrian throne in the Blue Chinese Salon *(p172)*
	1730 Palace is completed		**1916** Emperor Franz Joseph dies here, aged 86			
		1744–9 Nikolaus Pacassi adapts the building for Maria Theresa				

1650	1700	1750	1800	1850	1900	1950

1696 Leopold I commissions J B Fischer von Erlach to design a new palace			**1805 and 1809** Napoleon uses palace as headquarters		**1952** Reconstruction is completed after war damage
Emperor Leopold I		**1775** Gloriette is built			
		1752 Maria Theresa's husband, Franz Stephan, founds a menagerie, now the zoo		**1882** Palm House is built	

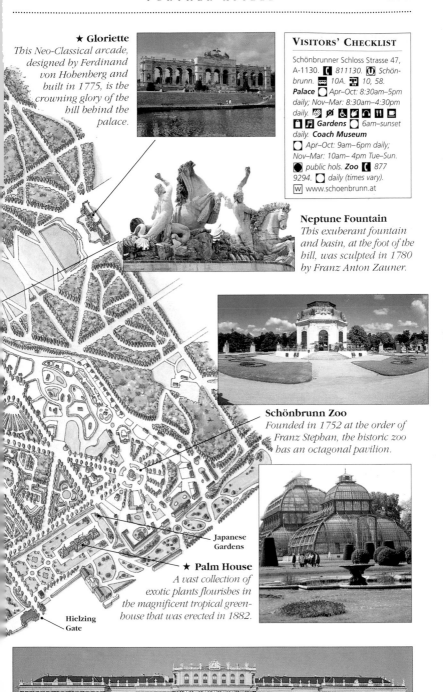

★ Gloriette

This Neo-Classical arcade, designed by Ferdinand von Hohenberg and built in 1775, is the crowning glory of the hill behind the palace.

Visitors' Checklist

Schönbrunner Schloss Strasse 47, A-1130. **(** 811130. **①** Schönbrunn. **🚌** 10A. **🚋** 10, 58. **Palace** ◯ Apr–Oct: 8:30am–5pm daily; Nov–Mar: 8:30am–4:30pm daily. 🚫 🔌 🛗 🔲 🎫 🏪 🔲 🏪 🎵 **Gardens** ◯ 6am–sunset daily. **Coach Museum** ◯ Apr–Oct: 9am–6pm daily; Nov–Mar: 10am–4pm Tue–Sun. ● public hols. **Zoo (** 877 9294. ◯ daily (times vary). Ⓦ www.schoenbrunn.at

Neptune Fountain

This exuberant fountain and basin, at the foot of the hill, was sculpted in 1780 by Franz Anton Zauner.

Schönbrunn Zoo

Founded in 1752 at the order of Franz Stephan, the historic zoo has an octagonal pavilion.

Japanese Gardens

★ Palm House

A vast collection of exotic plants flourishes in the magnificent tropical greenhouse that was erected in 1882.

Hielzing Gate

Façade of Schönbrunn Palace seen from the gardens

Inside Schönbrunn Palace

THE ROCOCO DECORATIVE SCHEMES devised by Nikolaus Pacassi dominate the Schönbrunn state rooms, where white panelling, often adorned with gilded ornamental framework, tends to prevail. The rooms vary from extremely sumptuous – such as the Millionen-Zimmer, panelled with fig wood inlaid with Persian miniatures – to the quite plain apartments occupied by Franz Joseph and Empress Elisabeth.

★ Round Chinese Cabinet
Maria Theresa used this room for private discussions with her State Chancellor. The walls are adorned with lacquered panels and vases.

★ Great Gallery
Once the venue for imperial banquets, the gallery was used for state receptions as recently as 1994.

Hidden staircase
which leads to the apartment of the State Chancellor on the floor above and was used for access to secret conferences.

Blue Chinese Salon
The room where Karl I abdicated in 1918 has hand-painted wallpaper with blue insets showing Chinese scenes.

Napoleon Room

Millionen-Zimmer

Memorial Room

First Floor

★ Vieux-Lacque Room
During her widowhood, Maria Theresa lived in this room, which is decorated with exquisite oriental lacquered panels.

Main entrance

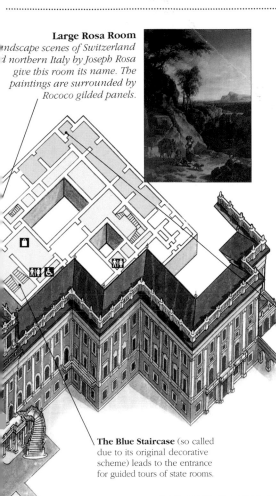

Large Rosa Room
Landscape scenes of Switzerland and northern Italy by Joseph Rosa give this room its name. The paintings are surrounded by Rococo gilded panels.

Breakfast Room
The imperial family's breakfast room has white wood panelling inlaid with appliqué floral designs worked by Maria Theresa and her daughters.

The Blue Staircase (so called due to its original decorative scheme) leads to the entrance for guided tours of state rooms.

STAR SIGHTS

- ★ **Round Chinese Cabinet**
- ★ **Great Gallery**
- ★ **Vieux-Lacque Room**

ROOM GUIDE
The state rooms open to the public are on the first floor. The suite of rooms to the right of the Blue Staircase were occupied by Franz Joseph and Elisabeth. Two galleries divide these from rooms in the east wing, which include Maria Theresa's bedroom and rooms used by Grand Duke Karl. The ground-floor Bergl rooms are only open on special occasions.

KEY

- ☐ Franz Joseph's apartments
- ☐ Empress Elisabeth's apartments
- ☐ Ceremonial and reception rooms
- ☐ Maria Theresa's rooms
- ☐ Grand Duke Karl's rooms
- ☐ Non-exhibition space

Portrait of Napoleon

Portrait of Maria Louisa

MARIA LOUISA AND THE KING OF ROME

After Napoleon's fall from power, his young son by his Austrian wife Maria Louisa was kept a virtual prisoner in Schönbrunn Palace. In 1832 at the age of 21, after a lonely childhood, he died of consumption in what is known as the Napoleon Room. He was called the Duke of Reichstadt, or the King of Rome, and the Memorial Room contains his portrait as a five-year-old and his effigy. There is also a crested larch under a glass dome; the unhappy boy claimed that he never had a single friend in the palace apart from this bird.

Day Trips from Vienna

WITHIN AN HOUR OR TWO'S JOURNEY from Vienna there is an astonishing range of countryside from Hungarian-style plains to alpine mountains, majestic rivers and idyllic lakes. Vienna is at the centre of Austria's wine-growing country and is surrounded by historic castles and churches, among which nestle picturesque wine-producing towns and villages. All the sights are accessible by bus or train and trips such as Baden and Gumpoldskirchen can easily be combined.

Mayerling and the Vienna Woods ❶

Vienna Sightseeing organizes trips (see p237). 🚌 *365 from Südtiroler Platz to Mayerling and Heiligenkreuz, or 265 to Heiligenkreuz.* **Mayerling Chapel** 📞 *02258 2275.* ⏱ *1 Apr–1 Oct: 9am–12:30pm, 1:30–5:45pm Mon–Sat, 10am–12:30pm, 1:30–5:45pm Sun; 2 Oct–31 Mar: 9am–12:30pm, 1:30–4:45pm Mon–Sat, 10am–12:30pm, 1:30–4:45pm Sun. Ring bell for attention.* ⏺ *1 Jan, Good Friday, 25 Dec.* **Heiligenkreuz Abbey** 📞 *02258 8703131. Phone to check opening hours.* 📷 *obligatory.*

WHERE THE LOWER slopes of the Alps meet the Danube and Vienna Woods there are several interesting sights.

The Mayerling hunting lodge, now the chapel, was the scene in 1889 of the double suicide of Crown Prince Rudolf *(see p32)*, heir to the Austro-Hungarian throne, and his 17-year-old lover Mary Vetsera, daughter of the diplomat Baron Albin Vetsera. Their tragic deaths shook the entire Austro-Hungarian empire and were the subject of the Viennese musical *Elisabeth* by the Hungarian Sylvester Levay. After his son's death, the distraught Emperor Franz Joseph gave the hunting lodge to a Carmelite convent and it was completely rebuilt. Some of Crown Prince Rudolf's furniture remains in the chapel.

A few miles north of Mayerling is the medieval Cistercian abbey of Heiligenkreuz. Much of the abbey was rebuilt in the Baroque period, having been largely destroyed during attacks by the Turks in 1529 and 1683. Inside is a 12th-century nave and a 13th-century chapter house (with Baroque wall paintings). Fine Baroque features include the bell tower and Trinity Column. The abbey houses the tombs of 13 of the Babenbergs who ruled in Austria during the medieval period *(see pp22–3)*.

Baden ❷

🚌 *552, 360W or 1134 (Mariazell) from Wien Mitte.* 🚆 *or* 🚊 *from Südbahnhof.* 🚋 *Badner Bahn (WLB) from Karlsplatz/Oper.* 🎫 *02252 4453157.*

TO THE SOUTH of Vienna are several spas and wine-growing towns in the hills of the southern Vienna Woods. The most famous is Baden, a spa with curative hot springs dating back to Roman times. As well as bathing in sulphurous water and mud to treat rheumatism, you can enjoy hot pools of 36°C (97°F).

In the early 19th century Baden was popular with the Imperial Court of Vienna. Then many elegant Biedermeier

Gumpoldskirchen wine festival

villas, baths, town houses and a square were built, and the gardens of the Kurpark laid out. The park extends from the town centre to the Vienna Woods and has a rose garden and a memorial museum to Beethoven and Mozart. Today you can sample local wines in Baden's restaurants.

KEY

■	City centre
▢	Greater Vienna
✈	Airport
▬	Motorway
▬	Major road
▬	Minor road

25 kilometres = 15 miles

Gumpoldskirchen ❸

🚆 *or* 🚊 *from Südbahnhof or Baden.* 🎫 *02252 63536.*

TYPICAL WHITE WINES are available from the pretty medieval village of Gumpoldskirchen, where many houses dating from the 16th century are still in use as *Heurige* (wine taverns). Twice a year, in late June and at the end of August, the main streets are converted into one enormous *Heuriger* for the famous Gumpoldskirchen wine festivals. There are also magnificent walks among the surrounding vineyards.

Eisenstadt ❹

🚌 *566 or 766 from Wien Mitte to Eisenstadt Domplatz.* 🚆 *from Südbahnhof; change at Bruck an der Leitha.* 🎫 *02682 63384.* **Schloss Esterházy** 📞 *02682 7193000.* ⏱ *Apr–Oct: 9am–6pm daily; Nov–Mar* 📷 *only, 10am & 2pm Mon–Fri.* **Haydn Museum** ⏱ *Easter–Oct: 9am–noon, 1–5pm daily.* **Jewish Museum** ⏱ *May–Oct: 10am–5pm Tue–Sun.*

TO THE SOUTHEAST of Vienna lies Burgenland, Austria's easternmost province and part of Hungary until 1918. Here

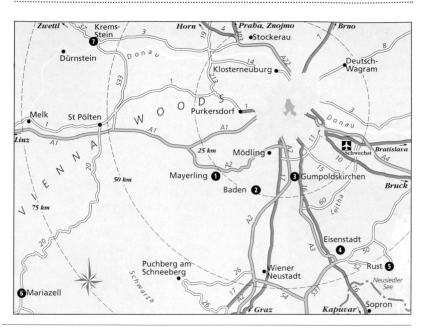

you can see the imposing residence of the Esterházy Princes, who claimed to be descended from Attila. Schloss Esterházy was built for Prince Paul Esterházy in 1663–73 and contains the Haydnsaal, a great hall of state decorated with 18th-century frescoes. Joseph Haydn (*see pp38–9*) conducted the prince's orchestra here and lived nearby on Haydngasse; his house is now a museum. He is buried in the Bergkirche, west of Schloss Esterházy.

Until World War II, Eisenstadt had a significant Jewish population, and there is a Jewish Museum near the palace.

Rust and Lake Neusiedl **5**

🚌 566 or 766 from Eisenstadt; 666 from Wien Mitte. 🛈 02685 502.

TEN MILES (15 km) east of Eisenstadt lies the 320 sq km (124 sq mile) Lake Neusiedl, part of which is in Hungary. The lake is surrounded by reeds, the home of dozens of species of wild birds. The reeds are used locally for folk crafts from thatching to basketwork. Around the lake are several wine villages and resorts, of which the prettiest is the town of Rust. It is known for the storks which nest on its roofs and towers, and for its wine.

Mariazell **6**

🚌 552 via Baden or 1150 from Wien Mitte. 🚉 from Westbahnhof, change at St Pölten to Mariazell alpine railway. 🛈 03882 2366. **Basilica** ◯ 6am–8pm daily. 📷 🛈 0388 22595 for tours. **Steam tram** 🛈 0388 23014. ◯ Jul–Sep: 10:30am–4:30pm Sat, Sun & hols.

THE JOURNEY to Mariazell from St Pölten is by the Mariazell alpine railway. The town has been Central Europe's main Catholic pilgrim site and a Gothic and Baroque basilica, enlarged in the 17th century, testifies to its religious significance. Inside is a wealth of Baroque stucco, painting and decoration. The treasury also forms part of the church.

A cable car up the mountain leaves every 20 minutes from the town centre. The world's oldest steam tram, built in 1884, runs between Mariazell railway station and a nearby lake.

River Trip from Krems to Melk **7**

See pp176–7.

View of Mariazell, where a virgin cult began in 1377

River Trip from Krems to Melk ❼

Some 80 km (50 miles) west of Vienna is one of the most magnificent stretches of river scenery in Europe. Castles, churches and wine-producing villages rise up on either side of the Danube valley and breathtaking views unfold. Redolent with history (it has been settled for over 30,000 years), this stretch from Krems to Melk is called the Wachau. A river trip is the best way to take in the landmarks, either with one of the tours organized by Cityrama, Vienna Line, Vienna Sightseeing or DDSG Shipping *(see p237)*, or independently *(see box)*.

The perfectly-preserved medieval town of Dürnstein ④

Krems to Dürnstein

The beautiful Renaissance town of Stein has in modern times merged into one with Krems, which has a medieval centre ①. At the end of Steinerstrasse is the house of the Baroque artist Kremser Schmidt. Climb one of the narrow hillside streets and look across the Danube for a fine view of Göttweig Abbey ②, an excellent example of Austrian Baroque, and in the 17th century a centre of the Counter-Reformation. You can also see the small town of Mautern ③, which

developed from a 1st-century Roman fortification, and now boasts the gourmet restaurant Bacher in Südtirolerplatz.

Once on board, after about 8 km (5 miles) you will pass the perfectly-preserved medieval town of Dürnstein ④, with a Baroque church overlooked by the ruins of a castle. From 1192 to 1193, after his return from the Third Crusade, England's King Richard the Lionheart was held prisoner in the castle by Duke Leopold V of Babenberg *(see p23)*. He was released only on payment of a huge ransom. Dürnstein has conserved much of its medieval and Baroque character and has splendid river views and side streets leading to charming river walks. A separate visit is advisable if you want to see the town at leisure.

Wine-producing towns from Rossatz to Wösendorf

On the opposite bank to Dürnstein lies Rossatz ⑤, which has been making wine for centuries and was once a busy port. Findings of Neolithic and Roman remains testify to early settlement. In the 10th century it belonged to a Bavarian convent, but passed to the Babenbergs and became part

Vineyards at Weissenkirchen ⑥

Das Rote Tor

1,000-Eimer Berg

Venus of Willendorf

Schönbühel Castle

0 km		5
0 miles		3

KEY

🚢	River boat boarding point
🚉	Railway station
—	Railway line
〜	River
▬	Major road
▬	Minor road

The church at Weissenkirchen which was fortified to hold off the Turks ⑦ of their Austrian domain. The Renaissance castle and Gothic church were transformed to Baroque around 1700.

At Weissenkirchen ⑥ the church dates mainly from the 15th and 16th centuries. The town is also renowned for its wine, as are Joching ⑦ and Wösendorf ⑧.

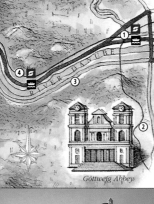

The ruined castle above the river at Aggstein ⑯

Churches and ruins

Clearly visible on top of a hill, the fortified Church of St Michael ⑨ was built between 1500 and 1523. An unusual architectural detail is the stone hares on its tower. Local folklore tells how, once, so much snow fell here that hares were able to leap onto the roof.

On the same side of the river is a ruined arch on a hill, Das Rote Tor ⑩, a fragment of a 14th-century gate through which the Swedes walked on their way to Spitz in 1645 during the 30 Years War *(see p25)*. The town of Mitterarnsdorf ⑪ has Roman remains.

Spitz to Aggsbachdorf

Spitz ⑫ is another pretty wine town and was also a Protestant stronghold during the Reformation. It lies at the foot of the 1,000-Eimer Berg (1,000-Bucket Mountain), so called because it is claimed that in a good year the vine-clad hills can produce enough wine to fill 1,000 buckets.

Further on is a wall-like rocky precipice jutting out from the bank, the Teufelsmauer or Devil's Wall ⑬. It has given rise to a number of legends. One tells how the devil's grandmother wanted to stop pilgrims and crusaders by creating a dam. At Schwallenbach ⑭ the church was rebuilt after the Bohemians devastated the village in 1463. Although you cannot see it from the boat, you will pass very close to the village of Willendorf ⑮, famous for the prehistoric findings made nearby, including the statue and fertility symbol Venus of Willendorf *(see pp20 and 126)*.

Aggstein ⑯ has a ruined castle high above the river. Georg Scheck von Wald, follower of Duke Albrecht I, rebuilt and enlarged the original castle in 1429. Legend has it that he called a rock, placed at the highest point of the castle, his rose garden. He would force his imprisoned enemies to leap to their deaths if the ransom he demanded failed to arrive. Aggsbachdorf ⑰ was settled by the Romans in the 2nd century and owned by the Kuenringer robber-barons during the Middle Ages.

Schönbühel Castle to Melk

The picturesque castle of Schönbühel ⑱ stands on a rocky outcrop overlooking the Danube. Although it has been on record since the 9th century, its present form dates from the early 19th century. Further

The Benedictine abbey of Melk dominates the river and town ⑳

on, at the mouth of the 70-km long (43-mile) River Pielach ⑲, 30 Bronze Age tombs and the foundations of a Roman tower have been excavated.

The high point of the trip is the Benedictine abbey of Melk ⑳. The pretty town has Renaissance houses, romantic little streets, old towers and remnants of a city wall built in the Middle Ages. The Baroque abbey, where Umberto Eco's novel *The Name of the Rose* begins and ends, is a treasure trove of paintings, sculptures and decorative art. The great library contains 2,000 volumes from the 9th to the 15th centuries alone. The church has a magnificent organ, and skeletons dressed in luxurious materials inside glass coffins. Some of the Abbey's treasures are not on permanent view.

TIPS FOR INDEPENDENT TRAVELLERS

Starting points: *Krems, Dürnstein, Melk or any river trip boarding point if you have a car. River trip tickets are on sale at these points.*
Getting there: *Take the national network train from Franz-Josefs-Bahnhof to Krems or Dürnstein. For Melk, depart from Westbahnhof.*
Stopping-off points: *Dürnstein has a variety of Heurige, restaurants, cafés and shops. Melk Abbey has a restaurant.* **Melk Abbey** 02752 5550. *Palm Sunday–1st Sun after All Souls: 9am–5pm (May–Sep: 9am–6pm). 11am & 2pm throughout year.*
Cycling: *A cycle path runs along the Danube. Bikes for hire at Krems, Melk, Spitz and Dürnstein train stations (reduction with train ticket), or from river trip boarding points. Take your passport for identification.*

Göttweig Abbey

FOUR GUIDED WALKS

VIENNA IS a comparatively small city, with several main attractions within easy walking distance of each other. All six sightseeing areas in this guide have a suggested short walk marked on a Street-by-Street map. Yet the city's suburbs are also worth exploring on foot. The following guided walks take you

Makart statue *(p180)*

through some of the best walking areas in and around the city, all easily accessible by public transport. The first walk takes you through the town itself. Starting in the Stadtpark, it continues past the Karlskirche to the elegant Wagner Apartments and the colourful Naschmarkt on the Linke Wienzeile. The bus journey to the start of our second walk at Kahlenberg

is in itself a pleasure. The bus runs along the scenic Höhenstrasse and through the Vienna Woods. Below Kahlenberg, Nussdorf and Grinzing are a far cry from the imperial splendours of the city centre, and have kept their identities as ancient wine villages. The fourth walk takes you to Grinzing via Heiligenstadt, where there are a number of buildings by well-known 20th-century architects. Hietzing, near Schönbrunn, with its quiet streets lined with Biedermeier and Jugendstil villas, is our third walk. There are also signposted routes through the Vienna Woods and the Prater, marked *Stadtwanderwege*. For details of these walks, phone or write to the Wiener Fremdenverkehrsamt *(see p237)*.

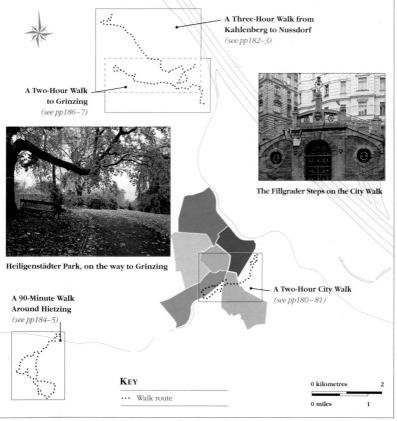

A Three-Hour Walk from Kahlenberg to Nussdorf
(see pp182–3)

A Two-Hour Walk to Grinzing
(see pp186–7)

The Fillgrader Steps on the City Walk

Heiligenstädter Park, on the way to Grinzing

A Two-Hour City Walk
(see pp180–81)

A 90-Minute Walk Around Hietzing
(see pp184–5)

KEY

··· Walk route

0 kilometres   2

0 miles   1

◁ **The winding Kahlenberger Strasse pathway** *(see p182)*

A Two-Hour City Walk

THIS WALK SKIRTS the southwestern perimeter of the inner city, following part of the course of the River Wien. It begins with a leisurely stroll through the Stadtpark, which was laid out in English landscape style when the Ringstrasse was built *(see p32)*. Continuing past Schwarzenbergplatz and Karlsplatz through the lively Naschmarkt, it ends with a glance at some masterpieces of Jugendstil architecture on the Linke Wienzeile.

Jugendstil portal in the Stadtpark, built in 1903–4 as part of the flood defences along the river ⑪

The Stadtpark

Begin at the entrance to the Stadtpark opposite Weihburggasse. Almost facing you is an impressive side entrance ① with sculpted portals which was designed between 1857 and 1862.

No. 38 Linke Wienzeile ㉑

On the city side, the park contains many monuments to musicians and artists. The first is the gilded statue of Johann Strauss II *(see p39)* playing his violin (1921) ②. Go left past this monument, and left again, into a paved circular seating area with a fountain dedicated to the Sprite of the Danube ③. Turn right out of this area and you come to an iron bridge across the River Wien, from the middle of which you get a view of the embankments ④.

Walk back to the nearby lake ⑤. On its southern side a statue of the Viennese landscape painter Emil Jakob Schindler (1895) ⑥ sits in the bushes. Follow the path until

it peters out into a culvert then go left across the bridge. Turn left again until you come to a monument to Franz Schubert (1872) by Karl Kundmann ⑦. Take the path past the lake and turn right at the clocktower. The painter Hans Makart, who dominated the visual arts in Vienna in the 1870s and 1880s, strikes a rhetorical pose in Viktor Tilgner's 1898 statue ⑧. Walk on past the entrance to the park. On the right is the bust of Franz Lehár, composer of *The Merry Widow* ⑨. Walk towards the Kursalon ⑩, which opened for concerts, balls and waltzes in the 1860s. Continue past the Kursalon, leaving the park through one of the Jugendstil portals *(see p57)* ⑪.

Statue of Johannes Brahms (1908) by Rudolf Weyr, in the Ressel Park ⑯

Fillgrader Steps

FILLGRADER GASSE · FILLGRADERSTRASSE · GUMPENDORFER STRASSE · STEGGASSE · KÖSTLERGASSE · LAIMGRUBENGASSE · WIENZEILE · LINKE WIENZEILE · RECHTE WIENZEILE · SCHLEIFMÜHLGASSE · HEUMÜHL · KETTENBRÜCKENG · FRANZENSGASSE · Kettenbrücken-gasse · OPERNGASSE · WIEDNER HAUPTSTRASSE · LEHÁRGASSE · MILLÖCKERG · Kar ㉔ ㉓ ㉖ ㉕ ⑳ ㉒ ㉑

TIPS FOR WALKERS

Starting point: *Weihburggasse Tram 1 or 2 (on Parkring).*

Length: *3 km (1½ miles).*

Getting there: *Trams 1 or 2, which circulate around the Ringstrasse and Franz-Josefs-Kai; or Stubentor U-bahn, then walk.*

Stopping-off points: *The Kursalon in the Stadtpark serves tea, coffee and cakes on the terrace and has a beer garden to one side. There are also many benches where you can rest. There are cafés in Ressel Park and the Naschmarkt; towards the end of the walk you will find Café Sperl on Gumpendorfer Strasse.*

Schwarzenbergplatz

Walk straight ahead, crossing the road into Lothringerstrasse. A monument to Beethoven (1880), showing him surrounded by figures alluding to the Ninth Symphony, stands on the right ⑫. Cross the road to the Konzerthaus (1912–13), home to the Vienna Symphony Orchestra *(see p226)* ⑬.

Cross the busy intersection to get a striking vista of Schwarzenbergplatz to your left, at the end of which is a fountain. It was erected in 1873 to celebrate the city's supply of pure drinking water which comes from the mountains. Behind it is the Memorial to the Red Army which liberated Austria in 1945 ⑭.

The Neo-Renaissance Kursalon ⑩

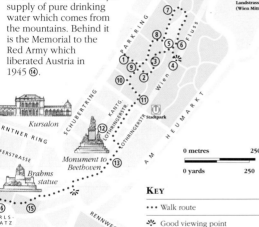

KEY

••• Walk route

🔆 Good viewing point

Ⓤ U-Bahn station

market and cross the road to look at Otto Wagner's Apartments *(see p137)* with golden medallions by Kolo Moser at No. 38 ㉑, and the Majolikahaus at No. 40, so called because of its floral tiles ㉒. As you turn into Köstlergasse alongside No. 38 it is worth pausing to admire the entrance.

Confession box, Karlskirche ⑰

Ressel Park

Continue along Lothringerstrasse, pass the Historical Museum of the City of Vienna *(see p144)* ⑮, into Ressel Park. On the left is a statue of Brahms with his muse at his feet (1908) by Rudolf Weyr ⑯. Look left past Brahms to the Karlskirche *(see p146–7)* ⑰. Go on, noting Otto Wagner's pavilions *(see p144)* at road level ⑱. Pass the Neo-Classical Technical High School ⑲ to leave the park. Cross Wiedner Hauptstrasse, go straight ahead then left into Operngasse, crossing the road. Walk through Bärenmühlendurchgang passage in the building facing you and cross the road into the Naschmarkt ⑳.

Naschmarkt

A lively food market *(see p136)*, originally held in the Karlsplatz, moved here after this part of the river was paved over in the late 19th century. It is a good vantage point from which to admire the elegant 19th-century buildings along the left bank, or Linke Wienzeile. Leave the

Papageno Gate of the Theater an der Wien ㉕

Gumpendorfer Strasse

Turn right at the end of Köstlergasse and walk up Gumpendorfer Strasse. Look left up Fillgradergasse for a glimpse of the Fillgrader Steps ㉓. Continue on to the historic Café Sperl *(see p58)*, once the haunt of the composer Lehár ㉔. Go on and turn right into Millöckergasse to see the famous Papageno Gate of the Theater an der Wien *(see p136)* ㉕. The sculpture above the entrance shows the theatre's first owner, Emanuel Schikaneder, in the character of Papageno from Mozart's *The Magic Flute*. Continue down Millöckergasse to the Linke Wienzeile. Bear left, passing the Secession Building *(see p136)* ㉖, and go on to Karlsplatz U-Bahn.

A Three-Hour Walk from Kahlenberg to Nussdorf

T HIS WALKS STARTS at the top of Kahlenberg, a summit of around 500 m (1,600 ft) at the northeastern edge of the Vienna Woods. From here there is a marvellous panorama over the city and its environs. A gradual descent through woods and vineyards leads to the wine village of Nussdorf and the most northern part of Heiligenstadt, an area rich in Beethoven associations, since this is where the composer spent many of his summers. The walk is mainly downhill, though it may be done in reverse.

St Florian

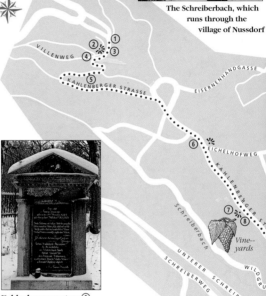

The Schreiberbach, which runs through the village of Nussdorf

Kahlenberg

The walk starts at the summit of Kahlenberg in Am Kahlenberg square ①. Kahlenberg itself was once called Sauberg (Sow Hill) because of the wild boar that roamed here. From the summit café terrace ②, you can admire distant views of the Alps to the south, plains stretching towards Hungary to the east, and the river Danube snaking through the middle. In the square itself at Josefsdorf is the Baroque church of St Joseph ③, where Jan Sobieski, the King of Poland, is said to have celebrated mass before he went into battle to defeat the Turks in 1683. For another view of Vienna you can climb the recently-restored Stefanie Warte ④, or lookout tower.

Kahlenberger Strasse

To the right of the café is the winding path of Kahlenberger Strasse which leads down to the slopes below the summit. After a couple of minutes you reach the small Kahlenberg cemetery ⑤, almost hidden in the woods to your left. It

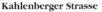

Kahlenberg cemetery ⑤

contains the grave of Karolina Trauernwieser, said to have been the most beautiful girl in the city at the time of the Congress of Vienna in 1815.

Her tomb bears the admirer's words: "Ye that ere lost an angel, pity me". A few steps on, the trees clear to reveal a stunning view over the Danube plain ⑥ while further along, on the right, is another view over the city ⑦. Kahlenberger Strasse carries on through vineyards ⑧ where grapes for the local *Heurige* are grown.

Nussdorf and Heiligenstadt

After a while, houses along the road announce that you have arrived at the village of Nussdorf. Follow a bend towards the right and then, passing Frimmelgasse, take

View towards Vienna from Kahlenberger Strasse ⑦

the right-hand fork, where the Schreiberbach (Schreiber brook) emerges from underground, to arrive at the Beethoven Ruhe ⑨ (Beethoven's peace); there is a statue of the composer here dating from 1863. Cross the stream by turning left over the bridge, then turn right into Beethovengang. At the end of this street you come to Eroicagasse, named after Beethoven's *(see p38)* Third Symphony. Turn right and then go downhill, crossing Kahlenberger Strasse. The road curves round, leading into Pfarrplatz.

Pfarrplatz

Immediately on your left at No. 2 is a pleasant *Heuriger*, Mayer am Pfarrplatz ⑩, where Beethoven is said to have stayed in

1817 while working on his Ninth Symphony. A statue of St Florian in soldier's costume and bearing a standard can be seen in a niche on the corner wall of the *Heuriger*. Also here is the church of St James ⑪, built in the 12th century on a Roman site, but rebuilt after its destruction by the Turks in the 17th century. From Pfarrplatz follow Probusgasse west towards No. 6 at the far end, which is the Heiligenstadt Testament House ⑫. This is where in 1802 Beethoven wrote a long and despairing letter to his brothers, giving a moving

Heiligenstadt Testament House ⑫

turn right into Kahlenberger Strasse, which has a pleasant old-world feel to it, especially at its eastern end. No. 26 ⑭, built around 1750 and with a Rococo façade, is where Beethoven stayed on two occasions during the summer of 1817 and in 1824. Further along, on the same side of the road at No. 10, is a pretty *Heuriger* with a figure above its door ⑮ dating from 1636. On the other side of the road, a plaque on the front of Nos. 7–9 ⑯ celebrates 100 years of *Schrammel* music *(see p39)*, a type of Viennese folk song often associated with *Heurige*.

Beethoven Ruhe memorial ⑨

account of his deafness. Turn right into Armbrustergasse, which curves upwards and passes the new Slovakian Embassy ⑬, until you come to a crossroads. Here,

St James parish church ⑪, rebuilt in the 17th century

Statue of Beethoven

Mayer am Pfarrplatz

Heiligenstadt Testament House

KEY

••• Walk route

∿ Good viewing point

🔲 Bundesbahn station

🔲 Schnellbahn station

0 kilometres 1

0 miles 0.5

TIPS FOR WALKERS

Starting point: *Kahlenberg summit.*

Length: *3.5 km (2 miles).*

Getting there: *The 38A bus from Heiligenstadt U-Bahn (on the U6 and U4 lines) takes you to the summit. The Schnellbahn at Nussdorf, or the D tram at Schatzgasse takes you back into town.*

Stopping-off points: *The café at the summit of Kahlenberg has a terrace from where you can enjoy the wonderful view of the Danube and the Alps.*

The Mayer am Pfarrplatz Heuriger at Pfarrplatz 2 (see p217) serves wine and meals in a shady courtyard. There is also a restaurant serving full meals in the same square, as well as other Heurige in Probusgasse and Kahlenberger Strasse. At Kahlenberger Strasse 10, there is a café and Heuriger in the same building.
St Joseph's Church 📞 *320 3029.* ⭘ *9:30am–noon, 1:30–4:30pm daily.* **Stefanie Warte Observatory** ⭘ *May–Oct: 9am–8pm Sat, Sun & public hols.* **Heiligenstadt Testament House** 📞 *370 5408.* ⭘ *9am–12:15pm, 1–4:30pm Tue–Sun.*

A 90-Minute Walk Around Hietzing

THE FORMER VILLAGE of Hietzing runs along the western edge of the extensive grounds of Schönbrunn Palace *(see p170–73)*. In Maria Theresa's time it was a fashionable area where the nobility went to spend their summers; later it became a suburb for the wealthy middle classes. The quiet streets contain a marvellous mix of Biedermeier and Jugendstil villas, while the square around the parish church retains an intimate small-town atmosphere.

From the station to Am Platz

Take the Hadikgasse exit from Hietzing U-Bahn ① and cross the tram tracks and road to Kennedybrücke. Turn right down Hadikgasse and after a minute you arrive at Otto Wagner's Kaiser Pavilion *(see p169)* ②, a former station designed for the use of the imperial family when they were at Schönbrunn. Retrace

The Kaiserstöckl opposite the Park Hotel, now a post office ⑥

your steps to the U-Bahn and cross the road into Hietzinger Hauptstrasse. Notice the attic of No. 6 with cherubs hugging the columns. The building dates from 1901–2, but the lower storey has been altered to accommodate shops ③. On your left through the railings are long avenues of trees at

the side of Schönbrunn ④. Just across the road is the Park Hotel, its ochre façade echoing that of the palace buildings ⑤. Facing it is the Kaiserstöckl (1770) or Emperor's Pavilion ⑥. Today it is a post office, but it used to be the holiday venue of Maria Theresa's foreign ministers. Continue to Am Platz with its plague column dating from 1730 ⑦. Next door to this is the parish church of Maria Geburt ⑧, originally built in the 13th century, and remodelled in the 17th century. The Baroque interior contains altars by the sculptor Matthias Steindl and ceiling frescoes by Georg Greiner. The church was used by Maria Theresa when she was in residence at Schönbrunn, and her box can be seen in the right-hand wall of the choir. In front of the church stands a statue of Franz Joseph's brother

Façade of the Park Hotel ⑤

Villa Primavesi

```
0 metres        250
0 yards         250
```

KEY

••• Walk route

Ⓤ U-Bahn station

TIPS FOR WALKERS

Starting point: Hietzing U-Bahn.
Length: 5 km (3 miles).
Getting there: the U4 and Tram 58 go to Hietzing. **Note:** On Sundays you may need to retrace your steps a short distance if the Maxing Gate is locked.
Stopping-off points: the BAWAG café in Hietzing's Am Platz is a pleasant place to stop for a coffee.
Hietzing Heimat Museum
⬜ 9am–noon 2–6pm Wed, 2–5pm Sat, 9:30am–noon Sun.
⬤ Jul–Aug. **Schönbrunn Palace and Park** (see pp170–73).
Villa Primavesi ⬤ to public.

Elaborate altar by Matthias Steindl in the Maria Geburt Kirche ⑧

Maximilian, the Emperor of Mexico who was executed in 1867 ⑨. Nearby is a Neo-Classical building housing the Hietzing Heimat Museum ⑩, and outside the museum is Vienna's last gas lamp.

Trauttmansdorffgasse and Gloriettegasse

Turn left into Maxingstrasse, named after Maximilian, then right into Altgasse. Almost facing Fasholdgasse is an old *Heuriger*, a Biedermeier building with ochre walls ⑪.

Detail from the majolica façade of the Lebkuchenhaus ⑲

Plaque on No. 50 Trauttmans-dorffgasse ⑭

Turn down Fasholdgasse into Trautt-mansdorffgasse, a street full of interesting houses. No. 40 is a beautifully-restored, long and low Biedermeier villa ⑫, while

across the road, at No. 27, is the house where the composer Alban Berg (*see p39*) once lived ⑬. Nos. 48 and 50 are contrasting examples of Viennese turn-of-the-century architecture ⑭. More examples of Biedermeier style can be seen at Nos. 54 and 56 ⑮.

At the end of the road, turn right into Gloriette-gasse. On the right at Nos. 14 and 16 is a villa with sculpted figures in the pediments, built in 1913–15 by Josef Hoffmann for the financier Robert Primavesi ⑯. Note the monumental sculpted figures resting in the pediments.

Cross the road to pass a terrace of Biedermeier houses – Nos. 38 and 40 have lunettes above the windows ⑰. No. 21 is the Villa Schopp, designed by Friedrich Ohmann in 1901–2 ⑱. Turn left down Wattmanngasse to see No. 29, the extraordinary Lebkuchen-haus (Gingerbread House) ⑲, so-called because of its dark brown decoration in majolica. It was built in 1914 to designs by a pupil of Otto Wagner (*see pp54–7*). Turn back into Gloriettegasse. At its southern junction with Wattmann-gasse, at No. 9, is the

Sculpted figure in a pediment of the Villa Primavesi ⑯

house that belonged to Katharina Schratt, the actress and confidante of Emperor Franz Joseph during his later years. It is said that the Emperor was in the habit of arriving here for breakfast ⑳.

Maxing Park and Schönbrunn Park

Walk to the end of Gloriette-gasse, then turn right up Maxingstrasse and cross the road at Maxing Park. If you would like to add another half hour to the walk, Hietzing cemetery, a little further up the hill, contains the graves of Otto Wagner, Gustav Klimt, Kolo Moser and Franz Grillparzer, among others. Alternatively, enter Maxing Park ㉑ and follow the main path upwards towards the right. At the top, go through the gates marked *Zum Tiergarten Schönbrunn*, passing the forestry research institute on your left. Although you are actually in the grounds of Schönbrunn, this heavily wooded area feels very remote from the formal gardens and you may catch a glimpse of deer. At the crossroads in the path turn left, signposted to the Botanical Garden. You soon arrive at a little wooden hut, which was Crown Prince Rudolf's playhouse ㉒.

The path eventually leads to the formally planted Botanical Garden ㉓, which was laid out in 1848 under Emperor Franz I. Take the path through the garden, keeping to tthe boundary wall with Hietzing. Exit into Maxingstrasse (this gate may be locked on Sundays) and continue north. At No. 18 is the house where Johann Strauss II wrote *Die Fledermaus* in 1874 ㉔. Carry on north along Maxingstrasse and retrace your steps to Hietzing U-Bahn.

A Two-Hour Walk to Grinzing

THIS WALK THROUGH part of Vienna's 19th district begins at the site of one of the most important monuments of 20th-century Vienna, the public housing development of the Karl Marx Hof. It then takes you through a pretty 19th-century park to the old wine village of Grinzing. Although the village suffered destruction at the hands of the Turks in 1529 and 1683 and from Napoleon's army in 1809, and is now feeling the effects of modern tourism, its pretty main street preserves its charm.

Façade of the 16th-century
Reinprecht *Heuriger* ⑮

Karl Marx Hof to Heiligenstädter Park

Facing you as you step out of Heiligenstadt station is the long ochre, terracotta and mauve façade of the Karl Marx Hof (*see p159*), a huge housing project designed by the city architect Karl Ehn and built from 1927 to 1930 during the Red Vienna period ①. It sprawls for 1.2 km (¾ mile) and has 1,265 flats.

Cross the road and pass through one of the four arches facing you into 12 Februar Platz to see the main façade from the other side. On the keystone of each arch stands a large figure sculpture by Joseph Riedl (1928) ②. Continue through the square, past a statue (1928) by Otto Hofner of a man sowing seeds ③, and you come to Heiligenstädter Strasse. Turn right, cross the road at the second pedestrian crossing and walk through the square opening in the building facing you. Go up the steps and take the path on the left into Heiligenstädter Park. When you come to a fork, take the left path that winds up a hill, going through woods. Turn right at the top into the formal part of the park ④. From here, you get a good view of the vine-clad slopes of the Kahlenberg ⑤.

Figure on the Karl Marx Hof ①

Steinfeldgasse

Take the second small path on the right, which descends gradually into Steinfeldgasse, where there is a cluster of houses built by the Secessionist

designer Josef Hoffmann. The first one you come to is the Villa Moser-Moll at Nos. 6–8, designed for Carl Moll and Kolo Moser ⑥. Next to it is the Villa Spitzer ⑦, then the more classical Villa Ast, built in 1909–11 ⑧. Where Steinfeldgasse meets Wollergasse is the Villa Henneberg of 1901 ⑨, and at No. 10 Wollergasse ⑩ is the Moll House II of 1906–7. Its black and white details are charming.

Steinfeldgasse to Grinzinger Strasse

At the point where Steinfeldgasse and Wollergasse meet, there is a path leading down through some woods. Follow this and descend the steps to the Church of St Michael, Heiligenstadt ⑪, which has striking

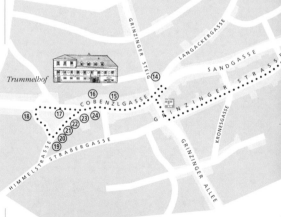

Trummelhof

modern stained-glass windows. Walk past the church, cross Hohe Warte and go up Grinzinger Strasse. You quickly arrive at No. 70, the house where Albert Einstein stayed from 1927 to 1931 ⑫. On the same side of the road is No. 64, the late 18th-century house where Beethoven and the Viennese playwright Franz Grillparzer lodged during the summer of 1808 while Beethoven was composing the Pastoral Symphony ⑬. Continue up Grinzinger Strasse, passing a number of attractive Biedermeier houses, until you arrive at Grinzinger

Lawns and trees in the Heiligenstädter Park ④

Allee. Turn right past a series of wine gardens and immediately right again to get a quick glimpse of the upper part of Sandgasse, where there are a number of more authentic *Heurige* ⑭.

Grinzing

Turning back on yourself and towards the centre of Grinzing, ascend Cobenzlgasse, the upper fork of Grinzing's main street. The Reinprecht *Heuriger* at No. 22 Cobenzlgasse is a 16th-century house, the façade of

Cobenzlgasse, Grinzing's main street

0 metres	500
0 yards	500

Courtyard at the Passauer Hof, an old wine press house ⑰

TIPS FOR WALKERS

Starting point: *Heiligenstadt station.*

Length: *3.5 km (2 miles).*

Getting there: *Heiligenstadt station is served by U-Bahn lines U4 and U6, trains S40 and S45 and buses 10A, 11A, 38A and 39A. Tram D stops on Heiligenstädter Strasse.*

Stopping-off points: *There are numerous Heurige (see pp216–17), coffee shops and restaurants in Grinzing. Avoid the larger Heurige – the smaller ones sell their own wine. Those at the top of Sandgasse tend to be good.*

KEY

• • • Walk route

☀ Good viewing point

🚋 Tram terminus

Ⓤ U-Bahn station

Ⓢ Schnellbahn station

═ Railway line

which has a tablet commemorating the composer Robert Stolz ⑮. No. 30 Cobenzlgasse is the Baroque Trummelhof, standing on the site of an 1835 brewery ⑯. Further up on the left, at No. 9, is the Passauer Hof, an old wine press house that contains fragments of a far older, Romanesque building ⑰. On the corner of Cobenzlgasse and Feilergasse is the Altes Presshaus, whose cellar contains an old wine press ⑱.

Turn left into Feilergasse, and you soon come face to face with the impressive white Jugendstil façade of

Nos. 41–3 Himmelstrasse ⑲. Continue down Himmelstrasse to No. 35, another *Heuriger*, Das Alte Haus, which has a charming plaque of the Virgin Mary above its door ⑳. There is another such painting at No. 31, which shows a holy man carrying a cross, bible and a bunch of grapes ㉑. No. 29 ㉒ is another *Heuriger* with a tablet to Sepp Fellner, a *Schrammel* musician *(see p39)* described as "The Schubert of Grinzing". Ironically, at No. 25, a grand building with shields above the doorway, there is a memorial to the real Schubert, described as "The Prince of Song, who loved to tarry in Grinzing" ㉓. Grinzing also has an attractive late Gothic church with a copper cupola and much-restored interior ㉔. Continue down the road to the tram terminus, where the No. 38 tram goes back to town.

Plaque of a holy man on the façade of No. 31 Himmelstrasse ㉑

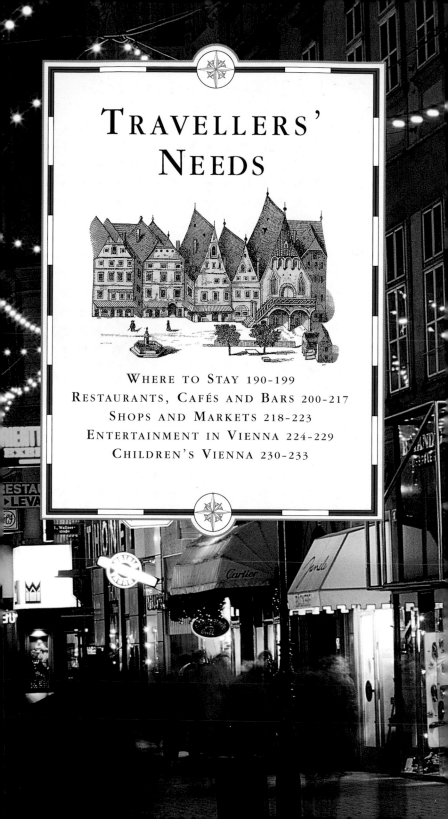

TRAVELLERS' NEEDS

WHERE TO STAY

ITH MORE THAN 500 hotels and pensions available, Vienna offers accommodation for everyone. From palaces to spartan lodgings, the city has some of the grandest European city hotels as well as numerous small boarding-houses. Hotels are generally larger and better equipped (some also have business facilities), and pensions are always bed and breakfast establishments. From a survey of different types of accommodation in all price brackets, we have selected 40 of the best. The chart *Choosing a Hotel* on page 195 will help you find a hotel to suit your needs: hotels are listed by area and in order of price category. For more details of facilities and for a short description, turn to the listings on pages 196–9. For further types of accommodation available in and on the outskirts of Vienna, see page 193.

Baroque façade of the Mailberger Hof on Annagasse *(see p197)*

WHERE TO LOOK

O NE OF THE JOYS of visiting Vienna is that you can stay grandly or cheaply right in the city centre. Almost all the famous hotels – the Sacher, the Bristol, the Imperial *(see Listings pp196–9)* – are on or just off the Ringstrasse, as are most of the large chain hotels. In the city centre lie a host of atmospheric and comfortable hotels and many pensions. Most are on fairly quiet side streets. The Townhall and Museum Quarter has a few good small hotels and is the most promising hunting ground for those travelling on a budget. A few hotels in or near the wine villages to the north *(see p199)* are also listed.

The **Österreich Werbung** (Austrian Tourist Board) publishes detailed leaflets listing over 500 hotels and pensions.

HOTEL PRICES

A CCOMMODATION IN Vienna is disproportionately expensive compared to other costs. Many hotels and pensions situated in prime locations are overpriced. There are a number of ways to cut costs. You can expect to pay approximately a fifth to a quarter less for a room in an establishment just outside the Ringstrasse, and less still if you stay further afield.

Most places have rooms at a variety of prices, depending on their size, aspect and, in pensions, whether they have en suite bathrooms. Single rooms tend to be about three-quarters the cost of double rooms. Some places will put an extra bed in the room on request. They may charge for this but it is likely to be a lot less than the cost of a single room. Other hotels have family or triple-bedded rooms.

Vienna's low season runs from November to March (excluding Christmas and New Year) and during July and August (when

Penthouse suite No. 663 in the Bristol Hotel *(see p198)*

residents go on holiday). Few hotels drop their prices in summer, but around half have winter rates up to 25% lower. Most of the large chain hotels reduce the room tariff when they are less busy and offer weekend specials, but even the lower rates compare badly with hotels of the same chain in the United States, for example.

Out of season, it may be worth asking if there's a discount for payment in cash. Many places offer discounts for longer stays (typically over a

Opulent lobby of the Imperial Hotel *(see p199)*

week), and it's possible to find packages such as three nights for the price of two or four nights for the price of three.

The **Österreich Werbung** has offices in the UK, USA, Canada, New Zealand and Australia. They have details of tour operators that provide all-inclusive packages to Vienna, and will be able to advise on the best available prices.

HIDDEN EXTRAS

WITH THE EXCEPTION of most five-star hotels, breakfast is included in the tariff. Rates will always include taxes such as VAT (or MWSt).

Beware if changing money at your hotel: the official exchange rate could well be as much as 10% better.

Parking fees can also mount up. Street parking within the Ringstrasse is restricted to 90 minutes and there are no private garages. Pensions generally leave you to your own devices to find an underground car park, but some hotels have designated spaces. At some hotels a reasonable amount is charged for parking, but at others it can be very expensive: it is a good idea to enquire in advance. Outlying districts do not have such stringent street parking restrictions, and garage parking is cheaper.

If you are cutting costs, try to avoid making phone calls from your room. Most hotels charge a flat rate per unit of time, even though the official rate varies from day-time to night-time and

Statue in the reception area of the Hotel Regina *(see p197)*

week-days to weekends. The surcharge may be up to three and a half times the standard rate, so it is often worth using a public telephone.

Every other Viennese on the street seems to have a four-legged friend in tow, so it's not surprising that many of the hotels allow dogs in the bedrooms. There may be a charge for this.

Wrought-iron balconies at the Museum pension *(see p198)*

HOW TO BOOK

EASTER, MAY, June, September, October, Christmas and New Year are considered peak season. During these times, many of the best hotels and pensions may be fully booked as much as two months in advance.

Making a reservation direct with any hotel is easy as most of the staff speak English. If you cancel once the booking has been made, you may be

charged for the room. Check in advance. If you are going to arrive after 6pm, let the hotel know or they may re-let your room to someone else.

The main **Wiener Touris-musverband** (Vienna Tourist Board) office can reserve hotel rooms in advance. It is also possible to book accommodation through most of their other offices, but only in person and for a small fee. These include the offices at No. 40 Kärntner Strasse; on the Westautobahn (A1) at the Wien-Auhof service station; and on the Südautobahn (A2) at the Zentrum exit. Otherwise, fax, telephone or write direct to the hotel. If the hotel accepts credit cards, a phone call to book will suffice; if not, you may have to send confirmation of the booking in writing. Different hotels in the city have different procedures.

The Anna Sacher restaurant at the Hotel Sacher *(see p198)*

FACILITIES

H OTELS ARE RATED one to five stars, pensions on a four-star system. As a rough guideline in terms of facilities, a three-star hotel corresponds to a four-star pension. The rating also attempts to cover the quality and ambience of the hotel or pension. Five-star hotels are all reliably smart and well-run. Many four- and three-star hotels proclaim themselves as *Palais*: while this may hold true in the Viennese sense of the word, don't expect anything more than a fine town house. At the cheaper end of the scale, small pensions above two stars are often more friendly and salubrious than cheap hotels. One- or two-star hotels and pensions tend to cater for travellers on a budget and are generally less pleasant.

Usually, only the top hotels have a full range of public rooms: a restaurant, bar, coffee shop and sitting room. In most smaller establishments the lounge is little more than an extension of the reception. Even if there is no bar, you may find that drinks are served. Almost all hotels and pensions have a breakfast room (though all too often it's in a dreary basement). Low-priced pensions provide continental breakfast, while most smart pensions and hotels offer gargantuan buffet feasts, with cheeses, meats, fruit, cakes and cereals.

As most hotels occupy old buildings, it's rare for two bedrooms to be the same. The simplest rooms almost always have a phone, though not necessarily a television. Mid-range hotel rooms often have cable TV and a minibar. Due to size constraints, many bathrooms have only a shower or a truncated tub bath. Many Viennese buildings back on to quiet courtyards, so you can choose between a peaceful room or a room with a view.

In the 19th century there was a restriction on the height of buildings. In order to circumvent the regulation, lower floors were (and still are) called *Hochparterre* and *Mezzanin*. Consequently you may find that the "first floor" is up three flights of stairs. In pensions, a communal lift (usually three-sided and therefore hazardous) serves the whole building.

The quality of service in the best luxury hotels is as good as anywhere in the world. Wherever you stay, it could be well worth befriending the concierge (by perhaps slipping him or her a tip early on in your stay). He or she can be invaluable in directing you to interesting restaurants and bars, and conjuring out of thin air a ticket to the Winter Riding School or a seat at the opera when they have been sold out for months. Most of the reception staff and many other staff speak English, but the standard of service is variable.

TRAVELLING WITH CHILDREN

A LMOST ALL THE HOTELS and pensions have cots (some charge) and can arrange a babysitter. Some may charge the same rate for putting a child's bed in the parents' room as they would for an adult's bed. Usually only the larger hotels allow children under various ages to stay free in their parents' room.

The handsome yellow exterior of the Hotel Josefshof *(see p198)*

DISABLED TRAVELLERS

INFORMATION about wheel-chair access to hotels relies on the hotel's own assessment of their suitability. The **Wiener Tourismusverband** also publishes a detailed leaflet.

HOSTELS

THERE ARE EIGHT youth hostels in the city. The **Wiener Tourismusverband**'s youth hostel and camping brochure lists their facilities. Those with better facilities cost around 10–15 euros a night for bed and breakfast. Most hostels expect residents to be in by midnight. You will need an International Youth Hostel Federation membership card, which can be obtained before you go or on the spot from any hostel. Contact **Österreichischer Jugendherbergsverband** for more information.

SAISONHOTELS

ANNUALLY FROM 1 July to 30 September two dozen students' hostels become Saisonhotels or seasonal hotels, rated on a scale of one to three stars. At the three-star level expect fairly decent rooms. You may make enquiries at any time of the year at two of the main chains, **Academia Hotels** and **Rosenhotels Austria**. Try to reserve well in advance and expect to pay up to 75 euros for a double room in one of the better places.

Elegant lobby at the Kaiserin Elisabeth Hotel *(see p196)*

One of the better chain hotels, the Vienna Marriott (see p197)

CAMPING

FIVE WELL-EQUIPPED campsites, one open throughout the year, can be found within a radius of 8–15 km (5–9 miles) from the city centre. Most camp-sites have kitchen facilities and some may have a supermarket. The **Wiener Tourismusver-band** produces a camping and youth hostel brochure which gives more details on sites. **Camping und Caravening Club Austria** and **Österreichischer Camping Club** can also provide more information.

SELF-CATERING

UNFORTUNATELY FOR those who are keen to "go it alone", there are limited opportunities for self-catering in the city. **Pego**, a company that rents homes throughout Austria, has two apartment blocks and a range of flats spread in and around the city; their brochure will give you all the details. You can book by telephone, by fax or in writing. Some apartments have a combined living and sleeping space and most also have a television and telephone. Expect to pay less per night than the price of a pension.

STAYING IN PRIVATE HOMES

SOME VISITORS CHOOSE to stay in a private home. You can book this type of accommo-dation through the **Wiener Tourismusverband**, but the booking has to be made in person. **Mitwohnzentrale** is a private company that offers the same service. Normally you need to stay a few nights and should expect to pay around 36 euros per person per night.

CHAIN HOTELS

CHAIN HOTELS are geared towards business people; rates usually vary according to their level of occupancy, rather than the season. Familiar names include the Vienna Hilton (*see p197*), the Inter-Continental Wien (*see p199*) and the Vienna Marriott (*see p197*) as well as the hotels listed on page 193.

View of a campsite at No. 40 Huttelbergstrasse

Choosing a Hotel

ALL OF THE HOTELS summarized here have been inspected and assessed. This chart shows some of the features that may affect your choice. The hotels are listed alphabetically within their price category. For more details, see pages 196–9.

Hotel	Price	NUMBER OF ROOMS	MOST BEDROOMS LARGE	BUSINESS FACILITIES	CHILDREN'S FACILITIES	RECOMMENDED RESTAURANT	CLOSE TO SHOPS AND RESTAURANTS	QUIET LOCATION	24-HOUR ROOM SERVICE	BEST VALUE FOR MONEY
STEPHANSDOM QUARTER *(see pp196–7)*										
Am Operneck	€	6	●				●			
Christina	€€	33			●		●	■		
Pension City	€€	19		■			●			
Amadeus	€€€	30			●		●	■		
Arenberg	€€€	22			●		●			
Austria	€€€	46	●		●		●	■	●	
Kärntnerhof	€€€	43			●		●	●	●	■
Wandl	€€€	138	●		●		●		●	■
Zur Wiener Staatsoper	€€€	22			●		●			
Kaiserin Elisabeth	€€€€	63			●		●	■		
K+K Palais	€€€€	66		■	●			■		
König von Ungarn	€€€€	33	●	■	●	■	●			■
Mailberger Hof	€€€€	35	●		●		●	■		
Am Schubertring	€€€€	39			●		●			
Römischer Kaiser Wien	€€€€€	24			●		●	■		
Vienna Marriott	€€€€€	313	●	■	●		●		●	
HOFBURG QUARTER *(see p197)*										
Nossek	€€	28	●	■	●		●			■
Pertschy	€€€	47			●		●	■		
Astoria	€€€€	118	●		●		●	■		
Ambassador	€€€€€	86	●		●		●	■		
SCHOTTENRING AND ALSERGRUND *(see p197)*										
Regina	€€€€	128			●		●			
MUSEUM AND TOWNHALL QUARTER *(see p198)*										
Wild	€	22					●			■
Graf Stadion	€€	40					●			
Museum	€€	15	●				●			
Altstadt Vienna	€€€	36	●		●		●			■
Josefshof	€€€	66		■	●		●	■		
Zipser	€€€	47			●		●			
K+K Maria Theresia	€€€€	133		■	●		●			
OPERA AND NASCHMARKT *(see p198)*										
Sacher	€€€€€	109	●	■	●	■	●		●	
BELVEDERE QUARTER *(see pp198–9)*										
Suzanne	€€	26			●		●			
Bristol	€€€€€	140	●	■	●	■	●		●	
Imperial	€€€€€	138	●	■	●	■	●		●	
Im Palais Schwarzenberg	€€€€€	44		■	●	■		■	●	■
FURTHER AFIELD *(see p199)*										
Altwienerhof	€€	25				■		■		■
Nordbahn	€€	78			●		●			
Gartenhotel Glanzing	€€€	18	●	■	●			■		
Landhaus Fuhrgassl-Huber	€€€	38			●			■		■
Biedermeier	€€€€	203	●		●		●	■		
Inter-Continental Wien	€€€€	453		■	●	■			●	
Vienna Hilton	€€€€€	600		■			●		●	

STEPHANSDOM QUARTER

Am Operneck

Kärntner Strasse 47, A-1010.
Map 4 D1 & 6 D4. **C** 5129310.
FAX 512931020. **Rooms:** 6. 🛏 1
⊞ TV ⚹ **MC, V.** €

This tiny pension opposite the
tourist office on Kärntner Strasse is
in the centre of the city. All but
one of the bedrooms are large,
comfortable and resolutely un-
stylish. The bathrooms, which have
showers, are somewhat cramped.
You can find quieter rooms
towards the back. Continental
breakfast is served in your room.

Christina

Hafnersteig 7, A-1010. **Map** 2 E5 &
6 E2. **C** 5332961. **FAX** 533296111.
Rooms: 33. 🛏 1 ⊞ TV ⚹ ⚹
DC, MC, V. €€ W www.
pertschy.com

The Christina is an unassuming
pension on a quiet, cobbled side
street just within the Stephansdom
Quarter. Though neither old nor
fashionable, it's the kind of place
where you'll be offered a cup of
coffee on arrival. It has been
renovated in Art Deco style and
larger rooms have proper baths.

Pension City

Bauernmarkt 10, A-1010. **Map** 2 E5
& 6 D3. **C** 5339521. **FAX** 5355216.
Rooms: 19. 🛏 1 ⊞ TV ⚹ ⚹
⚹ ⚹ 11 ⚹ AE, DC, MC, V. €€

This small, friendly hotel is housed
in a late 19th-century building in
the centre of Vienna, within easy
walking distance of Stephansdom
and Hoher Markt. It is also conveniently close to shops, bars and
restaurants. Some of the bedrooms
have good views and the hotel
can also offer some quiet rooms
away from the street.

Amadeus

Wildpretmarkt 5, A-1010. **Map** 2 E5
& 6 D3. **C** 5338738. **FAX** 533873838.
Rooms: 30. 🛏 1 TV ⚹ ⚹
AE, DC, MC, V. €€€
@ amadeus.vienna@mcnon.com

This spruce, modern hotel could
have been better named, as other
famous musicians such as Brahms
and Schubert used to frequent a
tavern on this site. But the hotel's
décor matches Mozart's era: the red
carpets, upholstery and lampshades
are complemented by chandeliers
and murals on the stairs. The
Amadeus is located close to the
Stephansdom on a handsome,
wide street with fashionable shops.

Arenberg

Stubenring 2 , A-1010. **Map** 2 F5 &
6 F3. **C** 5125291. **FAX** 5139356.
Rooms: 22. 🛏 1 ⊞ TV ⚹ ⚹
⚹ ⚹ AE, DC, MC, V. €€€
@ arenberg@ping.at

A seemingly dull office building
on the northeast corner of the
Ring houses one of the city's most
civilized and friendly pensions. An
honesty bar (help yourself and mark
your drinks down on a tab) sets the
tone. Expect rugs on parquet floors
and bedrooms with antique wallpaper and more prosaic furniture.

Austria

Fleischmarkt 20, A-1010. **Map** 2 E4 &
6 D2. **C** 51523. **FAX** 51523506.
Rooms: 46. 🛏 42. 1 ⊞ 24 TV
⚹ ⚹ ⚹ AE, DC, MC, V, JCB.
€€€ @ office@hotelaustria-wien.at

Up a cul-de-sac and close to the
Old University is the roomy and
somewhat dowdy Austria Hotel.
A plus point is that it is extremely
quiet. Downstairs, there are a
couple of small sitting-rooms and
a breakfast room arranged around
a fountain decorated with shells.
High-ceilinged, spacious bedrooms with modern furniture and
decent, old-fashioned bathrooms
ring a central courtyard.

Kärntnerhof

Grashofgasse 4, A-1011. **Map** 2 E5 &
6 E3. **C** 5121923. **FAX** 513222833.
Rooms: 43. 🛏 41. 1 ⊞ 24 ⚹
⚹ ⚹ P ⚹ AE, DC, MC, V, JCB.
€€€ @ karntnerhof@netway.at

A couple of cafés adjoin this well-
run and affordable cul-de-sac
address: a gate at the end leads to
the lovely Heiligenkreuzerhof *(see
p75)* where you can park the car.
The 19th-century building's best
feature behind its imposing yellow
façade is a fine Art Deco lift,
enclosed within a spiral staircase.
The better bedrooms have recently
been renovated. Breakfast is served
in rustic, beamed surroundings.

Wandl

Petersplatz 9, A-1010. **Map** 2 D5 &
5 C3. **C** 534550. **FAX** 5345577.
Rooms: 138. 🛏 134. 1 ⊞ 24 TV
⚹ ⚹ ⚹ ⚹ ⚹ ⚹ AE, DC,
MC, V, JCB. €€€ W www.hotel-
wandl.com

Close to the Peterskirche in the
very centre of the city is the
characterful, old-fashioned Wandl
Hotel. It has been in the same
family for several generations. Some
of the building's finer features
were wiped out by bombs so only
parts of its stuccoed style remain,
notably in a few bedrooms and in
the covered courtyard that serves

as the breakfast room. Other bedrooms are plainer but generally
large and with parquet floors.

Zur Wiener Staatsoper

Krugerstrasse 11, A-1010. **Map** 4 E1
& 6 D5. **C** 5131274. **FAX** 513127415.
Rooms: 22. 🛏 1 ⊞ TV ⚹ ⚹
⚹ AE, MC, V. €€€
@ office@zurwienerstaatsoper.at

A tall, thin 19th-century building
on a pedestrian street off Kärntner
Strasse houses this simple little
hotel. Its façade is great fun:
caryatids show off over the porch
and faces peer out of the plasterwork above. Inside, the breakfast
room, bedrooms and bathrooms
(all with showers) are squeezed into
the limited space available.

Kaiserin Elisabeth

Weihburggasse 3, A-1010. **Map** 4 E1
& 6 D4. **C** 51526. **FAX** 515267.
Rooms: 63. 🛏 1 ⊞ TV ⚹ ⚹
⚹ P ⚹ AE, DC, MC, V, JCB.
€€€€ @ kaiserin@ins.at

This fetching town house is in a
side street only yards from the
Stephansdom. It dates from the
14th century and in the 1800s
hosted many famous musicians
such as Wagner and Liszt. Persian
rugs lie on parquet floors in the
elegant public rooms. The *fin-de-
siècle*-style bedrooms are smart.
Smaller double rooms and singles
have showers only in the bath-
room. You may find it less friendly
than other similar city centre hotels.

K+K Palais

Rudolfsplatz 11, A-1010. **Map** 2 E4 &
6 D1. **C** 5331353. **FAX** 533135370.
Rooms: 66. 🛏 1 ⊞ TV ⚹ ⚹
⚹ P ⚹ AE, DC, MC, V, JCB.
€€€€ @ kk.palais.hotel@kuk.at

Canary yellow walls abound in
this successful modern establishment set within a fine 19th-century
building. An impressive glass-
fronted lobby leads through to a
smart breakfast room cum bar and
up a marble staircase to simple,
fresh bedrooms with white duvets
and wicker chairs. The hotel is
situated in a quiet, grassy square
in a business area.

König von Ungarn

Schulerstrasse 10, A-1010. **Map** 2 E5
& 6 D3. **C** 515840. **FAX** 515848.
Rooms: 33. 🛏 1 ⊞ TV ⚹ ⚹
⚹ P ⚹ 11 ⚹ AE, DC, MC,
V, JCB. €€€€ W www.kvu.at

Atmospheric and extremely good
value, the König von Ungarn
(The King of Hungary) is highly
recommended. Framed signatures
of famous visitors from past
centuries cover its walls, and

Mozart is said to have composed *The Marriage of Figaro* in a part of the building now known as the Figarohaus *(see p72)*. The covered central courtyard with its elegant bar/sitting room is one of the city's loveliest. Well-prepared traditional specialities are served in the vaulted red dining rooms. Most bedrooms are large with appealing rustic furniture; more peaceful rooms are to the rear.

Mailberger Hof

Annagasse 7, A-1010. **Map** 4 E1 & 6 D4. **⟦** 51206410. **FAX** 512064110.
Rooms: 35. ⟦⟧ 34. ① ⊞ TV ⚡ ⟦
⟦ ⟦ **P** ⟦ ⟦ AE, DC, MC, V.
€€€€€ W www.mailbergerhof.at

Virtually opposite the Römischer Kaiser Wien *(see below)*, the Baroque Mailberger Hof is a lovely hotel converted from medieval houses. You can dine in its fine open courtyard under parasols, or in the striking, vaulted restaurant. A wide, stone staircase leads to the bedrooms; most overlook the courtyard, are tastefully furnished and have plenty of space.

Am Schubertring

Schubertring 11, A-1010. **Map** 2 F5 & 6 D5. **⟦** 717020. **FAX** 7139966.
Rooms: 39. ⟦⟧ ① ⊞ TV ⚡ ⟦
⟦ ⟦ **P** ⟦ ⟦ AE, DC, MC, V, JCB. €€€€
@ hotel.amschubertring@cello.at

This Ringstrasse-style building contains one of the few Jugendstil hotels in the city. Art Deco prints, murals and lamps decorate the smart bar, breakfast and sitting rooms. The hotel's bedrooms on the sixth floor have thick carpets and high-quality reproduction furniture. Some are furnished in Jugendstil fashion with dark wood, others in lighter Biedermeier style. Quiet rooms at the back are available. Every detail has been carefully considered, and the staff show an equal amount of care.

Römischer Kaiser Wien

Annagasse 16, A-1010. **Map** 4 E1 & 6 D4. **⟦** 51277510. **FAX** 512775113.
Rooms: 24. ⟦⟧ ① ⊞ TV ⟦ ⚡
⟦ ⟦ ⟦ AE, DC, MC, V, JCB.
€€€€€ W www.bestwestern-ce.com

This terraced house, a classic example of a Viennese miniature Baroque palace, was built for the Imperial Chancellor in 1684. Stylish public rooms with chandeliers and rugs on tiles occupy the ground floor. Upstairs, the bedrooms are cheerful, creamy concoctions; there are also cheaper attic rooms. Bicycles can be hired at the hotel.

Vienna Marriott

Parkring 12a, A-1010. **Map** 4 D1 & 6 E4. **⟦** 515180. **FAX** 515186736.
Rooms: 313. ⟦⟧ ① ⊞ 24 TV ⚡
⟦ ⟦ ⟦ ⟦ ⟦ ⟦ **P** ⚡
⟦ ⟦ AE, DC, MC, V, JCB.
€€€€€ W www.marriot.com

A panoply of shops, cafés, bars and restaurants fill the open-plan atrium of this modern glass hotel, situated on the Ringstrasse. There are fairy lights and waterfalls to try to soothe the frenetic atmosphere. Although the hotel lacks a dedicated business centre, it does have business facilities, and is one of the few establishments in the city to have a swimming pool. The bedrooms are generally large, but despite sound-proofing and air-conditioning, those looking on to the Stadtpark can be noisy.

HOFBURG
QUARTER

Nossek

Graben 17, A-1010. **Map** 2 D5 & 5 C3. **⟦** 53370410. **FAX** 5353646.
Rooms: 28. ⟦⟧ 26. ① ⊞ ⟦ ⟦
⟦ ⟦ €€ @ pension.nossek@faxvia.net

You will need to book months in advance to procure a room with a balcony overlooking the Graben in this elegant, but simple, family-run pension. It is spread over three floors and most bedrooms, though short on facilities and with rudimentary bathrooms, are rather special: rugs cover the parquet floors and period furniture and tasteful paintings abound. Equally attractive are the yellow breakfast room, with its brass chandeliers, and the adjacent sitting room.

Pertschy

Habsburgergasse 5, A-1010. **Map** 2 D5 & 5 C3. **⟦** 534490. **FAX** 5344949.
Rooms: 47. ⟦⟧ ① ⊞ TV ⚡ ⟦
⟦ AE, DC, MC, JCB, V. €€€
W www.pertschy.com

This pension is an endearing combination of rather dowdy décor and a fine 300-year-old building. You enter a courtyard through ancient gates and ascend a wide, stone staircase. A green, carpeted walkway connects the bedrooms, each newly renovated with Rococo-style furnishings and adorned with crystal chandeliers. The breakfast room is decorated in mahogany in coffee house style. The clip clop of the hooves of *Fiaker* horses *(see p250)* clattering along the street where the hotel is located adds to the atmosphere.

Astoria

Führichgasse 1, A-1015. **Map** 5 C4. **⟦** 515770. **FAX** 5157782.
Rooms: 118. ⟦⟧ ① ⊞ TV ⚡ ⟦
⟦ ⟦ ⟦ **P** ⟦ ⟦ ⟦ AE, DC, MC, V, JCB. €€€€
W www.austria-trend.at

Perhaps the many opera stars who pop in here for a drink do so not only because it is just a stone's throw away from the auditorium, but also because this cosy turn-of-the-century hotel is less in the limelight than some of the more famous places close by. The panelled Jugendstil foyer leads to a rather grand dining room on the first floor. There are some splendid bedrooms, many with their own brass letterboxes. It is worth paying a little more for the extra space and period furnishings.

Ambassador

Neuer Markt 5, A-1010. **Map** 4 D1 & 6 D4. **⟦** 96161. **FAX** 5132999.
Rooms: 86. ⟦⟧ ① ⊞ TV ⚡ ⟦
⟦ ⟦ ⟦ **P** ⟦ ⟦ AE, DC, MC, V, JCB. €€€€€
W www.ambassador.at

The city's best-located 5-star hotel has a 19th-century, Ringstrasse-style façade looking on to Kärntner Strasse, with an al fresco café terrace. Marble, pillars, tapestries, chandeliers and a superfluity of regal crimson and gold endow the hotel with an ostentatious, dated magnificence. Visiting presidents and princes have stayed in the best bedrooms. Some of these have their own sitting rooms, which are screened behind heavy drapes.

SCHOTTENRING AND
ALSERGRUND

Regina

Rooseveltplatz 15, A-1096. **Map** 1 C4 & 5 A1. **⟦** 404460. **FAX** 4088392.
Rooms: 128. ⟦⟧ ① ⊞ TV ⚡ ⟦
⟦ ⟦ ⟦ ⟦ AE, DC, MC, V, JCB.
€€€€€ W www.kremslehuer.hotels.or.at

This huge 19th-century building, just outside the Ringstrasse, has enough stature to live comfortably next to the Votivkirche *(see p111)*. Inside there's a certain grandeur too, with brass chandeliers and classical statues. The building has been a hotel since 1896. In the restaurant there is a photo of its staff in 1913, while an ancient wine press dominates the café. Today, the hotel caters mainly for tourist groups. The old-fashioned bedrooms are rather lacking in modern comforts and are a bit of a let down.

MUSEUM AND TOWNHALL QUARTER

Wild

Lange Gasse 10, A-1080. **Map** 3 B1.
C 4065174. **FAX** 4022168.
Rooms: 22. 1 ⊞ ⬆ P ♿ AE,
DC, MC, V. € W www.pension-wild.com

This pension, in the heart of the Josefstadt area, is our cheapest recommendation by some margin. It is run by an extremely friendly woman and her son. The small bedrooms are all spotlessly clean, properly furnished and have a washbasin. A toilet and a shower are shared between every two or three rooms. There is a kitchen on each floor and a breakfast room by the reception area.

Graf Stadion

Buchfeldgasse 5, A-1080. **Map** 1 B5.
C 4055284. **FAX** 405011184.
Rooms: 40. ⬆ 1 ⊞ TV ♿ ⬆
⬆ P ♿ AE, DC, MC, V. €€
W www.graf-stadion.com

An unsung Biedermeier building *(see pp30–31)* on an atmospheric backstreet contains the low-key, inexpensive Graf Stadion hotel. Some of the house's features are lovely, such as a vaulted breakfast room (likewise ground-floor bedrooms) and a superb Art Deco lift with an upholstered seat and frosted glass. The bedrooms are pleasantly simple, with chrome bedsteads, but lack mod cons.

Museum

Museumstrasse 3, A-1070. **Map** 3 C1.
C 5234426. **FAX** 523442630.
Rooms: 15. ⬆ 1 ⊞ ♿ P TV
⬆ ⬆ ♿ AE, DC, MC, V. €€
@ hotel.museum@surfen.at

Behind a fine façade coated with *putti* and wavy wrought-iron balconies, and set above a cinema showing black-and-white movies, this is a classic Viennese pension. It is right on the doorstep of the main museums. The spartan but massive bedrooms have high ceilings and wooden floors, and the sitting and breakfast rooms have furry chairs, ornate fireplaces and, of course, chandeliers.

Altstadt Vienna

Kirchengasse 41, A-1070. **Map** 3 B1.
C 52633990. **FAX** 5234901.
Rooms: 36 (11 suites). ⬆ 1 ⊞
♿ TV ⬆ ♿ ⬆ P ♿ ♿ AE,
DC, MC, V. €€€
W www.altstadt.at

Situated in an interesting old quarter just west of the main museums, the Altstadt, open since 1991, has already become extremely popular. Designer lighting, boldly-coloured walls and striking modern furnishings bring life to the ample rooms of this 19th-century patrician house. The polished herringbone-patterned floors and high ceilings are very attractive. The bedrooms at the rear of the hotel couldn't be more peaceful, while those at the front overlook a church and tiled roofs. The buffet breakfast is good, the service excellent.

Josefshof

Josefsgasse 4-6, A-1080. **Map** 1 B5.
C 40419. **FAX** 40419150. *Rooms:* 66.
⬆ 1 ⊞ TV ♿ ♿ ⬆ ♿ ♿
♿ ♿ AE, DC, MC, V. JCB. €€€
W www.josefshof.com

The handsome yellow façade of the Biedermeier Josefshof rises to a bell-shaped flourish. It is just down the road from Vienna's English Theatre *(see p228)* in a quiet backstreet. A marble and glass hallway suggests more grandeur than really exists, but the breakfast room, opening on to a garden courtyard, is pleasant. The bedrooms are smart with high-quality reproduction furniture and parquet flooring. The out-of-season rates are generally better value than those in high season.

Zipser

Lange Gasse 49, A-1080. **Map** 1 B5.
C 404540. **FAX** 408526613.
Rooms: 47. ⬆ 46. 1 ⊞ TV ♿
♿ ⬆ P ♿ ♿ AE, DC, MC, V.
JCB. €€€ W www.nethotels.com

This pension in the Josefstadt area does not have as much character as some of the others in Vienna, but it does have smart modern carpets and furniture throughout, and the atmosphere is very friendly. Ask for one of the larger bedrooms at the rear of the hotel: they have excellent bathrooms and big wooden balconies which are high up and overlook an attractive leafy courtyard. These rooms are quieter too.

K+K Maria Theresia

Kirchberggasse 6-8, A-1070.
Map 3 B1. **C** 521230. **FAX** 5212370.
Rooms: 133. ⬆ 1 ⊞ TV ♿ ♿
♿ ⬆ ⬆ P ♿ ♿ ♿ AE, DC,
MC, V. €€€€ W www.kuk.com

The sister to the K+K Palais *(see p196)* is more popular with tourist groups. The modern building offers a similar overwhelmingly yellow experience and has striking modern furnishings – black leather, ethnic rugs and abstract

prints. A few of the bedrooms have balconies; some others have commanding city views. Avant-garde furniture shops and galleries abound in the surrounding streets.

OPERA AND NASCHMARKT

Sacher

Philarmonikerstrasse 4, A-1010.
Map 4 D1 & 5 C5. **C** 51456.
FAX 51456810. *Rooms:* 109. ⬆ 1
⊞ 24 TV ♿ ♿ ♿ ♿ ♿
P ♿ ♿ ♿ AE, DC, MC, V, JCB.
€€€€€ W www.sacher.com

Vienna's most famous hotel, the Sacher *(see p136)* has been a haunt for the regal and wealthy ever since it opened in 1876. Now its café is full of tourists thanks to the eponymous chocolate cake *(see p207)*. The many-panelled public rooms, in marble and red velvet, hung with oil paintings, maintain an intimate scale. The more expensive bedrooms are equally opulent, while the standard rooms, though hardly less comfortable, are less evocative. Whether you go for a slice of *Torte* or stay for a weekend, you will receive outstanding service.

BELVEDERE QUARTER

Suzanne

Walfischgasse 4, A-1010. **Map** 4 D1
& 6 D5. **C** 5132507. **FAX** 5132500.
Rooms: 26. ⬆ 1 ⊞ TV ♿ ♿
⬆ P ♿ ♿ AE, DC, MC, V. €€
W www.pension-suzanne.at

This popular pension lies just steps from Kärntner Strasse and the Opera House. It is hidden away behind an ugly concrete block and sited over a flower shop and a sex shop. However, the bedrooms, with paintings and comfortable armchairs, have old-fashioned charm and are spread over a number of floors. The more expensive have kitchenettes.

Bristol

Kärntner Ring 1, A-1015. **Map** 4 D2 &
6 D5. **C** 515160. **FAX** 51516550.
Rooms: 140. ⬆ 1 ⊞ 24 TV ♿
♿ ♿ ♿ ♿ ⬆ P ♿ ♿ ♿
AE, DC, MC, V, JCB. €€€€€
W www.westin.com

The *fin-de-siècle* Bristol is a very luxurious hotel. The location is superb: on the Ringstrasse and opposite the opera (though just within the Belvedere Quarter). The style – marble, gilt, antiques and paintings everywhere – is of dignified opulence. Each public room is an institution: the famous Korso restaurant for dining *(see p213)*, the gold-pillared sitting room for afternoon tea. Bedrooms divide into top-floor penthouses, superb business suites, and the rest.

Imperial

Kärntner Ring 16, A-1015. **Map** 4 D2 & 6 D5. **C** 501100. **FAX** 50110410. **Rooms:** 138. ▣ 🔲 1 🔲 24 TV ✦ ✦ 🔳 🛏 🔳 🔳 P Y ❚❚ 🔳 AE, DC, MC, V, JCB. €€€€€ W www.luxurycollection.com

If you stay at the Imperial you may well be sleeping under the same roof as a head of state or two. The grandest of Vienna's top hotels exudes an air of exclusivity in its famous, panelled restaurant and its wonderful café (full of elderly ladies). Its over-the-top Ringstrasse style *(see pp32–3)* is best displayed in a monumental marble staircase. In the 1950s, two extra floors were added, containing smaller rooms designed in cherry wood.

Im Palais Schwarzenberg

Schwarzenbergplatz 9, A-1030. **Map** 4 E2. **C** 7984515. **FAX** 7984714. **Rooms:** 44. ▣ 🔲 1 🔳 24 TV ✦ 🔳 🛏 🔳 🔳 P Y ❚❚ 🔳 AE, DC, MC, V, JCB. €€€€€ W www.palais-schwarzenberg.com

Occupying a portion of the huge Baroque Schwarzenburg Palace *(see p148)* in its 18-acre (7.5-ha) landscaped park, this hotel has an undeniably breathtaking setting. Honeymoon territory for some, and a getaway from the hurly-burly of Vienna's busier luxury hotels for others, this hotel is surprisingly intimate. Each of its imaginative vaulted public rooms, including its conservatory dining room, are cosy and relaxing. The main building has the larger, better bedrooms, with antiques and fine paintings. The adjacent stable block has smaller, more modern rooms.

FURTHER AFIELD

Altwienerhof

Herklotzgasse 6, A-1150. **C** 8926000. **FAX** 89260008. **Rooms:** 25. ▣ 18. 🔲 1 🔳 TV 🔳 🔳 ❚❚ 🔳 AE, DC, MC, V. €€ W www.altwienerhof.at

The Kellners' restaurant-with-rooms lies some way from the centre but close to an underground stop. Many of the overnight guests are French – understandable when outstanding cuisine is the order of the day. Formal dining takes place

in impressive mahogany and tapestry-panelled rooms, a lovely conservatory and, in summer, a tree-lined courtyard; one option for residents is a no-choice half-board meal. Old-fashioned, comfortable bedrooms, ranging from stylish suites to simple rooms with just a basin, offer very good value.

Nordbahn

Praterstrasse 72, A-1020. **C** 211300. **FAX** 2113072. **Rooms:** 78. ▣ 🔲 1 🔳 TV ✦ 🛏 🔳 🔳 P Y 🔳 AE, DC, MC, V. €€ W www.hotel-nordbahn.at

The famous Ferris Wheel at the Prater *(see pp160–61)* and the underground are both about five minutes' walk from the Nordbahn. Situated on the busy, tree-lined Praterstrasse, this rather characterless but roomy hotel boasts a small bar, a terrace of sorts, a free car park and a library. The bedrooms offer comfort rather than style and it is a good idea to ask for a room away from the main road. Max Steiner, who wrote the film scores for *Gone With The Wind* and *Casablanca*, was born here on 10 May 1888.

Gartenhotel Glanzing

Glanzinggasse 23, A-1190. **C** 47042720. **FAX** 470427214. **Rooms:** 18. ▣ 🔲 1 🔳 TV ✦ 🔳 🛏 🔳 P 🔳 AE, DC, MC, V. €€ W www.gartenhotel-glanzing.at

Built in the 1930s, this interesting ivy-festooned hotel has a rambling garden and stands in leafy suburbs close to the wine villages. Many of the guests are from the American Embassy nearby. Transport to the centre is a five-minute walk away. A civilized retreat, the hotel has a grand piano in the main room, and big bedrooms which make the most of great views. Some bedrooms are modern, others are in Biedermeier style. The hotel stresses its conviviality and extends its welcome to children.

Landhaus Fuhrgassl-Huber

Neustift am Walde, Rathstrasse 24, A-1190. **C** 44030336. **FAX** 4402714. **Rooms:** 38. ▣ 🔲 1 🔳 TV ✦ 🔳 🛏 🔳 P Y 🔳 AE, MC, V. €€

The accordion tunes and rustic décor of this faultlessly spruce hotel may make a welcome, down-to-earth break from classical music and Baroque frippery. The hotel lies in a typical wine village: there's a *Heuriger (see p216)* next door, and the hotel owner has his own just up the street. In addition, he owns the vineyards behind the

hotel. His daughter and son-in-law are the managers, and the hotel is prettily decked out in pine, with tiled floors and stencilled furniture. A bus to the centre stops virtually outside and the journey takes a little over 30 minutes.

Biedermeier

Landstrasser Hauptstrasse 28, A-1030. **Map** 4 F1. **C** 716710. **FAX** 71671503. **Rooms:** 203. ▣ 🔲 1 🔳 TV ✦ 🔳 🛏 🔳 🔳 P Y ❚❚ 🔳 AE, DC, MC, V, JCB. €€€€ W www.dorint.de

This hotel occupies the whole complex of a superbly restored narrow, yellow Biedermeier passage courtyard. It offers guests a Vienna in microcosm: a plank-floored tavern, a *Heuriger* wine cellar and a traditional coffee house that spreads into a bar and restaurant. The large, spacious bedrooms, almost all looking down on the pedestrianized, cobbled passage, are particularly quiet. The hotel lies off one of Vienna's main shopping streets, less than ten minutes on foot from the Ringstrasse.

Inter-Continental Wien

Johannesgasse 28, A-1037. **Map** 4 E1 & 6 E5. **C** 711220. **FAX** 7134489. **Rooms:** 453. ▣ 🔲 1 🔳 24 TV ✦ ✦ 🔳 🛏 🔳 🔳 🔳 P Y ❚❚ 🔳 AE, DC, MC, V, JCB. €€€€ W www.vienna.intercontinental.com

So cosmopolitan is the efficient Inter-Continental that it even offers Japanese dishes for breakfast. Other aspects are more Viennese: a pianist and violinist play nightly in the bar area of the elegant, chan-deliered foyer, and the heralded Vier Jahreszeiten restaurant *(see p214)* serves local specialities in nouvelle-cuisine style. The hotel is a two-minute walk from the Ringstrasse. The upper-floor bedrooms in this modern block have good views across the Stadtpark.

Vienna Hilton

Am Stadtpark, A-1030. **Map** 4 F1 & 6 F4. **C** 717000. **FAX** 7130691. **Rooms:** 600. ▣ 🔲 1 🔳 24 TV ✦ 🔳 🛏 🔳 🔳 🔳 P Y ❚❚ 🔳 AE, DC, MC, V, JCB. €€€€€ W www.hilton.com

This unprepossessing tower block is well situated just off the Ringstrasse and on top of the airport shuttle terminal. Focused around a multi-coloured, glass-roofed foyer, you can find bars, shops, a pleasing café cum restaurant and a business centre. The higher you go, the better the views and the plusher and pricier the bedrooms.

RESTAURANTS, CAFÉS AND BARS

VIENNA IS AN international city, probably to a greater extent than any other city in central Europe. As well as the rich and varied local cuisine, there are also Chinese, Greek, Turkish, Indian and other types of restaurant. Eating out is a popular local pastime.

The restaurants in the listings *(see pp211–14)* have been selected from the best Vienna can offer, across all price ranges. They are organized by area and price. Most restaurants serve lunch from noon to 2pm and many offer

Papier-mâché waitress outside restaurant

a fixed-priced menu. In the evenings, the Viennese start to eat from 6pm, and most restaurants close around 10pm. Many establishments serve food throughout the day, and some others offer mid-morning snacks. *Light Meals and Snacks* on pages 215–17 lists some of the city's best bars, wine bars, snack bars and *Café-Konditoreien*. Coffee houses *(see pp58–61)* are a Viennese institution: serving coffee, drinks and snacks, there are also plenty of newspapers to read. The *Phrase Book* on pages 287–8 will help you when ordering meals.

WHAT TO EAT

AS AN IMPERIAL CAPITAL, Vienna was influenced by the customs and foods brought to it by its far-flung population. Thus the local cuisine is an amalgamation of styles and traditions from Poland, Italy, Hungary and Bohemia, as well as from Austria itself.

Wine cellar sign

Many of the famous dishes actually originated elsewhere. *Wiener Schnitzel*, for example, came from Byzantium via Italy, and *Gulasch* came from Hungary *(see p205)*. When a restaurant anywhere in Austria is proud of its cuisine, it proclaims that it offers *Wiener Küche* (Viennese cuisine). In recent years, country cooking

has become more popular, and many top Austrian chefs have developed their own individual styles.

The Viennese relish boiled beef and their *Schnitzel* (breaded escalopes of veal or pork) are deservedly famous *(see p205)*. In winter most restaurants offer a good range of goose and game, and the puddings and pastries are sumptuous. Seasonal foods such as wild mushrooms are popular. At snack bars and delicatessens (which double up as informal eateries) you can eat open sandwiches, hors d'oeuvres and salads utilizing the many varieties of breads with smoked fish, hams and smoked meats. See also *Reading the Menu* on p202.

Local musician at the Augustinerkeller *(see p217)*

TYPES OF RESTAURANTS AND SNACK BARS

IT IS POSSIBLE to eat at any time of the day in Vienna. The word for the afternoon pause for a snack is known as *Jause*, and the mid-morning snack is known as *Gabelfrühstück (see p215)*. The city's eating establishments cater for between-meal eating and a wide range of restaurants, bars and snack bars offer modest or grand meals in the morning, afternoon and evening, as well as at lunchtime.

There is a large number of luxurious restaurants, most of them in or near the Stephansdom Quarter. Some, including those in the large hotels, offer international menus. Other restaurants concentrate on local

Open sandwiches available at Zum Schwarzen Kameel *(see p212)*

cuisine. They offer sufficient variety to entice gastronomes, and some of the best of them present specialities from other parts of Austria. These include such dishes as filled dumplings from Carinthia – at Bei Max *(see p212)* – or the beef and pumpkin oil dishes from Styria at the Steirereck *(see p214)*.

Most people, of course, do not eat routinely at the grander and relatively costly establishments. The basic eating house in the city is the *Beisl*. Quality varies from simple and dull to inventive and stylish. Most have plain interiors, with wooden floors and simple furnishings and tableware. Menus are usually confined to straightforward dishes, with a range of local soups and meats. Few bottled wines are available, but there are always wines by the glass, of variable quality, and good beer. *Beisln* are usually open all day, and

Garden scene at a *Heuriger (see p216)* where local wine growers are licensed to sell their own wine

Typical sausage stand (or *Wurststand*) in the city centre

residents will often refer to their favourite establishment of this kind as their *Lokal* (neighbourhood restaurant). There are also many *Wirtshäuser* or inns, and some *Gasthäuser*, slightly more sophisticated restaurants.

There are ethnic restaurants scattered throughout the city, but they are sparse within the Ringstrasse. For good Turkish and Greek food, the best hunting ground is the Schottenring and Alsergrund area. Many of the best Japanese restaurants are found in the streets near the Opera House.

The city's coffee houses *(see pp58–61)* are regarded as institutions. You can order a coffee and cake, have a drink or eat a full meal. They usually offer a range of simple dishes,

and most of them offer a three-course set lunch. The cooking is rarely outstanding, but the coffee house is convenient and familiar.

Many *Café-Konditoreien*, though better known for coffee, cakes and pastries, also offer a choice of simple meals and alcoholic drinks. The Stephansdom Quarter has many high-quality snack bars, which are often linked to grocery shops, and cafés – the latter tend to be less expensive. Pizzerias are now popular in Vienna and buffets offer simple sandwiches at affordable prices.

Wine bars, wine cellars and wine-growers' establishments called *Heurige (see p216)* all offer light meals at sensible prices. The latter are on the city outskirts in the wine-growing villages. Here wine is served at your table in a glass mug, and you fetch your food from a buffet. If fir branches are displayed outside it means the place is open and serving the home-pressed vintage. *Heuriger* is also the name used for wine of the most recent vintage.

MAKING RESERVATIONS

IN GENERAL it is wise to make a reservation if you are keen to patronize a particular restaurant. Even a simple *Beisl* can have a large and faithful

local clientele and you may be disappointed if you wander in and expect to find a free table. Coffee houses do not take reservations. If you are going to a *Heuriger* in a group you will need to book a table.

DRESS CODE

THE OLDER GENERATION of Viennese tend to dress formally when going out to eat at a good restaurant, but more casual clothes are also acceptable. In luxury or hotel restaurants it is wiser to err on the side of conservatism. In the city's grander restaurants, smarter clothes are invariably expected; while in the more informal places like *Beisln* or *Wirtshäuser*, and especially in *Heurige* where the Viennese go to let their hair down, you can wear whatever you feel comfortable in.

A trendy city bar, the Tunnel *(see p217)*, on Florianigasse

Do & Co restaurant *(see p211)* overlooking the Stephansdom

READING THE MENU

Menus can be hard to decipher, even for those who speak German, as the Viennese have their own terms for certain dishes *(see* Phrase Book *pp287–8).* Many waiters speak European languages and will be pleased to translate.

For a first course you can order soup *(Suppe)* or a cold or warm starter *(Kalte Vorspeise* or *Warme Vorspeise).* The main courses will be listed as *Hauptspeisen,* and desserts as *Mehlspeisen.* Most main courses in Viennese snack bars and restaurants are served with vegetables, but it is quite common to order a side salad as well. Cheese is usually eaten as an alternative to dessert, though there is nothing to stop you from ordering both if you prefer.

Wines and beers in simple restaurants are usually listed on the main menu. Elsewhere you should ask for the wine list, which will generally include an extensive range of Austrian wines as well as an international selection. Italian wines are popular in Austria, and there is usually a large choice in restaurants. Most restaurants serve wine by the glass. If you like dessert wine, try some *Eiswein* – so-called because the grapes are left on the vine until the first frost.

The Lehmann *(see p217),* one of the city's many *Café-Konditoreien*

HOW MUCH TO PAY

The huge variety of eating establishments in Vienna cater to every whim and pocket. At the cheaper end of the scale, such as in snack bars, you can eat well for around five euros. By choosing from one of the buffets at a wine cellar *(Weinkeller)* you can, depending on your selection, eat and drink satisfyingly for eight euros upwards. Coffee houses tend to be more expensive, and you should expect to pay about 12 euros or more for a light lunch in one of the more famous ones.

In a *Beisl* or a simple restaurant, soup generally costs from three euros, salads or first courses anything from around three to ten euros, and main courses from 8 to 15 euros. A three-course meal with a glass of wine or beer usually costs 18 euros upwards each. However, portions tend to be generous, and two courses are often sufficient. The fixed-price lunch is invariably good value.

Luxury restaurants and hotel restaurant prices are much higher, with fixed-price lunches costing about 30 euros. Yet these can be bargains in terms of service and quality. More elaborate set menus are sometimes available in the evenings, but prices are generally double. Eating à la carte can be expensive.

A decent bottle of wine in an average restaurant will cost 15 euros or more, but wines by the glass are nearly always available at around two euros. In a luxury restaurant a glass from a top estate will cost five to seven euros for the same quantity. Beer is generally reasonably priced: a ⅓ litre bottle costs two to three euros.

Although a service charge is sometimes included in the bill, you will be expected to leave an additional sum of up to 10% for service.

Credit cards are accepted in most of the luxury and hotel restaurants with a regular international clientele, but the majority of *Beisln* and standard Viennese restaurants only take cash.

SERVICE

SERVICE IS VARIABLE, with many waiters eager to take your order and advise you on the restaurant's specialities, while others may ignore you until you deliberately catch their eye. Although service can seem somewhat aloof, even the most busy waiter usually spares a moment to ask whether you are happy with your meal. Snack bars do not usually have waiters.

VEGETARIAN FOOD

THE VIENNESE are avid meat-eaters, so vegetarian restaurants are not common. Fortunately the few that do exist are of good quality (see *Choosing a Restaurant* on page 210). Salads are popular, and many places, such as *Heurige*, offer buffets with vegetarian dishes.

SMOKING

FEW RESTAURANTS have areas for non-smokers, but many restaurant owners are aware that foreigners may find smoking unacceptable while eating. If you make your preference clear when reserving a table, you should be placed in an area where you will be least affected.

Traditional Austrian musicians in a garden restaurant

CHILDREN

WELL-BEHAVED CHILDREN are generally welcome even in the grandest of restaurants. Children's portions are rarely specified on the menu, but almost every restaurant will be happy to provide a half-portion of most dishes. Do not expect children's favourites such as french fries and hamburgers, except at the fast food chains which often have a specific children's menu *(see p231)*. Children are expected to eat the same food as their elders.

Krah Krah bar sign

WHEELCHAIR ACCESS

THE VIENNESE are adept at manoeuvring wheelchairs over steps, but it is best to mention your needs when making a reservation. Some of the older establishments have narrow corridors or steps.

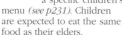

USING THE LISTINGS

The restaurant listings are on pages 211–14. Places to eat are listed according to area and price. Symbols after the address summarize facilities the restaurant offers. *Choosing a Restaurant* on page 210 is a quick-reference chart to help you decide where to eat.

🍽 fixed-price menu
V vegetarian food available
👶 caters for children
♿ wheelchair access
★ highly recommended
💳 credit cards accepted:
AE American Express
DC Diners Club
MC Mastercard/Access
V Visa
JCB Japanese Credit Bureau

Price categories for a three-course meal for one, including a ¼ litre of house wine, tax and service:
€ under 20 euros
€€ 21–30 euros
€€€ 31–40 euros
€€€€ 41–50 euros
€€€€€ over 50 euros

Restaurant in the Altwienerhof Hotel on Herklotzgasse *(see p214)*

What to Eat: Savoury Foods

Salzstangerl (right)

Siebenkorn-brot (left)

Hausbrot (right)

Kaiser-semmel (left)

Vollkorn Bauernbrot

VIENNESE COOKING is surprisingly varied, a reflection of imperial days when culinary traditions from many parts of Europe influenced the city's cooks. *Schnitzel* may have come to Austria via Milan, which was once under Austrian control. Soups are rich and flavoursome, and often include *Knödel* (dumplings). In winter, roast goose and duck appear on many menus as well as game dishes such as *Rehrücken* (saddle of venison). Seasonal vegetarian specialities include *Eierschwammerl* (chanterelle mushrooms) in autumn and *Spargel* (asparagus) in the summer months.

Frankfurter mit Senf
Frankfurters are one of the many types of sausage sold throughout the city. They are often served with mustard.

Leberknödelsuppe
This clear beef broth includes small dumplings made with liver, seasoned with parsley and marjoram.

Frittatensuppe
Thin strips of lightly seasoned pancakes are added to a clear beef soup.

Eierspeise
Served in the pan, this is like a scrambled omelette.

Smoked ham

Roast pork

Sauerkraut with juniper

Bauernschmaus
This simple country platter of hot meats can be found in many Viennese restaurants and is usually served with dumplings. The meats include frankfurters, a selection of ham, smoked pork, and roast pork or pork cutlet.

Eierschwammerl
Chanterelle mushrooms are picked in autumn and may be served in a salad.

Rindsgulasch
Originally from Hungary, this paprika-seasoned beef stew comes with dumplings.

Gefüllte Kalbsbrust
Breast of veal is filled with a variety of meat or vegetable stuffings.

Erdäpfelgulasch
This potato goulash often includes frank-furter sausages.

Wiener Schnitzel
The breaded veal escalope is fried until golden.

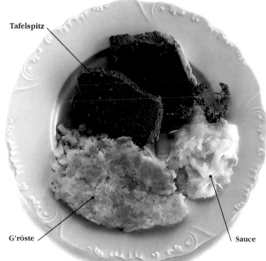

Tafelspitz

G'röste

Sauce

Tafelspitz mit G'röste
A favorite cut of beef is thickly sliced, boiled and served with fried grated potatoes and an apple and horseradish sauce. It is a typical lunchtime dish and was allegedly eaten every day by the Emperor Franz Joseph.

Gemischter Salat
Mixed salad ingredients are often arranged side by side.

Heringsalat
Herring is traditional on Ash Wednesday and served year-round. In salads, it is pickled.

Beef and rice stuffing

Tomato sauce

Gefüllte Paprika
Green peppers are stuffed with ground beef and rice and cooked in a tomato sauce.

What to Eat: Sweet Foods

F EW CITIES IN THE WORLD can rival Vienna's devotion to all things sweet. The Viennese enjoy cakes mid morning or afternoon, and set time aside for between-meal snacks – the afternoon coffee break is known as *Jause*. The finest *Torten* (gâteaux), pastries and cakes such as *Bischofsbrot* (Bishop's bread, which is sponge cake filled with nuts, raisins, glacé fruit and chocolate pieces) tend to be found in *Konditoreien (see p215)* and are usually consumed with a cup of coffee. Traditional Viennese puddings can be found in all good Viennese restaurants *(see pp211–14)* and are typically rich. Some innovative chefs have created their own versions.

Many *Konditoreien* offer cakes baked on the premises

DESSERTS

F ROM SWEET *Topfentascherl* (curd cheese envelopes) to *Kastanienreis* (chestnut purée), Vienna's dessert cuisine incorporates rich and varied ingredients. Some recipes are simple, others very extravagant. Fruits such as plums and apples fill featherlight dumplings, pancakes, fritters or strudels, and although *Mehlspeisen* (puddings) translates literally as "dishes with flour", ground almonds or hazelnuts can replace the flour. As well as the selection here there are less obvious choices such as sweet "pasta" served with poppyseeds to create *Mohnnudeln*.

Apfelstrudel
Apple and raisins are encased in a light strudel pastry dusted with icing sugar. The strudel is served warm or cold.

Palatschinken
Thicker than a French crêpe, the Austrian pancake is filled with fruit, curd cheese, chocolate sauce – or simply jam, as here.

Reisauflauf mit Äpfeln
Reisauflauf *is a rich rice soufflé. It can be cooked in a creamy and light style, or as a heartier dessert. Here it includes apple and is served with raspberry syrup.*

Mohr im Hemd
This rich chocolate pudding is steamed and served with hot chocolate sauce. Chilled whipped cream, usually scented with vanilla sugar, is added just before serving.

Topfenknödel
Light curd cheese dumplings are coated with breadcrumbs (or ground walnuts) which have been fried crisply in butter, and served hot with a fruit compôte or purée.

CAKES AND PASTRIES

Sachertorte is the best-known Viennese *Torte* but there are dozens of others, such as *Dobostorte*, a sponge cake sandwiched together with chocolate butter cream. Many cakes and pastries include chocolate, coffee or cream, while others use fresh fruit and wafer-thin strudel pastry. *Linzertorte* is a classic almond and jam pastry and *Guglhupf* is traditionally made with yeast, though there are many variations. The hollow centre may be filled with flowers for birthdays. *Faschingskrapfen* are deep-fried apricot doughnuts made in the pre-Lenten Carnival time known as *Fasching* (see p65).

Dobostorte
Invented by pâtissier Josef Dobos in Hungary in 1887, this rich cake alternates equal layers of sponge and chocolate butter cream and is glazed with caramel. Doboschnitten are exactly the same but sold in individual rectangles.

Linzertorte
A sweet almond pastry case is filled with raspberry, apricot or redcurrant jam and decorated with a pastry criss-cross pattern.

Sachertorte
The famous Sachertorte *has a layer of apricot jam beneath the thick, smooth chocolate coating.*

Mohnstrudel
The sweet, moist, yeast-based dough is spread with ground poppy seeds and raisins and folded over into a roulade.

Guglhupf
Baked in a fluted ring mould, variations on Guglhupf *include this marbelized chocolate version, Marmorguglhupf.*

Rehrücken
Shaped like the saddle of venison after which it is named, this chocolate cake is studded with almonds.

Esterházytorte
Available as a round cake or in rectangular slices, this sweetest of gâteaux is coated with feathered icing.

ORIGINAL SACHERTORTE

This celebrated chocolate gâteau was invented in 1832 by Prince Metternich's pastry chef, Franz Sacher. It has always been available from the Hotel Sacher shop in Kärntner Strasse, which sells it in a variety of sizes and packings. When the nearby Demel Konditorei claimed their *Sachertorte* was authentic on the grounds that a member of the Sacher family had sold them the recipe, the assertion provoked a protracted court case. Sacher won the right to the term "original *Sachertorte*" but was not able to stop the cake from being imitated in Vienna and all over the world.

What to Drink in Vienna

AUSTRIA is a source of excellent wine and good rich beers. Vienna itself is a wine-growing region. It is surrounded by vineyards which supply the *Heurige (see p216)* in villages on the edge of the city with young local wines. Fine Austrian wines are found in good restaurants *(see* Choosing a Restaurant, *p210)*. Home-produced wine is mainly white. Local red wines are improving, especially those from the Burgenland and Carnuntum districts. Sweet *Eiswein* is made from grapes left on the vines until the first frosts. Some first-class brandies are also produced – fruit brandies and schnaps are typical national beverages.

Beyond the villages north and west of Vienna lie vineyards producing *Heurige* wines

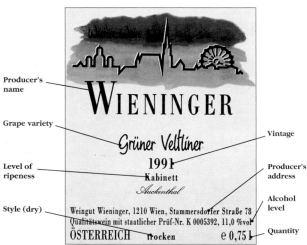

Chardonnay from Styria and sparkling wine from Lower Austria

AUSTRIAN WINES

THE MOST popular wine in Austria is Grüner Veltliner *(see below)*. Other wines include superb dry Rieslings, especially from the Wachau, and rich Weissburgunder (Pinot Blanc) from Burgenland. Red wines tend to be soft and lush – robust reds come from the Blaufränkisch grape *(see below)*. Among recent vintages, 1990 and 1992 were good.

Riesling from the Wachau can be light, or full bodied like the Smaragd style.

Producer's name
Grape variety
Vintage
Level of ripeness
Producer's address
Alcohol level
Style (dry)
Quantity

Grüner Veltliner is a fresh, fruity white wine. It is widely grown in Austria and is usually made in a dry style. It also makes excellent *Eiswein*.

St Laurent is a soft red wine; at its best it is rich and stylish.

Blaufränkisch is a quality local red – the best comes from Burgenland.

Krügel or ½ litre tankard

Seidl or standard ⅓ litre measure

Krügel or ½ litre of pale beer

Pfiff or ⅛ litre beer glass

Austrian Beers

Vienna has been producing good malty beers for more than 150 years. Viennese lagers are bronze in colour and sweet in flavour. They make an excellent accompaniment to the hearty soups and stews found in *Beisln (see p201)*. The local Ottakring brewery's *Gold Fassl* is typical of the style, although lighter Bavarian-type beers such as *Weizengold* are also commonly available. One of Austria's most popular beers is *Gösser*, produced in Styria and found in the pubs and restaurants of Vienna. Speciality beers include the Styrian *Eggenberger Urbock*, one of the strongest beers in the world. It is made by the Schloss Eggenberg brewery founded in the 17th century.

Kaiser beer, a light beer

Weizengold wheat beer

Gösser Spezial is rich

Bierhof beer mat advertising a pub in the Haarhof.

Null Komma Josef is a local alcohol-free beer.

Other Austrian Drinks

Austria offers a good range of non-alcoholic fruit juices such as *Himbeersaft* (raspberry syrup) or *Johannisbeersaft* (blackcurrant juice). Fruit is also the basis of many types of schnaps (sometimes called *Brand*). This powerful eau de vie is distilled from berries such as juniper and rowan as well as apricots *(Marillen)* and quince *(Quitten)*. It's worth paying the extra to sample the exquisite fruit schnaps produced by the dedicated specialists. *Almdudler* (herbal lemonade) is also a speciality. For a few weeks in autumn, fermenting grape juice, *Sturm*, is available. Milky in colour and quite sweet, it is more alcoholic than its grape flavour suggests.

Apricot schnaps

The Wiener Rathauskeller *(see p213)* is a popular restaurant serving a number of beers

Choosing a Restaurant

THE RESTAURANTS IN this book have been chosen for their good value or exceptional food. The key on page 203 explains the symbols used in the listings on pages 211–14.

Restaurant	Price	Ethnic Cuisine	Fixed Price Menu	Good Wine List	Late Opening	Outdoor Tables	Vegetarian Meals
STEPHANSDOM QUARTER (see p211–12)							
Zum Bettelstudent	€		■		■	●	■
Lustig Essen	€	●			■		
Zu den Drei Hacken	€€				■	●	■
Figlmüller	€€						
Griechenbeisl	€€				■	●	■
Haas & Haas	€€					●	■
Hedrich	€€					●	
MAK Café	€€				■		
Pfudl	€€				■		
Weibel's Wirtshaus	€€			●	■		■
Wrenkh	€€		■		■	●	■
Zum Kuckuck	€€€		■		■		
Schimanszky	€€€						■
Zum Schwarzen Kameel	€€€			●			■
Plachutta	€€€€					●	■
Do & Co	€€€€€			●	■	●	■
HOFBURG QUARTER (see p212)							
Bei Max	€€		■		■		
Ilona-Stüberl	€€	●				●	
Palmenhaus	€€				■	●	■
Prima	€€				■	●	
Stadtbeisl	€€				■	●	■
Yugetsu	€€	●	■		■		
SCHOTTENRING AND ALSERGRUND (see p212)							
Lokanta Sarikoç	€€	●			■		
Stomach	€€				■	●	■
TOWNHALL AND MUSEUM QUARTER (see p212)							
Spatzennest	€		■	●	■	●	■
Witwe Bolte	€€				■	●	■
Kupferdachl	€€€				■	●	■
Schnattl	€€€		■	●	■		
Schubertstüberl	€€€		■		■		
Wiener Rathauskeller	€€€				■		■
Grotta Azzurra	€€€€	●	■	●	■		
OPERA AND NASCHMARKT (see p213)							
Hunger-Künstler	€		■		■		■
Hansy (Smutny)	€€		■		■	●	
BELVEDERE QUARTER (see p213)							
Do & Co	€€€						
Imperial	€€€€		■	●	■		■
Korso	€€€€€		■	●	■		
Palais Schwarzenberg	€€€€€			●		●	
FURTHER AFIELD (see p214)							
Gmoa Keller	€		■	●	■	●	■
Zum Herkner	€€					●	
Marxer Stub'n	€€				■	●	■
Eckel	€€€			●		●	■
Hietzinger Bräu	€€€			●			
Vikerls Lokal	€€€		■	●	■	●	
Vincent	€€€		■	●	■		■
Niky's Kuchlmasterei	€€€€		■	●	■	●	
Altwienerhof	€€€€€			●	■	●	
Steirereck	€€€€€		■	●			■

STEPHANSDOM QUARTER

Zum Bettelstudent

Johannesgasse 12. **Map** 4 E1 & 6 D4.
(5132044. ○ 10am–2am daily.
¶ **V** **☐** AE, MC, V, DC, JCB. **€**

The original owner of this restaurant included a number of cheap and filling dishes on the menu to attract students. Today, the clientele is more varied and most of the food is Viennese. The goulash and beefsteak on toast, served with a salad, are good, and there is a large selection of beers.

Lustig Essen

Salvatorgasse 6. **Map** 2 D5 & 6 D2.
(5333037. ○ 11:30am–midnight daily. **V** **☐** MC. **€**

This smart airy restaurant serves a wide range of dishes in small portions. The food is not exclusively Viennese: you can eat snails here, or *tsatsiki*, or chicken curry with coconut. Whatever you order will be tasty and well presented.

Zu den Drei Hacken

Singerstrasse 28. **Map** 4 E1 & 6 D3.
(5125895. ○ 9am–midnight Mon–Sat. **V** **☐** AE, DC, MC, V. **€€**

It is claimed that Schubert and other denizens of Biedermeier Vienna frequented this wood-panelled *Beisl*. Today it offers a quiet, informal refuge just a few minutes' walk from the centre of the city. The menu features Italian as well as Viennese dishes.

Figlmüller

Wollzeile 5. **Map** 2 E5 & 6 D3.
(5126177. ○ 11am–10:30pm daily. ● Aug. **€€**

Figlmüller's is certainly touristy. It prides itself on serving the largest *Wiener Schnitzel* in Vienna and there is no reason to dispute this claim, as the breaded escalopes of pork spill over the edges of the plate and they are very tasty. The offal and steaks can also be excellent. All wines come from the owner's vineyards in Grinzing, where he also runs a *Heuriger*.

Griechenbeisl

Fleischmarkt 11. **Map** 2 F5 & 6 D2.
(5331941. ○ 11:30am–11:30pm daily. **V** **☐** AE, DC, MC, V, JCB. **€€**

There has been an inn here for 500 years, and its association with *Der Liebe Augustin (see p81)* has guaranteed a constant stream of tourists. The interior is charming, a maze of small panelled rooms through which the waiters carry heaped trays of food at amazing speed, and the Viennese cooking is adequate. The Griechenbeisl is popular – cosy and bustling.

Haas & Haas

Stephansplatz 4. **Map** 2 E5 & 6 D3.
(5122666. ○ 9am–8pm Mon–Fri, 9am–6:30pm Sat. **V** **☐** DC, V, MC. **€€**

This is a tea room and café rather than a formal restaurant, but its delightful courtyard garden offers a lovely spot for a light meal. The menu is limited but often includes local fish such as *Zander* (pike-perch) and Viennese classics such as *Tafelspitz (see p205)*. You can also order from a range of sandwiches and pastries.

Hedrich

Stubenring 2. **Map** 6 F3. **(** 5129588.
○ 11am–3pm, 6–10pm Mon–Fri.
★ **€€**

Richard Hedrich is one of Vienna's acclaimed chefs. His restaurant is small and thriving, even though it is only open on weekdays. Hedrich is most popular at lunchtime. The modern cooking has a delicate touch, yet portions are generous. Veal dishes such as sweetbreads and liver are particularly good, and so are the desserts. There are some good wines, too, which are also available by the glass.

MAK Café

Stubenring 5. **Map** 2 F5 & 6 F3.
(7140121. ○ 10am–2am Tue–Sun. **V** **€€**

The main attraction of this café, located in the Austrian Museum of Applied Arts *(see pp82–3)*, is its splendid interior, with a painted wooden ceiling and sparkling modern bars. The menu of light meals is varied, featuring prosciutto and guacamole, which make a change from the Viennese staples.

Pfudl

Bäckerstrasse 22. **Map** 6 D3.
(5126705. ○ 9am–2am Mon–Sat. **V** **☐** AE, DC, MC, V, JCB. **€€**

Seated in this rustic eatery, you could easily imagine yourself to be in the heart of the Austrian countryside. The cooking is traditional, with a large range of Viennese dishes, as well as seasonal specialities. This is a reasonably-priced, reliable restaurant, with generous portions. The wines come from Pfudl's own vineyards.

Weibel's Wirtshaus

Kumpfgasse 2. **Map** 6 E4.
(5123986. ○ 11:30am–midnight Mon–Sat. ● public hols. **V** **☐** AE, MC, V. **€€**

Hans Weibel owns the successful wine bar Vis-à-Vis *(see p217)* and in 1993 opened this Wirtshaus in an old house in a quiet lane in the Inner City. He has used the word Wirtshaus slightly tongue in cheek as the standard of food is higher than you would generally expect in a Wirtshaus. The menu is Viennese with a modern touch. However, most of the customers come especially for Weibel's selection of excellent Austrian and Italian wines, many available by the glass.

Wrenkh

Bauernmarkt 10. **Map** 2 E5 & 6 D3.
(5331526. ○ 11:30am–3pm 6pm–midnight Mon–Fri, 11:30am–3pm 6–11pm Sun and hols. **¶** **V** **☐** AE, DC, MC, V, JCB. **€€**

Wrenkh has a reputation as the best vegetarian restaurant in Vienna, and there are plenty of dishes, such as the risotto of wild mushrooms, that would satisfy all but the most dogged carnivores. The dessert menu, however, confirms that puritanism is not part of Wrenkh's philosophy. The interior is comfortable and the service helpful and efficient. There are good wines available by the glass.

Zum Kuckuck

Himmelpfortgasse 15. **Map** 4 E1 & 6 D4. **(** 5128470. ○ noon–2pm, 6pm–11pm Mon–Sat. **¶** **☐** AE, DC, MC, V, JCB. **€€€**

Zum Kuckuck is a charming little restaurant with painted banquettes. It is the perfect location for an intimate supper and at lunchtime the set menu is a true bargain. The dishes are mostly Viennese, with a few international touches. The game and fish dishes and the fruit desserts can be outstanding.

Schimanszky

Biberstrasse 2. **Map** 2 F5 & 6 E3.
(5134543. ○ noon–2pm, 6–10:30pm Mon–Fri, 6–10:30pm Sat. ● 2nd week Jul–2nd week Aug. **V** **☐** AE, DC, MC, V, JCB. **€€€**

Despite the modern art on the walls, Schimanszky is somewhat staid. The food is tasty, presenting attractive modern versions of traditional Viennese dishes. The menu is small and constantly changing and there are some intriguing combinations, such as scampi with raw ham, as well as traditional dishes such as pork with horseradish and root vegetables.

For key to symbols *see p203*

Zum Schwarzen Kameel

Bognergasse 5. **Map** 5 C3.
📞 5338967. ⏰ 8:30am–11:30pm
Mon–Sat. 🅥 ♿ 🈂 AE, DC, MC, V.
€€€

Purveyor of fine foods and wines since 1618, this is one of Vienna's oldest institutions. Beethoven was a regular customer at the shop and the Viennese have been visiting the famous snack bar *(see p217)* for centuries. The restaurant opened over 100 years ago, and the food is Viennese cuisine at its best.

Plachutta

Wollzeile 38. **Map** 2 E5 & 6 E3.
📞 5121577. ⏰ 11:30am–11pm
daily. 🅥 ♿ 🈂 DC, MC, AE, V.
€€€€

Plachutta is a smart, modern restaurant, with green and yellow décor and waiters in uniforms to match. The dish to eat here is *Tafelspitz (see p205)*. Or try the *Kruspelspitz*, which in this restaurant allows you to sample two types of boiled beef in the same dish. The wine list is unexciting.

Do & Co

Haas Haus, Stephansplatz 12.
Map 6 D3. 📞 5353969.
⏰ noon–3pm, 6pm–midnight
daily. 🅥 ♿ 🈂 V. €€€€€

With a roof terrace overlooking the Stephansdom, Do & Co has to have the most spectacular view in Vienna. Its international menu includes American steaks, Thai soups, sushi, and exotic fruits. The cooking is straightforward, sometimes even bland, rarely matching the elegant surroundings. The service can also be erratic. Come for the visual experience rather than the cuisine. A more reasonably priced branch of Do & Co is located in the Belvedere Quarter *(see p213)*.

(see p213)

HOFBURG QUARTER

Bei Max

Landhausgasse 2. **Map** 5 B3.
📞 5337359. ⏰ 11am–11pm
Mon–Fri, 11am–5pm Sat. ● 2 weeks
at Christmas (phone to check dates).
🅥 🍴 ♿ ★ 🈂 AE, DC, MC, V.
€€

Bei Max specializes in Carinthian dishes such as *Fleischnudel* or *Kasnudel*, which are pastry pockets stuffed with meat or cheese. There are four modestly-priced set menus as well as an à la carte menu. The cooking is reliable, portions are more than adequate and definitely good value. The wine list may be short but there are some interesting Austrian wines on offer.

Ilona-Stüberl

Bräunerstrasse 2. **Map** 5 C4.
📞 5339029. ⏰ noon–11pm daily.
🅥 ♿ 🈂 AE, DC, MC, V. €€

Located just off the Graben, this tiny wood-panelled eatery serves Hungarian food. The dishes are rich, tasty and filling. You'll find stuffed peppers and goulash on the menu, as well as delicious filled pancakes. There is also a good selection of beers on offer.

Palmenhaus

Burggarten. **Map** 4 D1 & 5 B4.
📞 5331033. ⏰ 10am–2am daily.
🅥 ♿ 🈂 AE, DC, MC, V, JCB. €€

This tasteful addition to Vienna's restaurant scene is housed in the newly restored Palmhouse of the Imperial Palace Gardens. The beautiful setting complements the inspired cuisine, which features fish and other dishes with a Mediterranean slant. The restaurant is particularly appealing during fine weather in the summer, when you can dine on the terrace, which seats up to 130 people.

Prima

Neuer Markt 2. **Map** 5 C4. 📞 5129-
202. ⏰ 9:30am–midnight daily. ♿
🈂 🅥 🈂 AE, DC, MC, V, JCB. €€

Although hot food is available here throughout the day, Prima is most popular with late-night diners emerging from the Opera. The menu is crammed with Viennese specialities, including potato soup, *Tafelspitz*, and *Gefüllte Kalbsbrust (see p205)*. Prima, which used to be called Halali, is also known for its wide selection of game dishes.

Stadtbeisl

Naglergasse 21. **Map** 2 D5 & 5 C3.
📞 5333507. ⏰ 10am–midnight
daily. 🅥 🈂 V. €€

Situated in a lovely 18th-century house with vaulted and panelled rooms, the Stadtbeisl serves hearty food. There are many wholesome pork dishes, as well as game and desserts such as fruit pancakes. The restaurant is popular with tourists and is reasonable value.

Yugetsu

Führichgasse 10. **Map** 5 C4.
📞 5122720. ⏰ noon–3:30pm,
6pm–midnight daily. ● Sun Jan–Mar.
🍴 ♿ 🈂 AE, DC, MC, V, JCB. €€

Located close to the Opera, this Japanese restaurant, probably the best in Vienna, is popular with Japanese tourists and locals alike. Although you can eat from an extensive à la carte menu, there are also a number of set-price menus. The set meals all feature sashimi and tempura, but sushi is reserved for the more expensive menus.

SCHOTTENRING AND ALSERGRUND

Lokanta Sarikoç

Währinger Strasse 18. **Map** 1 C4.
📞 3199987. ⏰ 11am–midnight
daily. 🅥 ♿ ♿ 🈂 AE, DC, MC, V.
€€

There is no shortage of Turkish and Greek restaurants in Vienna, and this is one of the best. Both waiter and buffet service are available, so the Sarikoç is ideal either for a full meal or a snack. There is a huge range of starters, with an equally large selection of grilled meats and kebabs to follow. Vegetarians will find plenty of choice and there are children's portions. The speciality of the house, served only on Wednesday evenings, is lamb on the spit.

Stomach

Seegasse 26. **Map** 1 C3. 📞 3102099.
⏰ 6pm–midnight Wed–Sat, 10am–
10pm Sun. 🅥 ♿ 🈂 €€

The food here is eclectic, with some standard Viennese dishes, but also a good selection of risottos and pasta dishes and an unusually large vegetarian section. Portions are huge and the cooking shows little refinement, but this is hearty cooking that deservedly attracts a strong following. The courtyard garden offers outdoor dining and is very pretty. Wines are available by the glass, and there are excellent beers.

MUSEUM AND TOWNHALL QUARTER

Spatzennest

Sankt-Ulrichs-Platz. **Map** 3 B1.
📞 5261659. ⏰ 10am–11:00pm
Sun–Thu. ● first half Aug. 🍴 🍴
🎴 🅥 ♿ ♿ ★ 🈂 AE, V. €

Located on a quaint Baroque square with a lovely church, this delightful restaurant is set in an 19th-century building with outdoor tables in the garden. The distinctive interior has a homely feel. The traditional Austrian food is excellent and the staff friendly. A menu in English is available.

Witwe Bolte

Gutenberggasse 13. **Map** 3 B1.
C 5231450. ☐ 11:30am–11:30pm
daily. **V ☆ ☎** AE, DC, MC, V.
€€

There are many restaurants in the
renovated Spittelberg district (see
p124), but this ancient and old-
fashioned establishment is one of
the most enjoyable, especially in
summer when the garden is open.
The cooking is solidly Viennese,
with a few international dishes
thrown in. This is a good place for
goulash, pork, salads, rich desserts
and copious draughts of beer.

Kupferdachl

Schottengasse 7. **Map** 5 B2.
C 533938114. ☐ 11:30am–3pm,
6pm–midnight Mon–Fri, 6pm–
midnight Sat. ● public hols, late Jul
& Aug. **V ☆ ☎** AE, DC, MC, V,
JCB. €€€

Occupying several cellar rooms
and an attractive garden, the décor
of this popular eatery is a blend of
rustic and martial. The cooking is
solid and dependable. Specialities
include dishes such as Barbary
duck and Ochsenmaulsalat (sliced
ox cheek in vinaigrette, which is
tastier than it sounds).

Schnattl

Lange Gasse 40. **Map** 1 B5.
C 4053400. ☐ 11:30am–2:30pm,
6pm–midnight Mon–Fri. **¶●¶ V ☆**
★ ☎ AE, DC. €€€

Wilhelm Schnattl has succeeded in
transforming a large house on
Lange Gasse into a very
fashionable restaurant. There are
few more pleasant spots in Vienna
than the sheltered courtyard here.
This highly talented chef's
interpretation of standard
Viennese dishes is fresh and
innovative, with excellent
ingredients impeccably cooked.
The desserts, mostly fruit-based,
are delicious. The wine list is
excellent and prices are reasonable. The only drawback is the
service, often maddeningly slow.

Schubertstüberl

Schreyvogelgasse 4–6. **Map** 5 B2.
C 5337187. ☐ 11:30am–3pm
6–11:30pm Mon–Sat. ● public hols.
¶●¶ V ☆ ☎ AE, DC, MC, V, JCB.
€€€

Located near the Burgtheater (see
pp130–1), this large restaurant is
quite formal. The menu features
both typical Viennese dishes, such
as Leberknödelsuppe (see p204)
and Apfelstrudel (see p206), and
more international cuisine. Drinks
and snacks are served all day.

Wiener Rathauskeller

Rathausplatz 1 (beneath the Neues
Rathaus, on the corner of Felder-
strasse). **Map** 1 C5. **C** 4051219.
☐ 11:30am–3pm, 6–11:30pm
Mon–Sat. **V ☎** AE, DC, MC, V,
JCB. €€€

Tourists generally flock here for
the buzzing atmosphere rather
than for the food. The restaurant
occupies a number of splendid
vaulted cellars decorated with
old wine casks. Live music is
performed here every evening.
The cooking is international,
though there is a selection of
delicious Austrian desserts.

Grotta Azzurra

Babenbergerstrasse 5. **Map** 5 B5.
C 58610440. ☐ noon–3pm,
6:30–11pm daily. **¶●¶ V ☆**
☎ AE, DC, MC, V, JCB. €€€€

The interior of this 19th-century
building has been stylishly transformed into a light and spacious
Italian restaurant. Grotta Azzurra
offers a range of classic Italian
cooking, elegantly presented. The
antipasto is mouthwatering, and
specialities include gnocchi and
beef dishes. The wine list is
lengthy and exclusively Italian.

OPERA AND NASCHMARKT

Hunger-Künstler

Gumpendorfer Strasse 48.
Map 3 B2. **C** 5879210.
☐ 6pm–1am daily. **¶●¶** lunch only.
V ☆ ☎ MC, V. €

This simple neighbourhood Beisl
with its wood panelling offers a
varied menu of traditional Austrian
and Italian dishes. It is a quiet and
unpretentious venue and is one of
the few places in this area that
stays open until late.

Hansy (Smutny)

Elisabethstrasse 8. **Map** 4 D2 & 5 B5.
C 5871356. ☐ 10am–midnight
daily. **¶●¶ / ☆ ☎** AE, DC, MC, V.
€€

Hansy is a useful standby for a
late-night meal. Despite its garish-
ness, the old-fashioned, green-tiled
interior makes a change from sleek,
modern establishments. The service
can be somewhat slow and the
food can scarcely be described as
refined, but there is a good
selection of robust Viennese and
Czech dishes. There is also a wide
range of beer on offer. The
restaurant is now called Hansy,
though the sign still reads Smutny.

BELVEDERE QUARTER

Do & Co

Akademiestrasse 3. **Map** 4 E1 & 6 D5.
C 74000144. ☐ 10:30am–7:30pm
Mon–Fri, 10am–6pm Sat. **☆ ☎**
AE, DC, MC, V. €€€

The sister establishment to the
roof-top restaurant in Haas Haus
(see p212) is designed on a more
modest scale and operates on a
different principle. It is essentially
a delicatessen that also offers light
meals and snacks. The fish and
seafood are particularly good, as
are the fruit-based desserts. The
cooking is a deft blend of
Viennese and Italian, and the
elegance of the cuisine matches
the stylish décor. Wine and champagne are available by the glass.

Imperial

Kärntner Ring 16. **Map** 4 D1 & 5 C5.
C 501100. ☐ 6pm–midnight daily.
¶●¶ ▼ ☆ V ☆ ☎ AE, DC,
MC, V, JCB. €€€

This restaurant is set within the
oldest hotel in Vienna (see p199).
The menu ranges from the
traditional to the international. The
bar area has tables outside, whilst
the restaurant itself is indoors where
you eat amid wood panelling,
which lends to the cosy and
intimate atmosphere. The staff are
friendly with impeccable service.

Korso

Hotel Bristol, Mahlerstrasse 2.
Map 4 D1 & 6 D5. **C** 51516546.
☐ noon–2pm, 7–11pm Mon–Fri &
Sun, 7pm–midnight Sat. ● first 3
weeks in Aug. **¶●¶ V ☆ ☎**
☎ AE, DC, MC, V, JCB. €€€€€

The celebrated chef Reinhard Gerer
presides over this well-known restaurant. The spacious dining room
is discreet and comfortable, the
wine list is magnificent (with prices
to match), and the cooking a confident display of modern Viennese
haute cuisine. The emphasis is on
the finest and freshest ingredients
rather than on very complex dishes.
The service is efficient but not
particularly friendly. The cooking,
however, is undeniably of a very
high standard.

Palais Schwarzenberg

Hotel im Palais Schwarzenberg,
Schwarzenbergplatz 9. **Map** 4 E2.
C 7984515. ☐ 6–10:30am, noon–
2:30pm, 6–10:45pm daily. **☆ ☎**
AE, DC, MC, V, JCB. €€€€€

The large dining room overlooking
the palace park is one of the most
tranquil places to eat in Vienna. The

cooking is unashamedly luxurious, with ample use of ingredients such as truffles, caviar and champagne, which expresses perfectly the style of the essentially Viennese cooking served here. More opulent international-style dishes include the pigeon cassoulet with fresh foie gras and lobster in a Chablis sauce. Very good Austrian wines are available by the glass.

FURTHER AFIELD

Gmoa Keller

Heumarkt 25. [7125310. ◯ 11am–midnight Mon–Sat. ◉ Aug and public hols. ▮◉▮ ▮ ▮ ▮ Thu. ▮▮
▮ ▰ AE, DC, MC, V. €

Under its previous owners, the sisters Nowak, this restaurant was the haunt of Vienna's rich and famous and that reputation still hangs in the air. The traditional *wirtshaus* interior is matched by a changing menu of traditional Austrian dishes and hospitality. There is a good wine list to choose from and friendly service.

Zum Herkner

Dornbacher Strasse 123. [4854386. ◯ 11:30am–2:30pm, 6–10pm Mon–Fri. ◉ Jul & Aug. ▮ ▮ €€

Heinz Herkner's unpretentious inn on the edge of the Vienna Woods enjoys a cult status among Viennese who come out here for a touch of rusticity: wooden floors, paper napkins and simple cutlery are all features. The cooking is pure Viennese, with dishes like *Kalbsvögerl* (shin of veal) as well as *Rehragout* (venison stew). Booking is recommended.

Marxer Stub'n

Marxergasse 5. [7124208. ◯ 9am–11:30pm Mon–Fri; also Oct–Apr: 11:30am–2:30pm Sun. ▮▮
▮ ▮ ▮ V. €€

This unpretentious neighbourhood restaurant, which caters at lunchtime to local office workers, offers a good range of dishes, including seasonal delicacies such as *Eierschwammerl* (chanterelle mushrooms) and regional dishes such as Styrian beef salad.

Eckel

Sieveringer Strasse 46. [3203218. ◯ 11:30am–2:30pm, 6–10:30pm Tue–Sat. ◉ 2 weeks in Aug & 3 weeks in Jan. ▮ ▮ ▮ ★
▰ AE, DC, V. €€€

In summer there are few more pleasant places to sit down and eat a meal than in the garden at

Eckel's. The large menu is traditional Viennese, but stylishly presented. The fish and seafood, especially lobster, are particularly good, and so is the veal. On the dessert menu it is worth looking out for the *Pfannkuchen* (soufflé omelettes). The wine list is superb, and wines are offered by the glass.

Hietzinger Bräu

Auhofstrasse 1. [87770870. ◯ 11:30am–3pm, 6–10:30pm daily. ▮ ▮ V ★ ▰ DC, MC, V. €€€

It's worth the short excursion to Hietzing just to eat the *Tafelspitz* at the Hietzinger Bräu. Here, an astonishing ten different cuts of beef are on offer, never salted or treated, and each described in detail on the menu. Although the atmosphere here is formal, this restaurant is comfortable, the service is good and the wine list is impressive.

Vikerls Lokal

Würffelgasse 4. [8943430. ◯ 11:30am–2:30pm, 6–11pm Tue–Sat, 11am–3pm Sun. ▮◉▮ ▮
★ €€€

Situated just beyond the Gürtel, this is a delightful family-run inn where you can dine in wood-panelled rooms. In summer tables are set outside in a pleasant garden. Prices are not especially cheap, but the raw materials are first rate, the sauces delicate, the portions ample, and the welcome from Frau Weidinger warm and friendly. The cooking is sophisticated and tasty: *Schmankerl von Kalb*, for example, is a delicate blend of veal fillet, kidneys and sweetbreads with a thyme and rosemary sauce. The selection of wines, served by the glass, is good and reasonably priced.

Vincent

Grosse Pfarrgasse 7. **Map** 2 E3. [2141516. ◯ 6pm–12.30am Mon–Sat. ◉ 4 weeks mid-summer. ▮◉▮ V ▮ ▮ ★ ▰ AE, DC, MC, V, JCB. €€€

Hidden away in the Leopoldstadt district is this excellent modish restaurant, its dark interior made more atmospheric by the gallery of modern Austrian art hung on the walls. Frank Gruber is an impassioned restaurateur who will, if you wish, abandon the menu and serve you a selection of the best dishes from his kitchen, each course accompanied by a different glass of wine. At its best the cooking is exquisite, and is always light and delicate. It goes without saying that there are superb Austrian wines available.

Niky's Kuchlmasterei

Obere Weissgerberstrasse 6. [7129000. ◯ 11:30am–midnight Mon–Sat. ▮◉▮ ▮ ▮ ▰ AE, DC, MC, V, JCB. €€€€

Easily the most exotically decorated restaurant in Vienna, Niky's will either appal or delight. The menu, however, is not so extreme. Modern Viennese in character, it is broad and includes such dishes as snails, dried hams and crêpes. The portions are generous and the service attentive. To accompany the meal there is Niky's cellar from which to select your wine. With around 18,000 bottles, it is one of the best in Austria.

Altwienerhof

Herklotzgasse 6. [8926000. ◯ noon–2pm, 6:30–11pm Mon–Fri, 6–10:30pm Sat. ◉ first 3 weeks in Jan. ▮ ▮ ★ ▰ AE, DC, MC, V. €€€€€

The gruff but friendly Altwienerhof chef, Rudolf Kellner, is inventive and very accomplished and his dishes are elaborately composed. He offers a number of set menus, using such luxury ingredients as goose liver, lobster, turbot and game. The portions are not too large – you are expected to order a number of different courses though this is by no means obligatory. The extensive cheese board includes a good selection of Austrian cheeses and the wine list is exceptional, with more than 1,000 different wines including rare old Burgundies and fine Austrian bottles. Compensating for the restaurant's downmarket location, the dining rooms are beautifully, if formally, decorated and there is a lovely garden courtyard used in summer.

Steirereck

Rasumofskygasse 2. [7133168. ◯ noon–2:30pm, 7–11pm Mon–Fri. ▮◉▮ V ▮ ★ ▰ AE, DC, MC, V. €€€€€

From the moment you walk into the Steirereck, you feel confident that you are in for a treat. The flower-filled rooms, the light, airy conservatory, the staff's welcome, and the tasty *amuse-gueules* brought swiftly to your table are just the beginning. The chef prepares exquisite food with unusual combinations and a strong Styrian influence – for example caviar on a jelly of red cabbage. The wine list is outstanding and the sommelier especially helpful. *Gabelfrühstück* (see p215) is served here and there is a well-priced set lunch, considered by many to be one of the city's bargains.

Light Meals and Snacks

Since the viennese are used to eating at any time of the day, Vienna offers a large selection of places where you can get a reasonable and quick meal. Many serve food from early morning until about 10pm. From the famous coffee houses (see pp58–61) to cheerful stand-at-a-counter snack bars, there is plenty of choice. Take-away pizzas, sausage stands and the small snack bars that double up as grocery stores are all convenient if you are pushed for time.

The city also boasts numerous drinking places: try a traditional *Heuriger* on the city outskirts, or spend an evening in one of the more sophisticated wine cellars. There are also plenty of bars to choose from, some offering live music, others with food as well as drink, and most open until the early hours of the morning.

SNACKS

Although coffee houses (see pp58–61) usually offer light meals throughout the day, this is rarely an economical way to eat. Better value, though less comfortable, are the snack bars, especially those attached to the top delicatessens, such as **Wild** in the Neuer Markt. Near the Graben is the **Lukullus Bar**, allied to Julius Meinl, Vienna's best-known chain of grocers. **Zum Schwarzen Kameel** offers superb miniature open sandwiches, platters of smoked fish and fresh salads, and a few warm dishes; wines by the glass are from the best estates. There is rarely anywhere to sit, but counters are provided where you can place your food and prop up a newspaper. Such establishments are ideal for travellers who do not wish to spend long in a restaurant, but seek a quick bite to eat without sacrificing quality.

Pizzerias are found in many of Vienna's busy streets. Of the cafeterias, the **Naschmarkt** chain is reliable and sensibly priced and the **Rosenberger Markt** has a wide choice with fresh ingredients. It includes a coffee house, *Heuriger*, bistro and a market restaurant.

Buffets too are handy – the **Trzesniewski** on Dorotheergasse is the most famous, offering good, cheap open sandwiches. Butchers' shops often provide similar amenities where you can enjoy sausages or roast chicken with a glass of beer at a stand-up counter. A specifically Viennese addition to the range of meals is the *Gabelfrühstück*, literally "fork breakfast", which is a selection of small, well-composed dishes offered by some restaurants during the morning, usually from 10:30am onwards. Dishes often include offal concoctions, which in the hands of restaurants such as the Steirereck (see p214) and Do & Co (see p213) can be utterly delicious.

CAKES AND COFFEE

Cafe-konditoreien are coffee houses that offer a large selection of cakes and pastries. They are almost always fully licensed, too. *Konditoreien* tend to be more cramped than most coffee houses, and you will not be expected to linger for as long. Although some stock newspapers, they will not have a wide selection. On the other hand the cakes should be among the best in the city and the coffee of equally exacting quality; prices tend to be slightly lower than in the classic coffee houses.

Demel Konditorei is the most famous example, and also the most expensive. It is renowned for its superb cakes, its unhelpful staff, and the fact that one of its former owners was sent to prison.

The excellent **Heiner** has two branches: both are cosy, comfortable places for a snack and their special cakes and confections produced for festivals such as Easter and Christmas are particularly imaginative. **Gerstner** has outdoor tables in summer. **Lehmann** has the best pastries on the Graben, and close to the Neues Rathaus is **Sluka**. Here they serve cakes for diabetics as well as delicious chestnut specialities in winter. At Easter, Christmas and other festivals, *Café-Konditoreien* usually make special sugar pastries and chocolate specialities for children.

Konditoreien are daytime establishments, closing around 7pm. Many serve light lunches and open sandwiches.

TAKE-AWAY FOOD

Most sandwich and snack bars, including the more expensive ones, sell dishes to take away, as do pizzerias and fast-food chains. Up-market snack bars and delicatessens provide delicious open sandwiches using a wide range of ingredients, from fresh shellfish to smoked meats and hams. Fried spring chicken is a staple Viennese speciality, available from take-away venues such as the **Wienerwald** chain. Inexpensive open sandwiches and filled rolls are available from food shops such as **Superimbiss Duran**.

Food stands, located in most busy streets, are the easiest source of take-away foods. At a sausage stand (*Würstelstand*) you can eat tasty *Bratwurst*, frankfurter (see p204), or other sausages and a roll, or there are many first-rate stands serving shellfish and other foods in the Naschmarkt (see p136 and Directory p217).

The Viennese are well served by ice-cream parlours. One of the best is **Tichy's**.

WINE BARS

Wine bars, as opposed to wine cellars, are relative newcomers to Vienna. The best, such as **Vis-à-Vis**, tend to be small and crowded, and they usually serve a wide range of outstanding wines and good simple snacks. The **Wein-Comptoir** is a wine bar and restaurant. Most such establishments are only open during the evenings.

WINE CELLARS

AUSTRIA IS FULL of splendid Baroque monasteries and most of them have their own extensive vineyards. Almost all of them have premises in the Stephansdom Quarter, beneath which are large wine cellars where food is served. Although the food is rarely of outstanding quality, it is fine for a midday snack or for a quick bite before a theatre or opera performance.

The **Augustinerkeller** near the Opera House is typical of the best: situated in the basement, it has an ample buffet from which you can select a snack of meat or cheese to accompany glasses of wine, usually from the monastery's own estates. They sometimes have *Schrammel* musicians playing popular Viennese tunes. The **Esterházykeller** operates on an identical principle, except that its wines come from a princely estate rather than a monastic one.

HEURIGE

THE HEURIGER is a uniquely Austrian establishment. Literally translating as "this year's", the word *Heuriger* has two meanings: it refers to the youngest available vintage of the local wine, and it also refers to the venues that sell such wines by the glass. Wine is *Heuriger* until St Martin's Day – 11 November – of the year after harvest.

The venues that sell the wine were established by Imperial decree in 1784, as places where owners were allowed to sell the wine grown in their own vineyards. They are found throughout Austria's wine regions and around Vienna. The most celebrated are in the wine villages to the north and west of Vienna.

There are almost 200 *Heurige* in the vicinity of Vienna and all are strictly regulated: in theory, the proprietors can only sell wine they have produced themselves from their own vineyards, and only during certain hours on certain days. Most only open in the afternoon, although those catering mainly to the tourist trade also open for lunch. Some *Heurige* close at certain times of the year to allow the proprietors to tend to their vineyards. For example, **Winzerhof Leopold** only opens in alternate months, beginning in February.

Long ago you could bring your own food to a *Heuriger*, which would provide the wine. Nowadays most *Heurige* have a full restaurant licence and many are permitted to offer wine and food from any source – if you go to Grinzing (*see p159*), the most famous *Heuriger* village, you will find it hard to sample local wines. On the other hand you will have a far greater choice of food and wine than in the more authentic venues found elsewhere. (If you are looking for an authentic *Heuriger*, look for a sign reading *Eigenbau* by the entrance – this indicates that the wine is made from the owner's vineyards.)

At a *Heuriger* you choose from a wide range of meats, cheeses, salads and breads at a buffet, and take your food to a table, where your wine order will be taken. Many Viennese will spend hours lingering at a *Heuriger*, snacking as the hours go by and the glasses of wine are emptied. It is perfectly possible to eat a full dinner at a *Heuriger*, and usually the larger the party the merrier. Most *Heurige* have gardens or courtyards, so are popular in warm weather, but they can be just as enjoyable in winter when the clientele moves indoors, often into cosy, panelled rooms.

The most popular *Heurige* are in Grinzing (*see p159*) and Heiligenstadt (*see p182–3*). They may not be the most authentic, but you will find a wide range of wine and ample seating both indoors and in the gardens. Among the better Grinzing *Heurige* are **Martin Sepp** and the **Reinprecht**. In Heiligenstadt **Zimmermann**, and **Mayer am Pfarrplatz** in the church square, are the best known. The *Heurige* of Neustift tend to have better-quality wine. **Fuhrgassl-Huber** and **Zeiler am Hauerweg** are excellent. Zeiler has beautiful gardens and Fuhrgassl-Huber some of the best wines to be found in a *Heuriger*. If you want to sample outstanding local wines and are not too concerned about the food, then head for Stammersdorf. The facilities are less opulent than Grinzing, but the clientele is mostly local and the wine at places such as **Hans Peter Göbel** is excellent.

BARS

VIENNESE BARS range from the exclusive haunts of the Austrian aristocracy to noisy places that stay open until the early hours of the morning. The latter type of establishment tend to come and go, although some of them, in nightlife districts such as the Bermuda Triangle (*see p84*), have been open for decades and are deservedly popular. Many also serve food – **Ma Pitom** in Seitenstettengasse is a good place for pizza. They come to life late at night, when bars such as **Relax**, **Kaktus**, **Rasputin** and **Krah Krah** are packed out. Many offer live music. The **Roter Engel** has music every night, and the raffish **Tunnel** in Florianigasse also has live bands playing several nights a week.

One of the most elegant bars in Vienna is the tiny **American Bar** (*see p105*). Designed by Adolf Loos, it has recently been restored to pristine condition. The staff discourage casual visits, and you must ring the bell to gain admission. Drinks are very expensive, but this is certainly one of the most beautiful bars in Europe and it is worth a visit for the décor alone. **Demel's Vis-à-Vis** in Kohlmarkt is a pricey seafood bar, but also doubles up as an ideal place for a glass of sparkling wine in elegant surroundings.

Midway between the trendy Triangle bars and the late-night drinking bars are the bohemian haunts such as the **Alt Wien** along Bäckerstrasse. These are distinguished more by their clientele and atmosphere than by their décor or food. Nonetheless they can offer entertainment for an evening.

DIRECTORY

STEPHANSDOM QUARTER

Café-Konditoreien
Aida
Rotenturmstrasse 24.
Map 2 E5 & 6 E2.
5331933.
One of several branches.

Gerstner
Kärntner Strasse 11–15.
Map 4 D1 & 6 D4.
5124963.

Heiner
Wollzeile 9.
Map 2 E5 & 6 D3.
51248380.
Kärntner Strasse 21–3.
Map 4 D1 & 6 D4.
51268630.

Snack Bars
Superimbiss Duran
Rotenturmstrasse 11.
Map 2 E5 & 6 D3.
5337115.

Wienerwald
Annagasse 3.
Map 4 D1 & 6 D4.
5123766.
One of several branches.

Zum Schwarzen Kameel
(See p212).
Map 5 C3.
5338967.

Wine Cellars
Urbanikeller
Am Hof 12.
Map 2 D5 & 5 C2.
5339102.

Wiener Rathauskeller
(See p213).
Map 1 C5.
4051219.

Zwölf Apostel Keller
Sonnenfelsgasse 3.
Map 6 E3.
5126777.

Wine Bars
Vis-à-Vis
Wollzeile 5.
Map 2 E5 & 6 D3.
5129350.

Wein-Comptoir
Bäckerstrasse 6.
Map 2 E5 & 6 D3.
5121760.

Bars
Alt Wien
Bäckerstrasse 9.
Map 2 E5 & 6 D3.
5125222.

Daniel Moser
Rotenturmstrasse 14.
Map 2 E5 & 6 D3.
5132823.

Kaktus
Seitenstettengasse 5.
Map 6 D2.
5331938.

Krah Krah
Rabensteig 8.
Map 6 D2.
5338193.

Ma Pitom
Seitenstettengasse 5.
Map 6 D2.
5354313.

New Bora
Johannesgasse 12.
Map 4 E1 & 6 D4.
5122784.

Oswald und Kalb
Bäckerstrasse 14.
Map 2 E5 & 6 E3.
5121371.

Rasputin
Seitenstettengasse 3.
Map 6 D2.
5353387.

Relax
Seitenstettengasse 5.
Map 6 D2.
5338506.

Roter Engel
Rabensteig 5.
Map 6 D2.
5354105.

HOFBURG QUARTER

Café-Konditoreien
Demel Konditorei
Kohlmarkt 14.
Map 2 D5 & 5 C3.
5335516.

Lehmann
Graben 12.
Map 2 D5 & 5 C3.
5121815.

Oberlaa
Neuer Markt 16.
Map 5 C4.
5132936.

Snack Bars
Akardenbar
Naglergasse 1.
Map 2 D5 & 5 C2.
5323334.

Trzesniewski
Dorotheergasse 1.
Map 2 D5 & 5 C3.
5123291.

Wild
Neuer Markt 10–11.
Map 5 C4.
5122179.

Cafeteria
Rosenberger Markt
Maysedergasse 2.
Map 5 C4.
5123458.

Wine Cellars
Augustinerkeller
Augustinerstrasse 1.
Map 4 D1 & 5 C4.
5331026.

Esterházykeller
Haarhofgasse 1.
Map 5 C3.
5333482.

Bar
**American Bar
(Loos Bar)**
Kärntnerdurchgang 10.
Map 4 D1 & 6 D3.
5123283. (See p105).

SCHOTTENRING AND ALSERGRUND

Bar
Tunnel
Florianigasse 39.
Map 1 B5.
4053465.

TOWNHALL AND MUSEUM QUARTER

Café-Konditorei
Sluka
Rathausplatz 8.
Map 1 C5 & 5 A2.
4057172.

OPERA AND NASCHMARKT

Snack Bar
Nordsee
Naschmarkt 1–4.
Map 4 D2.
5861420.

BELVEDERE QUARTER

Cafeteria
Naschmarkt
Schwarzenbergplatz 16.
Map 4 E2.
5053115.
Another branch at Schottengasse 1.

FURTHER AFIELD

Ice-Cream Parlour
Tichy's
Reumannplatz 13.
6044446.

Heurige
Fuhrgassl-Huber
Neustift am Walde 68.
4401405.

Hans Peter Göbel
Hagenbrunner Strasse 57,
Stammersdorf.
2948420.

Herbert Schilling
Langenzersdorfer Strasse
54, Strebersdorf.
2924189.

Martin Sepp
Cobenzlgasse 34,
Grinzing.
3203233.

Mayer am Pfarrplatz
Pfarrplatz 2,
Heiligenstadt.
3701287.

Reinprecht
Cobenzlgasse 22,
Grinzing.
3201471.

**Winzerhof Leopold,
Familie Leopold**
Stammersdorfer Strasse
18, Stammersdorf.
2921356.

Wolf-Köller
Langackergasse 11,
Grinzing.
3203002.

Zeiler am Hauerweg
Rathstrasse 31,
Neustift am Walde.
4401318.

Zimmermann
Armbrustergasse 5,
Heiligenstadt.
37022110.

SHOPS AND MARKETS

SINCE VIENNA IS a compact city, it is a pleasant place to shop. The main shopping area is pedestrianized and full of pretty cafés, and although it is not in the same league as London, Paris and New York when it comes to international stores, you can browse around at a more leisurely pace. Austrian-made glassware, food and traditional crafts all make for good buys. However, the shops tend to

Augarten porcelain Lipizzaner

cater for comparatively conventional and mature tastes and purses. Vienna has a range of markets selling a variety of produce and wares from exotic fruit to old trinkets. The pedestrian shopping areas of Kärntner Strasse, the Graben, and Kohlmarkt house the more expensive shops and are pleasant to wander around. For more details of shops and markets see the *Directory* on page 223.

BEST BUYS

MANY OF THE BEST buys in Vienna are small and readily transportable: coffee addicts shouldn't forget to buy freshly ground coffee – the city imports some of the best.

If you have a sweet tooth, you couldn't be in a more appropriate city. It is justly famous for its cakes, pastries and *Torten (see p206–7)* and any good *Café-Konditorei* (cake shop and café) will post cakes back home for you. In November and December, try the buttery Advent *Stollen* available from **Julius Meinl** *(see p221)* or any good baker. Stuffed with fruit and nuts and dusted with icing sugar, it is a tasty Christmas loaf. Alternatively, buy some prettily-packaged *Sachertorte (see p207)*, available year round. The specialist chocolate shops *(see p221)* are worth a visit, both for the unusual packaging and the chocolate itself.

Sweet *Eiswein* (so-called because the grapes are left on the vines until the first frosts) is an unusual and delicious dessert wine. **Zum Schwarzen Kameel** *(see p221)* sells the rarer red version as well.

Other Austrian-made goods include clothes manufactured in the felt-like woollen fabric known as *Loden (see p221)*. If you feel like treating yourself and have space in your car or suitcase, buy custom-made sheets or high-quality down pillows or duvets made in Austria *(see p220)*. Petit point embroidery, which adorns anything from powder compacts to handbags, is a Viennese speciality *(see p220)*.

Glassware – including superb chandeliers – and **Augarten** porcelain *(see p220)* tend to be highly original, although expensive. Many people collect crystal ornaments made by Swarovski. **Rasper & Söhne** *(see p220)* is a good glass and porcelain shop for such items.

Trachten (Austrian costume) shops *(see p221)* are fun; they have a wide selection of hats, children's dresses, jackets and blouses. **Gilhofer** *(see p221)* stocks old prints and maps. Early editions of works by writers such as Freud, Kraus or Rilke can be found in Vienna's antique bookshops *(see p221)*.

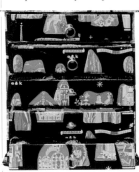

Chest of drawers chocolate box from Altmann & Kühne *(see p221)*

OPENING HOURS

SHOPS USUALLY OPEN at 8:30am or 9am and close at 6pm or 7pm. Some of the smaller shops close for an hour at lunch. Traditionally stores were required to close at noon on Saturday, a routine that some still follow, though most now stay open until 5pm. Shops are still closed on Sundays and public holidays, although you can buy items such as groceries, flowers, camera film, books and newspapers at the major railway stations. The supermarket at the airport is open seven days a week.

J & L Lobmeyr's glass shop on Kärntner Strasse *(see p220)*

HOW TO PAY

VIENNA IS NOW more credit card-orientated, with many shops accepting the major cards. Some also take Eurocheques (with a card), but it is still wise to carry some cash as an alternative.

WHERE TO SHOP

THE PEDESTRIAN SHOPPING areas of Graben, Kohlmarkt and Kärntner Strasse have many of the most well-known and expensive shops in Vienna, providing a largely car-free and relaxed environment.

The more cheaply-priced area is along Mariahilfer Strasse, with department stores selling household goods, and well-known chain stores such as C & A, Hennes, The Body Shop and Marks & Spencer.

RIGHTS AND SERVICES

IF A PURCHASE is defective you are usually entitled to a refund, provided you have proof of purchase. This is not always the case with goods bought in the sales – inspect them carefully before you buy. Many shops in Vienna will pack goods for you – and often gift-wrap them at no extra charge – and send them anywhere in the world.

VAT EXEMPTION

VAT (VALUE ADDED TAX) or MWSt (Mehrwertsteuer) is normally charged at 20%. If you buy goods during your stay in Austria and are normally resident outside the European Union (EU), you are entitled to claim back the VAT. This is only the case, however, if the total purchase price (which may be the sum of prices paid for a number of articles in any one shop) exceeds 73 euros. Take along your passport when shopping and ask the shopkeeper to complete Form U34 at the time of sale. This should also bear the shop's stamp and have the receipt attached. You may have the refund credited to your credit card account, have it posted home, or pick it up at the airport.

View down Kohlmarkt, one of Vienna's pedestrian shopping streets

Purchased goods must not be used prior to exportation. If you leave Vienna by air, present the form at Customs before checking in, and have it stamped as proof of export. You may also have to show your purchases at Customs, so pack them somewhere accessible. Then post the stamped form to the Austrian shopkeeper or collect the refund at the airport (there is a handling fee). If leaving by car or train, present the form to Customs at the border, where you can also claim a refund. If you are not disembarking the train at the border, there is sometimes a customs official on the train to stamp your form.

One of the famous *Loden* coats from Resi Hammerer *(see p221)*

When you have goods sent directly to your home outside the EU, VAT is deducted at the time of purchase.

Since Austria joined the EU in 1995, EU citizens can no longer claim back VAT.

SALES

THE BI-ANNUAL SALES are held in January and July. The best bargains can usually be found in fashions. Electrical and household goods are also much reduced.

SHOPPING CENTRES

SHOPPING CENTRES are a fairly recent innovation in Vienna. The most modern are the splendid **Haas Haus** and the spruced-up **Generali Centre**. Built in the same style as the Café Central *(see pp58–61)*, **Freyung Passage** is an arcade of elegant shops in the Palais Ferstel *(see pp108 and 110)*.

ADDRESSES

Generali Centre
Mariahilfer Strasse 77–79. **Map** 3 A3.

Haas Haus
Stock-im-Eisen-Platz 4.
Map 2 D5 & 5 C3.

Freyung Passage
Palais Ferstel 1, Freyung 2.
Map 2 D5 & 5 B2.

Shops and Boutiques

EVEN IF VIENNA DOES NOT BOAST the wide range of shops you find in many other European capitals, it does offer certain goods that are hard to beat elsewhere. Austrian glassware is justly famous and cut-glass gifts are of a high quality. A few shops, such as **Knize** (in the Graben), designed by Adolf Loos, are in themselves worth a visit simply to admire the Jugendstil architecture. It's best to speak English in shops unless you are fluent in German – you will probably receive quicker service!

SPECIALITY SHOPS

VIENNA STILL manufactures leather goods, although nowadays a lot are imported from Italy. **Novotny** have their own workshops as well as firms working exclusively for them. **Robert Horn** designs and manufactures leather travel cases and accessories. He maintains that even he has been unable to improve on the design of a briefcase carried by Metternich at the Congress of Vienna, which he has only slightly modernized.

Petit point embroidery is another Viennese speciality. Some of the most attractive can be found at **Petit Point** (where even the shop's door handle is embroidered) and at **Maria Stransky**.

A marvellous place for party tricks, and much beloved by practical jokers, is **Zauberklingl. Kober** (see p230) is a "serious" toy shop which sells well-made dolls and toys. Or combine a visit to the novelty and joke shop called **Witte** with a trip to the Naschmarkt. Witte stocks masks, fancy dress outfits, and beautiful old-fashioned paper decorations that are ideal for festivals. **Metzger**, a shop specializing in beeswax, sells its own candles and candlesticks. It also stocks certain gift items, such as honey cakes and boxes of chocolates.

MUSIC

AS YOU WOULD expect in "the City of Music", the range of recordings available is rich and varied. **EMI** and **Gramola** have a wonderful choice – there is some superb operetta as well as opera music on sale – and **Arcadia** has a great selection of classical recordings by Austrian artists as well as other nationalities. Shop staff are usually very knowledgeable. For pop music, the **Virgin Megastore** on Mariahilfer Strasse is well stocked, although CDs and tapes are more expensive here than in other countries in Europe.

JEWELLERY

VIENNESE JEWELLERS have long been famous for their fine workmanship. Fruit and flower brooches carved in semi-precious stones and sometimes studded with diamonds, are a more recent Austrian innovation. **Juwel** always has a good selection in a wide price range. Both **Köchert** and **Heldwein** were jewellers to the Imperial Court and still produce beautiful jewellery in their own workshops today. Köchert also sells antique pieces and Heldwein are known for their multi-coloured chains of semi-precious stones. A few years ago, one of the pieces designed by **Schullin** won the prestigious Diamonds International award organized by De Beers for innovative design. Their small window usually attracts a crowd of admirers to view their latest creations. Don't let that put you off – prices start at a reasonable level.

GLASSWARE

THE CHANDELIERS at Vienna's Opera House and the Metropolitan Opera in New York are by **J & L Lobmeyr**, as are the chandeliers in numerous palaces throughout the world – including the Kremlin. This company – now run by a fifth generation of the same family – has produced beautiful glasses and crystal chandeliers since the early 19th century, often commissioning famous artists. One range of glasses still in production today was designed by Josef Hoffmann (see p56) in Jugendstil style. Its famous *Musselinglas*, a type of glass so fine that it almost bends to the touch, is exquisite. There is a small but superb glass museum on the first floor and, apart from its own glassware, Lobmeyr also sells select items of Hungarian Herend porcelain.

INTERIORS

VIENNA'S PORCELAIN makers, **Augarten**, are the second oldest in Europe. The company was founded in 1718 and taken over by the House of Habsburg in 1744. Ever since, its products have been marked with their banded shield coat of arms. Each piece of porcelain at **Schloss Augarten** is still hand finished and painted: patterns and shapes are based on original models from the Baroque, Rococo, Biedermeier and Art Deco periods and on designs created by present-day artists. The Schloss Augarten factory is open to visitors. **Rasper & Söhne** stocks glass and porcelain as well as kitchenware, and is good for gifts.

Founded in 1849, **Backhausen** is known for its exclusive furnishing fabrics, woven in the original Jugendstil patterns, and for its silk scarves and matching velvet handbags. In addition it has a good selection of duvets and household linens. Quality bedding and linens are available at **Gans**, which conveniently has a shop at Vienna's Schwechat airport for last-minute purchases. **Gunkel** stocks household linen and bath robes, and for generations the Viennese have patronized **Zur Schwäbischen Jungfrau**, founded in 1720, where fine linens can be made to order as well as purchased ready-made.

Härtel has the largest and possibly the most beautiful selection of braids of all kinds: confined seemingly to the smallest premises of any shop in Vienna, it also sells tassels, fringes and other decorative materials.

FOOD AND WINE

TWO OF VIENNA'S most renowned and almost revered food and wine shops, **Wild** and **Zum Schwarzen Kameel** *(see p212)*, sell mouth-watering produce. The former's wine cellars are magnificent and stretch three floors underground. Its selection of eaux de vie must be the best in Vienna. It also sells books on wine. Wild is worth a visit for its delicious goose liver alone.

Julius Meinl supermarket has branches all over Vienna, and indeed all over Austria, but its flagship is the Graben branch. Enter via its Lukullus Bar *(see p217)* in Naglergasse if you would like to stop for a snack and a drink.

Altmann & Kühne is famous for its tiny, hand-made chocolates sold in beautiful boxes shaped like miniature chests of drawers, books, horses and angels.

GIFTS

SUCCESSOR OF THE famous Wiener Werkstätten, the outfit called **Österreichische Werkstätten** has a selection of almost exclusively Austrian goods. In stock are a range of enamelled jewellery designed by Michaela Frey, ceramics, mouth-blown glass, candles and, from late autumn onwards, Christmas tree decorations. The arts and crafts markets *(see p222)* are also good hunting-grounds for picking up knick-knacks.

BOOKS

PRACTICALLY a Viennese information centre, **Georg Prachner** is one of Vienna's best bookshops and doubles up as a meeting place for regulars. It has a good selection of books in English, as does **Shakespeare & Co**.

For rare old books – as well as new ones – visit **Heck**. Old prints and maps are available at the specialist **Gilhofer**. **Taschenbuchladen** stocks paperbacks, and for a large selection of books in English there's the excellent **British Bookshop**.

NEWSPAPERS AND PERIODICALS

MOST NEWSPAPER kiosks within the Ringstrasse stock foreign newspapers – and so do the best coffee houses, where they can be read free of charge. There is no English-language Viennese newspaper. **Morawa** sells newspapers and periodicals in practically any language.

CLOTHES AND ACCESSORIES

VIENNESE CLOTHES are well-made and tend to be quite formal. **Resi Hammerer** is famous for jackets, coats and capes made from *Loden*. This is a warm, felt-like fabric traditionally in dark green or grey, but now produced in a range of colours.

Tostmann is best known for traditional Austrian costumes or *Trachten*: its *Dirndl* (dresses) are made from a variety of fabrics including beautiful brocades. Its clothes for children are particularly delightful. **Fürnkranz** has branches throughout Vienna, but its main shop for elegant day and evening wear is in Kärntner Strasse, with the shop at Neuer Markt stocking more

sporty styles. **Flamm** can always be relied upon for simply-tailored dresses and suits in silk and fine wool.

E Braun & Co was originally a purveyor of fine linens to the Imperial Court, but it now sells clothes. It is worth going into the shop if only to view the gilded birdcage of a lift. Another old-established Viennese name is **Knize**. A famous tailoring establishment in imperial times, the shop now stocks ready-to-wear clothes for men and women. It also sells its own scent. **Kettner** – almost hidden down a nearby side street – stocks casual daywear for both men and women at all its branches.

All the shoes at **Bellezza** are imported from Italy; the quality, as you would expect, is excellent. For young, fashionable styles, try **Stephan Kelian**: it has a good selection of Kelian shoes made in France.

Younger, trendier shoppers should head straight to Judengasse – this street has plenty of reasonably priced boutiques with styles to suit every taste. For menswear in particular, **D G Linnerth** stocks informal and sporty clothes designed for teenagers upwards.

An optician called **Erich Hartmann** bought a shop with a large stock of horn and tortoiseshell in 1980. Today he sells a range of hand-made spectacles, combs and chains, all made from horn. His shop looks like a coffee house and is well-known in the city.

SIZE CHART
For Australian sizes follow British and American convention.

Women's clothes

Austrian	36	38	40	42	44	46	48	50
British	10	12	14	16	18	20	22	24
American	8	10	12	14	16	18	20	22

Shoes

Austrian	36	37	38	39	40	41	42	43
British	3½	4	5	5½	6½	7½	8	9
American	5	5½	6½	7	8	9	9½	10½

Men's shirts

Austrian	44	46	48	50	52	54
British	34	36	38	40	42	44
American	S	M	M	L	XL	XL

Antiques, Auctions and Markets

MANY DISTRICTS in Vienna have their own markets – and a few have several – where you can buy arts and crafts, food, flowers and imported and second-hand goods. The city is also known for its Christmas markets, popular with locals in the evenings. If you are interested in antiques and bric-a-brac, it is worth looking in both the specialist antique shops and the main auction house. Alternatively, enjoy browsing round the bustling ethnic stalls and mix of cultures in the Naschmarkt, Vienna's main food market.

ANTIQUES

VIENNA IS JUSTLY FAMOUS for its antique shops. Most are located in the Stephansdom Quarter as well as along Schönbrunner Strasse, where stock ranges from valuable antiques to simply second-hand. The **Dorotheum** *(see Auctions)*, the **Kunst und Antikmarkt** and the Floh-markt *(see Artisan Markets)* should not be missed. Jewellery and antique paintings can be particularly good finds. One of the best shops for antique jewellery is the **Galerie Rauhenstein**. It stocks rare and beautiful pieces up to and including the 1940s.

If you are interested in old jewellery and silver and other antiques, **Herbert Asenbaum** is worth a visit. For larger pieces and shops on a larger scale, try **Mario Perco** on Spiegelgasse or **Reinhold Hofstätter** on Bräunerstrasse. They are both well established and have a good selection of fine antique furniture.

AUCTIONS

OPENED IN 1707 as a pawn-brokers for the "new poor", and appropriately called the *Armen Haus* (poor house), Vienna's **Dorotheum** is now the city's most important auction house. In 1788 it moved to the site of a former convent called the Dorotheerkirche, which had an altar-piece of St Dorothea in it – hence the name. This is an interesting place to browse around, and since buying is not restricted to auction times, you can often purchase items over the counter. It has other branches dotted around the city.

FOOD MARKETS

BETWEEN the Linke and Rechte Wienzeile, the **Naschmarkt** *(see p136)* is worth visiting even if you don't buy anything. Exotic fruit and vegetables, notably Greek, Turkish and Asian specialities, crowd the stalls and are piled high in the shops. It is a fascinating place to wander around and observe life. Open all year round, it acts as a meeting point for people of different nationalities who come to buy and sell fruit and vegetables, tea, herbs and spices. The section near the Karlsplatz contains the more expensive Viennese-run stalls. These gradually give way to stands run by colourful Turkish stallholders as you move further towards the flea market.

In addition to the exotic food stalls, you will see Czechs selling hand puppets, Russians selling Babushka dolls and Turks with stalls piled high with eastern clothes. The market is also a good spot for late-night revellers to feast on highly-spiced fish snacks in the early hours of the morning.

Food-lovers should not miss the farmers' market known as the **Bauernmarkt**. From March until the end of October on Tuesdays and Thursdays, a whole range of organic and other country produce is on sale here.

ARTISAN MARKETS

ANTIQUE MARKETS and arts and crafts markets are fairly new to Vienna, but the Flohmarkt (flea market) at the end of the **Naschmarkt** *(see p136)* and the **Kunst und Antikmarkt** are established hunting grounds for second-hand goods and antiques. The price quoted is probably not the price that you are expected to pay – it's usually assumed that you will bargain.

For the better quality hand-crafted goods, head to the Spittelberg market *(see p124)* near the Volkstheater. Here artists and craftspeople sell their own products rather than mass-produced factory goods. This is a fashionable and attractive part of Vienna and, although the market is small, you are likely to find gifts of good quality. There are also small galleries and cafés where artists exhibit their works.

The **Heiligenkreuzerhof** *(see p75)* art market is in a quiet, secluded courtyard where a small, select group of exhibitors is on hand should you wish to discuss the work. The stalls sell jewellery, ceramics and other hand-made goods. Further entertainment and atmosphere is provided by an Austrian folk singer dressed in traditional clothes playing his accordion.

FESTIVE MARKETS

CHRISTMAS MARKETS in Vienna are very special, the most famous of all being the **Christkindlmarkt** *(see p64)* held in front of the Rathaus. Attractions vary from year to year, but there are always sideshows, decorated trees, performances on a temporary stage and lots of stalls, as well as a workshop for making Christmas presents and baking goodies. Items for sale include honey cakes, bees-wax candles, Christmas decorations and various crafts, although the main attraction is the joyous atmosphere. It is especially magical at night when everything is lit up.

The **Alt Wiener Christ-kindlmarkt** *(see p64)* at the Freyung is a smaller affair. Two weeks before Easter there is also an Easter market here with a large selection of blown and hand-painted eggs. Four other Christmas markets take place in the Spittelberg area, in front of Schloss Schönbrunn, at Karlskirche and at the Heiligenkreuzerhof.

DIRECTORY

SPECIALITY SHOPS

Kober
Graben 14–15. **Map** 2 D5
& 5 C3. ◖ 53360180.

Maria Stransky
Hofburg Passage 2.
Map 5 C4. ◖ 5336098.

Metzger
Stephansplatz 7. **Map** 2 E5
& 6 D3. ◖ 5123433.
One of two branches.

Novotny
Spiegelgasse 6. **Map** 4 D1
& 5 C4. ◖ 5122336.

Petit Point
Kärntner Strasse 16.
Map 4 D1 & 6 D4.
◖ 5124886.

Robert Horn
Bräunerstrasse 7.
Map 5 C4. ◖ 5138294.

Witte
Linke Wienzeile 16.
Map 3 A4. ◖ 58643050.

Zauberklingl
Führichgasse 4. **Map** 5 C4.
◖ 5126868.

MUSIC

Arcadia
Kärntner Strasse 40.
Map 4 D2 & 5 C5.
◖ 5139568.

EMI
Kärntner Str 30. **Map** 4 D1
& 6 D4. ◖ 51236750.

Gramola
Graben 16. **Map** 2 D5 &
5 C3. ◖ 5335034.

Virgin Megastore
Mariahilfer Strasse 37–9.
Map 3 B2. ◖ 588370.

JEWELLERY

Heldwein
Graben 13.
Map 5 C3. ◖ 5125781.

Juwel
Kohlmarkt 1. **Map** 2 D5 &
5 C3. ◖ 5336021.

Köchert
Neuer Markt 15.
Map 5 C4. ◖ 51258280.

Schullin
Kohlmarkt 7. **Map** 2 D5 &
5 C3. ◖ 53390070.

GLASSWARE

J & L Lobmeyr
Kärntner Str 26. **Map** 2 D5
& 6 D4. ◖ 5120508.

INTERIORS

Augarten
Stock-im-Eisen-Platz 3–4.
Map 2 D5 & 5 C3.
◖ 5121494. *One of
several branches.*

Backhausen
Kärntner Strasse 33.
Map 4 D1 & 6 D4.
◖ 514040.

Gans
Brandstätte 1–3. **Map** 4 D1
& 6 D3. ◖ 5333560.
One of several branches.

Gunkel
Tuchlauben 11. **Map** 2 D5
& 5 C3. ◖ 53363010.

Härtel
Petersplatz 1. **Map** 5 C3.
◖ 5330906. *One of two
branches.*

Rasper & Söhne
Graben 15. **Map** 2 D5 &
5 C3. ◖ 534330.

Schloss Augarten
Obere Augartenstrasse 1.
Map 2 E2. ◖ 211240.

**Zur Schwäbischen
Jungfrau**
Graben 26. **Map** 2 D5 &
5 C3. ◖ 5355356.

FOOD AND WINE

Altmann & Kühne
Graben 30. **Map** 2 D5 &
5 C3. ◖ 5330927.
One of two branches.

Julius Meinl
Graben 19. **Map** 2 D5 &
5 C3. ◖ 5323334.

Wild
Neuer Markt 10–11.
Map 5 C4. ◖ 5122179.

**Zum Schwarzen
Kameel**
Bognergasse 5.
Map 5 C3. ◖ 5338125.

GIFTS

**Österreichische
Werkstätten**
Kärntner Str 6. **Map** 4 D1
& 6 D4. ◖ 5122418.

BOOKS

British Bookshop
Weihburggasse 24–6.
Map 4 E1 & 6 D4.
◖ 5121945.

Mariahilfer Strasse 4.
Map 3 C2.
◖ 5226730.

Georg Prachner
Kärntner Str 30. **Map** 4 D1
& 6 D4. ◖ 5285490.

Gilhofer
Bognergasse 2. **Map** 5 C3.
◖ 5334285.

Heck
Kärntner Ring 14. **Map**
4 E2 & 6 D5. ◖ 5055152.

Shakespeare & Co
Sterngasse 2. **Map** 2 E5 &
6 D2. ◖ 5355053.

NEWSPAPERS AND PERIODICALS

Morawa
Wollzeile 11. **Map** 2 E5 &
6 D3. ◖ 515620.

CLOTHES AND ACCESSORIES

Bellezza
Kärntner Str 45. **Map** 4 D1
& 5 C5. ◖ 5121953.

E Braun & Co
Graben 8. **Map** 2 D5 &
5 C3. ◖ 5125505.

Erich Hartmann
Corner of Lilieng.
Map 6 D3. ◖ 5121489.

Flamm
Neuer Markt 12.
Map 5 C4. ◖ 5122889.

Fürnkranz
Kärntner Str 39. **Map** 6 D4
& 5 C5. ◖ 4884426.
One of several branches.

Kettner
Seilergasse 12. **Map** 5 C4.
◖ 51322390. *One of
several branches.*

Knize
Graben 13. **Map** 2 D5 &
5 C3. ◖ 51221190.

Kurt Denkstein
Bauernmarkt 8. **Map** 6
D2. ◖ 5330460.

D G Linnerth
Lugeck 1–2. **Map** 6 D3.
◖ 5125888.

Resi Hammerer
Kärntner Str 29–31. **Map**
4 D1 & 5 C5. ◖ 5126952.

Tostmann
Schottengasse 3a.
Map 5 B2. ◖ 53353310.

ANTIQUES

Galerie Rauhenstein
Rauhensteingasse 3.
Map 6 D4. ◖ 5133009.

Herbert Asenbaum
Kärntner Str 28. **Map** 4 D1
& 6 D4. ◖ 5122847.

Mario Perco
Spiegelgasse 11. **Map** 4 D1
& 5 C4. ◖ 5135695.

Reinhold Hofstätter
Bräunerstrasse 12. **Map**
5 C4. ◖ 5335069.

AUCTIONS

Dorotheum
Dorotheergasse 17. **Map**
4 D1 & 5 C4. ◖ 51560.

MARKETS

**Alt Wiener
Christkindlmarkt**
Freyung. **Map** 2 D5 &
5 B2. ◯ Dec: 9:30am–
7:30pm daily.

Bauernmarkt
Freyung. **Map** 2 D5 & 5 B2.
◯ Mar–end Oct: 10am–
6:30pm Tue & Thu.

Christkindlmarkt
At the Neues Rathaus.
Map 1 C5 & 5 A2.
◯ Mid-Nov–24 Dec:
2–6:30pm Mon–Fri,
10am–6:30pm Sat & Sun.

Heiligenkreuzerhof
Map 2 E5 & 6 E3.
◯ Apr–Sep: first Sat &
Sun of each month; end
Nov–19 Dec: 10am–7pm
Sat, 10am–6pm Sun.

**Kunst und
Antikmarkt**
Donaukanal-Promenade.
Map 6 F2. ◯ May–end
Sep: 2–8pm Sat,
10am–8pm Sun.

Naschmarkt
Map 3 C2. ◯ 6am–
6:30pm Mon–Fri,
6am–2pm Sat.

Entertainment in Vienna

Vienna offers a wide range of entertainment, particularly of the musical variety. There is grand opera at the Opera House – Staatsoper *(see pp138–9)* – or the latest musical at the Theater an der Wien *(see p136)*. Dignified orchestral concerts and elegant Viennese waltzes take place at the great balls during the Carnival season, and waltzes are played in the relaxed atmosphere of the Stadtpark. Even the famous Lipizzaner horses perform to Viennese music and no visit to the city is complete without a trip to the

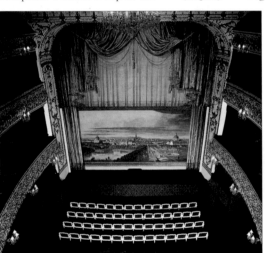

Pipo at the Ronacher (see p228)

Winter Riding School *(see pp98–9)*. Vienna also has excellent theatres, two of which perform in English, and several cinemas which specialize in classic films. Restaurants close early, but you can still be entertained around the clock at one of Vienna's many nightspots. Within the Ringstrasse, the city buzzes with late-night revellers enjoying jazz clubs, such as the Roter Engel, discos, casinos and bars with live music. Or you can end your day sipping coffee and nibbling pastries at a late-night café *(see also pp215–7)*.

The stage of the Theater in der Josefstadt *(see p116)*

PRACTICAL INFORMATION

A monthly guide to Vienna is issued free by the Wiener Tourismusverband (main Vienna Tourist Office – *see p237)*. Posters which list the weekly programmes for the opera houses and theatres are pasted on billboard columns and displayed in most hotel lobbies. They also list casts for all the performances. Each day the four main newspapers in the city, *Die Presse*, *Kronenzeitung*, *Standard* and *Kurier* *(see p239)* publish programme listings. All four also give details of daily cinema performances and concerts as well as the main sporting events.

BOOKING TICKETS

You can buy tickets direct from the appropriate box office (check opening hours, since these vary), or reserve them on the telephone. The phone numbers and addresses for the booking offices are listed in the Music, Theatre and Cinema directories *(see pp227–8)*. The four state theatres, the Burgtheater *(see p130)*, the **Akademietheater** *(see p228)*, the Opera House *(see pp138–9)* and the **Wiener Volksoper** *(see p227)*, all have one central booking office,

the **Bundestheaterkassen** *(see p227)*. Tickets usually go on sale a week before the performance. Phone reservations can be made from six days before the performance. Written applications for tickets for the state theatre must reach the Österreichische Bundestheater Verband (address as Bundestheaterkassen) at least three weeks in advance for the Volksoper and Opera House, and 10 days ahead for the Akademietheater and Burgtheater. Standing-room tickets (over 500 at the Opera House and 100 at the Volksoper) are sold at the evening box office one hour before the start of the performance. The state theatres also offer student concessions. About an hour before the start of a performance, and at the management's discretion, students under 27 can buy any unsold tickets very cheaply. Sometimes they will then sell their tickets to tourists for a mark-up.

Tickets for the state theatres, the Theater an der Wien *(see p136)* and **Raimund Theater** *(see p227)* can be used on public transport for two hours before, and six hours after, all performances. Agencies are reliable, try **Reisebüro Mondial** *(see p227)*, and hotel staff may be able to obtain tickets, if at higher prices. Otherwise try the box office for returns.

Billboard column

AT THE THEATRE

IF YOU VISIT THE theatre in person, you will be able to see the seating plan and make your choice accordingly. The monthly programme for the state theatres also contains individual seating plans and it is a good idea to have them in front of you when booking your tickets by telephone. Most hotel porters will also have copies of seating plans for the principal venues.

If you book by telephone remember that *Parkett* (stalls) are in front and are usually the most expensive. In some theatres the front rows of the stalls are known as *Orchestersitze*. The *Parterre* (back stalls) are cheaper and the dress circle (the grand or royal circle) is called *Erster Rang*, followed by the *Zweiter Rang* (balcony). At the Burgtheater and Opera House, there are two extra levels called the *Balkon* and *Galerie*. The higher you go, the cheaper the seats are.

Casino Wien in Esterházy Palace

Boxes are known as *Logen* and the back seats are always cheaper than the front seats.

At the **Wiener Volksoper** *(see p227)* they still have *Säulensitze*, seats where the view is partly obscured by a column. These cheap tickets are bought by music lovers who come to listen rather than to view. There are four tiers of boxes at the Volksoper, known in ascending order as *Parterre, Balkon, Erster Rang* and *Zweiter Rang*.

Buffets at Vienna's principal theatres provide alcoholic and non-alcoholic drinks, and tasty snacks which range from open sandwiches at the **Akademietheater** *(see p228)* and Volksoper to the more elaborate

Busker beneath the Pestsäule

concoctions at the Opera House and Burgtheater. Small open sandwiches with caviar, egg, smoked salmon, cheese and salami on Vienna roll-style bread are also common. Glasses of *Sekt*, a sparkling wine, are always available.

Buffets are usually open for up to one hour before the start of a performance and are often fairly empty. They are an ideal place for relaxing with a snack and a drink, and the coffee is extremely good.

It is not usual to tip ushers at theatres, unless you are being shown to a box, but you may round up the price of a theatre programme.

Coats and hats have to be left in the cloakroom before you go to your seat. There is usually no fixed charge, and tipping is at your discretion.

FACILITIES FOR THE DISABLED

A NUMBER OF VENUES offer wheelchair access or help for those with hearing difficulties. Be sure to make your needs very clear when booking tickets.

A booklet, *Wien für Gäste mit Handicaps* (Vienna for handicapped guests), is published by the Wiener Tourismus-verband *(see p237)* and provides information on facilities at entertainment venues, museums, hotels, restaurants, cafés, cinemas, post offices and so on.

TRANSPORT

BUSES AND TRAMS run until around 11pm, while the underground continues until about midnight *(see Getting Around Vienna, pp250–55)*. Night buses are a popular method of transport, with eight routes operating around the city and into the suburbs. They start at 12:30am from Schwedenplatz and continue every half hour until 4am. Tickets usually cost around one euro and are sold on the bus *(see p255)*.

You can phone for a taxi from your venue, or take one from outside. Taxis usually line up outside theatres after a performance, otherwise you can go to one of the many taxi ranks which are found on most street corners. Taxis which do not stop when hailed are already booked.

CASINOS

CASINOS AUSTRIA has become the hallmark for superbly run casinos all over the world (you will even find them aboard luxury liners), but **Casino Wien** is a showcase. It is set in the Baroque Esterházy Palace *(see p80)* and you can play French or American roulette, baccarat and poker there. The complex includes a bar, a restaurant and the **Jackpot Café**, which is a typically Viennese addition.

Casino Wien
Kärntner Strasse 41. **Map** 4 D1.
Casino ⬭ 3pm–4am daily.
Jackpot Café ⬭ 10am–1am daily.
📞 5124836.

Dancing at the grand Opera Ball *(see p139)*

Music in Vienna

THE VIENNA OPERA HOUSE *(see pp138–9)* is one of the greatest of its kind in the world and, like all four state theatres, is heavily subsidised. The acoustics are excellent – the world-famous conductor Arturo Toscanini advised on the rebuilding of the theatre after it was destroyed at the end of the last war. The house orchestra, the Vienna Philharmonic, performs while the Opera House is open from September until June. Most operas are sung in the original language. The city supports two principal orchestras, the Vienna Philharmonic and the Wiener Symphoniker. There are also a number of chamber music ensembles, such as the Alban Berg Quartet, and visiting artists. Church music is often of concert quality. You can hear more informal music in the Stadtpark, where a small orchestra regularly plays waltzes in summer. Live rock music is popular in discos, and there is an annual jazz festival *(see p63)*.

Performances are also held at the Stadthalle *(see p229)*, in places such as Schubert's birthplace in Nussdorf *(see p183)* and in many historic palaces.

The New Year's Concert *(see p65)* is televised live from the Grosser Musikvereinsaal in the Musikverein every year. You can apply for tickets by writing direct to the **Wiener Philharmoniker**. Applications must be received on 2 January (not before, not after) for the next year's concert. You can order from abroad by telegram.

Waltz concerts and operetta, with stars from the Vienna Volksoper, can be heard at the Musikverein, the Neue Burg *(see p95)* and the Konzerthaus on Tuesdays, Thursdays and Saturdays from April until October. Mozart and Strauss concerts are performed on Wednesdays at the Neue Burg. All tickets are the same price, so get there early to choose the best seat. Among seasonal events, in July the Wiener Klassik festival *(see p63)* features the works of great composers who have worked in Vienna *(see pp38–9)*, and from July to September you can attend the Vienna Music Festival *(see p62)*.

OPERA AND OPERETTA

SEAT PRICES AT the Vienna Opera House range from 4 to 145 euros. Tickets are sold one week in advance, except standing-room tickets which are on sale one hour before the performance starts. These are good value, since the most expensive ticket is around two euros, but there is usually a long queue. After buying your ticket, if you find a spot near a side rail, you can mark your space by tying a scarf round it – leaving you free to wander around. The New Year's Eve performance is always *Die Fledermaus*, and famous guests sometimes make surprise appearances during the second act.

The **Wiener Volksoper** is renowned for its superb operetta productions ranging from Strauss, Millöcker and Ziehrer to Lehár and Kálmán. There are also performances of musicals and light opera by Mozart, Puccini and Bizet, sung in German. The same singers also appear at the Opera House and vice versa – often singing the same role. Prices can range from 3 to 58 euros, and the season is the same as the Opera House.

Concealed in a small side street in the Stephansdom Quarter is one of Vienna's great little opera houses the **Wiener Kammeroper**. Many international singers such as Waldemar Kmentt, Eberhard Waechter and Walter Berry

started their careers here. You can expect anything from the early works of Rossini to classic operetta, as well as rock versions of familiar operas such as *Tales of Hoffmann* and *Carmen,* and opera parodies.

The historic Theater an der Wien *(see p136)* and the large **Raimund Theater** are part of the Vereinigte Bühnen Wien, the City's own theatres. Both of these specialize in grand and lavish musicals. The Wiener Festwochen *(see p62)* is held in May and June, and includes productions by guest companies, which are staged at these two theatres as part of the festival programme.

Throughout July and August the Wiener Kammeroper perform evening operas by Mozart, such as *The Marriage of Figaro* and *Don Giovanni*, at **Schönbrunner Schlosspark** *(see also pp170–71)*. From mid-July until mid-August the Wiener Kammeroper also play at the **Soirée bei Prinz Orlofsky** festival at the Schönbrunner Schlosstheater *(see p63)*. The festival **Seefestspiele Mörbisch** *(see p63)* takes place every weekend in July and August on a stage projecting onto Lake Neusiedl.

CLASSICAL CONCERTS

THE PRINCIPAL VENUES for classical concerts are the **Musikverein** (including the recently-restored Brahmssaal there) and the concert halls of the **Konzerthaus**.

CHURCH MUSIC

DETAILS OF the many church concerts performed in Vienna are published in all the daily newspapers. Look out particularly for details of Sunday mass at the following places: Augustinerkirche *(see p102)*, Minoritenkirche *(see p103)*, the Karlskirche *(see p146)*, Stephansdom *(see p76)* and Michaelerkirche *(see p92)*. In July and August, many other churches hold organ recitals.

The Vienna Boys' Choir *(see p39)* can be heard during mass at the Burgkapelle *(see p103)* every Sunday and religious holiday at 9:15am except from July to about mid-September. (The box office is open the Friday before). You can also hear them at the **Konzerthaus** every Friday at 3:30pm in May, June, September and October. Tickets are available from hotel porters and from **Reisebüro Mondial**. Book well in advance for major events.

Informal Music

THE DESCRIPTION just outside **Konzert-Café Schmid Hansl** reads, "the home of Viennese song". The original owner of this small café, which serves hot food until it closes, was Hansl Schmid, a very fine singer and musician. Guests would often visit the café just to hear him sing, and sometimes a famous artist might join him in a duet or give a solo performance. The present owner, Hansl Schmid's son, once a member of the Vienna Boys' Choir, has kept up this tradition, and you may well encounter opera stars coming in to perform unexpectedly.

Another Viennese favourite is the **Wiener Kursalon**. Here you sit on a terrace overlooking the Stadtpark and listen to old and new tunes and excerpts from the latest musicals. In the evening or in bad weather, the concert is transferred indoors. Sadly, this venue is under threat of closure.

Rock, Pop and Jazz

WHAT IS POPULAR one week in Vienna's lively music scene may very well be out of fashion the next. Many discos have live music on certain nights or for a limited period. **Atrium** is easily the oldest-established disco in Vienna and plays music from the 1960s and 1970s.

U4 disco has a different style every night (from industrial to flower power) and Thursday is gay night. **Roter Engel** in the Bermuda Triangle has live music every night and there is a midnight show at **Nachtwerk**.

Live concerts are held at the **Café Szene** and **Liquid/Olympic Studies** has five separate bars and the latest music. You can also hear live music at **Chelsea** on Sundays and on several nights at the **Jazzland**. **New Bora** and **Queen Anne** are under the same ownership: New Bora has live music, and Queen Anne is quieter. **Tanzcafé Volksgarten**, with its many dance floors, is popular, as are **Scotch Club** and **Take Five**.

For jazz fans there is also the **Jazzfest** held in the first two weeks of July, with concerts in various venues such as the Opera House *(see pp138–9)*, the Volkstheater *(p228)* and the Neues Rathaus *(p128)* as well as many open-air events.

Directory

Opera and Operetta

Bundestheaterkassen
Central Ticket Office. Hanuschgasse 3, A-1010. **Map** 5 C4. *Reservations:* *514440.* *8am–6pm Mon–Fri, 9am–noon Sat, Sun & public hols.*

Raimund Theater
Wallgasse 18, A-1060. *599770.*

Reisebüro Mondial
Faulmanngasse 4. **Map** 4 D2. *58804141.*

Schönbrunner Schlosspark
Schönbrunner Schloss Strasse, A-1130. *5120100.*

Seefestspiele Mörbisch
Mörbisch am Neusiedlersee, Burgenland. *02685 8181 (Jul & Aug).*

Soirée bei Prinz Orlofsky
Schönbrunner Schlosstheater, Schönbrunn. *5120100.*

Wiener Kammeroper
Fleischmarkt 24, A-1010. **Map** 2 E5 & 6 D2. *5130851.*

Wiener Volksoper
Währinger Strasse 78, A-1090. **Map** 1 B2. *514443318.*

Classical Concerts

Musikverein
Bösendorferstrasse 12. **Map** 4 E2 & 6 D5. *5058190.*

Wiener Hofburg-Orchester
Margaretenstrasse 3. **Map** 4 D2. *5872552.*

Wiener Philharmoniker
Bösendorferstrasse 12, A-1010. **Map** 4 E2 & 6 D5. *50565250.*

Raimund Theater
See Opera and Operetta.

Church Music

Konzerthaus
Lothringerstrasse 20, A-1030. **Map** 4 E2 & 6 E5. *7121211.*

Informal Music

Konzert-Café Schmid Hansl
Schulgasse 31. **Map** 1 A2. *4063658.* *9pm–4am Tue–Sat.*

Rock, Pop and Jazz

Atrium
Schwarzenbergplatz 10. **Map** 4 E2. *5053594.*

Café Szene
Hauffgasse 26. *7493341.*

Chelsea
Stadtbahnhofen 29–31, A-1080. **Map** 4 D2. *4079309.*

Gmoa Keller
Heumarkt 25. *7125310.*

Jazzfest
See text for venues. *588660 for information.*

Jazzland
Franz-Josefs-Kai 29. **Map** 2 E5 & 6 E2. *5332575.*

Nachtwerk
Dr-Gonda-Gasse 9. *6168880.*

New Bora
Johannesgasse 12. **Map** 4 E1 & 6 D4. *5122784.*

Queen Anne
Johannesgasse 12. **Map** 4 E1 & 6 D4. *5120203.*

Roter Engel
Rabensteig 5. **Map** 6 D2. *5354105.*

Scotch Club
Parkring 10. **Map** 4 E1 & 6 E4. *5129417.*

Take Five
Annagasse 3a. **Map** 4 D1 & 6 D4. *5129277.*

Tanzcafé Volksgarten
Burgring/Heldenplatz. **Map** 3 C1 & 5 B4. *5330518.*

U4
Schönbrunner Strasse 222. **Map** 3 A4. *8158307.*

Theatre and Cinema

VIENNA HAS A GOOD CHOICE of theatres, with an eclectic mix of styles ranging from classical drama to the avant-garde. Some places, like the Theater in der Josefstadt (see p116) or the recently restored Ronacher, are well worth visiting for their architecture alone. You can see productions in English at the English Theatre or, if you understand German, you can go and watch one of the many fringe performances. Some cinemas screen films in their original language. The classic film which is usually showing somewhere in the city is *The Third Man*, set in Vienna during the Allied occupation.

THEATRES

VIENNESE THEATRE is some of the best in Europe and the Burgtheater (see p130), one of the City's four state theatres, is the most important venue. Classic and modern plays are performed here and even if your understanding of German is limited, you will still enjoy a new production (which can often be avant-garde) of a Shakespeare play. For classic and modern plays go to the **Akademietheater**, part of the Burgtheater.

The Josefstadt Theater (see p116) is worth a visit for the interior alone. As the house lights slowly dim, the crystal chandeliers float gently to the ceiling. It offers excellent productions of Austrian plays as well as classics from other countries, and the occasional musical. **Kammerspiele** is the Josefstadt's "little house". The old and well-established **Volkstheater** offers more modern plays as well as the occasional classic and some operetta performances.

Vienna has a wide range of fringe theatre from one-man shows to *Kabarett* – these are satirical shows not cabarets – but fairly fluent German is needed to appreciate them. German-speakers will also enjoy the highly recommended **Kabarett Simpl**, which has recently reopened.

Theatres that give performances in English include the **English Theatre** and the very small **International Theater**. Plays at the English Theatre only run for a short period, but often feature famous international stars.

The **Ronacher** was once Vienna's most glamorous theatre. It became a variety theatre where the music-hall star Josephine Baker appeared among other entertainers. Stall seats were then replaced with tables and it became a restaurant. When the Burgtheater was destroyed in World War II, performances took place at the Ronacher until the Burgtheater was rebuilt. Recently restored, the Ronacher is once more a variety theatre.

CINEMAS

CINEMAS SCREENING the latest films in their original language are the **De France**, **Burg Kino** and **Top Kino Center**. The **Haydn Cinema**, **Artis International** and the **Flotten Center** show new releases in English only. Specializing in old and new classics as well as the more unusual films are the **Österreichisches Filmmuseum**, **Filmhaus Stöbergasse**, **Filmcasino**, and **Votiv-Kino** (which has a special cinema breakfast on Sundays). The **Apollo Center** is a modern complex with the largest cinema screen in Austria.

DIRECTORY

THEATRES

Akademietheater
Lisztstrasse 1, A-1010.
Map 4 E2.
Ticket Office: Hanuschgasse 3. **Map** 5 C4.
[514440.

English Theatre
Josefsgasse 12, A-1080.
Map 1 B5.
[4021260.

International Theater
Porzellangasse 8, A-1090.
Map 1 C3.
[3196272.

Kabarett Simpl
Wollzeile 36, A-1010.

Map 2 E5 & 6 E3.
[5124742.

Kammerspiele
Rotenturmstrasse 20, A-1010.
Map 2 E5 & 6 E2
[42700300.

Ronacher
Seilerstätte 9, A-1010.
Map 4 E1 & 6 D4.
[58885.

Volkstheater
Neustiftgasse 1, A-1070.
Map 3 B1.
[5247263.

CINEMAS

Apollo Center
Gumpendorfer Strasse 63.
Map 3 A4 & 5 B5.
[5879651.

Artis International
Schulgasse 5, A-1010.
Map 1 A2.
[5356570.

Burg Kino
Opernring 19.
Map 4 D1 & 5 B5.
[5878406.

De France
Schottenring 5.
Map 2 D4 & 5 B1.
[3175236.

Filmcasino
Margaretenstrasse 78.
Map 3 C3.
[5879062.

Filmhaus Stöbergasse
Stöbergasse 11–15.
Map 3 B5.
[5466630.

Flotten Center
Mariahilfer Strasse 85–87.
Map 3 A2.
[5865152.

Haydn Cinema
Mariahilfer Strasse 57.
Map 3 B2.
[5872262.

Österreichisches Filmmuseum
Augustinerstrasse 1.
Map 4 D1 & 5 C4.
[5337056.

Top Kino Center
Rahlgasse 1.
Map 3 C2 & 5 A5.
[5875557.

Votiv-Kino
Währinger Strasse 12.
Map 1 C4
[3173571.

Sport and Dance

OUTDOOR ACTIVITIES ARE extremely popular. Football is followed by many locals – especially since the pre-war victories of the famous "Wonder Team". Visitors who enjoy swimming can take advantage of the pools the city has to offer. Horse racing and ice-skating also attract many locals. Flat racing takes place at the Freudenau in the Prater. The well-equipped Stadthalle is ideal for spectator sports like boxing and wrestling and houses its own pool, bowling alleys and ice rink. Many of Vienna's dance schools hold special waltz classes during the Carnival season (see p65).

ICE-SKATING

OUTDOOR ICE-SKATING is very popular in Vienna. Locals make good use of the open-air rinks at the Eislaufanlage Engelmann and the Wiener Eislaufverein (see p232).

SWIMMING

VIENNA CAN BE very warm in summer and has many outdoor pools, including the Schönbrunner Bad in the Schönbrunn Palace park (see pp170–71). The Krapfenwaldbad has wonderful views over Vienna, and the Schafbergbad holds underwater gymnastics every Tuesday and Thursday. The Thermalbad Oberlaa has three open-air pools and an indoor pool. The Kinderfreibad Augarten (see p232) is popular with children, and they can be left at the Kinderfreibad to be watched by the attendants. Beach huts on the Alte Donau coast can be hired daily from Strandbad Gänsehäufel or Strandbad Alte Donau, where you can also hire boats. Strandbad Gänsehäufel has a beach, a heated pool, table tennis and Punch and Judy shows. For relaxing beaches, the world's longest water slide, barbecues and a night bus at weekends, visit Donauinsel.

FOOTBALL

THE VIENNESE ARE enthusiastic football fans, and there are two huge covered football stadiums in the city. The Ernst Happel Stadion (which seats 48,000) is in the Prater and the Hanappi Stadion (which seats 20,000) is at Hütteldorf.

HORSE RACING

THE PRATER OFFERS a wide range of activities (see pp160–61), including flat racing at the Freudenau and trotting races at the Krieau.

DANCING AND DANCE SCHOOLS

DURING THE Carnival season (see p65) many balls, and some fancy dress dances, are held in Vienna. Venues include the Hofburg, the Neues Rathaus (see p128) and the Musikverein (see p227). The grandest event is the Opera Ball (see p139), which takes place on the Thursday before Ash Wednesday. The opening ceremony includes a performance by the Opera House ballet. An invitation is not needed, you just buy a ticket. The Kaiserball is held at the Neue Burg on New Year's Eve (see pp65 and 95). A special ball calendar is issued by the Wiener Tourismusverband – Vienna Tourist Office (see p237).

The Summer Dance Festival (see p63) runs from July to August. You can learn a range of dances, including rock 'n' roll, at some dance schools in the city. During the Carnival season, some schools hold Viennese waltz classes. The Elmayer-Vestenbrugg also teaches etiquette.

DIRECTORY

GENERAL

Stadthalle
Vogelweidplatz 15.
Swimming pool
(981000.
◻ 8am–9:30pm Mon, Wed, Fri, 6:30am–9:30pm Tue & Thu, 7am–9:30pm Sat, 7am–6pm Sun & public hols.

ICE-SKATING

Eislaufanlage Engelmann
Syringgasse 6–8.
(4051425. ◻ 3rd week Oct–1st week Mar: 9am–6pm Mon, 9am–9:30pm Tue, Thu, Fri, 9am–7pm Wed, Sat, Sun.

SWIMMING

Krapfenwaldbad
Krapfenwaldgasse 65–73.
(3201501.
◻ May–Sep: 9am–8pm Mon–Fri, 8am–8pm Sat & Sun.

Schafbergbad
Josef-Redl-Gasse 2.
(4791593.

Strandbad Alte Donau
Strandbad Alte Donau 22, Arbeiterstrandbad-strasse 91.
(2633543.

Strandbad Gänsehäufel
Moissigasse 21.
(2699016.

Thermalbad Oberlaa
Kurbadstrasse 14.
(68009. ◻ 8:45am–10pm Mon–Sat, 7:45am–10pm Sun & public hols.

Donauinsel
U1 stop – Donauinsel.

FOOTBALL

Ernst Happel Stadion
Meiereistrasse 7.
(72808540.

Hanappi Stadion
Kaisslergasse 6.

HORSE RACING

Freudenau
Prater: flat racing
Freudenau 65.
(72895350.
(See pp62 & 161.)

Krieau
Prater: trotting
Sudportalstrasse 247.
(7269412 (enquiries).
(See pp64 & 160.)

DANCING AND DANCE SCHOOLS

Elmayer-Vestenbrugg
Bräunerstrasse 13.
Map 5 C4.
(5127197 (3–8pm).
◻ 3–8pm Mon–Sat, 5–10pm Sun.

CHILDREN'S VIENNA

TRADITIONALLY, the Viennese have a reputation for preferring dogs to children. But negative attitudes towards children are gradually disappearing as the number of families has increased since the 1960s baby boom. A few restaurants serve children's portions, and in some of the more expensive places they can eat Sunday lunch at half price. Eating out at a *Heuriger* is less formal, and you can sit outside in summer. Vienna has many playgrounds and some old-fashioned, yet entertaining, museums. Further out there are large parks, a zoo, swimming pools and ice rinks. Various children's activities are organized throughout the year.

Children pay half price on trams

PRACTICAL ADVICE

TRAFFIC IN VIENNA can be fast and drivers are not automatically obliged to stop at pelican crossings. Always cross the road at traffic lights, and watch out for speeding cyclists in the bicycle lanes.

Children up to the age of six can travel for free on public transport. Those between the ages of six and 14 must buy a half-price ticket. During the summer holidays (the end of June to the end of August) children under 18 can travel free provided they can show some form of identification when buying a ticket.

It is a good idea to carry some small change, as you will need it to use public lavatories. These are usually clean.

In shops, the assistants may offer children boiled sweets, but do not feel obliged to accept these.

The concierges at many hotels, particularly the larger establishments, can arrange for a baby-sitter. If they cannot, they may be able to suggest a reliable local agency. If you get back from an evening out after about 10 or 11pm, you may have to pay for the baby-sitter's taxi home.

CHILDREN'S SHOPS

TRADITIONAL Austrian clothing, which is still worn by some children in Vienna, can be purchased from **Lanz Trachtenmoden** on Kärntner Strasse. Traditional dress includes *Lederhosen*, leather shorts, for boys and the *Dirndl*, a traditional dress, for girls. The *Dirndl* is worn with a white lace blouse and an apron. A little bag is sometimes carried as well. Lanz Trachtenmoden also stocks a range of beautiful knitwear in a myriad of colours and designs. Children will particularly like the fine embroidered woollen slippers made in the Tyrol.

Dohnal sells Austrian-made clothes for children up to the age of 16, and the large international chains such as **012 Benetton** and **Jacadi** stock a wide selection of good-quality children's clothes.

Haas & Haas sells delightful craft-like presents, including wooden toys and puppets. Their conservatory-style tea house is an ideal place to treat your children to lunch, or a delicious cake or *palatschinken (see pp206–7)*.

Children on a day out visiting Josefsplatz in the Hofburg

The **Wiener Spielzeug-schachtel** sells imaginative wooden toys and children's books, while a more conventional toy shop is **Kober** on the Graben. Kober stocks a superb selection of toys and games, but at high prices.

Dressing up at the Maxim Kinderfest, part of Fasching (see p65)

012 Benetton
Goldschmiedgasse 9. **Map** 5 C3.
[5339005. One of several branches.

Dohnal
Kärntner Strasse 12.
Map 4 D1 & 6 D4. [5127311.
One of several branches.

Haas & Haas
Teehandlung, Stephansplatz 4.
Map 2 E3 & 6 D3. [5129770.

Jacadi
Trattnerhof 1. **Map** 5 C3.
[5358866.

Kober
Graben 14–15. **Map** 2 D5 & 5 C3.
[5336019.

Lanz Trachtenmoden
Kärntner Strasse 10.
Map 4 D1 & 6 D4. [5122456.

Wiener Spielzeugschachtel
Rauhensteingasse 5.
Map 6 D4.
[5124494.

The Vienna Marriott offers special Sunday lunch deals for families

EATING OUT

RESTAURANTS in Vienna are not as tolerant of noisy or boisterous children as establishments in many other cities, but there are still plenty of places where children are welcome. Some of the more expensive hotel restaurants offer special Sunday lunch deals for families. The best is probably the Vienna Marriott *(see p197)*, where children under six eat free and six to 12-year-olds eat for half price. There is also a playroom with a child minder. The **SAS Palais Hotel** offers a similar deal without the playroom.

Heurige, where you can sit outside in summer, are usually less formal. The best time for families is from 4pm, when most of them open, as they are less crowded. Heuriger Zimmermann *(see p217)* has a small zoo where children can stroke the animals.

There are also a number of fast-food restaurants, including **McDonald's** and **Pizza Hut**. Most of these have special children's menus and some offer free gifts for children, especially on their birthdays. The **Wienerwald** Viennese chicken restaurants also have a children's menu. They are more formal indoors, but some, like the branch in the Freyung, have a garden. Open until 11:30pm, **Lustig Essen** also caters for children.

Lustig Essen
Salvatorgasse 6. **Map** 2 E5 & 6 D2.
[5333037.

McDonald's
Singerstrasse 4. **Map** 4 E1 & 6 D3.
[5139279.
One of several branches.

Pizza Hut
Schottengasse 2.
Map 5 B2. [5331810.

SAS Palais Hotel
Parkring 16. **Map** 4 E1 & 6 E4.
[515170.

Wienerwald
Annagasse 3.
Map 4 D1 & 6 D4. [5123766.
Freyung 5, Schottenkeller.
Map 2 D5 & 5 B2. [5331420.
Two of several branches.

SIGHTSEEING WITH CHILDREN

VIENNA HAS A WEALTH of attractions that will appeal to children, including funfairs, museums, sports and the zoo.

It costs around half the adult entrance fee for children to get into museums. If children touch or get too close to the exhibits, the museum attendants are likely to make a fuss.

Vienna has plenty of parks, but some are designed more for admiring from the pathways than running around in. Watch out for signs warning *Bitte nicht betreten,* which means "Please don't walk on the grass". Details of some of the more child-friendly parks and nature reserves are given on page 232.

Children's playgrounds in Vienna are generally safe and well equipped. However, it is advisable to avoid the Karlsplatz play area, which is rather seedy and downmarket.

Family out cycling, a familiar sight at the Prater

Elephants at Tiergarten Schönbrunn in the palace gardens *(see pp170–71)*

THE ZOO, PARKS AND NATURE RESERVES

THE ZOO IS LOCATED in Schönbrunn Palace gardens *(see pp170–71)* and adults can admire the many Baroque animal houses which accommodate elephants and the like. There is a butterfly house and the gardens have playgrounds and sandpits.

In the Vienna Woods, the Lainzer Tiergarten *(see p169)*, once a hunting ground, is now a nature reserve where children can see deer, wild boar and horses. There are playgrounds and a pond. An easy walk takes you to Hermes Villa hunting lodge, with its café and nature-based exhibitions.

At Gänserndorf **Safari und Abenteuerpark**, you can feed elephants and giraffes from your car windows. One section has animals which children can stroke. There are shows such as performing sea lions and a snake parade.

Safari und Abenteuerpark
Siebenbrunnerstrasse Gänserndorf.
[02282 702610. *Safari park*
◯ 7 Apr–29 Oct: 9:30am–3:30pm
Mon–Fri, 9am–4:30pm Sat & Sun.
Abenteuerpark ◯ 7 Apr–
29 Oct: 9:30am–6:30pm daily.

FUNFAIRS

AN IDEAL VENUE FOR A family outing is the atmospheric Prater *(see pp160–61)*. Its big wheel is magical at night, and noisier and busier than by day. The Prater park has sandpits, playgrounds, ponds, streams, and a vast area for children to run around in.

The **Böhmische Prater**, a smaller funfair in the Laaerwald, has ponds, birdlife, meadows and playgrounds.

Böhmische Prater
Laaerwald, Favoriten.
[6898193.

CHILDREN'S SPORTS

VIENNA HAS SOME excellent swimming baths, free for children under six, such as the Dianabad *(see p229)*. The **Kinderfreibad Augarten** is a shallow pool and free for children between the ages of six and 15. However, it is not open to anyone else, except accompanying adults.

In summer, you can swim in the Donau Insel coves. During winter, you can bathe in the hot geysers at Thermalbad Oberlaa *(see p229)*.

Between October and March you can go ice-skating at **Wiener Eislaufverein** or at **Eislaufanlage Engelmann**. Then enjoy hot chocolate in a Ringstrasse coffee house like Café Prückel *(see pp58–61)* or Café Schwarzenberg *(see pp60–61)* on Kärntner Ring.

ICE-SKATING

Eislaufanlage Engelmann
Syringgasse 6–8. [4051425.
◯ 3rd week Oct–1st week Mar:
9am–6pm Mon, 9am–9:30pm Tue,
Thu, Fri, 9am–7pm Wed, Sat, Sun.

Wiener Eislaufverein
Lothringerstrasse 28. **Map** 4 E2.
[71363530. ◯ Oct–Mar: 9am–
9pm Tue, Thu, Fri, 9am–8pm Sat–
Mon, 9am–10pm Wed.

Ice-skating at **Wiener Eislaufverein**

SWIMMING

Kinderfreibad Augarten
Karl-Meissl-Gasse entrance, Augarten Park. **Map** 2 E1.
[3324258.
◯ 10am–6pm Mon–Fri.

The big wheel forms a familiar landmark in the Prater park *(see pp160–61)*

ENTERTAINMENT

ALTHOUGH MOST THEATRE is performed in German, the **Märchenbühne der Apfelbaum** marionette theatre sometimes puts on shows in English of favourite fairy tales. Fairy stories with music and song can also be seen at the **Lilarum** puppet theatre. The **Wiener Konzerthaus** holds concerts *Für Kinder und Kenner* (children and experts) six times a year on Saturday or Sunday afternoons. In January, watch out for the Maxim Kinderfest, part of Fasching *(see p65)*, when children can dress up in costume. In November and December the Opera House *(see pp138–9)* and the Wiener Volksoper *(see p227)* have traditional children's programmes *(Kinderzyklus)*. Productions include Mozart's *The Magic Flute* and Engelbert Humperdink's *Hansel and Gretel*.

Several cinemas in Vienna show films in the original languages – look in the *Standard* newspaper's foreign films section. See also *Entertainment in Vienna* on pp224–9.

Lilarum
Göllnergasse 8. **〔** 7102666.

Märchenbühne der Apfelbaum
Kirchengasse 41.
Map 3 B1.
〔 523172920.

Wiener Konzerthaus
Lothringerstrasse 20.
Map 4 E2 & 6 E5.
〔 7121211.

SPECIAL ACTIVITIES AND WORKSHOPS

THE RATHAUS *(see p128)* has children's activities once a month (details from the town hall), and from mid-November there is a Christmas market *(see pp222–3)* which includes a children's train, pony rides and stalls selling toys, chestnuts and winter woollens. A Christmas workshop is held at the Volkshalle in the Rathaus from 9am to 6pm (7pm at weekends). The activities include baking, silk painting and making decorations.

Attacus atlas at the Natural History Museum *(see pp126–7)*

A Christmas market stall in front of the Rathaus *(see p128)*

MUSEUMS

VIENNA'S MUSEUMS are generally better known for their old-fashioned charm than for modern hands-on exhibits, but there are still a range of places children will enjoy. The Natural History Museum dinosaur room boasts fossils and columns decorated with dinosaur sculptures *(see pp126–7)*. Housed in a World War II flak tower, the **Haus des Meeres** (Vienna Aquarium) contains over 3,000 sea creatures, including piranhas, crocodiles and sharks. Feeding time is 3pm.

Popular exhibits at the Völkerkundemuseum *(see p95)* include exotic musical instruments, some Native American artefacts and Montezuma's treasures. Children aged 13 and under are allowed to enter the **Kunsthaus Wien** free. Designed by Friedensreich Hundertwasser, this colourful private gallery has undulating floors and bright paintings.

The **Wiener Strassenbahnmuseum** (Vienna Tram Museum) houses the largest collection of vintage trams and buses in the world. Details of tours in a 1920s tram and tours of the museum are available from information offices at Karlsplatz and Westbahnhof *(see p237)*.

The Heeresgeschichtliches Museum *(see pp164–5)*, in the restored Arsenal, contains a range of war memorabilia. If you have a spare half hour, you may also like to visit the small Doll and Toy Museum *(see p86)* and the **Zirkus und Clownmuseum.**

A doll's house (about 1920) from the Doll and Toy Museum *(see p86)*

Haus des Meeres
Esterházypark. **Map** 3 B2.
〔 5871417. **◯** 9am–6pm daily.

Kunsthaus Wien
Untere Weissgerberstrasse 13.
〔 7120491. **◯** 10am–7pm daily.

Wiener Strassenbahnmuseum
Erdbergstrasse 109. **〔** 7909 44903.
◯ May–beginning Oct: 9am–4pm Sat, Sun & public hols. (For tours see p237).

Zirkus und Clownmuseum
Karmelitergasse 9. **Map** 2 E4 & 6 E1.
〔 2110602127. **◯** 5:30–7pm Wed, 2:30–5pm Sat, 10am–noon Sun.

Montezuma's headdress in the Völkerkundemuseum *(see p95)*

SURVIVAL GUIDE

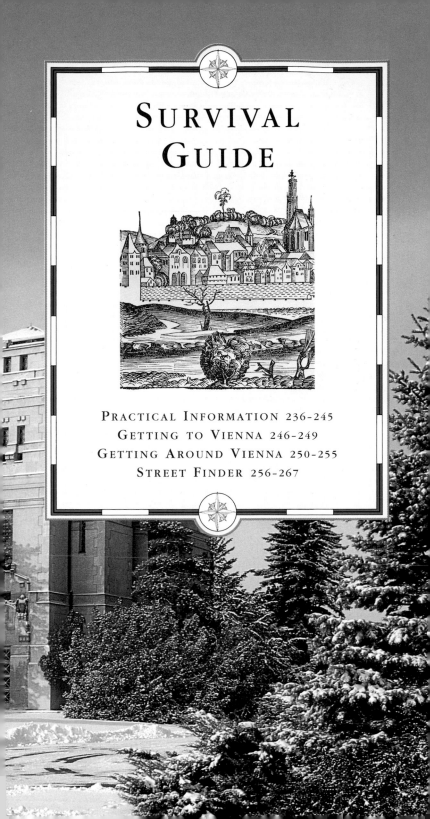

PRACTICAL INFORMATION

THE BEST WAY to get around the centre of Vienna is on foot, although from November onwards there is a lot of snow, ice and grit on the roads. If you are using public transport, buy the appropriate travel pass or ticket (see Getting to Vienna, pp248–51, Getting Around Vienna, pp252–7, and the underground and commuter train map on the inside back cover). Senior citizens pay less on public transport and at museums, and there are also a number of reductions for card-carrying students. Sights are sometimes being refurbished, so it may be a good idea to ring and check that they are open before visiting. Some shops close on Saturday afternoons and all are closed on Sundays. Banks are shut all weekend. Embassies and religious services are listed on page 239.

Sign for tourist information

Theatre ticket booking office

TOURIST INFORMATION

THERE ARE PLENTY of maps, information leaflets and brochures available in tourist offices at home and in Vienna. You can plan your trip in advance by getting in touch with travel agencies and the representatives of **Österreich Werbung** (the Austrian National Tourist Office) in your own country, or you can approach the **Wiener Tourismusverband** (Vienna Tourist Board) directly. For assistance in organizing day trips from Vienna (see p174–5), contact the Österreich Werbung. Tourist information is also available from the offices of Austrian Airlines (see p247). Information offices can be found at motorway exits (see Directory) and at **Westbahnhof** and **Südbahnhof** stations from where you can make hotel reservations. For air travellers, the arrivals hall at Schwechat Airport has a tourist information office where you can reserve rooms and pick up a free city map (these are widely available on request). The map highlights the most popular sights and contains network diagrams of the underground and the commuter trains (see also inside back cover).

For cheaper accommodation and information for young people about youth hostels or tickets for pop concerts, the multilingual team at **Jugendinformation Wien** provides assistance and leaflets in various languages including English, French and Italian.

SIGHTSEEING TIPS

VIENNA HAS approximately 70 museums and their entrance prices vary considerably. Any major exhibitions put on by the museums will involve an extra charge. Children pay roughly half price and there are also reductions for senior citizens and students with identity cards. There are no reduced-rate weekly or monthly passes. The only day on which the entrance fee is reduced or free is 26 October – the Austrian National Day.

Museums and galleries are often very crowded at weekends, so it is a good idea to plan your visits during the week if you can. Many museums close on a Monday, but it is wise to check the opening times in this guide or in the free museums leaflet available at tourist offices. It gives addresses, phone numbers and visiting times for memorials, museums and sights, and is updated every year. If you are still in doubt, ring the museum itself.

Booking for the Opera House, Burgtheater, Akademietheater and Volksoper is best done through the Bundestheaterkassen (see p227). Tickets for the Vienna Boys' Choir can be obtained from the Burgkapelle (see p103) or from Reisebüro Mondial (see p227). It is a good idea to write or phone well in advance. There are many booking agencies, but they are likely to add on a heavy surcharge. (See also Entertainment in Vienna pp224–9.)

City tour bus used by one of Vienna's leading tour operators

GUIDED TOURS AND EXCURSIONS

THE MAIN GUIDED tour operators are **Vienna Sightseeing** and **Cityrama**. Trams are a good way of seeing the 19th-century buildings in the Ringstrasse because, with the right ticket, you can choose where to get on and off (see p252).

The **DDSG Shipping Co** organizes tours on the Danube and Danube Canal to sights such as Otto Wagner's Nussdorf locks or Friedensreich Hundertwasser's decoration of Spittelau District heating plant.

In the summer there are about 50 guided walking tours, presented in English, French or Italian, with themes such as Vienna 1900.

From May to September, cycling enthusiasts can book tours through **Vienna Bike** or the bike hire company **Pedal**

A guided walking tour around the Hofburg (see pp96–101)

Power. The latter's 3-hour city tours leave from the Prater ferris wheel at 10am daily. Pedal Power also offer a tour of local *Heurige* at weekends. Tours are run in German or

English, but tours in Italian or French can also be arranged.

Tram tours in a 1920s tram (visiting the world's largest tram museum) are organized by **Oldtimer Tram** and leave from Otto Wagner's Pavilions on Karlsplatz (see pp144–5).

ETIQUETTE

FEMINISM HAS had little impact in Vienna. Women will have doors opened and even their hand kissed at a formal introduction, and handshaking is the norm. Titles and status are important, so don't be surprised if a Frau Doktor (often a woman married to someone with a doctorate) is served first in a restaurant or shop. When eating with Austrians, wait until everyone raises their glasses for a *Prost* before sipping your wine. Remember to call the waiter *Herr Ober* (Mr Head Waiter).

DIRECTORY

DIALLING CODE FOR VIENNA

From Great Britain
[00 43 1.
From the US & Canada
[011 43 1.
From Australia
[0011 43 1.

TOURIST OFFICES

Jugendinformation Wien
Babenbergerstrasse 1
A-1010.
Map 3 C1 & 5 B5.
[1799.
○ noon–7pm
Mon–Sat.

Österreich Werbung
Rilkeplatz 5.
[588660.
○ 9:30am–5pm
Mon–Wed & Fri,
9:30am–6pm Thu.

Schwechat Airport
Arrivals Hall.
[70072828 or
70072875.
○ 8:30am–9pm daily.

Wiener Tourismusverband
(Main office) Corner of Albertinaplatz, Tegethoffstrasse and Meysedergasse.
Map 4 D1 & 6 C4.
[211140.
○ 9am–7pm daily.

Obere Augartenstrasse 40.
Map 2 E3.
[211140.
○ 8am–4pm Mon–Fri.

East Motorway (A1 exit)
Wien/Auhof motorway.
[9791271 or 9791272.
○ Nov–Mar: 10am–6pm daily; Apr–Oct: 8am–10pm daily.

South Motorway (A2)
Zentrum motorway exit.
[6160070 or 6160071.
○ Easter–Jun: 9am–7pm daily; Jul–Sep: 8am–10pm daily; Oct: 9am–7pm daily.

Südbahnhof
Map 4 F4.
[5053132.
○ winter: 6:30am–9pm; summer: 6:30am–10pm daily.

Westbahnhof
[8923392.
○ 7am–10pm daily.

TRANSPORT INFORMATION

Wiener Linien
(Vienna Transport Authority Information).
Erdbergstrasse 202.
[79090.

FOREIGN AUSTRIAN TOURIST OFFICES

London
30 St George Street,
London
W1R 0AL.
[071 629 0461.

New York
500 Fifth Avenue,
Suite 2009–2022,
New York,
N Y 10110.
[212 944 6880.

Sydney
36 Carrington Street,
1st floor,
Sydney,
NSW 2000.
[02 299 3621.

Toronto
2 Bloor Street East,
Suite 3330, Toronto,
Ontario
M4W 1A8.
[416 967 3381.

TOUR OPERATORS

Cityrama
Börsegasse 1.
Map 2 D4 & 5 B1.
[534130.

DDSG Shipping Co
Handelskai 265.
[7268123.

Pedal Power
Ausstellungsstrasse 3.
[7297234.

Vienna Bike
Wasagasse 28/2/5.
[3191258.

Vienna Sightseeing
Stelzhamergasse 4–11.
Map 4 F1 & 6 F3.
[7124683.

Oldtimer Tram
Schwendgasse 51.
[89213340.

INFORMATION FOR DISABLED VISITORS

SERVICES FOR the disabled, as with many major cities, are rather disappointing, but if you contact museums in advance they will help with wheelchairs. Most of the main sights are quite close together and accessible by wheelchair. Just plan your route carefully. There is a useful book, *Wien für Gäste mit handicaps* (Vienna for handicapped guests), available from tourist offices (*see p237*). Unfortunately, trams and buses cannot accommodate wheelchairs. At train stations, ask about lifts when you get your ticket. Facilities vary at underground stations, so check first. The main travel agent that books rooms for the disabled in Vienna is **Egnatia Tours**.

STUDENT INFORMATION

ALL OF VIENNA'S main theatres offer cheap standing-room tickets sold at the evening box office prior to the performance. For popular shows you may need to queue for several hours. Unsold tickets can be bought shortly before the performance starts. As well as an international student card, you will need to bring your university identity card. An international student card also entitles students to discount rail passes, special fares on local transport, student charter flights and discounts at museums and sports events.

Any tourist office will provide up-to-date information about the cheaper hotels and pensions as well as a list of Vienna's youth hostels, *Jugendherbergen (see p193)*.

Signs for womens' (above) and mens' lavatories

Information office for use by young people and students

TIME

VIENNA IS on Central European Time, which puts it two hours ahead of Greenwich Mean Time in summer and one hour ahead in winter.

OPENING HOURS

THIS GUIDE PROVIDES the opening times for each individual sight. Most businesses start work at around 8am and close at about 4pm. On Friday afternoons, many businesses close early and, even if they do not, it is hard to get anything done.

Most shops are open from Monday to Friday, 8am to 6pm with a one- or two-hour break at midday, although shops in the centre tend not to close for lunch. Some shops still close at 1pm on Saturdays, but most now stay open until 5pm. Shops also close on Sundays and public holidays.

PUBLIC LAVATORIES

THERE ARE 330 public lavatories in Vienna and they are open between 9am and 7pm. They are generally clean, but are not free, so it a good idea to carry some small change. The Jugendstil lavatory on the Graben was designed by Adolf Loos and is worth a visit. Other usefully located WCs are in the Opernpassage and the Rathaus Park, opposite the Burgtheater. All underground stations have lavatories.

FRONTIER FORMALITIES AND CUSTOMS

NATIONALS FROM most European and many overseas countries do not need a visa to enter Austria. Dogs and cats require a rabies vaccination certificate with a German translation. Motorists need a Green Card as proof of third-party insurance. Details can be obtained from car clubs.

TAX-FREE GOODS

NON-RESIDENTS from outside the European Union (EU) can obtain a refund of up to 20% of the price on the VAT paid on purchases of over 73 euros in any one shop. When you buy the goods, get a receipt to reclaim the tax. This must be stamped by a customs official. Try to keep the goods with you for possible inspection. You can get on-the-spot refunds at tax points at airports, border crossings and railway stations listed on the tax-free envelope, or post the receipt (*see p219*).

Duty-free limits apply to alchoholic drinks such as Eiswein, if unopened

DUTY-FREE LIMITS

EVERY NON-EU CITIZEN over the age of 17 can import duty-free goods totalling 200 cigarettes (or 50 cigars or 250 g of tobacco), 2 litres of wine and 1 litre of spirits. They may also bring in other commodities to a value of 175 euros duty free.

At the beginning of 1995 Austria joined the European Union and duty-free limits for EU citizens entering or leaving Austria are now in line with those for other EU countries.

RADIO AND NEWSPAPERS

AUSTRIA HAS two main radio stations. Ö1 plays classical music and transmits the news in English, French and German every day at 8am. Ö3 plays popular music and transmits

Austrian two-pin electric plug

regular traffic bulletins. Radio FM4 transmits in English from 1am to 2pm daily on 103.8 MHz. It covers regional and international news as well as cultural events. There are also several private radio stations playing mainly pop music. Cable stations carry BBC World Service broadcasts 24 hours daily; Vienna Cable Radio transmits on FM 108.8.

The main listings magazine is *Falter*, but the two chief newspapers, *Die Presse* and *Standard*, list films daily. You can buy papers in a *Tabak Trafik* (newsagent), a kiosk or, on Sundays, on street corners. Foreign film cinemas include Burg Kino, Top Kino, Haydn, Flotten and the De France *(see p228)*.

Foreign newspapers, including the *European, Financial Times, Herald Tribune, International Guardian* and *Economist*, are available from central kiosks.

There are also several English-language bookshops, including the **British Bookshop, Gerold & Co** and **Shakespeare & Co**.

Foreign newspapers are on sale at central kiosks

ELECTRICAL ADAPTORS

THE VOLTAGE in Austria is 220V AC. Plugs have two small round pins. It is a good idea to buy a multi-adaptor before coming to Vienna, as they are not easy to find in Austria. Some of the more expensive hotels may offer guest adaptors, but only for electric shavers.

CONVERSION CHART

Imperial to Metric

1 inch	= 2.54 centimetres
1 foot	= 30 centimetres
1 mile	= 1.6 kilometres
1 ounce	= 28 grams
1 pound	= 454 grams
1 pint	= 0.57 litres
1 gallon	= 4.6 litres

Metric to Imperial

1 millimetre	= 0.04 inches
1 centimetre	= 0.4 inches
1 metre	= 3 feet 3 inches
1 kilometre	= 0.6 miles
1 gram	= 0.04 ounces
1 kilogram	= 2.2 pounds
1 litre	= 1.8 pints

DIRECTORY

EMBASSIES & CONSULATES

Australia
Mattiellistrasse 2–4.
Map 4 E2.
☎ 51285800.

Canada
Laurenzerberg 2.
Map 6 E2.
☎ 531383000.

Ireland
Hilton-Center,
16th Floor, Landstrasser
Hauptstrasse 2a.
Map 4 F1 & 6 F4.
☎ 7154246.

New Zealand
Springsiedlg 28.
☎ 3188505.

United Kingdom
Jaurèsgasse 12.
Map 4 F2.
☎ 716130.

United States of America
Boltzmanngasse 16.
Map 1 C3.
☎ 31339.

INTERNATIONAL BOOKSHOPS

British Bookshop
Weihburggasse 24–6.
Map 4 E1 & 6 D4.
☎ 5121945.

Gerold & Co
Graben 31.
Map 2 D5 & 5 C3.
☎ 53350140.

Shakespeare & Co
Sterngasse 2.
Map 2 E5 & 6 D2.
☎ 5355053.

RELIGIOUS SERVICES

Anglican
Christ Church 3,
Jaurèsgasse 17–19.
Map 4 F2.
☎ 7148900.

Islamic
Islamic Center 21,
Hubertusdamm 17–19,
Floridsdorf.
☎ 2630918.

Jewish
Seitenstettengasse 4.
Map 2 E5 & 6 D2.
☎ 531040.

Lutheran
Dorotheergasse 16.
Map 4 D1 & 5 C4.
☎ 5128392.

Methodist
Sechshauser Strasse 56,
Fünfhaus.
☎ 8958175.

Roman Catholic
Tourismus Pastoral 1,
Stephansplatz 6.
Map 2 D5 & 6 D3.
☎ 515523375.

TOURS FOR DISABLED VISITORS

Egnatia Tours
Piaristengasse 60.
Map 1 B5.
☎ 40553460.

Personal Security and Health

Pharmacy sign

VIENNA IS VERY SAFE compared to many European cities. Tourists are unlikely to encounter any violence and the police and emergency services are easy to contact. Pharmacists are respected and their advice is often sought by locals. A visit to the pharmacy, unless the problem is serious, is probably the easiest choice. Specialist services available include **Befrienders**, a telephone helpline for English speakers who may be feeling lonely, an **AIDS Helpline** and an English-speaking **Alcoholics Anonymous** group.

SOS sign on U-Bahn platforms

EMERGENCY NUMBERS

AIDS Helpline
4092300.

Alcoholics Anonymous
7995599.
Ask for English language AA.

Befrienders
7133374.

Dentist
5122078.
Night and weekend line.

Ambulance
144.

Doctor on Call
141.

Fire
122.

Police
133.

Vienna Medical Emergency Service
40144.

Motorway Breakdown
120.

PERSONAL SECURITY AND PROPERTY

THERE ARE A FEW places to steer clear of in Vienna. The underground is generally safe by day and night. Karlsplatz station, however, which is renowned as a drug centre, is quite unsavoury, particularly at night when it is best avoided. There may be some upsetting sights, although you are unlikely to be bothered. Last trains can be very crowded and the passengers a bit unruly. All under-ground stations have SOS points for emergencies from which you can call the station supervisor or halt trains. There has been an increase in the number of gypsies in recent years, some of whom may ask for money. Locals tend to ignore them and it is best to follow suit. In the Prater, care should be taken at night as it is known for pickpocketing and for fights. Areas around the main railway stations can be unpleasant, though not really dangerous. The red light district is on the Gürtel between the Westbahnhof and the Südbahnhof.

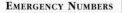

Red Cross sign

Take care of your property and do not go out with a lot of cash (travellers' cheques are the safest way of carrying large sums of money). For robbery, assault or missing persons, visit the nearest police station. Contact your consulate if you lose your passport.

MEDICAL TREATMENT AND INSURANCE

TICK-BORNE ENCEPHALITIS is a possible danger wherever there are deciduous trees in Austria and most Austrians and foreign residents are inoculated against it. Inoculation is done in stages, but is not usually recommended for tourists. Only a tiny proportion of ticks carry the disease, which may cause brain damage and in some cases lead to death. The risk is minimal, but to be on the safe side, if you are bitten you should not remove the tick but go to an outpatients department. The Lobau, the Lainzer Tiergarten and Vienna Woods are tick areas, so it is a good idea to wear a hat and long shirt sleeves here.

Britain has a reciprocal arrangement with Austria whereby emergency hospital treatment is free upon presentation of a British passport. In theory, visits to doctors, dentists or

Police motorcycle

Policeman

Fire engine

Police car

Ambulance

outpatient departments are also free, but obtaining free treatment can involve a lot of bureaucracy. It is best to take out full health insurance which will also cover flights home

Policewoman   **Fireman**

for medical reasons. There are several private hospitals in Vienna, but the main hospital (and the largest in Europe) is the Vienna General Hospital in the ninth district *(see p245)*. In the case of a medical emergency, call an ambulance *(Rettungsdienst)* or the local **Doctor on Call**.

PHARMACIES

I F YOU ARE NOT in an emergency, go to an *Apotheke* (pharmacy) for advice on medicines and treatment. They all display a red "A" sign and operate a night rota system. Any closed pharmacies will display the address of the nearest one open, and the **Pharmacy Information Line** also has details of some which are open. If the problem is serious, call **Vienna Medical Emergency Service**.

(see p245)

Façade of pharmacy

LOST PROPERTY

G O TO THE nearest police station in the first instance. If they do not restore your property within seven days (and you are still in Vienna), then try the lost property bureau. For property lost on the railways and the Schnell-bahn, ask at the Westbahnhof, which is open from 8am to 3pm Monday to Friday. You have to go there in person.

Banking and Local Currency

Creditanstalt bank logo

IN THE PAST TEN years, Viennese financial systems have become more accessible. There are now several money-changing machines *(see Directory)*, and you can take any amount of euros or foreign currency in or out of the country. Cash tends to be used rather than credit cards.

BANKING AND EXCHANGE

THE BEST PLACE to change money is at a bank. Although you can use travel agents and hotels, the banks give you a better rate. Exchanging a large amount of money at one time can save on commission because there is often a minimum charge.

Most banks stay open from 8am to 12:30pm and from 1:30pm to 3pm (5:30pm on Thursdays). A few of them (for example, the main Creditanstalt bank on Schotten- gasse) do not close for lunch. Some banks, generally those at the main railway stations and at airports *(see Directory)*, stay open longer than usual.

You can pay for items with major credit cards such as VISA, Mastercard, American Express and Diners Club in most hotels, shops and major restaurants, but they are not used as frequently as, for instance, in the UK or France, so it is a good idea to have some cash on you. If you are planning to use a credit card, make sure it is accepted first.

Austrian banks operate a large network of money dispensers, many of which take foreign credit cards with PIN codes. This facility will be clearly stated on the front of

the machine. There are also a few automatic money changing machines (Change-o-mats) which will accept foreign bank notes. Both sets of machines give instructions in German, English and French, and some may also have instructions in Italian, Swedish and Spanish.

Traveller's cheques are the safest way to carry large sums of money, with the advantage that you can change as much or as little as you need at the time. Choose a well-known name such as Thomas Cook, American Express or cheques issued through a bank. They can be changed for cash in most Austrian banks and are useful for paying for your room at many of the larger hotels. There is, however, a minimum commission charge, which may make changing small sums of money uneconomical. It is worth checking the exchange rates before you travel to decide whether sterling, dollar or euro cheques are the most appropriate for your trip.

AUSTRIAN BANK ACCOUNTS

IT IS NOT WIDELY KNOWN that Austria, like Switzerland, offers facilities for confidential bank accounts. Many Austrians

and foreign nationals open anonymous savings and securities accounts here. These accounts are accessed by a password, which is the equivalent of a numbered Swiss account. However, the Austrian authorities are now starting to crack down on international money-laundering practices, and foreigners who deposit large amounts of cash are obliged to identify themselves.

DIRECTORY

AFTER-HOURS EXCHANGE COUNTERS

City Air Terminal (Hilton Centre)
Map 4 F1 & 6 F4. ☐ *8am–12:30pm, 2–6:30pm daily.*

Opera-Karlsplatz Passage
Map 4 D1 & 5 C5.
☐ *8am–7pm daily.*

Schwechat Airport
☐ *6am–9pm daily.*

Südbahnhof
Map 4 F4.
☐ *7am–9pm daily.*

Westbahnhof
☐ *7am–10pm daily.*

AUTOMATIC MONEY-CHANGING MACHINES

Die Erste Bank, Graben 21.
Map 2 D5 & 5 C3.

Creditanstalt, Kärntner Ring 1.
Map 4 D2 & 6 C1.

Creditanstalt, Mariahilfer Strasse 54. **Map** 3 B2.

Bank Austria, Stephansplatz 2.
Map 1 D5 & 6 D3.

FOREIGN CREDIT CARD MACHINES

Creditanstalt, Schottengasse 6.
Map 1 C4 & 5 B2.

Creditanstalt, Schubertring 14.
Map 4 E2 & 6 D5.

AMERICAN EXPRESS

Kärntner Strasse 21–3.
Map 4 D1 & 6 D4. ☐ *515670.*

Autobank automatic money-dispensing machine

Currency conversion machine which accepts foreign banknotes

THE EURO

Twelve countries have replaced their traditional currencies, such as the Austrian Schilling, with the Euro. Austria, Belgium, Finland, France, Germany, Greece, Ireland, Italy, Luxembourg, Netherlands, Portugal and Spain chose to join the new currency: the UK, Denmark and Sweden stayed out, with an option to review their situation. The Euro was introduced on 1 January 1999, but only for banking purposes. Notes and coins came into circulation on 1 January 2002. A transition period has allowed euros and schillings to be used simultaneously, with national notes and coins being phased out by mid-2002. Euro notes and coins can be used anywhere inside the participating member states.

Bank Notes

Euro bank notes have seven denominations. The 5-euro note (grey in colour) is the smallest, followed by the 10-euro note (pink), 20-euro note (blue), 50-euro note (orange), 100-euro note (green), 200-euro note (yellow) and 500-euro note (purple). All notes show the stars of the European Union.

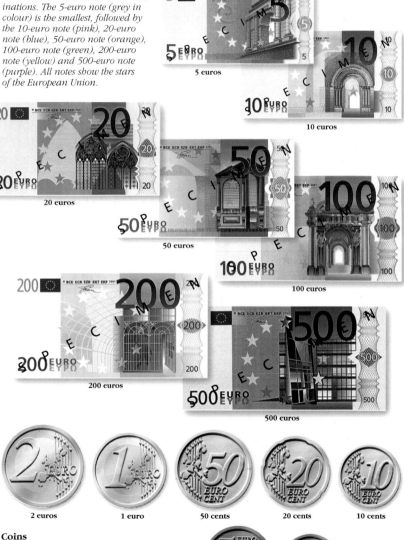

5 euros

10 euros

20 euros

50 euros

100 euros

200 euros

500 euros

2 euros   1 euro   50 cents   20 cents   10 cents

Coins

The euro has eight coin denominations: 1 euro and 2 euros; 50 cents, 20 cents, 10 cents, 5 cents, 2 cents and 1 cent. The 2- and 1-euro coins are both silver and gold in colour. The 50-, 20- and 10-cent coins are gold. The 5-, 2- and 1-cent coins are bronze.

5 cents

2 cents

1 cent

Communications

A USTRIA'S TELECOMMUNICATIONS network and postal service are now run by two separate companies. The many post offices are easily identified by the yellow post office sign. Phoning abroad at peak times can be problematic as there are not enough telephone lines, although the number is being increased. Many phone numbers have been changed as a result, so if you cannot get through ring directory enquiries *(see below)*. To phone outside Austria, try using a telephone booth at a post office. You do not need change as you pay at the counter.

Emergency phone sign

Coin-operated phone **Sign for cardphone**

USING THE TELEPHONE

T ELEPHONES ARE mainly push-button, and most of them have instructions in four languages: German, English, French and Italian. Austria has one of the most expensive telephone systems in Europe, so make sure you have plenty of change or take a phone-card with you. The coin-operated telephones take 10 cent, 20 cent, 50 cent, one and two euro coins.

Phonecards can be purchased from any post office or from newsagents. For international calls, it is best to avoid hotels as they tend to add a hefty surcharge on top of the cost of the call.

Cheap rate calling times from Vienna are between 6pm and 8am Monday to Friday and all day on Saturday, Sunday and public holidays. To make a reverse charge call, for which a fee is payable, go to the nearest post office.

Telephone boxes
There are telephone booths at every post office. Yellow-striped public telephone boxes take coins or phonecards and are found throughout the city. Directories are usually available in telephone boxes, but can be too tatty to use. If you need to find a number, post offices always have legible directories available or contact directory enquiries.

USING A CARD PHONE

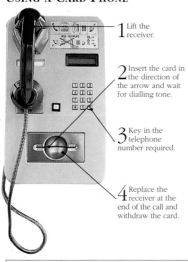

1 Lift the receiver.

2 Insert the card in the direction of the arrow and wait for dialling tone.

3 Key in the telephone number required.

4 Replace the receiver at the end of the call and withdraw the card.

USING A COIN-OPERATED PHONE

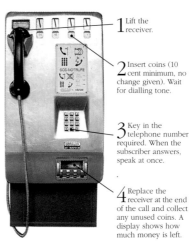

1 Lift the receiver.

2 Insert coins (10 cent minimum, no change given). Wait for dialling tone.

3 Key in the telephone number required. When the subscriber answers, speak at once.

4 Replace the receiver at the end of the call and collect any unused coins. A display shows how much money is left.

REACHING THE RIGHT NUMBER
- For Austrian and German directory enquiries, dial 11811.
- International or national telegrams, dial 0800100190.
- For telegram information, dial 5332565.
- For international information, dial 11812 for European countries and for overseas.
- For wake-up service, dial 11818.
- To ring the **USA,** dial 001 followed by the number.
- To ring the **UK**, dial 0044 then the number (omit the 0 from the area code).
- To ring **Australia**, dial 0061 then the number.
- To ring **New Zealand**, dial 0064 then the number.
- To ring the **Irish Republic**, dial 00353 then the number.
- The front pages of the A–H telephone directory list codes for each country. The cost of calls is available at post offices.

Mail and Postal Services

Decorative stamp

THE POST OFFICE provides postage stamps *(Briefmarken)*, telegrams and registered letters, as well as arranging the delivery of packages. There is also an express delivery *(Eilbriefe)* service, but this is a lot more expensive and may only be a day quicker. In addition, the post office sells phonecards and collectors' stamps. You can collect correspondence marked *Post Restante* or *Postlagernd* (to be called for) but you will need proof of identity, such as a passport. You can cash travellers' cheques and giro cheques up to a maximum of 180 euros per cheque. Main post offices will also change foreign currency into euros and vice versa. Many post offices also have fax machines.

Post office sign

standard vehicle country code (for example, "D" for Germany) before the post code.

E-MAIL AND THE INTERNET

VIENNA NOW HAS a variety of new internet cafés, where you can collect your email in relative comfort, often with a cup of coffee or a snack. Charges are most reasonable during off-peak times.

USEFUL ADDRESSES

Central Post Office
Fleischmarkt 19. **Map** 2 E5 & 6 D2.
515090.

Südbahnhof
Wiedner-Gürtel 10. **Map** 4 F4.
501810.

Westbahnhof
Gasgasse 2.
891150.

8921020 (for general information).
W www.post.at

Surland Internet Café
Krugerstrasse 10.
10am–11pm daily.

SENDING A LETTER

THE AUSTRIAN POSTAL system is reliable, verging on the pedantic, and posting a letter can take some time. Each

Display showing pick up times

Yellow letter box

individual letter is carefully weighed and every size and shape coded separately. Very few letters are sent at the set European rate of 51 cents.

Most post offices in Vienna are open between 8am and noon and 2pm and 6pm from Monday to Friday (but there

are no financial dealings after 5pm). Precise opening times are displayed at every post office. The main post office in each of the city's 23 urban districts *(Bezirke)* is open from 8am to 10am on Saturdays (but not for financial dealings). The **Central Post Office** in the first district is open 24 hours, and those at **Westbahnhof** and **Südbahnhof** open daily from 6am to 11pm and 7am to 10pm respectively, but not all services are available after normal opening hours. The airport post office is open from 7am to 8pm daily.

You can buy postage stamps at newsagents or post offices, which also have stamp-vending machines. Letters for Europe weighing up to 20 g cost 51 cents, as do postcards. Registered letters cost 2.03 euros. You should add the

Vienna's Districts

Vienna is divided into 23 urban districts or Bezirke, *as shown on this map. The district number is incorporated into the Vienna postcode. For example, the 23rd district is written as A-1230. The inset area shows the part of Vienna covered by our Street Finder maps 1–4 (see pp262–5).*

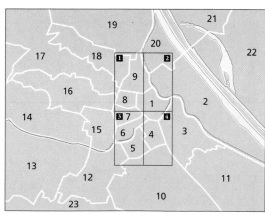

GETTING TO VIENNA

A S A POPULAR tourist destination and a major link between Eastern and Western Europe, Vienna is well served by air and rail. There are direct flights from every major European city as well as from North America, Canada, Japan and Australia. However, visitors from New Zealand need to change planes at London or Frankfurt and visitors from Ireland must transit at London or Munich. Vienna also has coach and rail links with the rest of Europe, but this usually involves overnight travel. If you are not eligible for student or special rates, travelling by train is not significantly cheaper. Vienna has good motorway routes to the rest of Europe, but if you are arriving from Germany, do not forget that the Austrian motorway speed limit is only 130 km (80 miles) per hour.

Austrian Airlines aeroplane

ARRIVING BY AIR

THERE ARE several flights a day between London's Gatwick and Heathrow airports and Vienna's airport at Schwechat. British Airways is the main British airline with regular flights to Vienna, and the main Austrian carrier is Austrian Airlines. Lauda Air, founded by former Formula 1 world racing champion Niki Lauda, operates no-smoking flights from Gatwick and Manchester to Vienna. If you fly from the United States, there are direct flights with Delta from New York and Orlando. Lauda Air runs flights from Los Angeles and Austrian Airlines from Chicago. There are also direct flights from Sydney and

USING SCHWECHAT AIRPORT

Schwechat International Airport is one of the most modern in Europe. A major rebuilding schedule in the early 1990s added an extra boarding pier. Facilities within the airport include restaurants, a supermarket, duty-free shops, banks and tourist information offices. Easily accessed by road, the airport lies 19 km (12 miles) southeast of Vienna.

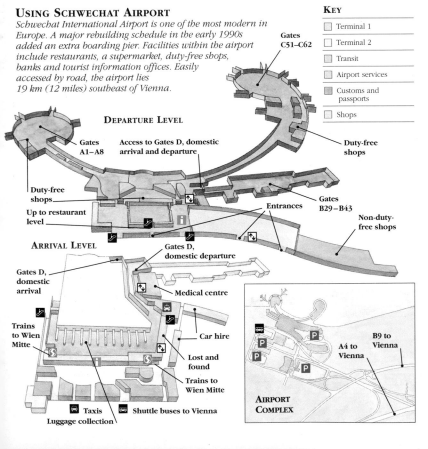

KEY

☐	Terminal 1
☐	Terminal 2
☐	Transit
☐	Airport services
☐	Customs and passports
☐	Shops

Gates C51–C62

DEPARTURE LEVEL

Gates A1–A8

Access to Gates D, domestic arrival and departure

Duty-free shops

Gates B29–B43

Duty-free shops

Up to restaurant level

Entrances

Non-duty-free shops

ARRIVAL LEVEL

Gates D, domestic departure

Gates D, domestic arrival

Medical centre

Trains to Wien Mitte

Car hire

Lost and found

Trains to Wien Mitte

Taxis

Shuttle buses to Vienna

Luggage collection

P

P

P

P

A4 to Vienna

B9 to Vienna

AIRPORT COMPLEX

The modern exterior of Schwechat International Airport

Toronto. It is not necessary to pay full price for a scheduled ticket. There are good deals if you shop around the discount agencies; you can get APEX tickets if you book two weeks in advance; and charters are available at very competitive prices. Weekend package offers, including the price of two nights at a good Viennese hotel, can be excellent value, sometimes costing less than the economy-class ticket price.

Schwechat International Airport transit area

SCHWECHAT AIRPORT

VIENNA HAS ONE airport, Schwechat International. It is 19 km (12 miles) from the city centre, about a 20–25 minute bus ride from the City Air Terminal, which is located in the same building as the Vienna Hilton, and is also easily accessible by train. This modern airport is very easy and quick to use. The airport supermarket is often used by Viennese caught out by the

restricted shopping times in the city and is open 7 days a week from 7:30am until 7pm including holidays.

GETTING INTO TOWN

THE SIMPLEST way to get to the centre is by taxi or bus. When you come out of customs you will see signs for taxis and buses straight ahead. There are always plenty of taxis and they take about 20 minutes to reach the centre of Vienna.

From 6:30am to 11:30pm shuttle buses run every 20 minutes between the airport and the City Air Terminal and near Wien Mitte Schnellbahn and U-Bahn stations. From 11:30pm to 6:30am buses depart every 30 minutes (but hourly, on the hour, from 1–4am), and the times are the same in each direction. There are also buses from 8:10am to 6:40pm, every 30 minutes, to the Südbahnhof and the Westbahnhof stations, though these are not as convenient for the city centre. Between these times they run roughly every hour, but exact timings can vary somewhat.

The fare is around 5 euros, including baggage, which you pay the driver when you get on. When you get to the City Air Terminal, there are

always plenty of taxis available. The Schnellbahn train, which departs from the basement level of the airport, is the cheapest option, but only goes once an hour. It takes about 30 minutes to connect with Wien Mitte and stops at Praterstern-Wien Nord.

Shopping mall at Schwechat International Airport

Arriving by Rail

L IKE LONDON and Paris, Vienna has several mainline railway stations, three of which serve international connections.

Most Eurocity services charge a supplement if you buy your ticket less than 72 hours before departure. Many of the train services to Vienna are overnight and, for a small fee, it is possible to reserve a seat or a bed up to two months before travelling. Often there are no buffet facilities on overnight trains, but snacks are sometimes sold by the steward.

Generally, the Westbahnhof handles trains from the west and includes some Budapest services. Southern and eastern

Rail route into Vienna with abbey at Melk (see p177) in the background

Sign at Westbahnhof showing how to get to the exit, Regionalbahn, Schnellbahn, ticket machines and Regionalbus station

Travel agency (*Reisebüro*) at Westbahnhof

areas are served by the Süd-bahnhof, and trains from the north arrive at Franz-Josefs-Bahnhof (*see* Major Rail and Coach Stations *opposite*).

Westbahnhof has interchanges with the U3 and U6 underground lines, the Schnell-

Exterior view of the Franz-Josefs-Bahnhof, which services trains from Prague and northern Austria

bahn and several tram and bus routes. The Südbahnhof is linked to the Schnellbahn and several tram and bus lines, while Franz-Josefs-Bahnhof is served by the Schnellbahn and the cross-city D tram, which goes directly to the Ringstrasse. All the stations have taxi ranks.

The travel agency (*Reisebüro*) at Westbahnhof is open from 8am to 7pm on weekdays and from 8am to 1pm on Saturdays and can provide information as well as helping with booking hotel rooms.

The travel agency at the Südbahnhof, which is open from 8am to 7pm on weekdays and from 8am to 1pm on Saturdays (with shorter hours from November to April), offers a similar service. In Vienna there is a telephone number for obtaining railway information in English.

Railway information
[C] *051717.*

Austrian Federal Railways
[C] *390 0000.*
[W] www.oebb.at

Arriving by Coach

S ERVICES RUN TO Vienna's main coach station, Wien Mitte, from Eastern European cities such as Bratislava and Budapest, along with domestic routes from eastern Austria (*see p255*). Eurolines run coaches from London Victoria

Eurolines coach

to Wien Mitte. Südbahnhof coach station handles routes from southern and southwestern Austria (*see p255*).

Arriving by Road

A LL DRIVERS IN AUSTRIA must carry their driver's licence, car registration document and insurance papers. Visitors need to carry an overseas extension of their annual insurance, such as a Green Card. An international driver's licence is required for people whose language is written in a script other than Roman. Wearing seatbelts is compulsory, and children up to the age of 12 or under 1.5 m (5 ft) may not sit on front seats unless with special child seats or seat belts. To travel on motorways in Austria you must have a

Sign on the Gürtel indicating the direction of the city centre

vignette sticker, available at petrol stations and tobacconists, attached to the inside of your windscreen. *Vignettes* are available for 10 days (7.5 euros), two months (22 euros) or one year (72.5 euros). All rented cars will have a *vignette* provided. Visitors arriving by road from the south arrive on the A2 and A23 southern motorways (Südautobahn), from the north on the A22 Danube motorway (Donauuferautobahn), from the west on the A1 western motorway

(Westautobahn) and from the east (including Schwechat International Airport) on the A4 eastern motorway (Ostautobahn). The city centre is marked Zentrum. The motorways converge on the outer ring road (Gürtel), sections of which are quite seedy. A *Parkscheine* is needed to park on inner-city streets and is available from tobacconists.

ARRIVING BY BOAT

From april to October you can arrive by boat along the Danube from Bratislava, the Wachau and Budapest.

Sign showing direction to the ferry terminal

The boat docks at the Donaudampfschiffsgesellschaft (DDSG) shipping line's landing station at the Reichsbrücke bridge *(see p237)*. It is close to the Vorgartenstrasse U-Bahn station on the U1 line. There is a DDSG information counter at the dock which can provide city maps.

DDSG ferry arriving in Vienna from eastern Europe

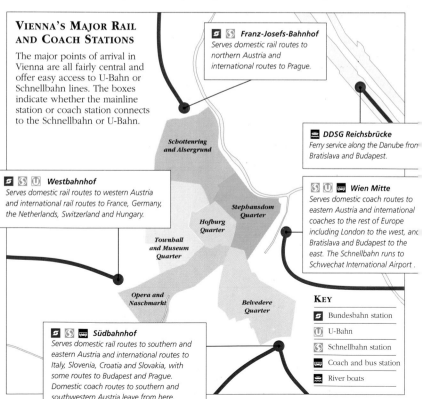

VIENNA'S MAJOR RAIL AND COACH STATIONS

The major points of arrival in Vienna are all fairly central and offer easy access to U-Bahn or Schnellbahn lines. The boxes indicate whether the mainline station or coach station connects to the Schnellbahn or U-Bahn.

Franz-Josefs-Bahnhof
Serves domestic rail routes to northern Austria and international routes to Prague.

DDSG Reichsbrücke
Ferry service along the Danube from Bratislava and Budapest.

Westbahnhof
Serves domestic rail routes to western Austria and international rail routes to France, Germany, the Netherlands, Switzerland and Hungary.

Wien Mitte
Serves domestic coach routes to eastern Austria and international coaches to the rest of Europe including London to the west, and Bratislava and Budapest to the east. The Schnellbahn runs to Schwechat International Airport .

Schottenring and Alsergrund

Stephansdom Quarter

Hofburg Quarter

Townhall and Museum Quarter

Opera and Naschmarkt

Belvedere Quarter

Südbahnhof
Serves domestic rail routes to southern and eastern Austria and international routes to Italy, Slovenia, Croatia and Slovakia, with some routes to Budapest and Prague. Domestic coach routes to southern and southwestern Austria leave from here.

KEY

Bundesbahn station

U-Bahn

Schnellbahn station

Coach and bus station

River boats

Getting Around Vienna

WALKING IS GENERALLY the easiest and most enjoyable way to get around the compact centre of Vienna. There is so much to see, and when you feel tired or hungry there is always a café or *Konditorei* just a few steps away. The good news for pedestrians is that the normally assertive Viennese drivers are dissuaded from driving through the city centre by a complicated and frustrating one-way system, pedestrian zones and

strict parking limits. If you would rather not walk around the main sights, a network of minibuses crisscrosses the city centre. The public transport system is clean, efficient and easy to use. Run by the City of Vienna Transport Authority, it consists of a tram, bus and underground network. All the services operate from 5am to 12:30am, but it is best to check individual timetables, which are very reliable, before travelling.

Viennese Fiaker

WALKING IN VIENNA

WALKING IS AN excellent way to see the city, but there are a few points to remember. Traffic rarely stops at pedestrian crossings so you should proceed with care. British and Australian visitors should remember that motorists drive on the right. On the Ringstrasse, trams run against the traffic, so it is necessary to look both ways. Try to use subways or crossings where there are signals. If you ignore the red figure meaning "Do not cross" you could be fined on the spot by a policeman, even if there is no sign of traffic at the time. Other Viennese pedestrians will also voice annoyance, as jay-walking is regarded as irresponsible. In addition, keep an eye out for cyclists; they share the pavement with pedestrians and, if they are travelling at some speed, may not have time to stop if you stray onto their section of the pavement.

Do not cross

Cross

There are at least 50 guided walking tours in and around Vienna on offer throughout the summer months. They explore themes such as Biedermeier, Baroque or Vienna 1900 and are available in German, English, French

and Italian. For a variety of information on walking tours, contact the Wiener Tourismusverband *(see p237)* .

THE CITY BY FIAKER

TRADITIONAL horse-drawn open carriages or *Fiakers*, many driven by a crusty, bowler-hatted and bewhiskered coachman, are a novel and relaxing way to get around. Take into account that part of the route is on the busy Ringstrasse. You can hire a *Fiaker* at Stephansplatz, Heldenplatz and Albertinaplatz, but to avoid an unpleasant surprise agree the terms (price and length of trip) before you set off. Even a short trip can be costly.

VIENNA BY BICYCLE

VIENNA IS great for cyclists, as long as you avoid the main roads and tramlines by sticking to the cycle paths. A 7-km (4-mile) cycle path round the Ringstrasse takes you past many sights and there are bike paths to the Hundertwasser Haus *(see p162)* and to the Prater *(see pp160–61)*. A booklet called *Rad Wege* shows all Vienna's cycle routes and is available from bookshops. Bikes can be hired at some train stations and a discount is often given if you have a train ticket. You will be asked to leave some identification as insurance. City cycle tours are run from May to September at Radverleih Salztorbrücke under the Salztor Bridge *(see p237)*.

Traffic signal for cyclists

Cycle lane

Cycling along bicycle lanes in the Prater

Anfang·

Beginning of no-parking zone

·Ende·

End of no-parking zone

Priority to traffic on the right cancelled

Priority to traffic on the right restored

DRIVING IN VIENNA

DRIVERS ARE aggressive in Vienna, so you will need to be alert as cars race and cut in front of you as a matter of course. Priority is always to the right unless a "yellow diamond" indicates otherwise. You must give way to trams, buses, police cars, fire engines and ambulances. It is useful to belong to an internationally affiliated automobile association or you will be charged by the ÖAMTC (the Austrian motoring association) for breakdowns or repairs. Traffic news is on radio station Ö3, and Blue Danube Radio broadcasts traffic news in English. The speed limit in Vienna is 50 km (30 miles) per hour. Police carry out checks with infra-red guns and can fine you on the spot. The limit for alcohol is 0.5 mg per ml of blood (about ¹⁄₃ litre of beer or 1–2 glasses of wine). There are spot checks and you could be fined a considerable sum and have your licence confiscated if you exceed the limit.

Only lead-free petrol and diesel are widely available. A few garages take credit cards, but tend to prefer cash.

PARKING PLACES

APART FROM Sundays, when shops are closed, finding a parking spot in Vienna is frustrating and time-consuming. *Anfang* and *Ende* signs can be seen everywhere. You are not allowed to park between them. Do look carefully as the *Ende* sign may be around a corner or facing the wrong way. If your car is clamped or towed away, telephone or go to the police, who will tell you which of the city's two pounds to go to. The City of Vienna operates a daytime park and pay scheme in districts 1, 4, 5, 6, 7, 8 and 9 *(see p245)*. You can buy parking disks from newsagents *(Tabak Trafiken)*, some banks and petrol stations. Usually, a maximum of two hours is allowed in any space. In other districts, a blue line by the kerb indicates a pay and display scheme. Car parks in Vienna tend to be expensive.

CAR HIRE

TO HIRE A CAR, you will need your passport and a driver's licence that has been issued for at least one year. International licences are required for languages in a script other than Roman.

Major car hire firms have outlets at the airport and in the city centre. Car hire is more expensive at the airport, but it is the only place where you will be able to hire a car late at night or at weekends.

(see p245)

TAXIS

Car park sign

YOU CAN RECOGNIZE a taxi by the TAXI sign on the roof. They are usually saloon cars, often Mercedes. If a taxi is for hire, the sign on its roof will be illuminated. In the centre of Vienna it is easier to get a taxi at one of the city's ranks, rather than by hailing one in the street. Alternatively you can call one of three numbers (31300, 40100 or 60160) to order a taxi, which will usually come in a few minutes. The operator tells you when to expect it and you should be waiting, as it may drive off if you are not there. A short trip costs from 5 to 10 euros. There are additional costs for more than one passenger, luggage, and late-night and weekend journeys. A trip to the airport costs up to 30 euros. It is usual to tip about 10% of the fare, rounding up the sum to the nearest euro.

Taxi meter

Basic fare / **Supplement fare**

Vienna's taxis are usually saloon cars, often Mercedes

TICKETS AND TRAVEL CARDS

FINDING YOUR WAY around Vienna's transport system is fairly simple, but buying the right ticket at the right price can be a bit more confusing. It is easiest to buy your tickets in advance, either from a newsagent (*Tabak Trafik*), from a ticket machine or over the counter at an underground or Schnellbahn booking office. A standard ticket covers all areas of Vienna (zone 100). With this you can change trains and lines as often as you like, and even change from the underground to a tram or a bus, but you are not allowed to break your journey.

A weekly season ticket is valid for all areas of Vienna (zone 100) and from Monday to Sunday. This is a good buy if you plan to use public transport for more than four

24-hour ticket

72-hour ticket

Weekly season ticket

Streifenkarte, or strip ticket, valid for four journeys

8-Tage-Karte valid for eight days' travel or for up to eight people on the same day

days. One advantage of this ticket is that it need not be used just by the person who bought it. More useful for parties of visitors are the green *8-Tage-Karte*. Each card consists of eight strips which, when stamped, are valid for a day on Vienna's public transport. This ticket is good for

several people travelling together as up to eight people may stamp the same ticket. It is important that you start with strip one – stamping strip eight first will invalidate the other seven. Also available are 24-hour tickets and 72-hour tickets, as well as a strip ticket for four rides.

1 Choose your ticket for the zone in which you wish to travel.

2 Choose your ticket type.

3 Insert coins or notes to the value of your ticket.

4 Collect your ticket and change.

Vienna Transport Authority ticket machine

Insert your ticket in the direction of the arrow. Wait for the pinging noise to confirm that your ticket has been validated.

Ticket-stamping machine

DIRECTORY

BIKE RENTAL

Pedal Power
Ausstellungstrasse 3.
[7297234.
○ Apr–Oct: 8am–8pm daily.

Südbahnhof
Map 4 F4.
[9300035787.
○ 6am–10pm daily
1 Apr–31 Oct.

Westbahnhof
[9300032985.
○ 4am–midnight daily
1 Apr–31 Oct.

CAR HIRE

Avis City
Opernring 3–5.
Map 5 B5 & 4 D1.
[5876241.
Airport [70072700.

Budget City
City Air Terminal
(at Vienna Hilton).
Map 4 F1 & 6 F4.
[7146565.
Airport [70072711.

Hertz City
Kärntner Ring 17.
Map 4 D1 & 5 C5.
[700732661.
Airport [70072661.

CAR PARKS

Wollzeile 7.
Map 2 E5 & 6 D3.

Am Hof.
Map 2 D5 & 5 C2.

Morzinplatz.
Map 2 E4 & 6 D2.

Dr-Karl-Lueger-Ring.
Map 1 C5 & 5 A2.

Börsegasse.
Map 2 D4 & 5 C1.

Other car parks are shown on the Street

Finder map (*see pp262–7*).

24-HOUR PETROL STATION

Börsegasse 11.
Map 2 D4 & 5 C1.

TAXIS

Taxi-Booking
[31300, 40100 and 60160.

Limousine Service
Flughafen-Taxi
[5127000.

Travelling by Underground

**U-Bahn
station symbol**

CONSTRUCTION OF VIENNA'S underground, or U-Bahn, system, one of the most modern in Europe, began in 1969 and continues to the present day. Though Vienna is a compact city and many of the major sights can be reached on foot or by tram and bus, the U-Bahn is a clean, fast and reliable way of crossing the city. It is also useful for travelling further afield. The U-Bahn currently comprises five lines, with line U2 running in a circle that corresponds to the outer edge of the Ringstrasse.

manually and you will need to pull hard as they are stiff and heavy. The U-Bahn is generally safe *(see p240)*, but in case of emergencies there are help points on most platforms. You are not allowed to smoke on U-Bahn platforms or on the trains (smoking is also forbidden on trams and buses).

**Emergency help point on a
Vienna U-Bahn platform**

THE UNDERGROUND SYSTEM

DISPLAYS ABOVE the train doors show stations and connections, and a recorded voice announces stops and also connections to trams and buses. Be aware, though, that this announcement may be a station behind. Prams can be stored by the doors; a picture of a pram indicates where. Bicycles are also allowed, but only on a few carriages and at set times. Doors are opened

---

MAKING A JOURNEY BY UNDERGROUND

1 To determine which line to take, travellers should look for their destination on a U-Bahn map. The five lines are distinguished by colour and number. Simply trace the line to your destination, making a note of where you need to change lines. Connections to other forms of transport are also shown.

2 Tickets can be bought from a newsagent, ticket vending machines or ticket offices. To get to the trains, insert your ticket into the ticket-stamping machine in the direction of the arrow. Wait for the ping indicating that it is validated, and pass through the barrier. Follow the signs (with the number and colour of the line) to your platform.

3 On the platform, check the direction and destination of the train on an electronic destination indicator.

4 Stops along the line are shown on a plan. A red arrow in the corner shows the direction in which the train enters the station.

5 At your destination follow the *Ausgang* signs to reach street level.

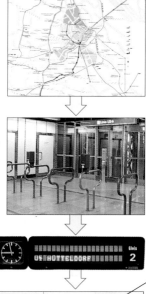

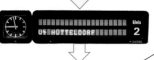

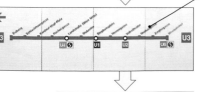

Pull handle to open door

The door opens out to the side

Sign showing stops on line 3 of the U-Bahn, including connecting stops

6 At stations with more than one exit, use the map of the city to check which street or square you will come out at.

Viennese tram

Travelling by Tram

THE CITY'S RED AND WHITE trams are a
familiar sight, and the Viennese know
winter has arrived when tram drivers put
up their leather screens against the icy
wind that blows through the doors. Sadly
many lines are being pulled up to make
way for cars, and development of the U-
Bahn means that some lines are no longer
needed. A visit to Vienna would not be complete without
a tram ride, as it offers not only an excellent view of
the city, but a nostalgic journey into Vienna's past.

USING A TRAM

USING VIENNA'S TRAMS is a
delightful way to get
around the city. There are still
some old-style trams in use
with wooden seats and old-
fashioned interiors. A recorded
voice announces the stops
(as on the underground and
buses), and each tram has its
route clearly displayed with
all the stops marked. The
doors are opened by pressing
the button beside them. Single-
journey tickets
can be bought
from machines
at the front of
the tram, but
regular pass-
engers tend to
use passes or

Tram stop

strip tickets *(see p252)*, which
work out cheaper and are
more convenient.

Tram exit button

Tram entrance button

SIGHTSEEING BY TRAM

A GOOD WAY to see the
parade of handsome
19th-century public buildings
on the Ringstrasse is on the
tram network. A trip on tram
lines 1 and 2 will take you

Trams in a busy Vienna street

past buildings ranging in style
from Greek Neo-Classical to
Jugendstil *(see p54–7)*. The
Tram Museum gives organ-
ized tours of Vienna in a
1920s tram (including a visit
to Vienna's Tram Museum
itself). The meeting point is
at Otto Wagner's Karlsplatz
Pavilions *(see p144)*, and
prospectuses are available
from information offices.
Private groups may also hire
a vintage tram (built between
1913 and 1958) to take them
to the Prater or a *Heuriger* or
simply to tour the city.

Tram Museum
⬛ 790944903.

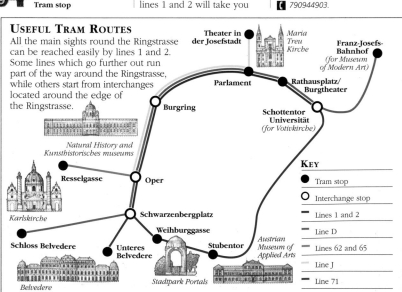

USEFUL TRAM ROUTES

All the main sights round the Ringstrasse
can be reached easily by lines 1 and 2.
Some lines which go further out run
part of the way around the Ringstrasse,
while others start from interchanges
located around the edge of
the Ringstrasse.

*Natural History and
Kunsthistorisches museums*

Resselgasse

Karlskirche

Schloss Belvedere

Belvedere

**Theater in
der Josefstadt**

*Maria
Treu
Kirche*

**Franz-Josefs-
Bahnhof**
*(for Museum
of Modern Art)*

Parlament

**Rathausplatz/
Burgtheater**

Burgring

**Schottentor
Universität**
(for Votivkirche)

Oper

Schwarzenbergplatz

Weihburggasse

**Unteres
Belvedere**

Stubentor

*Austrian
Museum of
Applied Arts*

Stadtpark Portals

KEY

● Tram stop

○ Interchange stop

━ Lines 1 and 2

━ Line D

━ Lines 62 and 65

━ Line J

━ Line 71

Travelling by Bus

Bus stop

Little hopper buses serve the centre of Vienna and larger buses go from the inner suburbs, Ringstrasse and Prater to the outer suburbs. Some buses run along old tram routes, and they are the same municipal red and white colour as the trams. Bus stops are also in the same red and white colours as tram stops.

8052

WH 8052 LO

Viennese hopper bus

Bus Tickets

Tickets for buses, like tram tickets, can be purchased when you get on, but it is more advisable to buy a pass or a strip ticket from Schnellbahn or U-Bahn stations, or from a newsagent, beforehand *(see p252)*. Ticket machines on trams and buses are identical. Tickets other than those bought on the bus or tram need to be stamped in the blue ticket-stamping machine in order to validate them. If you have already made part of your journey by tram or U-Bahn, there is no need to stamp your ticket again. Limited services run on holidays and Christmas Day. On New Year's Eve, buses and other forms of public transport run all night.

2 Insert money in the slot

1 Choose your ticket

3 Collect your ticket and change here

Bus ticket machine

Coaches

Vienna's main coach station is Wien Mitte *(see p248)*, where you can board one of the orange-coloured federal buses *(Bundesbusse)* that run to a variety of destinations in eastern Austria. Coaches to other regions of Austria depart from the Südbahnhof *(see p248)*. The main coach companies that organize excursions and tours in and around Vienna are Cityrama and Vienna Sightseeing *(see p237)*, and their buses and coaches, full of tourists, are a common sight on the roads of central Vienna, especially during the summer months.

Night Buses

Night buses operate every night of the week starting at half past midnight and then at 30-minute intervals until 4am in the morning. There is some variation in the service between weekday nights (Sunday night through to Thursday night) and that operating at the weekend and on public holidays. The buses go from Schwedenplatz to most suburbs of the city. If you are staying some distance from a night bus route, you can arrange for a taxi to pick you up from your destination stop at Schwedenplatz Transport Office.

Night bus stop

Schnellbahn logo

Bundesbahn logo

Travelling by Train

The Austrian Federal Railways or Bundesbahn, with its familiar red and white logo, has about 5,800 km (3,600 miles) of railways, and offers frequent direct connections to all European countries *(see p248)*. Within Austria, it offers good connections to tourist destinations such as Salzburg and Innsbruck. Further afield destinations *(see pp156–77)* can be reached by Schnellbahn or Bundesbahn lines.

The Schnellbahn (known as the S-Bahn for short), with its distinctive blue and white logo, is really a commuter service. It has stops in the centre of Vienna interconnecting with mainline railway stations *(see p249)*, but is of most use as a means of getting to sights that are further afield. The local Bundesbahn is also a commuter service, when it is sometimes called the Regionalbahn on maps and timetables in order to distinguish it from national routes. Timetable information is available from station information offices and is displayed on station departures and arrivals boards.

Schnellbahn train

STREET FINDER

THE MAP REFERENCES for all of the sights, hotels, restaurants, bars, shops and entertainment venues described in this book refer to the maps in this section. A complete index of street names and all the places of interest marked on the maps can be found on the following pages. The key map *(right)* shows the area of Vienna covered by the *Street Finder*. This map includes sightseeing areas as well as districts for hotels, restaurants and entertainment venues.

All the street names in the index and on the *Street Finder* are in German – *Strasse* translating as street and *Gasse* meaning lane. *Platz* or *Hof* indicate squares or courtyards. Throughout this guide, the numbers of the houses follow the street names, in the same way that you will find them in Vienna.

View of Vienna's roof tops from Am Hof *(see p87)*

KEY TO STREET FINDER

	Major sight
	Places of interest
	Other building
Ⓤ	U-Bahn station
🚆	Bundesbahn station
🚋	Badner Bahn stop
Ⓢ	Schnellbahn station
🚌	Bus and coach station
P	Parking
ℹ	Tourist information office
✚	Hospital with casualty unit
🚓	Police station
✝	Church
✡	Synagogue
⊠	Post office
═	Railway line
—	One-way street
—	Pedestrian street

SCALE OF MAPS
1–4 & 5–6 RESPECTIVELY

0 metres	250	
0 yards	250	**1:12,000**

0 metres	125	
0 yards	125	**1:7,000**

Section of the Austria fountain (1846) by Schwanthaler (left) and side view of the Schottenkirche *(see p110)*

0 kilometres	1
0 miles	0.5

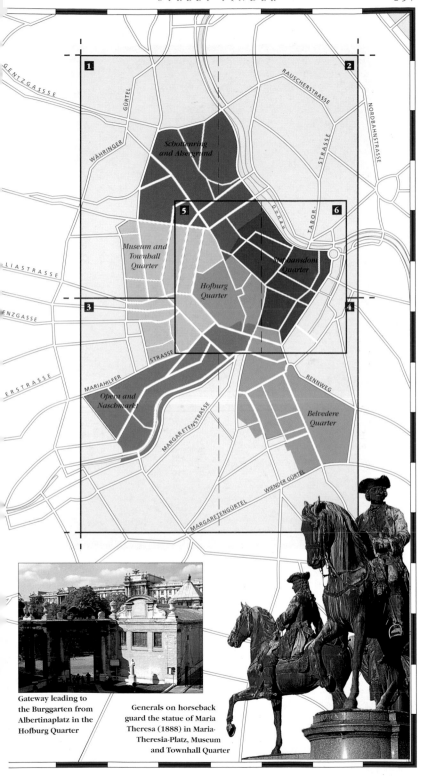

1

2

GENTZGASSE

RAUSCHERSTRASSE

GÜRTEL

WÄHRINGER

NORDBAHNSTRASSE

STRASSE

Schottenring
and Alsergrund

5

DOBL

TABOR

6

LIASTRASSE

Museum and
Townhall
Quarter

Stephansdom
Quarter

ENZGASSE

3

Hofburg
Quarter

4

STRASSE

ERSTRASSE

MARIAHILFER

RENNWEG

Opera and
Naschmarkt

Belvedere
Quarter

MARGARETENSTRASSE

WIENER GÜRTEL

MARGARETENGÜRTEL

Gateway leading to
the Burggarten from
Albertinaplatz in the
Hofburg Quarter

Generals on horseback
guard the statue of Maria
Theresa (1888) in Maria-
Theresia-Platz, Museum
and Townhall Quarter

Street Finder Index

VIENNA'S STREET and place names are generally spelt as one word; -platz, -strasse or -kirche are put at the end of the name, as in Essiggasse for example. Occasionally they are treated as separate words, for instance Alser Strasse. Abbreviations used in this index are Dr as in Doctor-Ignaz-Seipel-Platz, and St as in Sankt Josef Kirche. Some entries have two map references. The first refers to the smaller scale map that covers the whole of central Vienna, the second refers to the large-scale inset map that covers the Stephansdom and Hofburg Quarters.

USEFUL WORDS	
Gasse	street
Strasse	road
Platz	square
Hof	court
Kirche	church
Kapelle	chapel
Dom	cathedral
Denkmal	monument
Markt	market
(often the sight of an old market)	
Brücke	bridge

SEE PAGES 5 & 6 FOR ENLARGEMENT OF THIS AREA

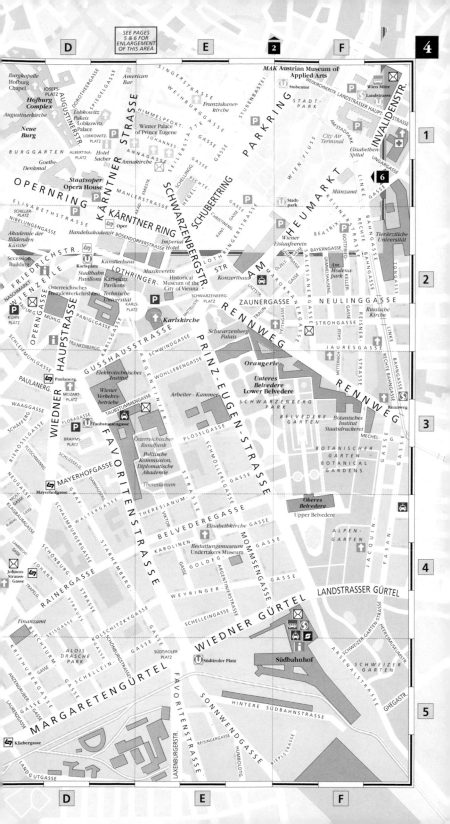

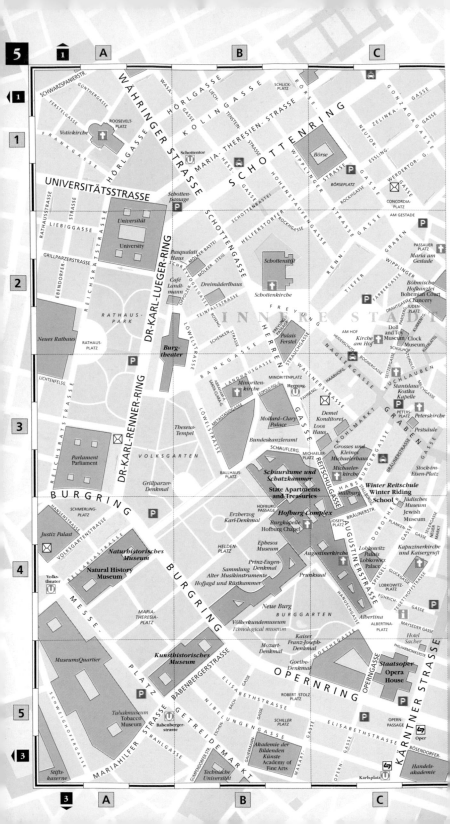

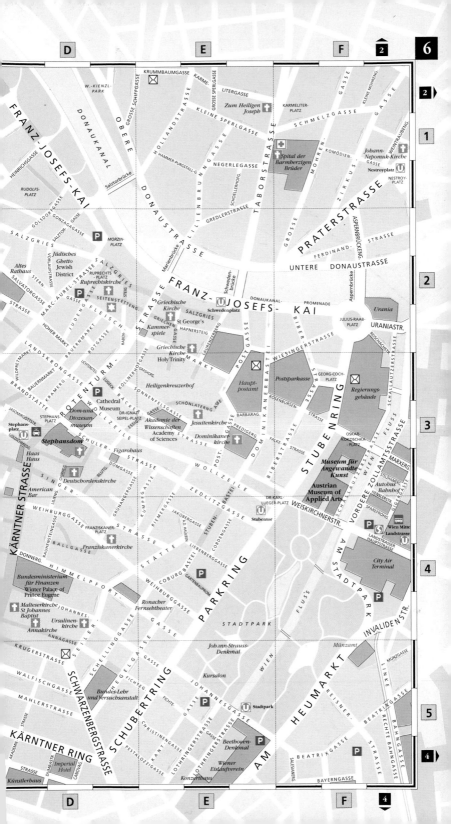

General Index

Acknowledgments

DORLING KINDERSLEY wishes to thank the following people who contributed to the preparation of this book.

MAIN CONTRIBUTOR
Stephen Brook was born in London and educated at Cambridge. After working as an editor in Boston, Massachusetts, and in London, he became a full-time writer in 1982. Among his many books are *New York Days, New York Nights, The Double Eagle, Prague* and *L.A. Lore.* He has also written books on wine and contributes articles on wine and travel to many newspapers and periodicals.

ADDITIONAL CONTRIBUTORS
Gretel Beer, Caroline Bugler, Dierdre Coffey, Fred Mawer.

PROOF READER
Diana Vowles.

DESIGN AND EDITORIAL
MANAGING EDITOR Carolyn Ryden
MANAGING ART EDITOR Steve Knowlden
SENIOR EDITOR Georgina Matthews
SENIOR ART EDITOR Vanessa Courtier
EDITORIAL DIRECTOR David Lamb
ART DIRECTOR Anne-Marie Bulat
CONSULTANT Robert Avery
LANGUAGE CONSULTANT Barbara Eichberger
Ros Angus, Tessa Bindloss, Chris Clouter, Carey Combe, Lucinda Cooke, Maggie Crowley, Fay Franklin, Sally Gordon, Emily Green, Alistair Gunn, Elaine Harries, Melanie Hartzell, Paul Hines, Joanne Lenney, Helen Partington, Alice Peebles, Robert Purnell, Ella Milroy, Nicki Rawson, Simon Ryder, Andrew Szudek, Samia Tadros, Lynda Warrington, Susannah Wolley Dod.

ADDITIONAL ILLUSTRATIONS
Kevin Jones, Gilly Newman, John Woodcock, Martin Woodward.

CARTOGRAPHY
Peter Winfield, James Mills-Hicks (Dorling Kindersley Cartography)
Colourmap Scanning Limited, Contour Publishing, Cosmographics, European Map Graphics, Street Finder maps: ERA Maptec Ltd (Dublin).
MAP CO-ORDINATORS Simon Farbrother, David Pugh
CARTOGRAPHIC RESEARCH Jan Clark, Caroline Bowie, Claudine Zante.

ADDITIONAL PHOTOGRAPHY
DK Studio/Steve Gorton, Poppy, Steve Shott, Clive Streeter.

SPECIAL ASSISTANCE
Marion Telsnig and Ingrid Pollheimer-Stadtlober at the Austrian Tourist Board, London; Frau Preller at the Heeresgeschichtliches Museum; Frau Wegscheider at the Kunsthistorisches Museum; Frau Stillfried and Mag Czap at the Hofburg; Herr Fehlinger at the Museen der Stadt Wien; Mag Schmid at the Natural History Museum; Mag Dvorak at the Österreischicher Bundestheaterverband; Dr Michael Krapf and Mag Grabner at the Österreichische Galerie; Robert Tidmarsh and Mag Weber-Kainz at Schloss Schönbrunn; Frau Zonschits at the Tourismusverband.

PHOTOGRAPHY PERMISSIONS
DORLING KINDERSLEY would like to thank the following for their kind permission to photograph at their establishments:

Alte Backstube, Bestattungsmuseum, Schloss Belvedere, Bundesbaudirektion, Deutschordenskirche and Treasury, Dom und Diözesanmuseum, Sigmund Freud Gesellschaft, Josephinum Institut für Geschichte der Medzin der Universität Wien, Kapuzinerkirche, Pfarramt St. Karl, Stift Klosterneuburg, Wiener Kriminalmuseum, Niederösterreichisches Landesmuseum, Österreichischer Bundestheaterverband, Österreichische Postsparkasse (P. S. K.), Puppen- und Spielzeugmuseum, Dombausekretariat Sankt Stephan, Spanische Reitschule, Österreichisches Tabakmuseum and Museum für Volkskunde. Dorling Kindersley would also like to thank all the shops, restaurants, cafés, hotels, churches and public services who aided us with photography. These are too numerous to thank individually.

PICTURE CREDITS
t = top; tl = top left; tc = top centre; tr = top right; cla = centre left above; ca = centre above; cra = centre right above; cl = centre left; c = centre; cr = centre right; clb = centre left below; cb = centre below; crb = centre right below; bl = bottom left; b = bottom; bc = bottom centre; br = bottom right; d = detail.

Works of art have been reproduced with the permission of the following copyright holders:
© DACS 1994: 34cbr, 90c, 105c, 153t; © THE HENRY MOORE FOUNDATION: 142b.

The Publishers are grateful to the following individuals, companies and picture libraries for permission to reproduce their photographs:

GRAPHIC SAMMLUNG ALBERTINA, Wien: 26–7; ANCIENT ART AND ARCHITECTURE COLLECTION: 24b(d), 25t, 29ca; ARCHIV FÜR KÜNST UND GESCHICHTE, Berlin: 8–9, 16(d), 17t, 19tc(d), 19br(d), 21b, 22–3, 24t, 24–5, 25cb, 25bl, 26ca, 26br(d), 27t, 28t, 28c, 28br(d), 29t, 28–9, 29cl, 29bl, 30t(d), 30cl, 32cl, 32br, 33b, 34br, 36tl, 38br, 55b(d), 67 inset, 87b(d), 98cla, 110b(d), 147ca, 150cb, 170b, 235 inset; Erich Lessing 38cb, 39cr, 98cla; AUSTRIAN AIRLINES: 246t; AUSTRIAN ARCHIVES: 35tl.

BILDARCHIV PREUSSISCHER KULTURBESITZ, Berlin: 23bl, 35cbl, 92t; CASA EDITRICE BONECHI, Firenze: 165ca; CHRISTIAN BRANDSTÄTTER VERLAG, Wien: 20ca, 31c(d), 33tl, 34bl, 83t, 99c; BRIDGEMAN ART LIBRARY, London: 131b(d); Albertina, Wien 46br; Bonhams, London 24ca; British Library, London 4t(d), 19bl(d); Kunsthistorisches Museum, Wien

19tr(d), 46cr; Museum der Stadt Wien 33tr, 38car(d), 38bcl, 39cl; Österreichische Galerie 35tr; HOTEL BRISTOL: 190cr; ©1999 BUNDESGÄRTEN, Wien: 170tl ; BUNDESMINISTERIUM FÜR FINANZEN: 27cb(d); BURGHAUPTMANNSCHAFT IN WIEN: 101ca, 101cb, 101b.

ARCHÄOLOGISCHER PARK CARNUNTUM: 21tr; CASINOS AUSTRIA: 225c; CEPHAS PICTURE LIBRARY: Mick Rock 159b, 208tl; Wine Magazine 238br; CONTRAST PHOTO: Milenko Badzic 65t; Franz Hausner 166b; Michael Himml/Transglobe 150tr, 174; Hinterleitner 225b; Peter Kurz 63b, 139tl, 231b; Boris Mizaikoffl/Transglobe 63t; Tappeiner/Transglobe 232c; H Valencak 176b.

DDSG-DONAUREISEN GMBH: 249c; ET ARCHIVE, London: 38br; Museum für Gestaltung, Zurich 34cl; Museum der Stadt Wien 26bl, 31tl, 38cal; EUROLINES (UK) Ltd: 248cb; EUROPEAN COMMISSION: 243; MARY EVANS PICTURE LIBRARY, London: 18tl, 18bl, 18br, 19tl, 22c, 25br, 27br, 30cr, 30bl, 30br, 32t, 35b, 38t, 39t, 76tr, 173b, 189 inset.

F. A. HERBIG VERLAGSBUCHHANDLUNG GMBH, München: 98bl, 98br, 99bl, 99br.

ROBERT HARDING PICTURE LIBRARY: Larsen Collinge International 42cb, 232t; Adam Woolfitt 62t, 135t, 148t, 176t, 254tl; HEERESGESCHICHTLICHES MUSEUM, Wien: 47b, 164t, 164b, 165t, 165cb, 165b; HISTORISCHES MUSEUM DER STADT WIEN: 17b, 20t, 21ca, 21cbr, 26t, 28cb, 32cr, 32bl, 33ca, 33cb, 43t, 47tl, 49c, 139tc, 139tr, 143ca, 167t; HULTON-DEUTSCH COLLECTION: 28bl, 36tr(d), 38bcr(d), 166ca; HUTCHISON LIBRARY: John G Egan 202t.

THE IMAGE BANK, London: GSO Images 11b; Fotoworld 41bl; HOTEL IMPERIAL: 190b.

JOSEFSTADT THEATRE: 224c.

WILHELM KLEIN: 23t, 26cb; KUNSTHAUS WIEN: Peter Strobel 48t; KUNSTHISTORISCHES MUSEUM, Wien: 24cb, 41cbr, 46cl, 48b, 56c, 95t, 95b, 99t, 100 all, 118–9 all, 120–1 all, 122–3 all, 173tl.

J & L LOBMEYR, Wien: 49t; LEOPOLD MUSEUM-PRIVATSTIFTUNG: *Selbstbildnis*, 1910, by Egon Schiele 46bla, *Hockender Weiblicher Akt*, 1910, by Egon Schiele 117tr; MAGNUM PHOTOS: Erich Lessing 18tr, 20c, 20bl, 20br, 21tl, 21cbl, 22cb, 23cal, 26c, 29br, 30–1, 31b; MANSELL COLLECTION,

London: 9 inset; MARRIOTT HOTELS: 194t, 231t; MUSEUM JUDENPLATZ: Votava/PID 86tl; MUSEUMSQUARTIER, Wien: Rupert Steiner/MQ E+B BesmbH 41br; NARODNI MUSEUM, Praha: 18bc; NATURHISTORISCHES MUSEUM, Wien: 46t, 126–7 except 127br, 233cb.

ÖSTERREICHISCHE BUNDESBAHNEN: 248t, 255b; ÖSTERREICHISCHE GALERIE, Wien: 47ca, 47cb, 152c, 153 all, 154bl, 155 all; ÖSTERREICHISCHES MUSEUM FÜR ANGEWANDTE KUNST, Wien: 28ca, 47tl, 56t, 57c, 82–3 all except 83t; ÖSTERREICHISCHE NATIONALBANK: 243cal, 243cac; ÖSTERREICHISCHE NATIONALBIBLIOTHEK, Wien: 20cb, 22t, 23cb, 36c; ÖSTERREICH WERBUNG: 5bl, 27ca, 31tc, 31tr, 34ca, 44b, 98cbl, 101t, 138b, 161cb, 161b, 170t, 177b, 203t, 230cr.

POPPERFOTO: 37tc; RAIFFEISENBANK WIEN: Gerald Zugman 34cr; RETROGRAPH ARCHIVE, London: Martin Ranicar-Breese 191br; REX FEATURES, London: Action Press 36bl, Adolfo Franzo 37tl, Sipa Press 37bl(d), Sokol/Sipa Press 125b; GEORG RIHA: 77t; RONACHER VARIETY THEATRE/CMM: Velo Weger 224t.

HOTEL SACHER: 192t; SCHLOSS SCHÖNBRUNN KULTUR- UND BETRIEBS GESMBH, Wien: Professor Gerhard Trumler 170c, 171 all except 171b, 172 all, 173tr; SCIENCE PHOTO LIBRARY, London: Geospace 10t; SYGMA: Habans/Orban 37tr, Viennareport 37ca; TRAVEL LIBRARY: Philip Entiknapp 66–7, 219t, 250t.

WERNER FORMAN ARCHIVE: Museum der Stadt Wien 60c; St Stephens Cathedral Museum 23car, WIENER SÄNGERKNABEN: 5cbr, 39b, 64b; WIENER STADT- UND LANDESBIBLIOTHEK, Wien: 36tc, 36bl; WIGAST AG: 194c, 194b.

VIENNASLIDE: Harald A Jahn 230b; Karl Luymair 230cl; MUSEUM FÜR VÖLKERKUNDE, Wien: 49b, 233b; VOTAVA, Wien: 161t; ZEFA: 151c; Anatol 98–9; Damm 248b; G Gro-Bauer 177t; Havlickek 175b; Sibelberbauer 62b; Streichan 37cb; Studio Mike 206t; V Wentzel 41cbc.

Jacket: all special photography except ZEFA front top and ROBERT HARDING PICTURE LIBRARY/Adam Woolfitt front bc.

All other images © Dorling Kindersley. For further information see: www.DKimages.com

Phrase Book

IN EMERGENCY

Help!	**Hilfe!**	hilf-er
Stop!	**Halt!**	hult
Call a doctor	**Holen Sie einen Arzt**	hole'n zee ine'n artst
Call an ambulance	**Holen Sie einen Krankenwagen**	hole'n zee ine'n krank'n-varg'n
Call the police	**Holen Sie die Polizei**	hole'n zee dee pol-its-eye
Call the fire brigade	**Holen Sie die Feuerwehr**	hole'n zee dee foy-er-vair
Where is the nearest telephone?	**Wo finde ich ein Telefon in der Nähe?**	voh fin-der ish ine tel-e-fone in dair nay-er?
Where is the nearest hospital?	**Wo ist das nächstgelegene Krankenhaus?**	voh ist duss next-g'lay-g'ner krunk'n-hows?

COMMUNICATION ESSENTIALS

Yes	**Ja**	yah
No	**Nein**	nine
Please	**Bitte**	bitt-er
Thank you	**Danke vielmals**	dunk-er feel-malse
Excuse me	**Gestatten**	g'shtatt'n
Hello	**Grüss Gott**	groos got
Goodbye	**Auf Wiedersehen**	owf veed-er-zay-ern
Goodnight	**Gute Nacht**	goot-er nukht
morning	**Vormittag**	for-mit-targ
afternoon	**Nachmittag**	nakh-mit-targ
evening	**Abend**	ahb'nt
yesterday	**Gestern**	gest'n
today	**Heute**	hoyt-er
tomorrow	**Morgen**	morg'n
here	**hier**	hear
there	**dort**	dort
What?	**Was?**	vuss?
When?	**Wann?**	vunn?
Why?	**Warum?**	var-room?
Where?	**Wo/Wohin?**	voh/vo-hin?

USEFUL PHRASES

How are you?	**Wie geht es Ihnen?**	vee gayt ess een'n?
Very well, thank you	**Sehr gut, danke**	zair goot, dunk-er
Pleased to meet you	**Es freut mich sehr, Sie kennenzulernen**	ess froyt mish zair, zee ken'n-tsoo-lairn'n
See you soon	**Bis bald/bis gleich**	bis bult/bis gleyesh
That's fine	**Sehr gut**	zair goot
Where is...?	**Wo befindet sich...?**	voe b'find't zish...?
Where are...?	**Wo befinden sich...?**	voe b'find'n zish...?
How far is it to...?	**Wie weit ist...?**	vee vite ist...?
Which way to...?	**Wie komme ich zu...?**	vee komma ish tsoo...?
Do you speak English?	**Sprechen Sie englisch?**	shpresh'n zee eng-glish?
I don't understand	**Ich verstehe nicht**	ish fair-shtay-er nisht
Could you please speak slowly?	**Bitte sprechen Sie etwas langsamer?**	bitt-er shpresh'n zee et-vuss lung-zam-er?
I'm sorry	**Es tut mir leid/ Verzeihung**	es toot meer lyte/ fair-tseye-oong

USEFUL WORDS

big	**gross**	grohss
small	**klein**	kline
hot	**heiss**	hyce
cold	**kalt**	kult
good	**gut**	goot
bad	**schlecht**	shlesh't
enough	**genug**	g'nook
well	**gut**	goot
open	**auf/offen**	owf/off'n
closed	**zu/geschlossen**	tsoo/g's hloss'n
left	**links**	links
right	**rechts**	reshts
straight on	**geradeaus**	g'rah-der-owss
near	**in der Nähe**	in dair nay-er
far	**weit**	vyte
up	**auf, oben**	owf, obe'n
down	**ab, unten**	up, oont'n
early	**früh**	froo
late	**spät**	shpate

entrance	**Eingang/Einfahrt**	ine-gung/ine-fart
exit	**Ausgang/Ausfahrt**	ows-gung/ows-fart
toilet	**WC/Toilette**	vay-say/toy-lett-er
free/unoccupied	**frei**	fry
free/no charge	**frei/gratis**	fry/grah-tis

MAKING A TELEPHONE CALL

I'd like to place a long-distance call	**Ich möchte ein Ferngespräch machen**	ish mer-shter ine fairn-g'shpresh mukh'n
I'd like to call collect	**Ich möchte ein Rückgespräch (Collectgespräch) machen**	ish mer-shter ine rook-g'shpresh (coll-ect-g'shpresh) mukh'n
local call	**Ortsgespräch**	orts-g'shpresh
I'll try again later	**Ich versuche es noch einmal etwas später**	ish fair-zookh-er ess nokh ine-mull ett-vuss shpay-ter
Can I leave a message?	**Kann ich etwas ausrichten?**	kunn ish ett-vuss ows-rikht'n?
Hold on	**Haben Sie etwas Geduld**	harb'n zee ett-vuss g'doolt
Could you speak up a little please?	**Bitte sprechen Sie etwas lauter?**	bitt-er shpresh'n zee ett-vuss lowt-er?

STAYING IN A HOTEL

Do you have a vacant room?	**Haben Sie ein Zimmer frei?**	harb'n zee ine tsimm-er fry?
double room with double bed	**ein Doppelzimmer mit Doppelbett**	ine dopp'l-tsimm-er mitt dopp'l-bet
twin room	**ein Doppelzimmer**	ine dopp'l-tsimm-er
single room	**ein Einzelzimmer**	ine ine-ts'l-tsimm-er
room with a bath/shower	**Zimmer mit Bad/Dusche**	tsimm-er mitt bart/doosh-er
porter	**Gepäckträger/ Concierge**	g'peck-tray-ger/ kon-see-airsh
key	**Schlüssel**	shlooss'l
I have a reservation	**Ich habe ein Zimmer reserviert**	ish harb-er ine tsimm-er rezz-air-veert

SIGHTSEEING

bus	**der Bus**	dair booss
tram	**die Strassenbahn**	dee stra-sen-barn
train	**der Zug**	dair tsoog
art gallery	**Galerie**	gall-er-ee
bus station	**Busbahnhof**	booss-barn-hofe
bus (tram) stop	**die Haltestelle**	dee hal-te-shtel-er
castle	**Schloss, Burg**	shloss, boorg
palace	**Schloss, Palais**	shloss, pall-ay
post office	**das Postamt**	dee pohs-taamt
cathedral	**Dom**	dome
church	**Kirche**	keersh-er
garden	**Garten, Park**	gart'n, park
library	**Bibliothek**	bib-leo-tek
museum	**Museum**	moo-zay-oom
information (office)	**Information (-sbüro)**	in-for-mut-see-on (-zboo-roe)
closed for public holiday	**Feiertags geschlossen**	fire-targz g'shloss'n

SHOPPING

How much does this cost?	**Wieviel kostet das?**	vee-feel kost't duss?
I would like...	**Ich hätte gern...**	ish hett-er gairn...
Do you have...?	**Haben Sie...?**	harb'n zee...?
I'm just looking	**Ich schaue nur an**	ish shau-er noor un
Do you take credit cards?	**Kann ich mit einer Kreditkarte bezahlen?**	kunn ish mit ine-er kred-it-kar-ter b'tsahl'n?
What time do you open?	**Wann machen Sie auf?**	vunn mukh'n zee owf?
What time do you close?	**Wann schliessen Sie?**	vunn shlees'n zee?
This one	**dieses**	deez'z
expensive	**teuer**	toy-er
cheap	**billig**	bill-igg
size	**Grösse**	grers-er
white	**weiss**	vyce
black	**schwarz**	shvarts
red	**rot**	roht
yellow	**gelb**	gelp
green	**grün**	groon
blue	**blau**	blau

TYPES OF SHOP

antique shop	**Antiquitätengeschäft**	un-tick-vi-**tayt**'n-g'**sheft**
bakery	**Bäckerei**	beck-er-**eye**
bank	**Bank**	bunk
book shop	**Buchladen/ Buchhandlung**	bookh-lard'n/ bookh-hant-loong
butcher	**Fleischerei**	fly-sher-**eye**
cake shop	**Konditorei**	kon-ditt-or-**eye**
chemist		
(for prescriptions)	**Apotheke**	App-o-**tay**-ker
(for cosmetics)	**Drogerie**	droog-er-**ree**
department store	**Warenhaus, Warengeschäft**	vahr'n-hows, vahr'n-g'**sheft**
delicatessen	**Feinkost (geschäft)**	fine-kost (g'**sheft**)
fishmonger	**Fischgeschäft**	fish-g'**sheft**
gift shop	**Geschenke(laden)**	g'**shenk**-er(**lahd**'n)
greengrocer	**Obst und Gemüse**	ohbst oont g'**moo**-zer
grocery	**Lebensmittelgeschäft**	**layb**'nz-mitt'l-g'**sheft**
hairdresser	**Friseur/Frisör**	freezz-**er**/freezz-**er**
market	**Markt**	markt
newsagent/ tobacconist	**Tabak Trafik**	tab-**ack** tra-feek
travel agent	**Reisebüro**	**rye**-z**er**-boo-roe
café	**Cafe, Kaffeehaus**	kaff-**ay**, kaff-**ay**-hows

EATING OUT

Have you got a table for... people?	**Haben Sie einen Tisch für... Personen?**	harb'n zee ine'n tish foor... pair-**sohn**'n?
I want to reserve a table	**Ich möchte einen Tisch bestellen**	ish **mer**-shter ine'n tish b'**shtell**'n
The bill please	**Zahlen, bitte**	**tsarl**'n **bitt**-er
I am a vegetarian	**Ich bin Vegetarier**	ish bin vegg-er-**tah**-ree-er
Waitress/waiter	**Fräulein/Herr Ober**	froy-line/hair **oh**-bare
menu	**die Speisekarte**	dee **shpize**-er-kart-er
fixed price menu	**das Menü**	duss men-**oo**
cover charge	**Couvert/Gedeck**	**koo**-vair/g'**deck**
wine list	**Weinkarte**	**vine**-kart-er
glass	**Glas**	glars
bottle	**Flasche**	**flush**-er
knife	**Messer**	**mess**-er
fork	**Gabel**	**garb**'l
spoon	**Löffel**	**lerff**'l
breakfast	**Frühstück**	**froo**-shtook
lunch	**Mittagessen**	**mit**-targ-ess'n
dinner	**Abendessen/ Dinner**	**arb**'nt-ess'n/ dee-**nay**
main course	**Hauptspeise**	**howpt**-shpize-er
starter, first course	**Vorspeise**	**for**-shpize-er
dish of the day	**Tageskarte**	**targ**-erz-kart-er
wine garden(s)	**Heuriger (Heurige)**	**hoy**-rigg-er (-e)
rare	**englisch**	**eng**-glish
medium	**medium**	**may**-dee-oom
well done	**durch**	**doorsh**

MENU DECODER

See also pp204 - 9.

Apfel	**upf**'l	apple
Almdudler	ahlm-**dood**-ler	herbal lemonade
Banane	bar-**nar**-ner	banana
Ei	**eye**	egg
Eis	**ice**	ice cream
Fisch	**fish**	fish
Fisolen	fee-**soul**'n	green beans (haricot)
Fleisch	**flysh**	meat
Garnelen	**gar**-nayl'n	prawns
gebacken	g'**buck**'n	baked/fried
gebraten	g'**brart**'n	roast
gekocht	g'**kokht**	boiled
Gemüse	g'**mooz**-er	vegetables
vom Grill	fom **grill**	grilled
Gulasch	**goo**-lush	stew
Hendl/Hahn/Huhn	hend'l/harn/hoon	chicken
Kaffee	kaf-**fay**	coffee
Kartoffel/Erdäpfel	kar-**toff**l/**air**-dupf'l	potatoes
Käse	**kayz**-er	cheese
Knoblauch	k'**nob**-lowkh	garlic
Knödel	k'**nerd**'l	dumpling
Kotelett	kot-**lett**	chop
Lamm	**lumm**	lamb
Marillen	mah-**ril**'n	apricot
Meeresfrüchte	**mair**-erz-froosh-ter	seafood

Mehlspeise	**mayl**-shpize-er	dessert
Milch	**milhk**	milk
Mineralwasser	minn-er-**arl**-vuss-er	mineral water
Obst	**ohbst**	fresh fruit
Öl	**erl**	oil
Oliven	o-**leev**'n	olives
Orange	o-**ronsh**-er	orange
frischgepresster Orangensaft	frish-g'**press**-ter o-**ronsh**'n-zuft	fresh orange juice
Paradeissalat	pa-ra-**dice**-sa-lahd	tomato salad
Pfeffer	**pfeff**-er	pepper
pochiert	posh-**eert**	poached
Pommes frites	pomm-**fritt**	chips
Reis	**rice**	rice
Rind	**rint**	beef
Rostbraten	rohst-**brart**'n	steak
Rotwein	**roht**-vine	red wine
Salz	**zults**	salt
Sauce/Saft	**zohss**-er/zuft	sauce
Schalentiere	**sharl**'n-tee-rer	shellfish
Schinken/Speck	**shink**'n/shpeck	ham
Schlag	**shlahgg**	cream
Schnecken	**shnek**'n	snails
Schokolade	shock-o-**lard**-er	chocolate
Schwein	**shvine**	pork
Semmel	**zem**'l	roll
Senf	**zenf**	mustard
Serviettenknödel	ser-vee-**ert**'n-k'**nerd**'l	sliced dumpling
Sulz	**zoolts**	brawn
Suppe	**zoop**-er	soup
Tee	**tay**	tea
Topfenkuchen	topf'n-**kookh**'n	cheesecake
Torte	**tort**-er	cake
Wasser	**vuss**-er	water
Weinessig	**vine**-ess-igg	vinegar
Weisswein	**vyce**-vine	white wine
Wurst	**voorst**	sausage (fresh)
Zucker	**tsook**-er	sugar
Zwetschge	**tsvertsh**-ger	plum
Zwiebel	**tsveeb**'l	onions

NUMBERS

0	**null**	**nool**
1	**eins**	**eye**'ns
2	**zwei**	**tsvy**
3	**drei**	**dry**
4	**vier**	**feer**
5	**fünf**	**foonf**
6	**sechs**	**zex**
7	**sieben**	**zeeb**'n
8	**acht**	**uhkht**
9	**neun**	**noyn**
10	**zehn**	**tsayn**
11	**elf**	**elf**
12	**zwölf**	**tsverlf**
13	**dreizehn**	**dry**-tsayn
14	**vierzehn**	**feer**-tsayn
15	**fünfzehn**	**foonf**-tsayn
16	**sechszehn**	**zex**-tsayn
17	**siebzehn**	**zeep**-tsayn
18	**achtzehn**	**uhkht**-tsayn
19	**neunzehn**	**noyn**-tsayn
20	**zwanzig**	**tsvunn**-tsig
21	**einundzwanzig**	**ine**-oont-tsvunn-tsig
22	**zweiundzwanzig**	**tsvy**-oont-tsvunn-tsig
30	**dreissig**	**dry**-sig
40	**vierzig**	**feer**-tsig
50	**fünfzig**	**foonf**-tsig
60	**sechzig**	**zesh**-tsig
70	**siebzig**	**zeep**-tsig
80	**achtzig**	**uhkht**-tsig
90	**neunzig**	**noyn**-tsig
100	**einhundert**	ine **hoond**'t
1000	**eintausend**	ine **towz**'nt

TIME

one minute	**eine Minute**	**ine**-er min-**oot**-er
one hour	**eine Stunde**	**ine**-er **shtoond**-er
half an hour	**eine halbe Stunde**	**ine**-er **hull**-ber shtoond-er
Monday	**Montag**	**mone**-targ
Tuesday	**Dienstag**	**deen**-starg
Wednesday	**Mittwoch**	**mitt**-vokh
Thursday	**Donnerstag**	**donn**-er-starg
Friday	**Freitag**	**fry**-targ
Saturday	**Samstag**	**zum**-starg
Sunday	**Sonntag**	**zon**-targ

FOR UPDATES TO OUR GUIDES, AND INFORMATION ON
<u>DK TRAVEL MAPS</u> & <u>PHRASEBOOKS</u>

VISIT US AT
eyewitnesstravel.dk.com

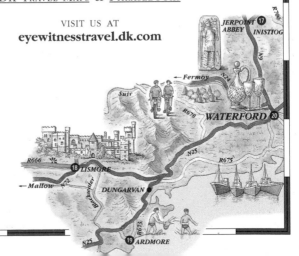

The Vienna Transport Network

THERE ARE FIVE U-Bahn lines running across the city, each identified by a number. The Schnellbahn is essentially a commuter service. Bundesbahn trains to the rest of Austria and Europe run from Vienna's mainline stations. The Badner Bahn operates between its terminal opposite the Opera, and Baden. For more details, see *Getting Around Vienna* on pages 250–55.